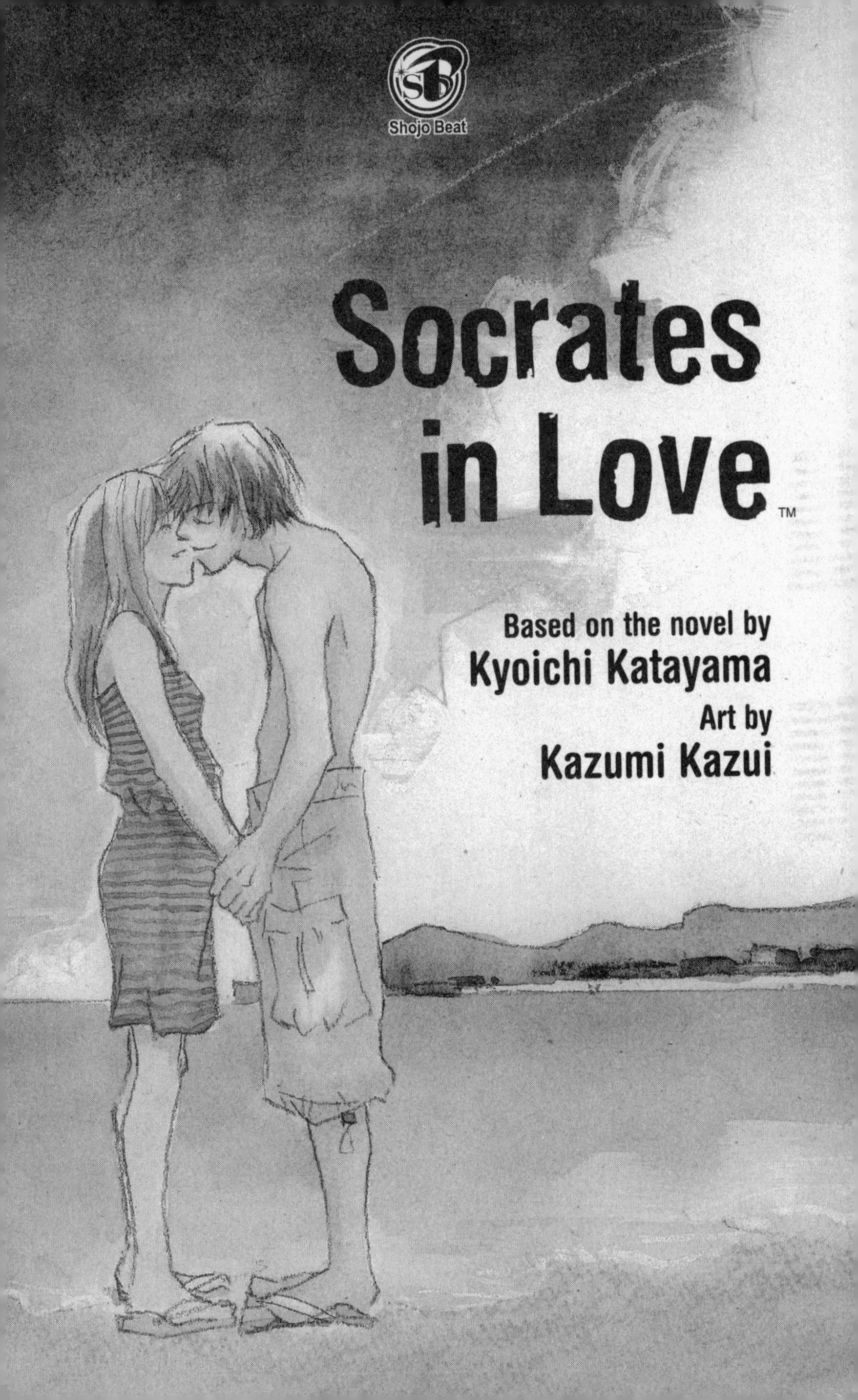

Shojo Beat

Socrates in Love™

Based on the novel by
Kyoichi Katayama

Art by
Kazumi Kazui

I MET AKI...
I LOST SIGHT OF
HER MANY TIMES FOR
VARIOUS REASONS.
BUT AKI WAS ALWAYS
BY MY SIDE, CALLING
OUT TO ME. IT TOOK
ME A WHILE TO
REALIZE THAT...

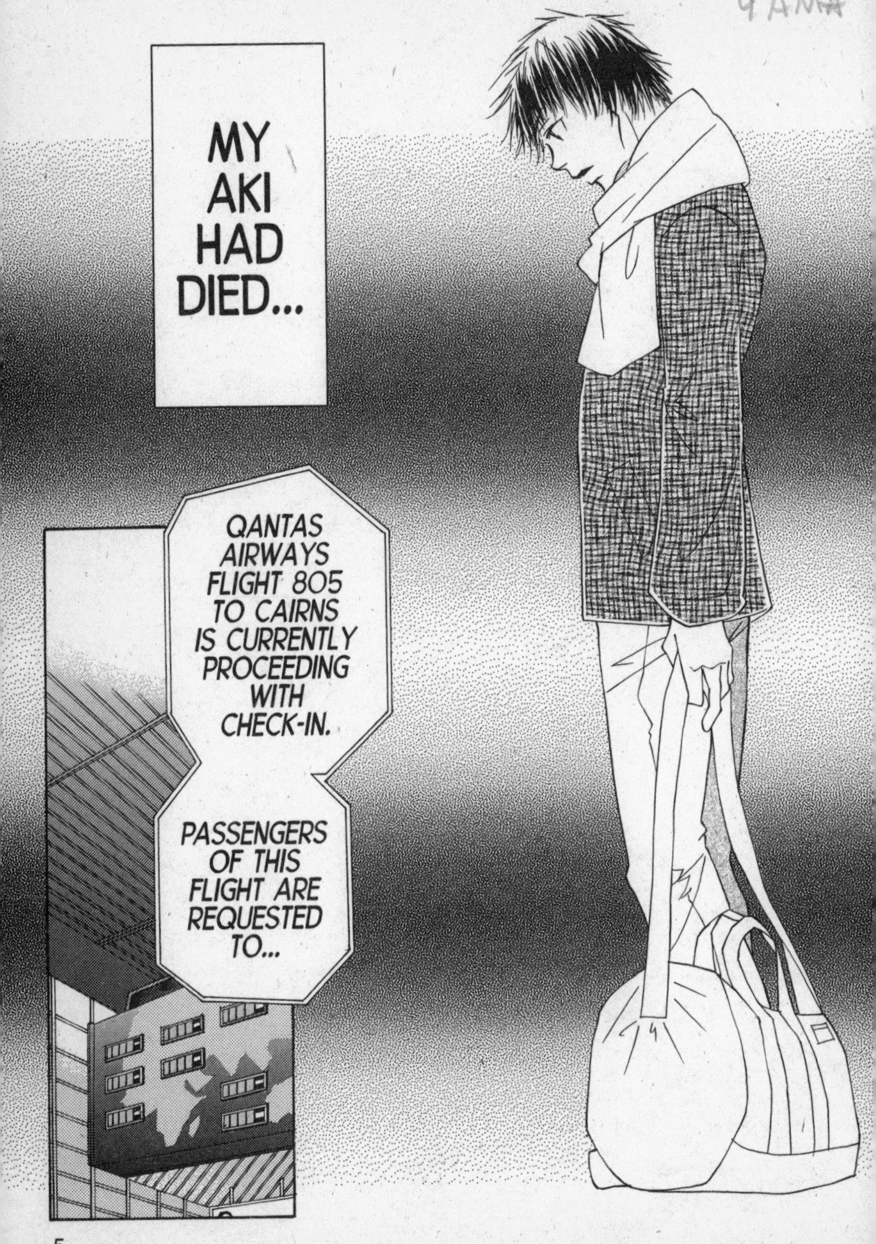
MY AKI HAD DIED...
QANTAS AIRWAYS FLIGHT 805 TO CAIRNS IS CURRENTLY PROCEEDING WITH CHECK-IN.
PASSENGERS OF THIS FLIGHT ARE REQUESTED TO...

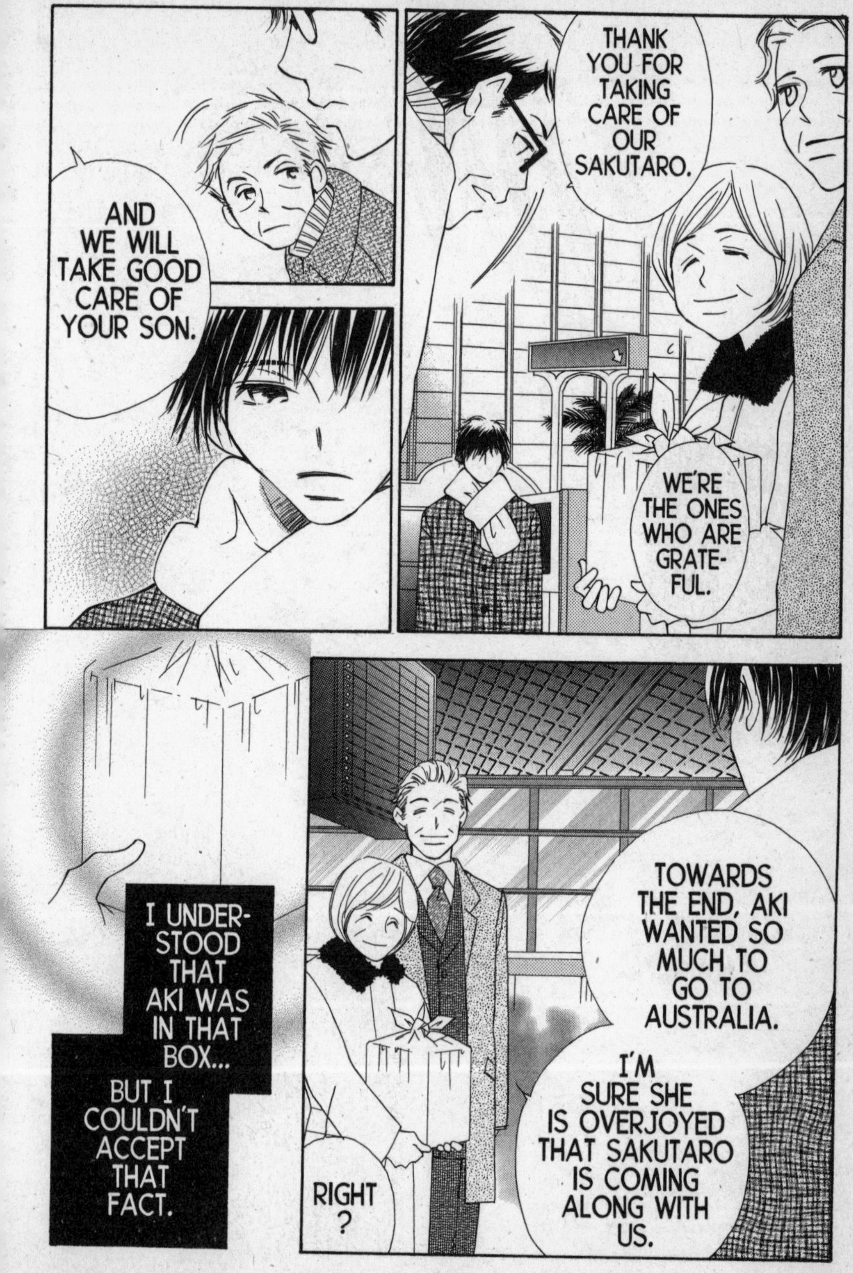
THANK YOU FOR TAKING CARE OF OUR SAKUTARO.
WE'RE THE ONES WHO ARE GRATE-FUL.
AND WE WILL TAKE GOOD CARE OF YOUR SON.
TOWARDS THE END, AKI WANTED SO MUCH TO GO TO AUSTRALIA.
I'M SURE SHE IS OVERJOYED THAT SAKUTARO IS COMING ALONG WITH US.
RIGHT?
I UNDER-STOOD THAT AKI WAS IN THAT BOX...
BUT I COULDN'T ACCEPT THAT FACT.

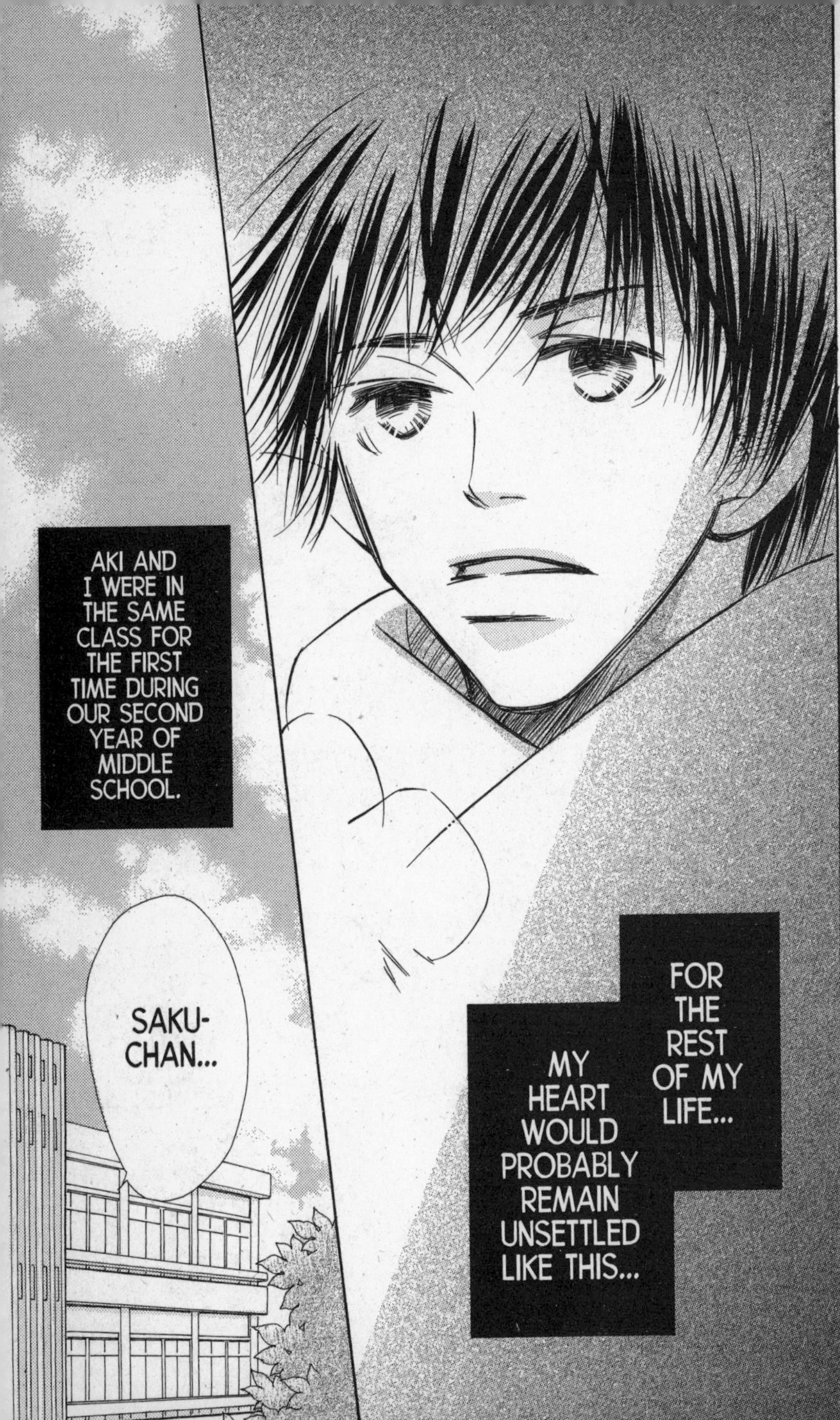
FOR THE REST OF MY LIFE...
MY HEART WOULD PROBABLY REMAIN UNSETTLED LIKE THIS...
AKI AND I WERE IN THE SAME CLASS FOR THE FIRST TIME DURING OUR SECOND YEAR OF MIDDLE SCHOOL.
SAKU-CHAN...

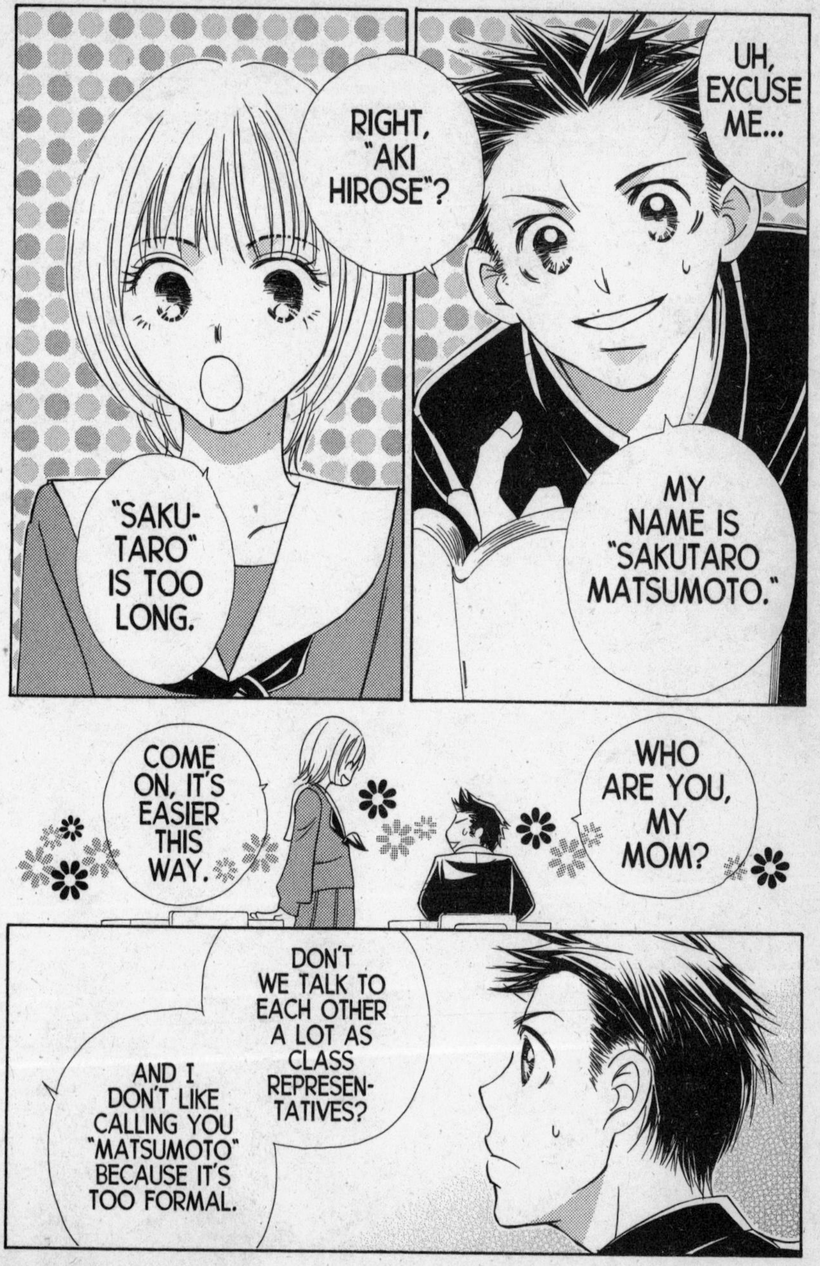
UH, EXCUSE ME...
MY NAME IS "SAKUTARO MATSUMOTO."
RIGHT, "AKI HIROSE"?
"SAKU-TARO" IS TOO LONG.
WHO ARE YOU, MY MOM?
COME ON, IT'S EASIER THIS WAY.
DON'T WE TALK TO EACH OTHER A LOT AS CLASS REPRESEN-TATIVES?
AND I DON'T LIKE CALLING YOU "MATSUMOTO" BECAUSE IT'S TOO FORMAL.

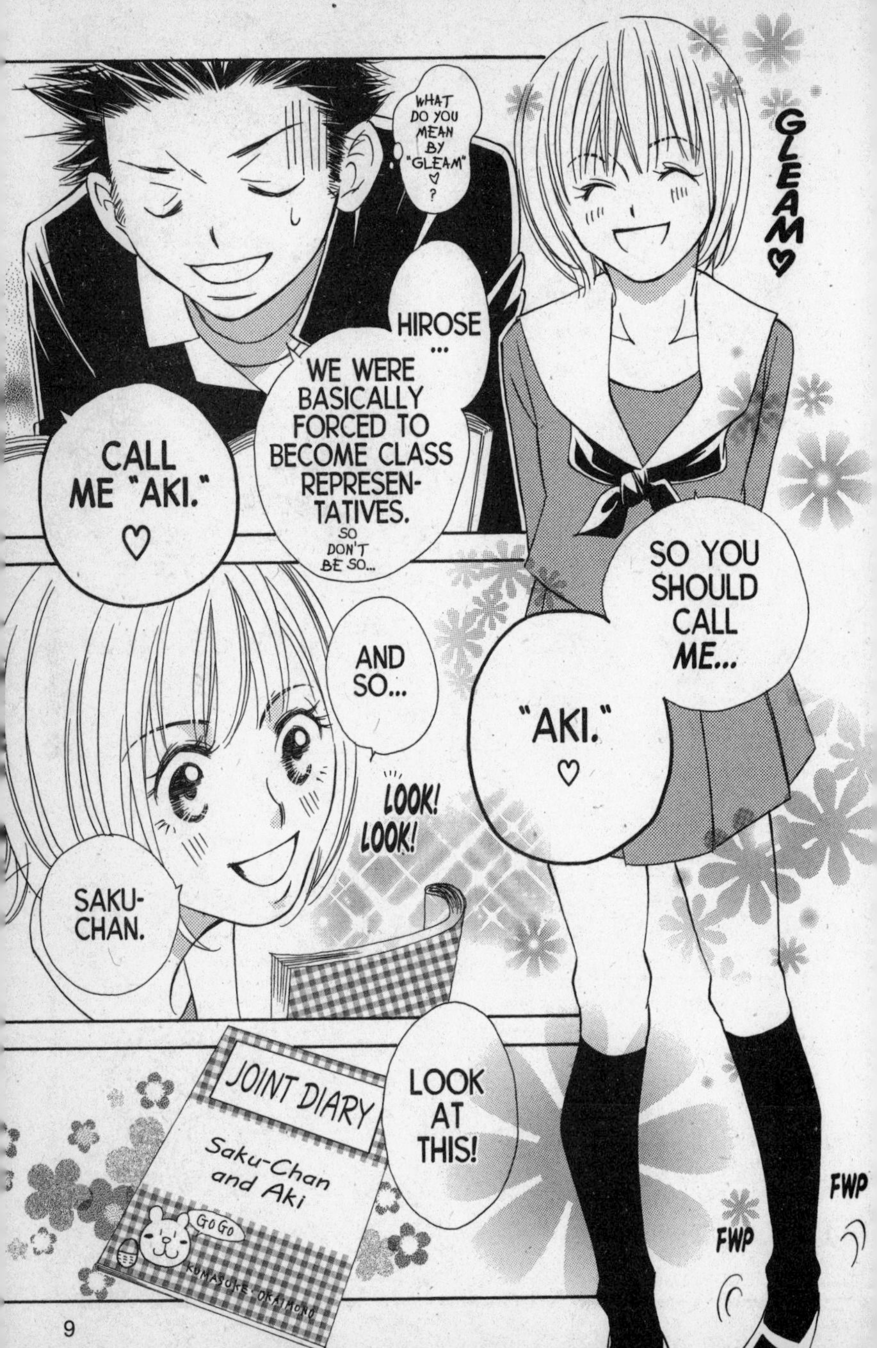
GLEAM♡
SO YOU SHOULD CALL ME...
"AKI." ♡
FWP
FWP
WHAT DO YOU MEAN BY "GLEAM"♡?
HIROSE...
WE WERE BASICALLY FORCED TO BECOME CLASS REPRESEN-TATIVES.
SO DON'T BE SO...
CALL ME "AKI." ♡
AND SO...
LOOK! LOOK!
SAKU-CHAN.
LOOK AT THIS!
JOINT DIARY
Saku-Chan and Aki
GO GO
KUMASUKE ORAIMONO

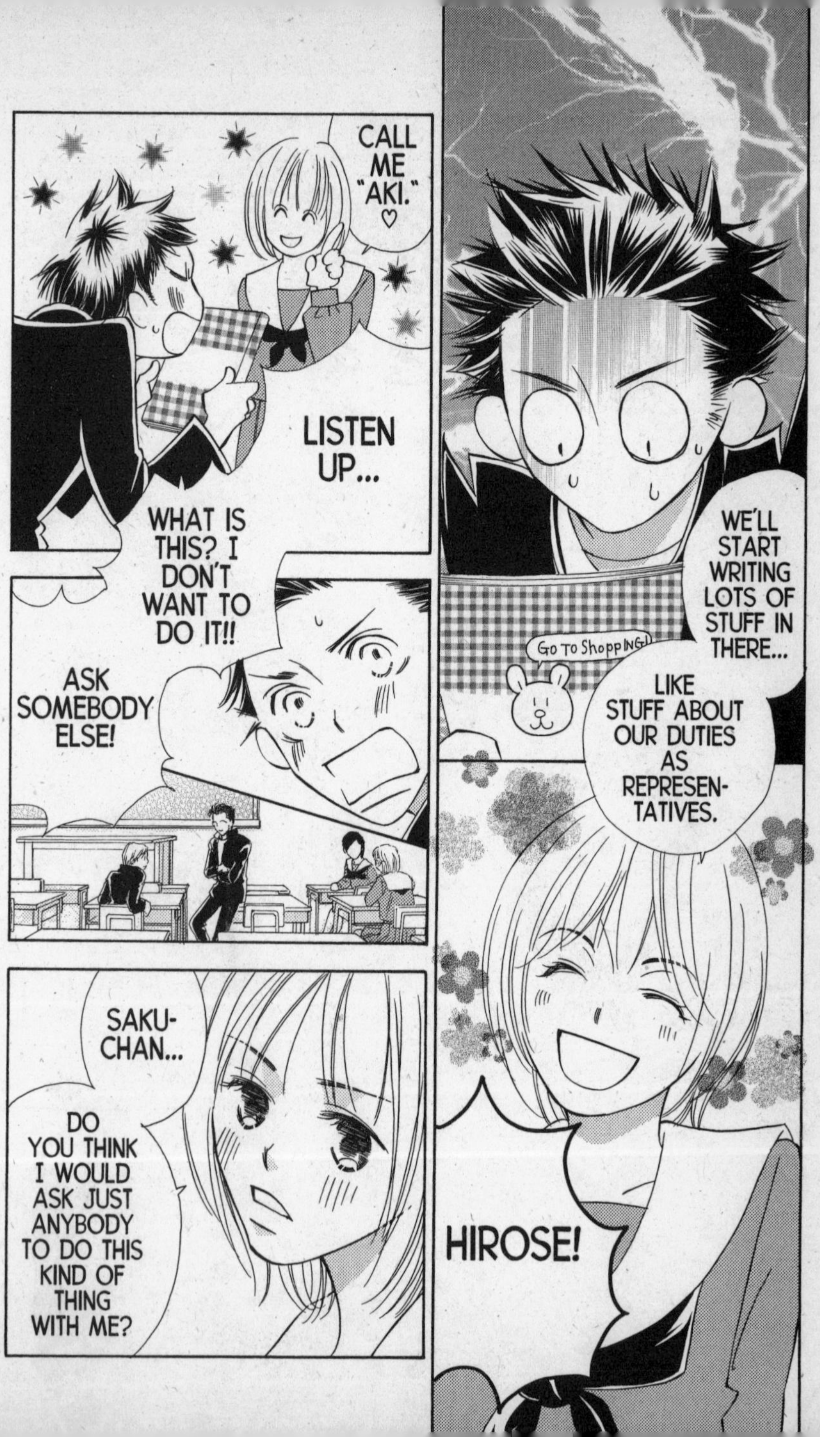
WE'LL START WRITING LOTS OF STUFF IN THERE...
GO TO SHOPPING!!
LIKE STUFF ABOUT OUR DUTIES AS REPRESEN-TATIVES.
HIROSE!
CALL ME "AKI." ♡
LISTEN UP...
WHAT IS THIS? I DON'T WANT TO DO IT!!
ASK SOMEBODY ELSE!
SAKU-CHAN...
DO YOU THINK I WOULD ASK JUST ANYBODY TO DO THIS KIND OF THING WITH ME?

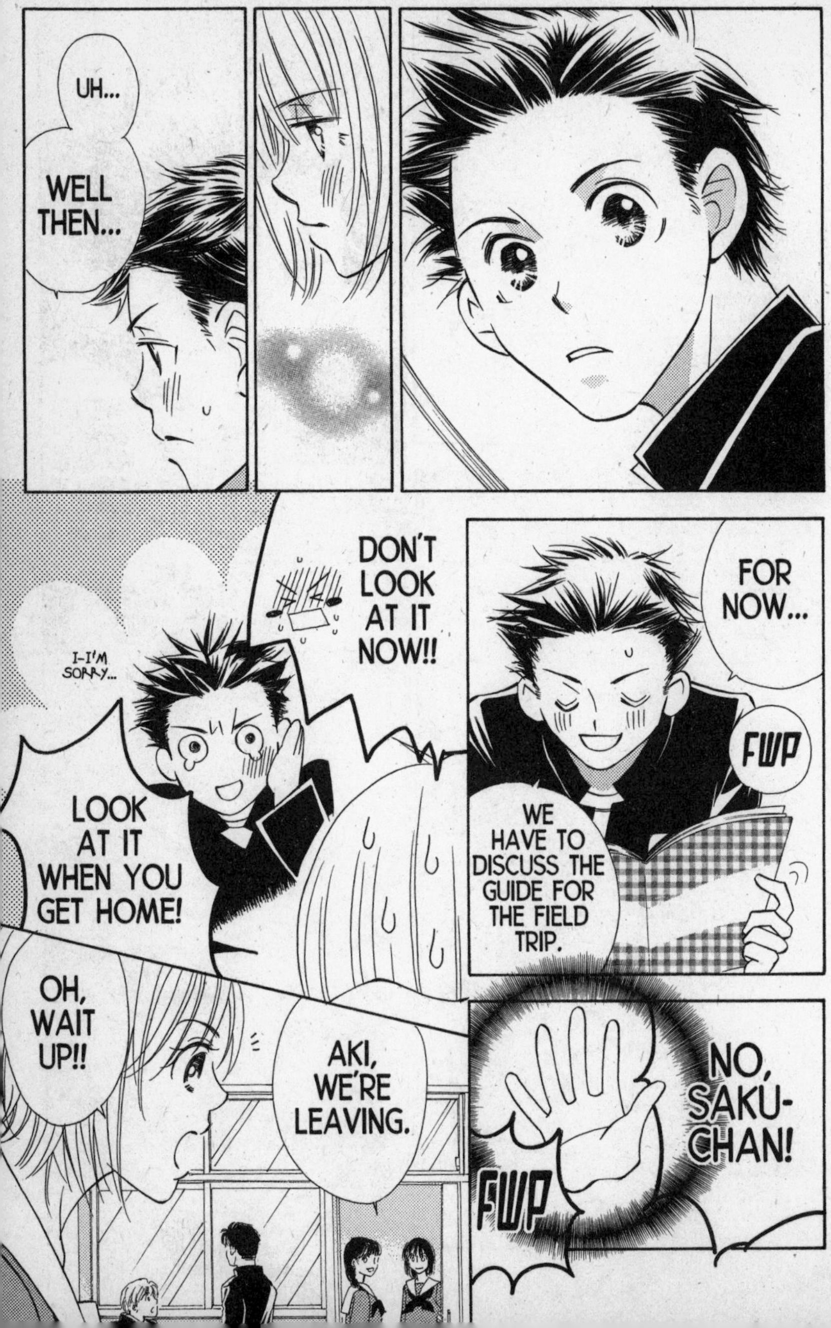
UH...
WELL THEN...
FOR NOW...
FWP
WE HAVE TO DISCUSS THE GUIDE FOR THE FIELD TRIP.
DON'T LOOK AT IT NOW!!
I-I'M SORRY...
LOOK AT IT WHEN YOU GET HOME!
NO, SAKU-CHAN!
FWP
AKI, WE'RE LEAVING.
OH, WAIT UP!!

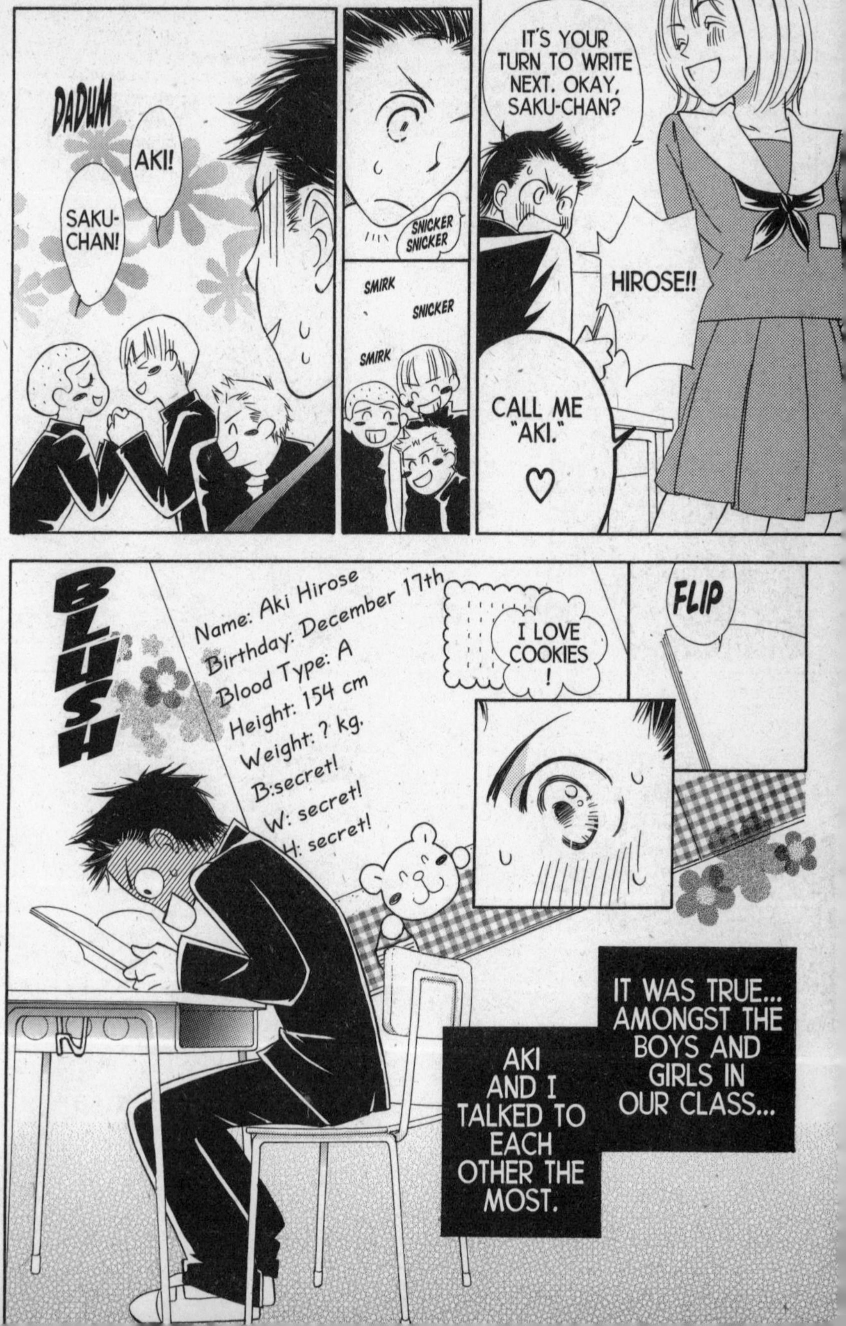
IT'S YOUR TURN TO WRITE NEXT. OKAY, SAKU-CHAN?
HIROSE!!
CALL ME "AKI." ♡
SNICKER SNICKER
SMIRK
SNICKER
SMIRK
DADUM
AKI!
SAKU-CHAN!
FLIP
Name: Aki Hirose
Birthday: December 17th
Blood Type: A
Height: 154 cm
Weight: ? kg.
B:secret!
W: secret!
H: secret!
I LOVE COOKIES!
BLUSH
IT WAS TRUE... AMONGST THE BOYS AND GIRLS IN OUR CLASS...
AKI AND I TALKED TO EACH OTHER THE MOST.

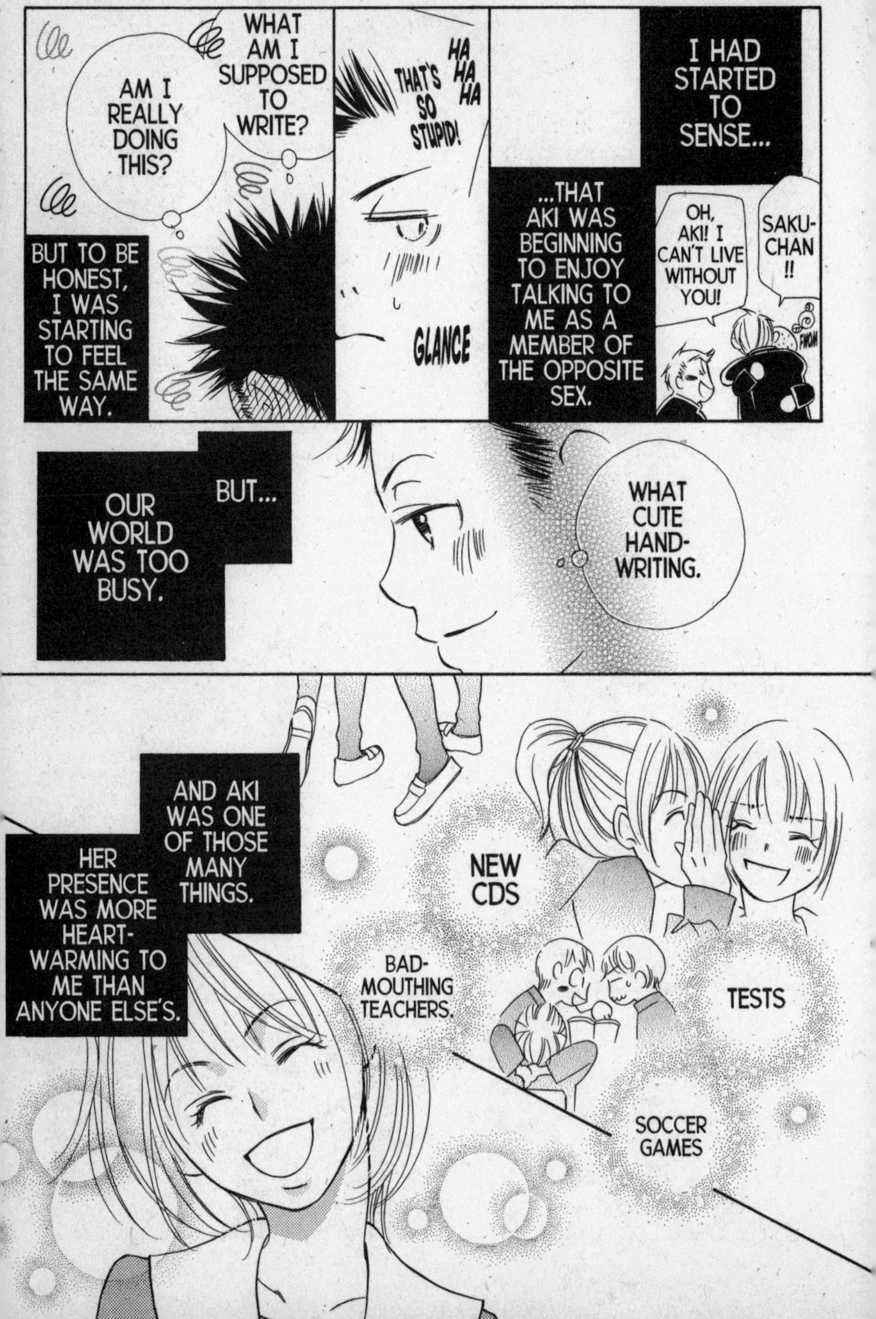
I HAD STARTED TO SENSE...
...THAT AKI WAS BEGINNING TO ENJOY TALKING TO ME AS A MEMBER OF THE OPPOSITE SEX.
SAKU-CHAN!!
OH, AKI! I CAN'T LIVE WITHOUT YOU!
FWOM
HA HA HA
THAT'S SO STUPID!
GLANCE
WHAT AM I SUPPOSED TO WRITE?
AM I REALLY DOING THIS?
BUT TO BE HONEST, I WAS STARTING TO FEEL THE SAME WAY.
WHAT CUTE HAND-WRITING.
BUT...
OUR WORLD WAS TOO BUSY.
NEW CDS
TESTS
SOCCER GAMES
BAD-MOUTHING TEACHERS.
AND AKI WAS ONE OF THOSE MANY THINGS.
HER PRESENCE WAS MORE HEART-WARMING TO ME THAN ANYONE ELSE'S.

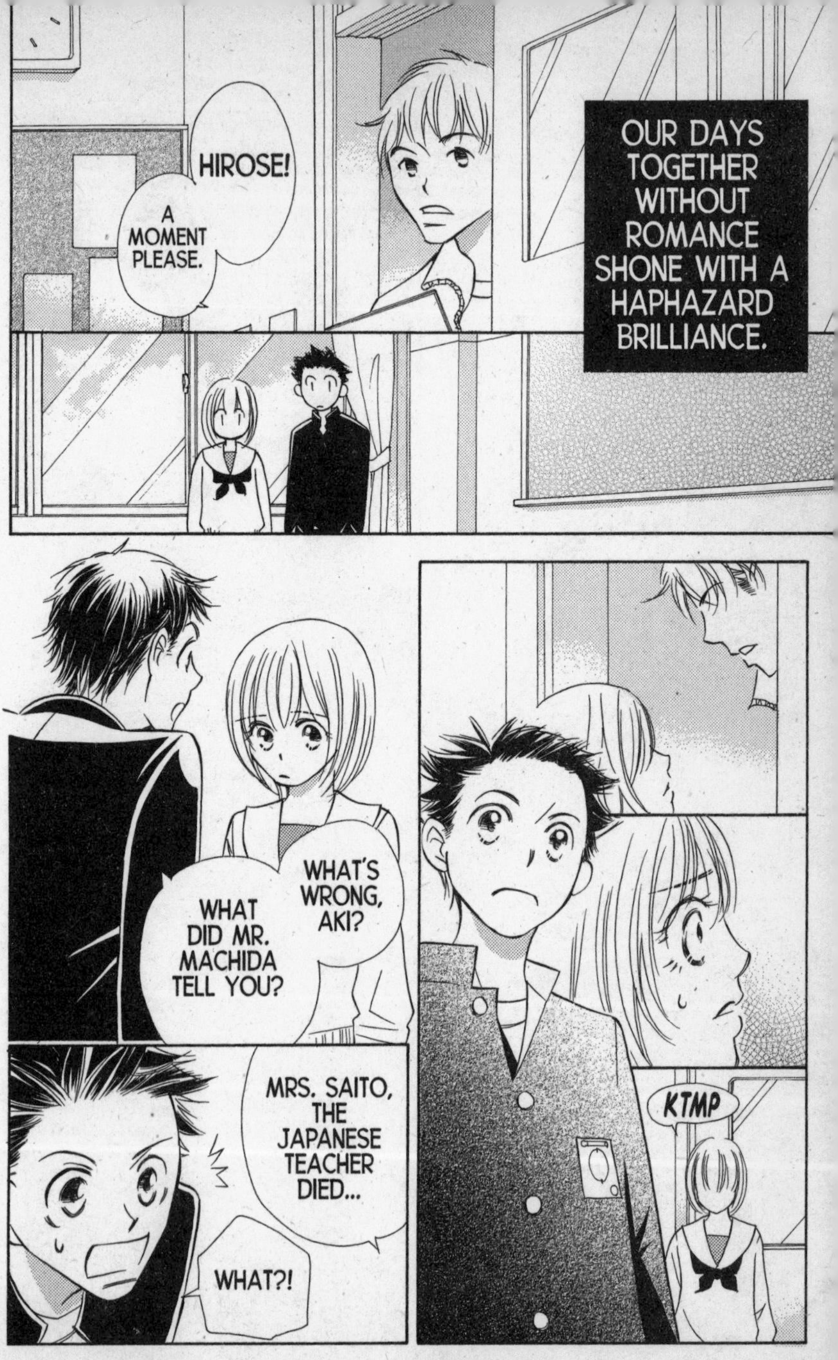
OUR DAYS TOGETHER WITHOUT ROMANCE SHONE WITH A HAPHAZARD BRILLIANCE.
HIROSE!
A MOMENT PLEASE.
KTMP
WHAT'S WRONG, AKI?
WHAT DID MR. MACHIDA TELL YOU?
MRS. SAITO, THE JAPANESE TEACHER DIED...
WHAT?!

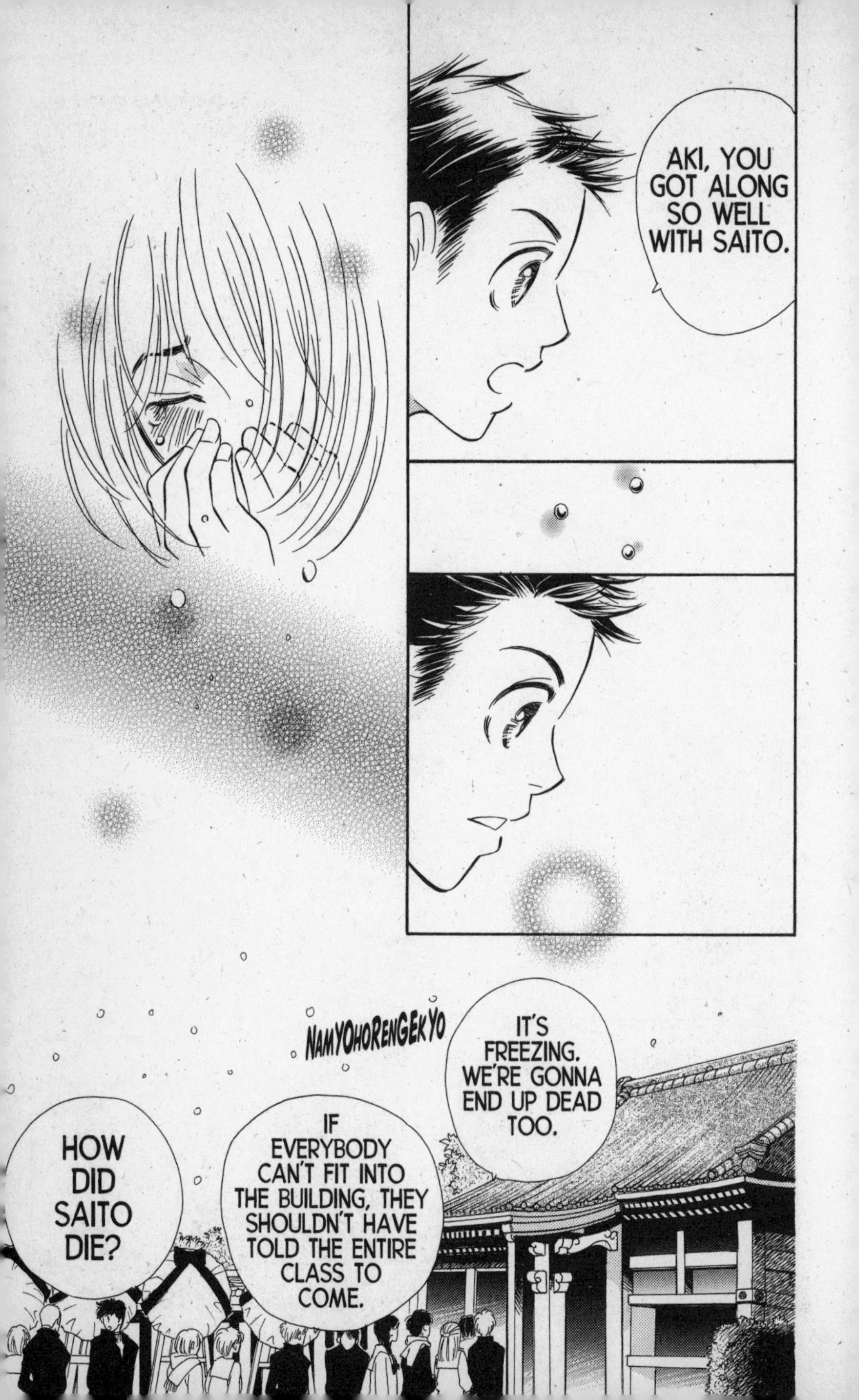
AKI, YOU GOT ALONG SO WELL WITH SAITO.
IT'S FREEZING. WE'RE GONNA END UP DEAD TOO.
NAMYOHORENGEKYO
IF EVERYBODY CAN'T FIT INTO THE BUILDING, THEY SHOULDN'T HAVE TOLD THE ENTIRE CLASS TO COME.
HOW DID SAITO DIE?

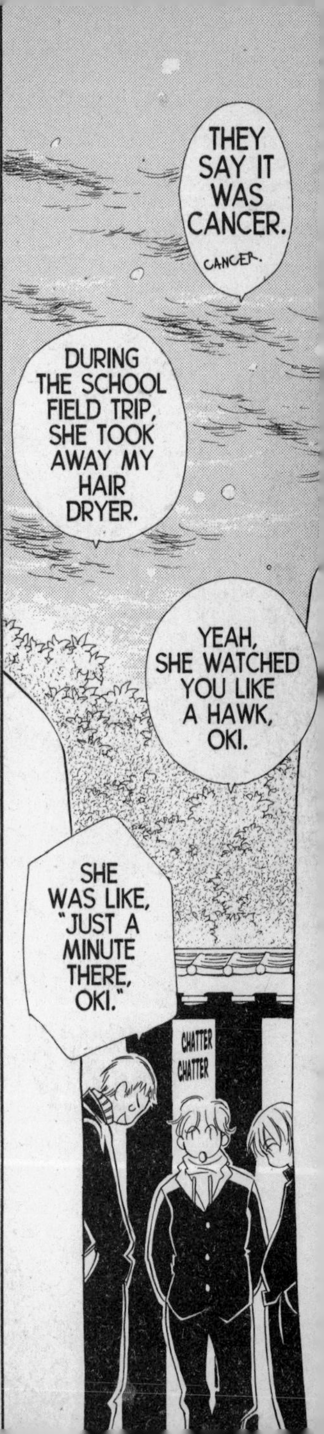
THEY SAY IT WAS CANCER.
CANCER.
DURING THE SCHOOL FIELD TRIP, SHE TOOK AWAY MY HAIR DRYER.
YEAH, SHE WATCHED YOU LIKE A HAWK, OKI.
SHE WAS LIKE, "JUST A MINUTE THERE, OKI."
CHATTER CHATTER
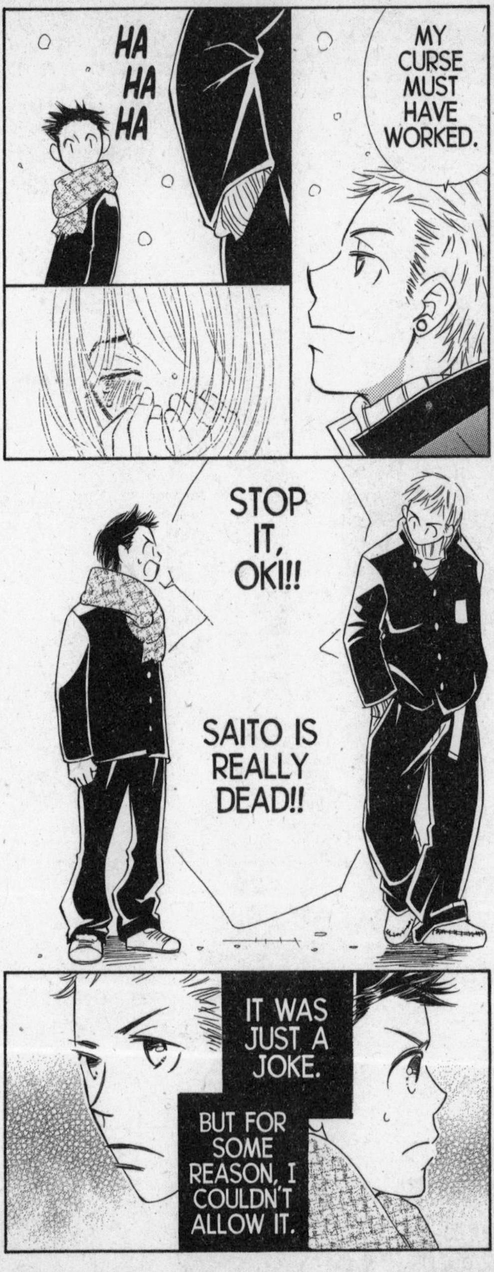
MY CURSE MUST HAVE WORKED.
HA HA HA
STOP IT, OKI!!
SAITO IS REALLY DEAD!!
IT WAS JUST A JOKE.
BUT FOR SOME REASON, I COULDN'T ALLOW IT.

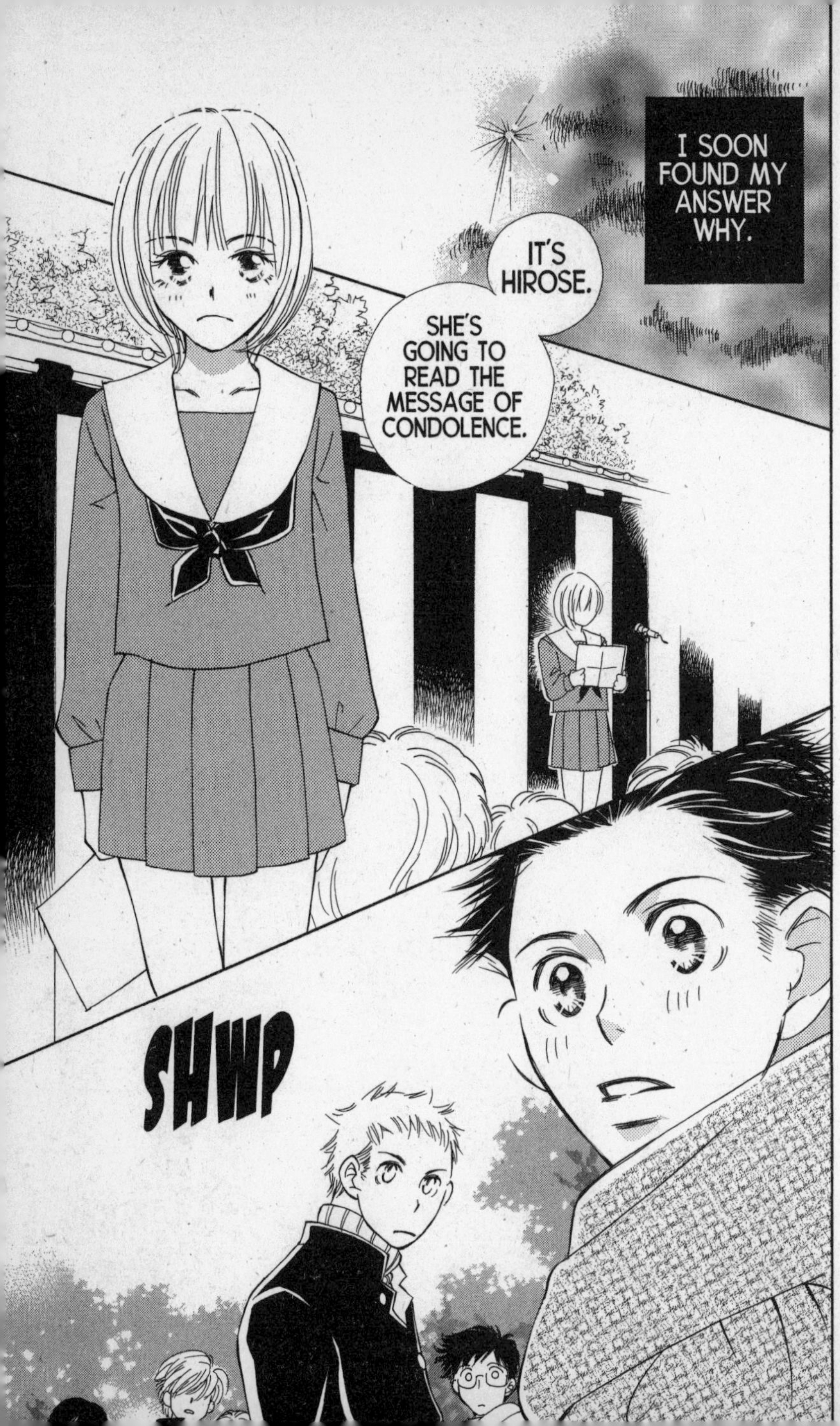
I SOON FOUND MY ANSWER WHY.
IT'S HIROSE.
SHE'S GOING TO READ THE MESSAGE OF CONDOLENCE.
SHWP

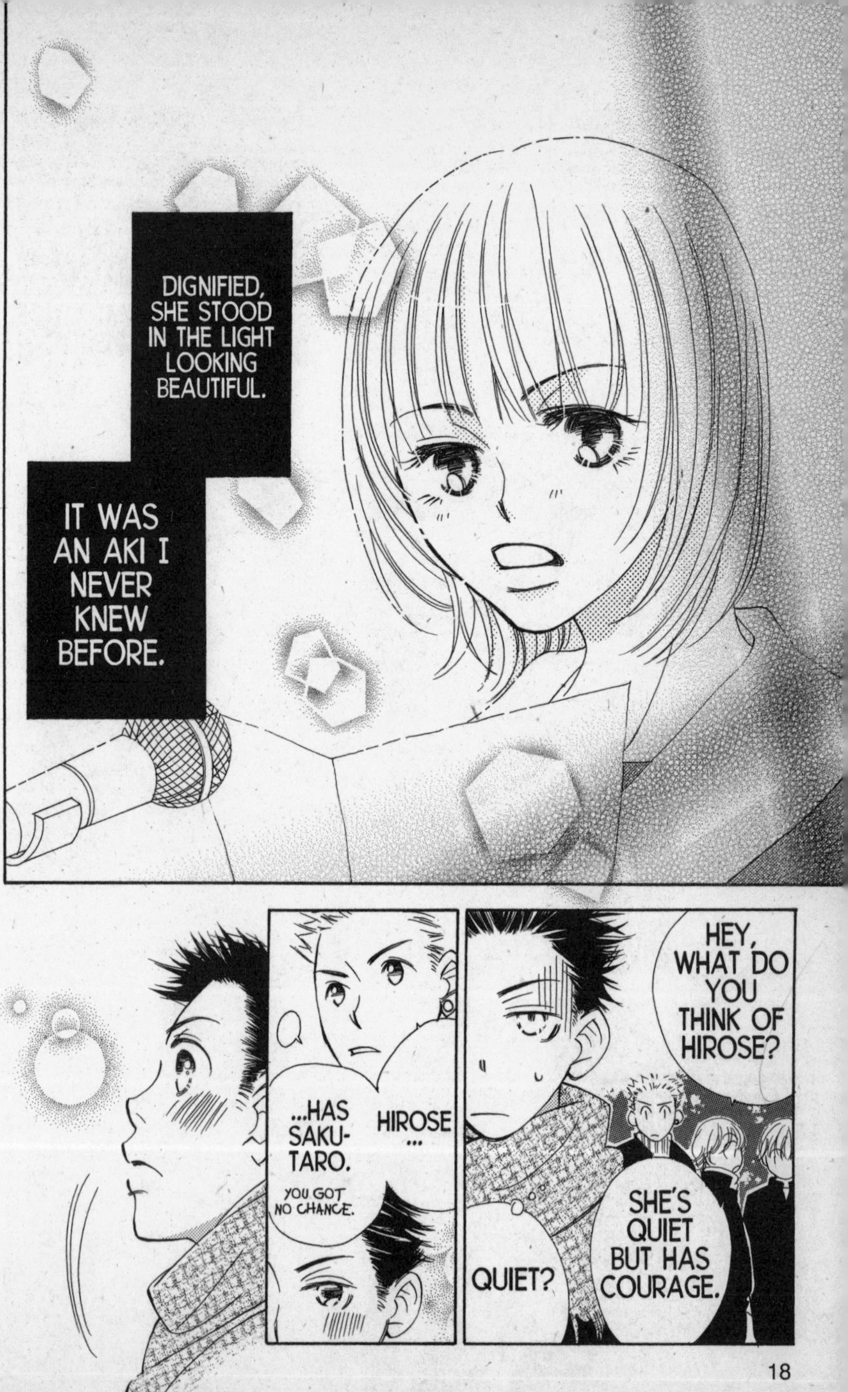
DIGNIFIED, SHE STOOD IN THE LIGHT LOOKING BEAUTIFUL.
IT WAS AN AKI I NEVER KNEW BEFORE.
HEY, WHAT DO YOU THINK OF HIROSE?
SHE'S QUIET BUT HAS COURAGE.
QUIET?
HIROSE...
...HAS SAKUTARO.
YOU GOT NO CHANCE.

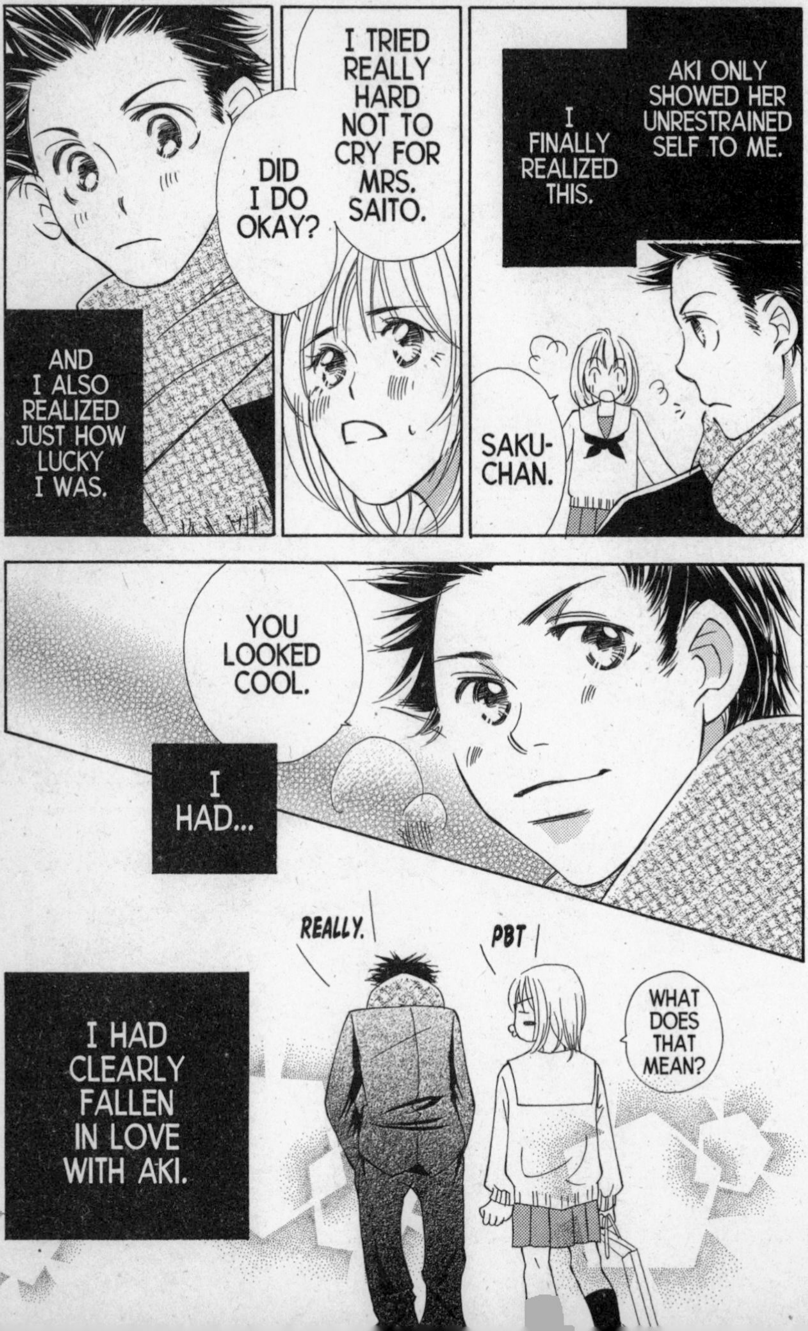
AKI ONLY SHOWED HER UNRESTRAINED SELF TO ME.
I FINALLY REALIZED THIS.
SAKU-CHAN.
I TRIED REALLY HARD NOT TO CRY FOR MRS. SAITO.
DID I DO OKAY?
AND I ALSO REALIZED JUST HOW LUCKY I WAS.
YOU LOOKED COOL.
I HAD...
WHAT DOES THAT MEAN?
PBT
REALLY.
I HAD CLEARLY FALLEN IN LOVE WITH AKI.

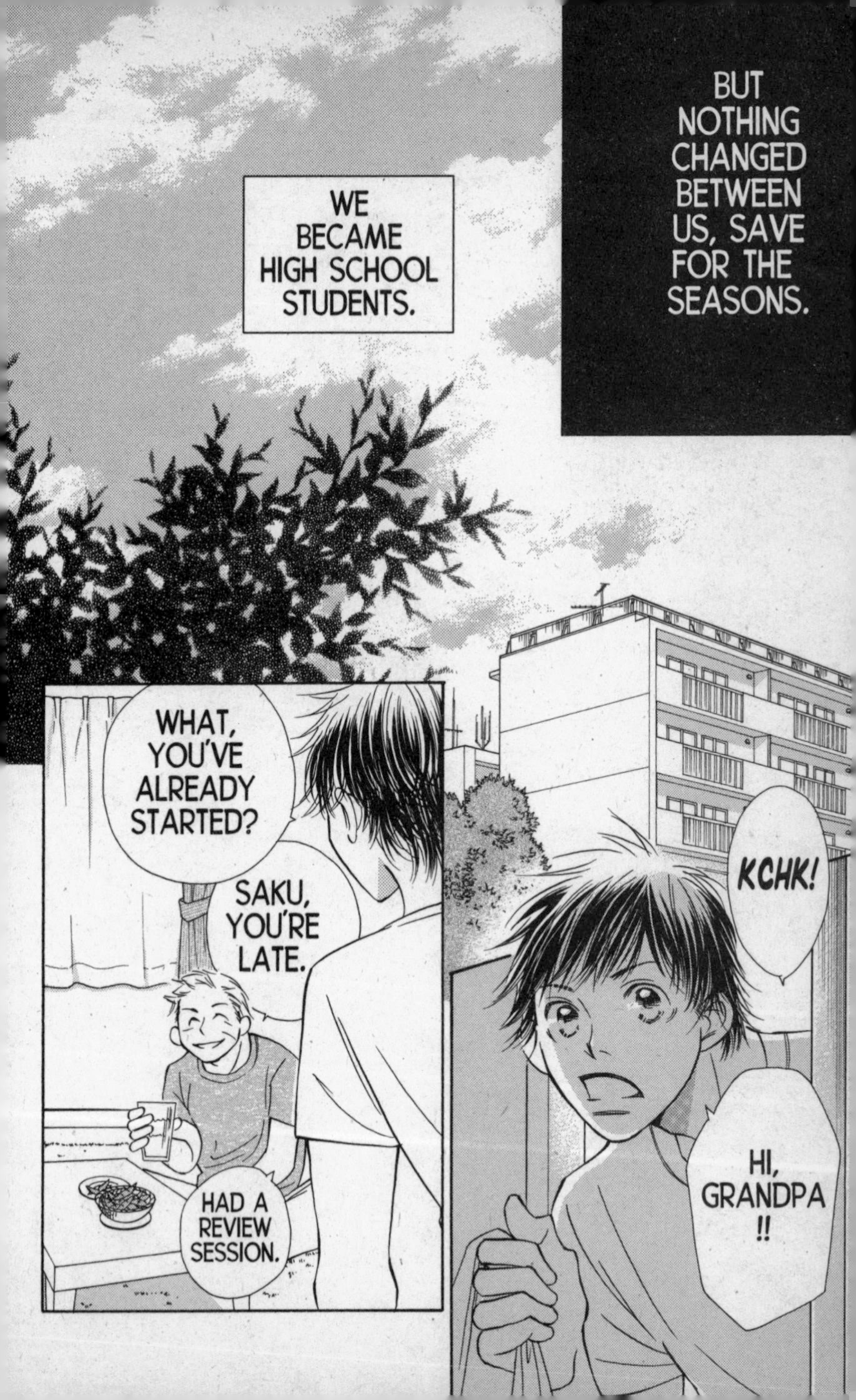
BUT NOTHING CHANGED BETWEEN US, SAVE FOR THE SEASONS.
WE BECAME HIGH SCHOOL STUDENTS.
KCHK!
HI, GRANDPA !!
WHAT, YOU'VE ALREADY STARTED?
SAKU, YOU'RE LATE.
HAD A REVIEW SESSION.

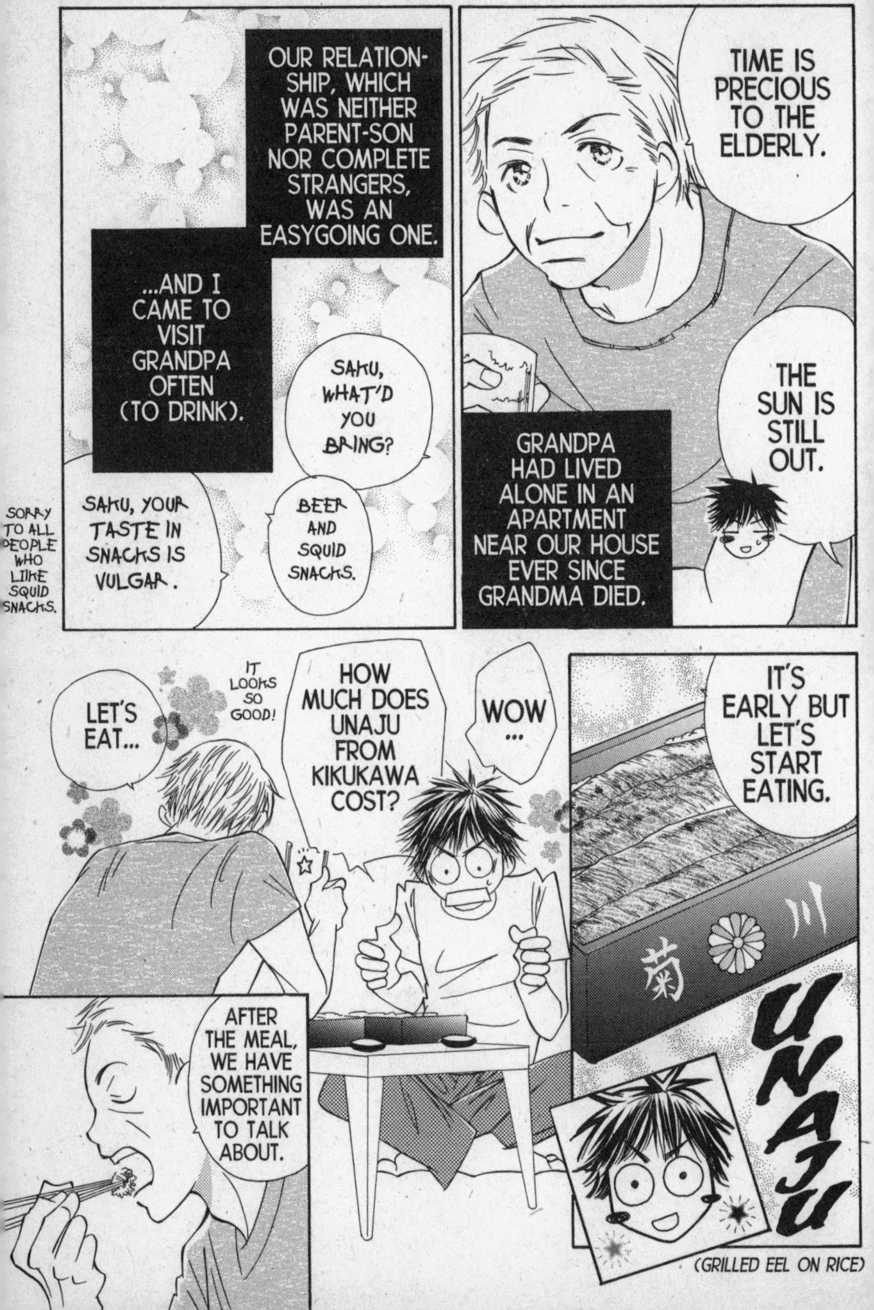
TIME IS PRECIOUS TO THE ELDERLY.
THE SUN IS STILL OUT.
GRANDPA HAD LIVED ALONE IN AN APARTMENT NEAR OUR HOUSE EVER SINCE GRANDMA DIED.
OUR RELATION-SHIP, WHICH WAS NEITHER PARENT-SON NOR COMPLETE STRANGERS, WAS AN EASYGOING ONE.
...AND I CAME TO VISIT GRANDPA OFTEN (TO DRINK).
SAKU, WHAT'D YOU BRING?
BEER AND SQUID SNACKS.
SAKU, YOUR TASTE IN SNACKS IS VULGAR.
SORRY TO ALL PEOPLE WHO LIKE SQUID SNACKS.
IT'S EARLY BUT LET'S START EATING.
UNAJU
(GRILLED EEL ON RICE)
WOW ...
HOW MUCH DOES UNAJU FROM KIKUKAWA COST?
IT LOOKS SO GOOD!
LET'S EAT...
AFTER THE MEAL, WE HAVE SOMETHING IMPORTANT TO TALK ABOUT.

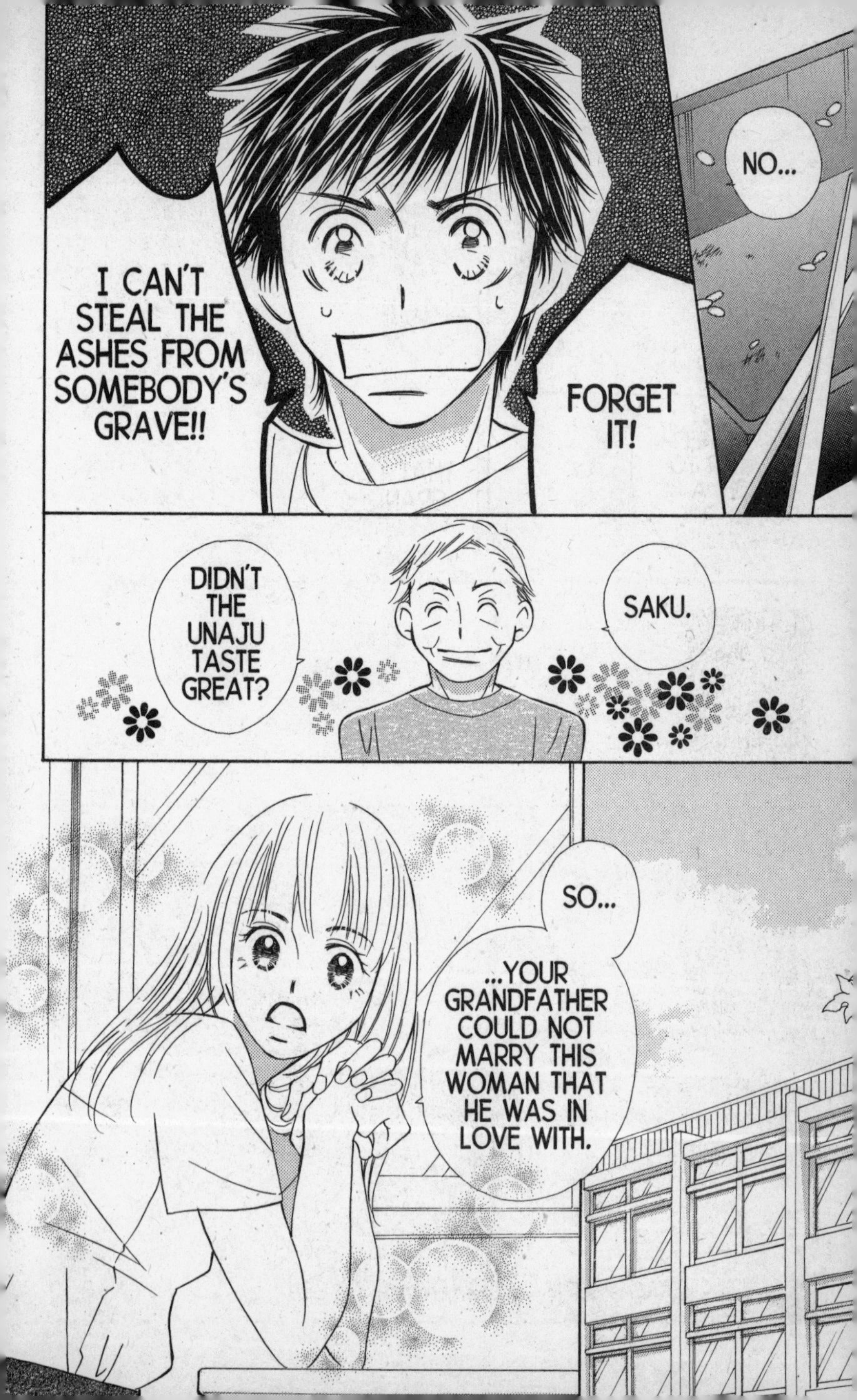
NO...
FORGET IT!
I CAN'T STEAL THE ASHES FROM SOMEBODY'S GRAVE!!
SAKU.
DIDN'T THE UNAJU TASTE GREAT?
SO...
...YOUR GRANDFATHER COULD NOT MARRY THIS WOMAN THAT HE WAS IN LOVE WITH.

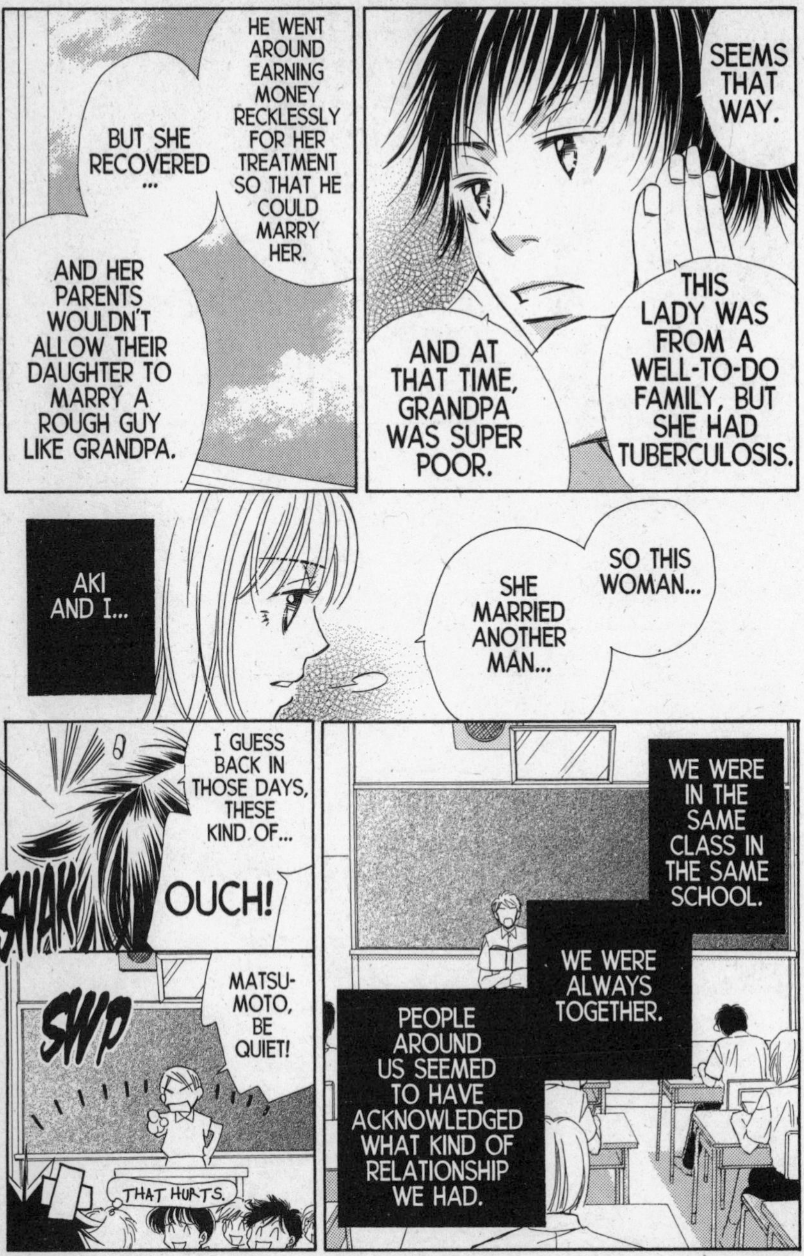
SEEMS THAT WAY.
THIS LADY WAS FROM A WELL-TO-DO FAMILY, BUT SHE HAD TUBERCULOSIS.
AND AT THAT TIME, GRANDPA WAS SUPER POOR.
HE WENT AROUND EARNING MONEY RECKLESSLY FOR HER TREATMENT SO THAT HE COULD MARRY HER.
BUT SHE RECOVERED...
AND HER PARENTS WOULDN'T ALLOW THEIR DAUGHTER TO MARRY A ROUGH GUY LIKE GRANDPA.
SO THIS WOMAN...
SHE MARRIED ANOTHER MAN...
AKI AND I...
WE WERE IN THE SAME CLASS IN THE SAME SCHOOL.
WE WERE ALWAYS TOGETHER.
PEOPLE AROUND US SEEMED TO HAVE ACKNOWLEDGED WHAT KIND OF RELATIONSHIP WE HAD.
I GUESS BACK IN THOSE DAYS, THESE KIND OF...
SWAK
OUCH!
MATSU-MOTO, BE QUIET!
SWP
THAT HURTS.

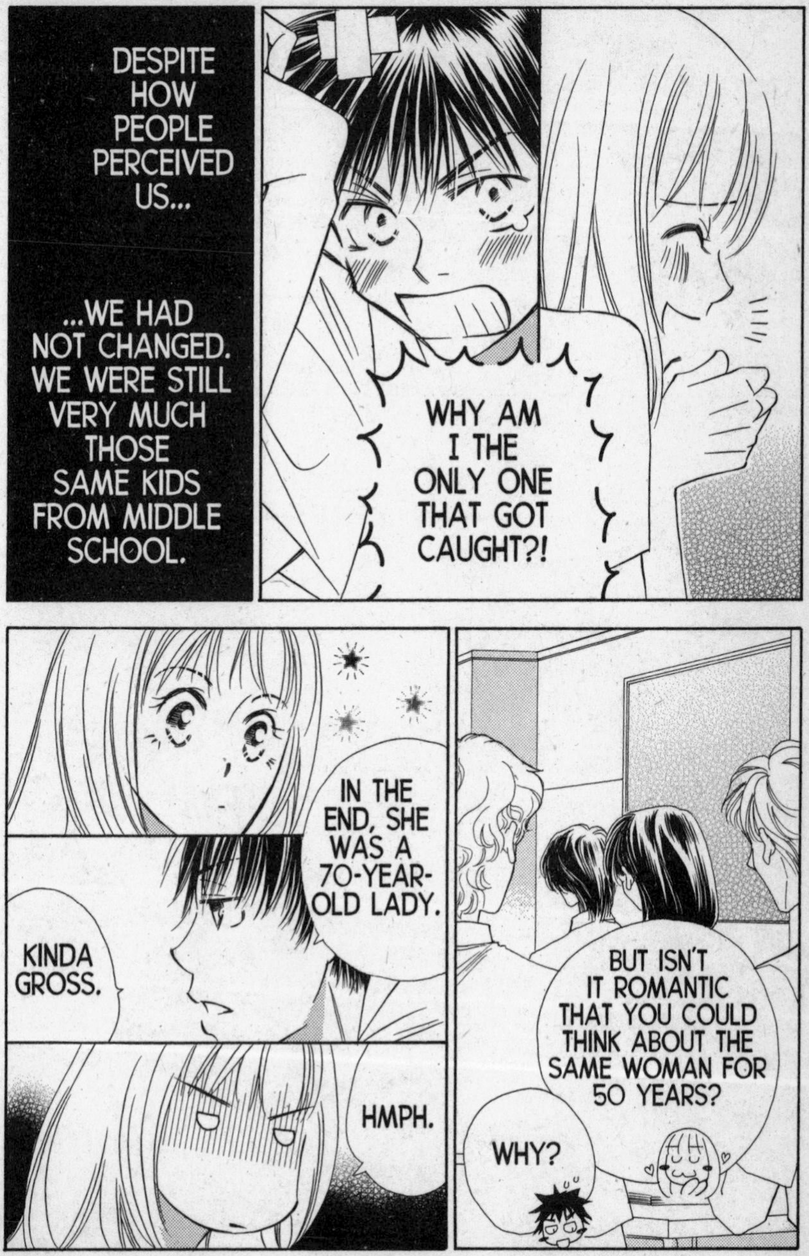
WHY AM I THE ONLY ONE THAT GOT CAUGHT?!
DESPITE HOW PEOPLE PERCEIVED US...
...WE HAD NOT CHANGED. WE WERE STILL VERY MUCH THOSE SAME KIDS FROM MIDDLE SCHOOL.
BUT ISN'T IT ROMANTIC THAT YOU COULD THINK ABOUT THE SAME WOMAN FOR 50 YEARS?
WHY?
IN THE END, SHE WAS A 70-YEAR-OLD LADY.
KINDA GROSS.
HMPH.

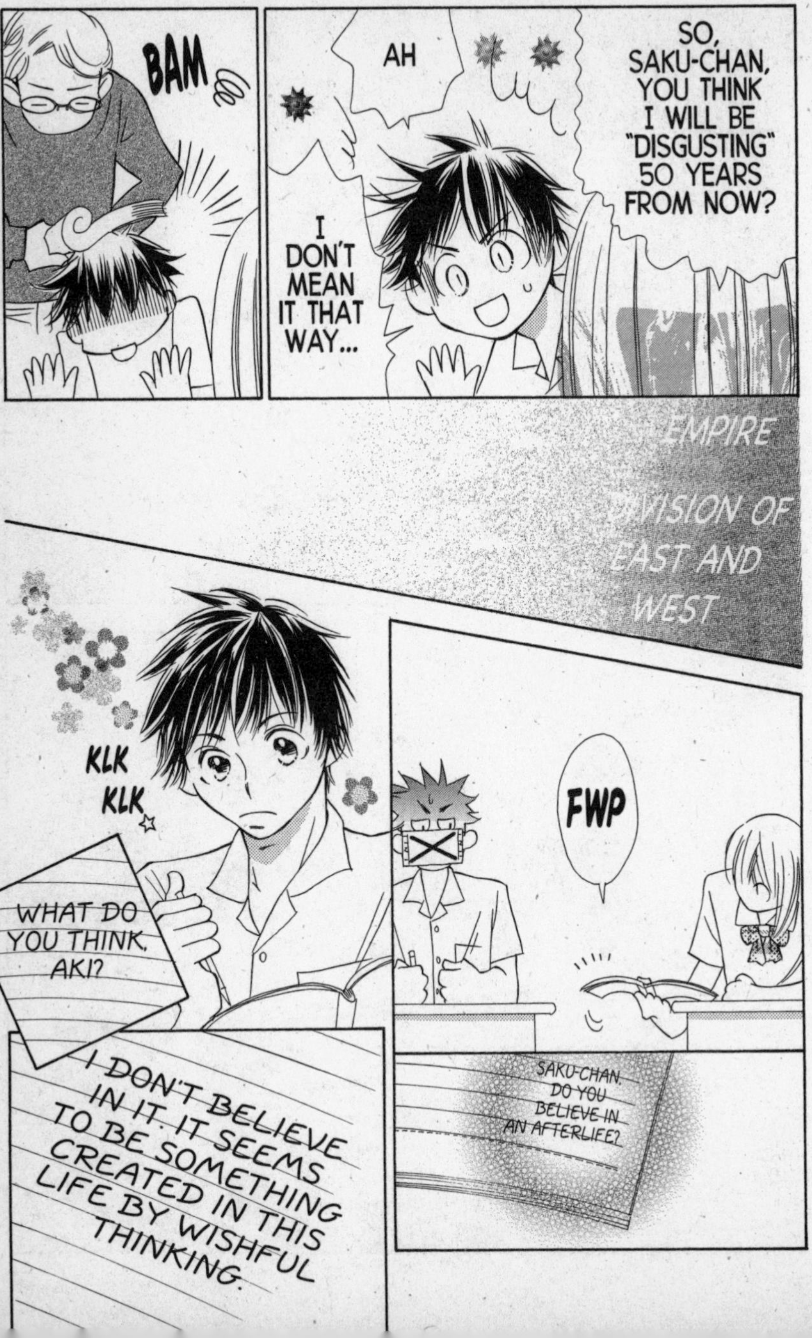
SO, SAKU-CHAN, YOU THINK I WILL BE "DISGUSTING" 50 YEARS FROM NOW?
AH
I DON'T MEAN IT THAT WAY...
BAM
EMPIRE
DIVISION OF EAST AND WEST
FWP
SAKU-CHAN, DO YOU BELIEVE IN AN AFTERLIFE?
KLK KLK
WHAT DO YOU THINK, AKI?
I DON'T BELIEVE IN IT. IT SEEMS TO BE SOMETHING CREATED IN THIS LIFE BY WISHFUL THINKING.

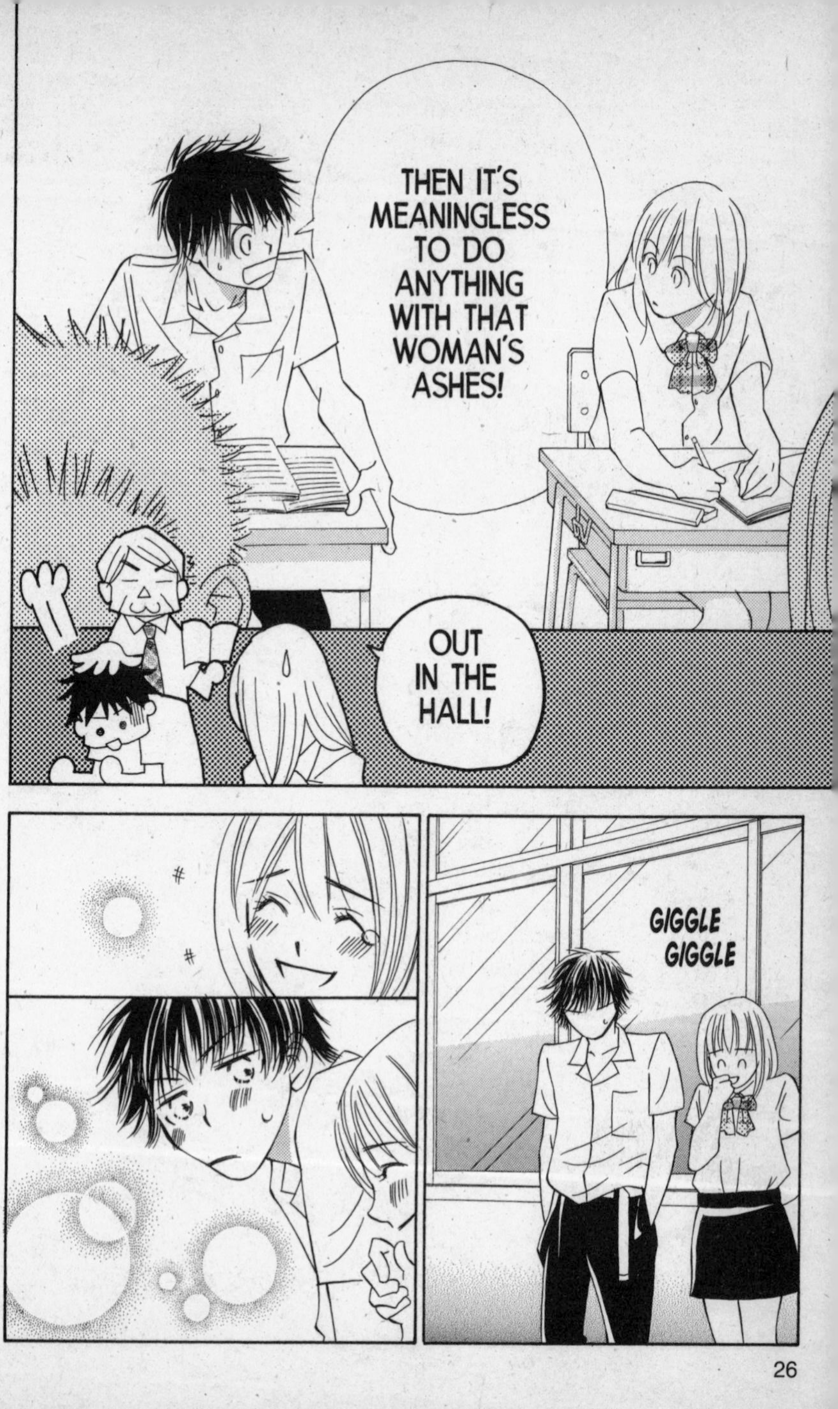
THEN IT'S MEANINGLESS TO DO ANYTHING WITH THAT WOMAN'S ASHES!
OUT IN THE HALL!
GIGGLE GIGGLE

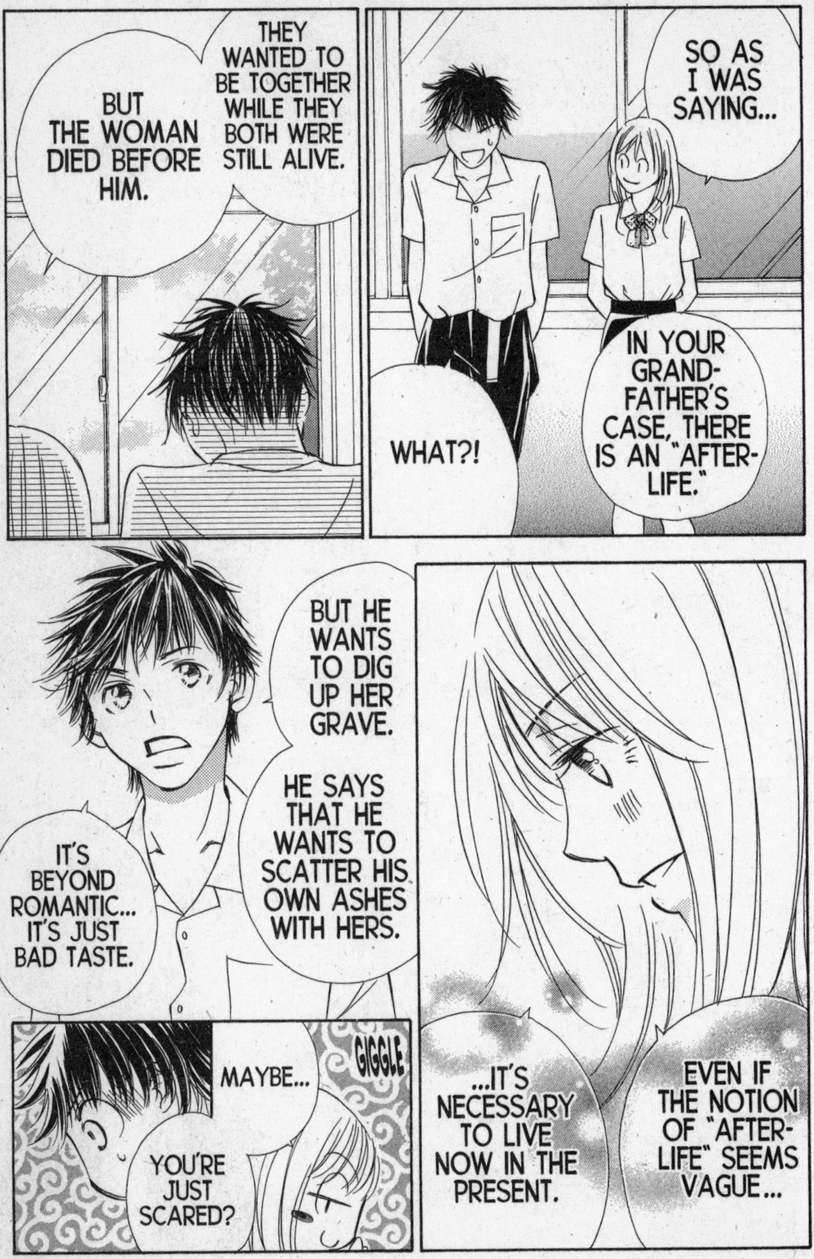
SO AS I WAS SAYING...
IN YOUR GRANDFATHER'S CASE, THERE IS AN "AFTERLIFE."
WHAT?!
THEY WANTED TO BE TOGETHER WHILE THEY BOTH WERE STILL ALIVE.
BUT THE WOMAN DIED BEFORE HIM.
EVEN IF THE NOTION OF "AFTERLIFE" SEEMS VAGUE...
...IT'S NECESSARY TO LIVE NOW IN THE PRESENT.
BUT HE WANTS TO DIG UP HER GRAVE.
HE SAYS THAT HE WANTS TO SCATTER HIS OWN ASHES WITH HERS.
IT'S BEYOND ROMANTIC... IT'S JUST BAD TASTE.
GIGGLE
MAYBE...
YOU'RE JUST SCARED?

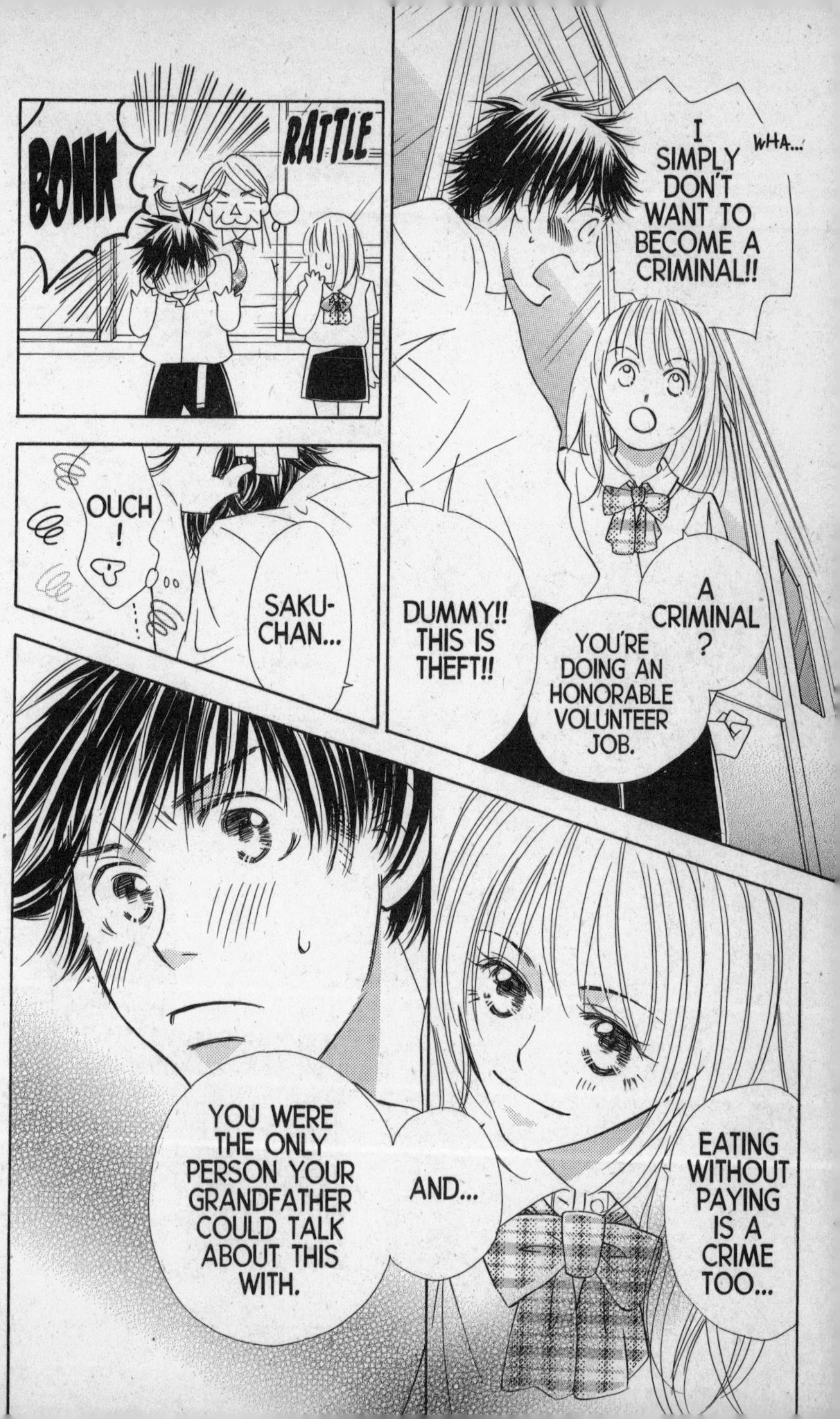
I SIMPLY DON'T WANT TO BECOME A CRIMINAL!!
WHA...
A CRIMINAL?
YOU'RE DOING AN HONORABLE VOLUNTEER JOB.
DUMMY!! THIS IS THEFT!!
RATTLE
BONK
SAKU-CHAN...
OUCH!
EATING WITHOUT PAYING IS A CRIME TOO...
AND...
YOU WERE THE ONLY PERSON YOUR GRANDFATHER COULD TALK ABOUT THIS WITH.

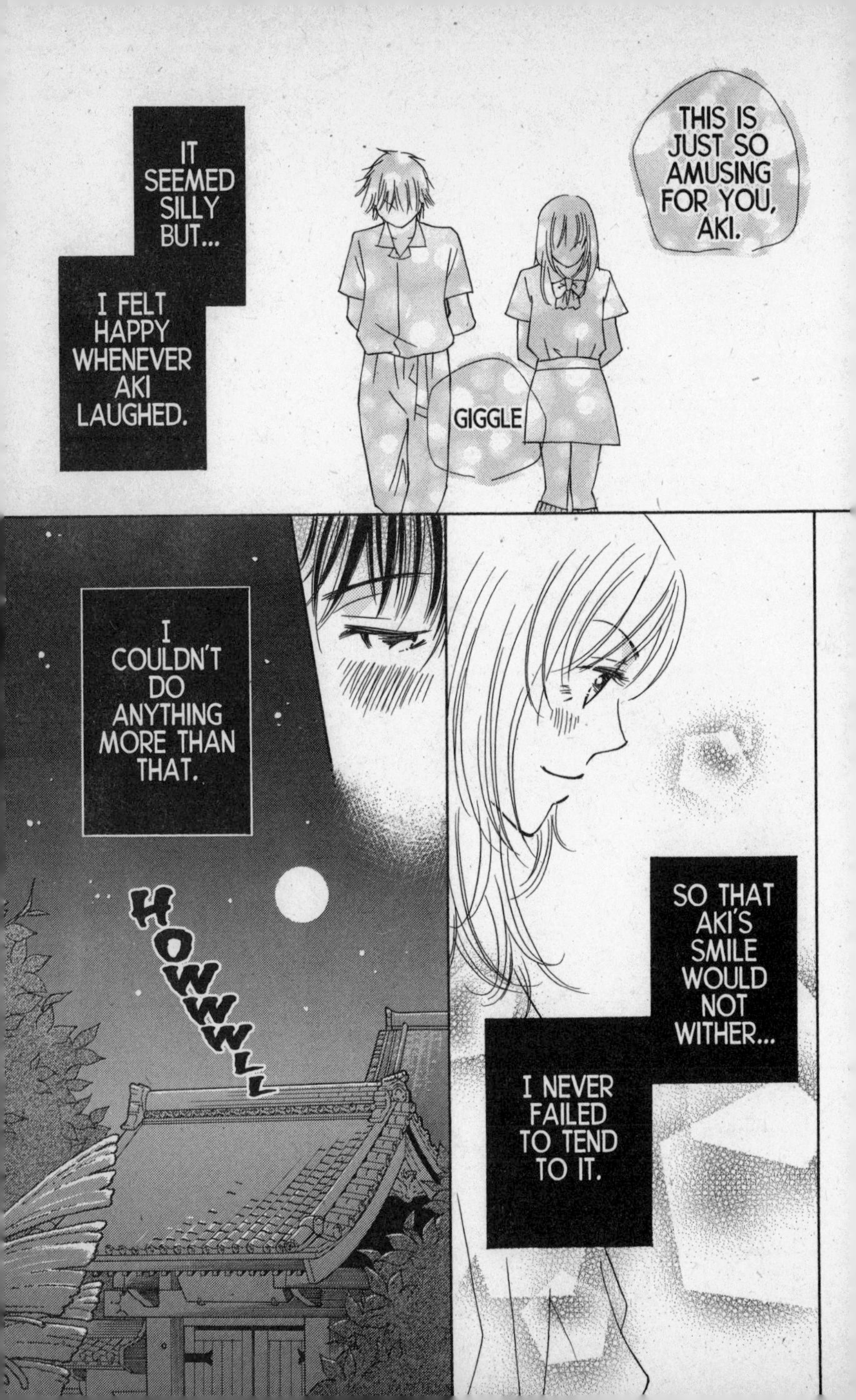
THIS IS JUST SO AMUSING FOR YOU, AKI.
GIGGLE
IT SEEMED SILLY BUT...
I FELT HAPPY WHENEVER AKI LAUGHED.
SO THAT AKI'S SMILE WOULD NOT WITHER...
I NEVER FAILED TO TEND TO IT.
I COULDN'T DO ANYTHING MORE THAN THAT.
HOWWLL

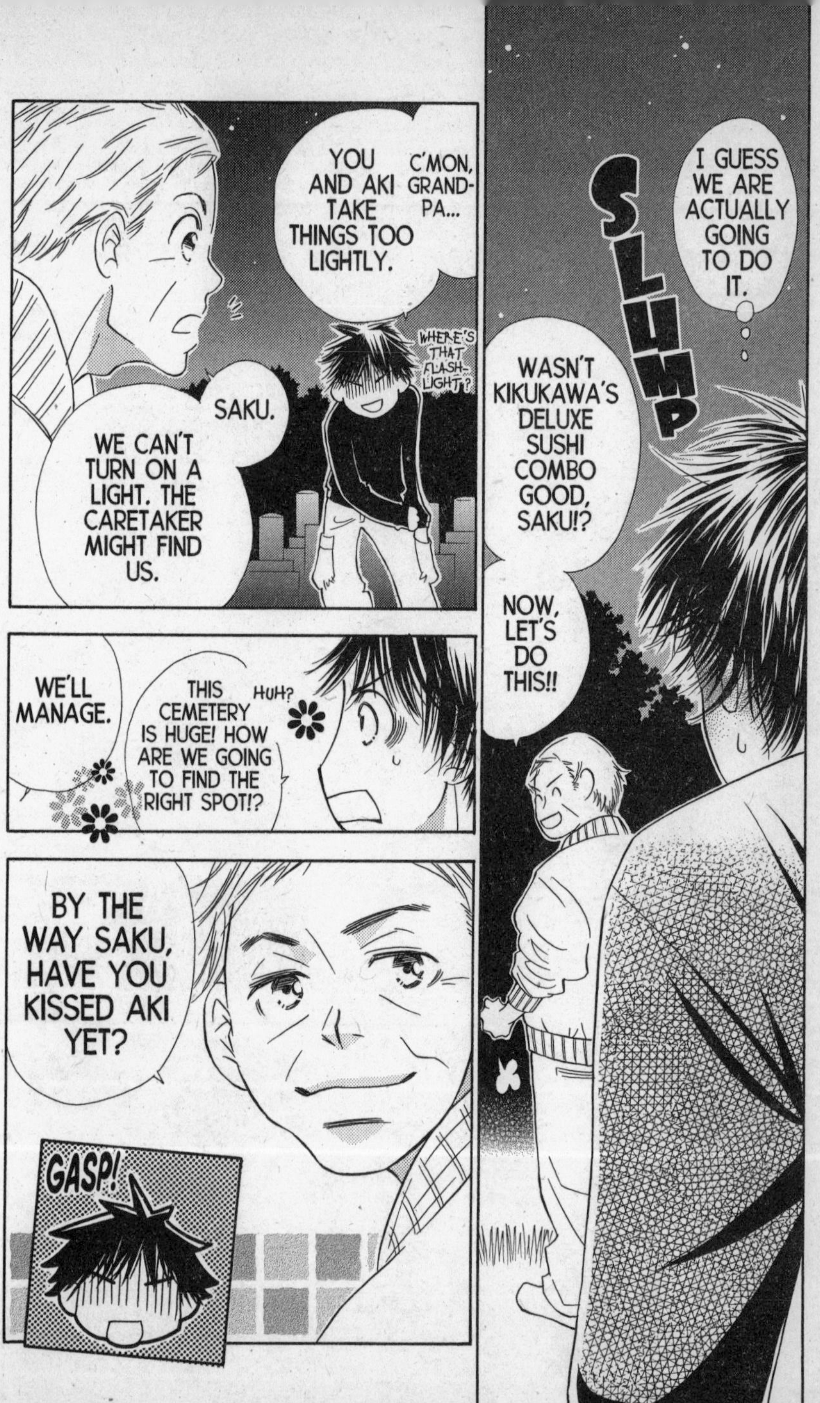
I GUESS WE ARE ACTUALLY GOING TO DO IT.
SLUMP
WASN'T KIKUKAWA'S DELUXE SUSHI COMBO GOOD, SAKU!?
NOW, LET'S DO THIS!!
C'MON, GRANDPA...
YOU AND AKI TAKE THINGS TOO LIGHTLY.
WHERE'S THAT FLASHLIGHT?
SAKU.
WE CAN'T TURN ON A LIGHT. THE CARETAKER MIGHT FIND US.
HUH?
THIS CEMETERY IS HUGE! HOW ARE WE GOING TO FIND THE RIGHT SPOT!?
WE'LL MANAGE.
BY THE WAY SAKU, HAVE YOU KISSED AKI YET?
GASP!

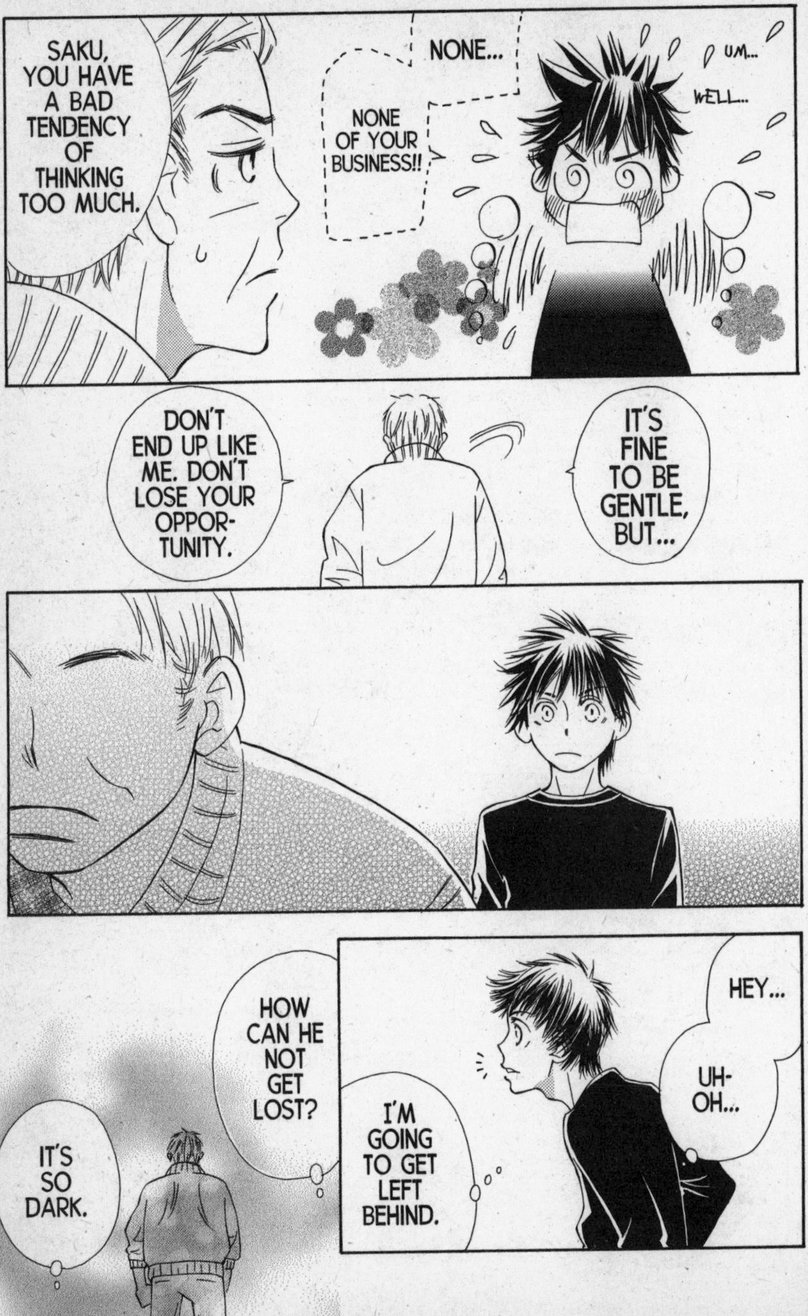
UM...
WELL...
NONE...
NONE OF YOUR BUSINESS!!
SAKU, YOU HAVE A BAD TENDENCY OF THINKING TOO MUCH.
IT'S FINE TO BE GENTLE, BUT...
DON'T END UP LIKE ME. DON'T LOSE YOUR OPPOR-TUNITY.
HEY...
UH-OH...
I'M GOING TO GET LEFT BEHIND.
HOW CAN HE NOT GET LOST?
IT'S SO DARK.

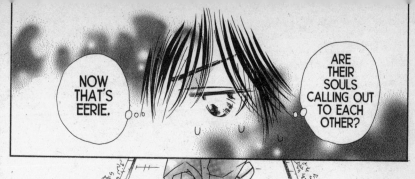

ARE THEIR SOULS CALLING OUT TO EACH OTHER?

NOW THAT'S EERIE.

HERE IT IS.

FIRST, WE OFFERED INCENSE...

SORRY, WE WILL BE DISTURBING YOU FOR A SHORT WHILE.

AFTER TEN MINUTES OF LABOR...

GRANDPA, IS YOUR BACK OKAY?

SHUFL

CAREFUL, DON'T DROP IT!!

SHUFL

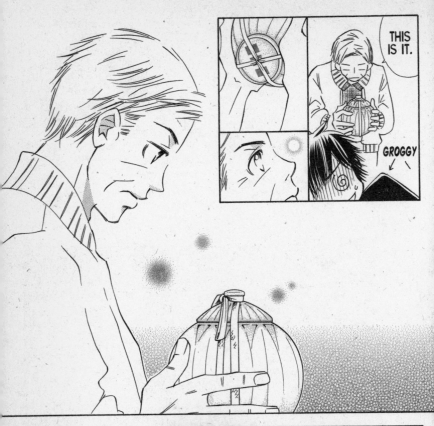

THIS IS IT.

GROGGY

GRAN--

GRANDPA, LET'S HURRY.

WE DON'T WANT TO GET CAUGHT...

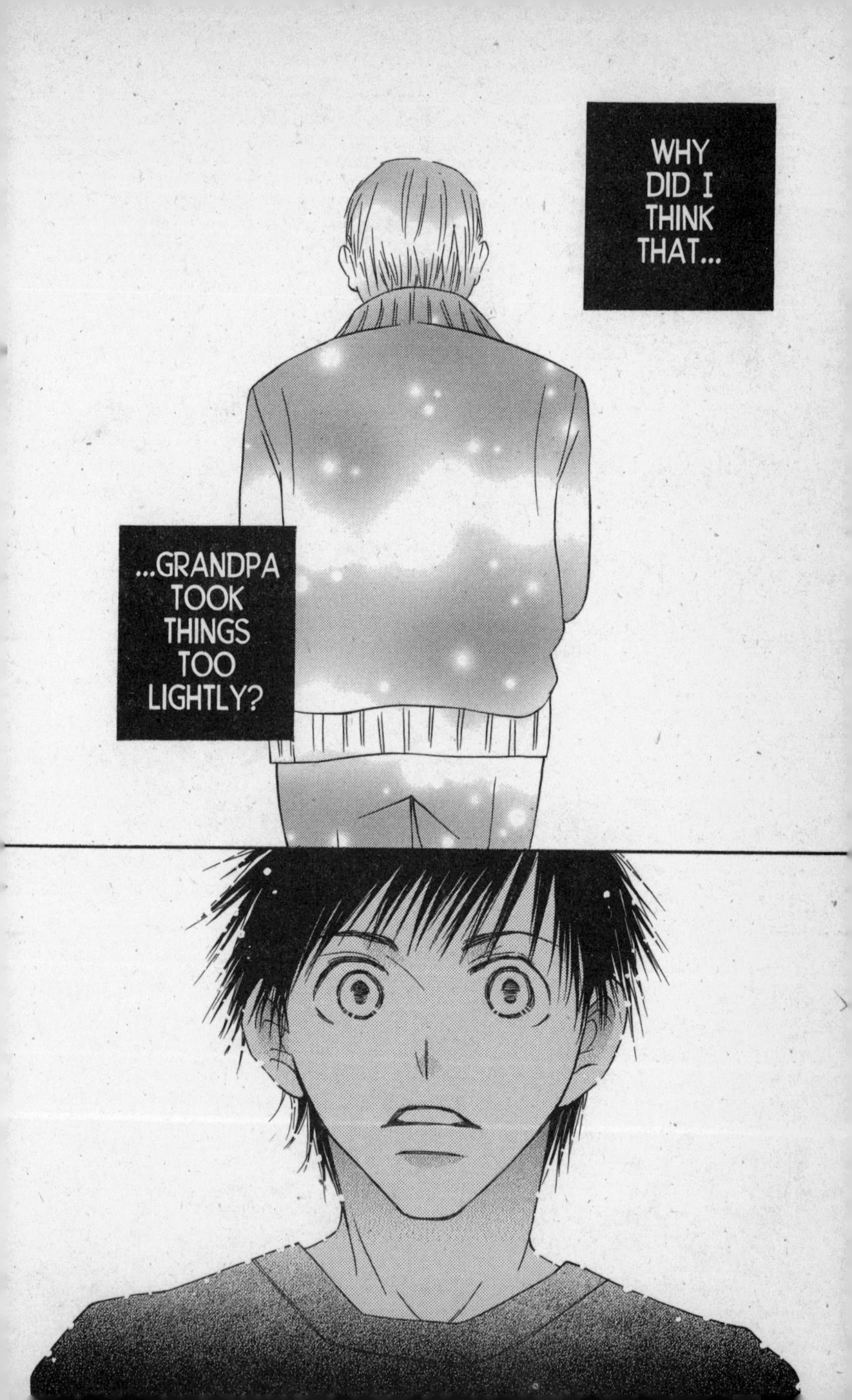
WHY DID I THINK THAT...
...GRANDPA TOOK THINGS TOO LIGHTLY?

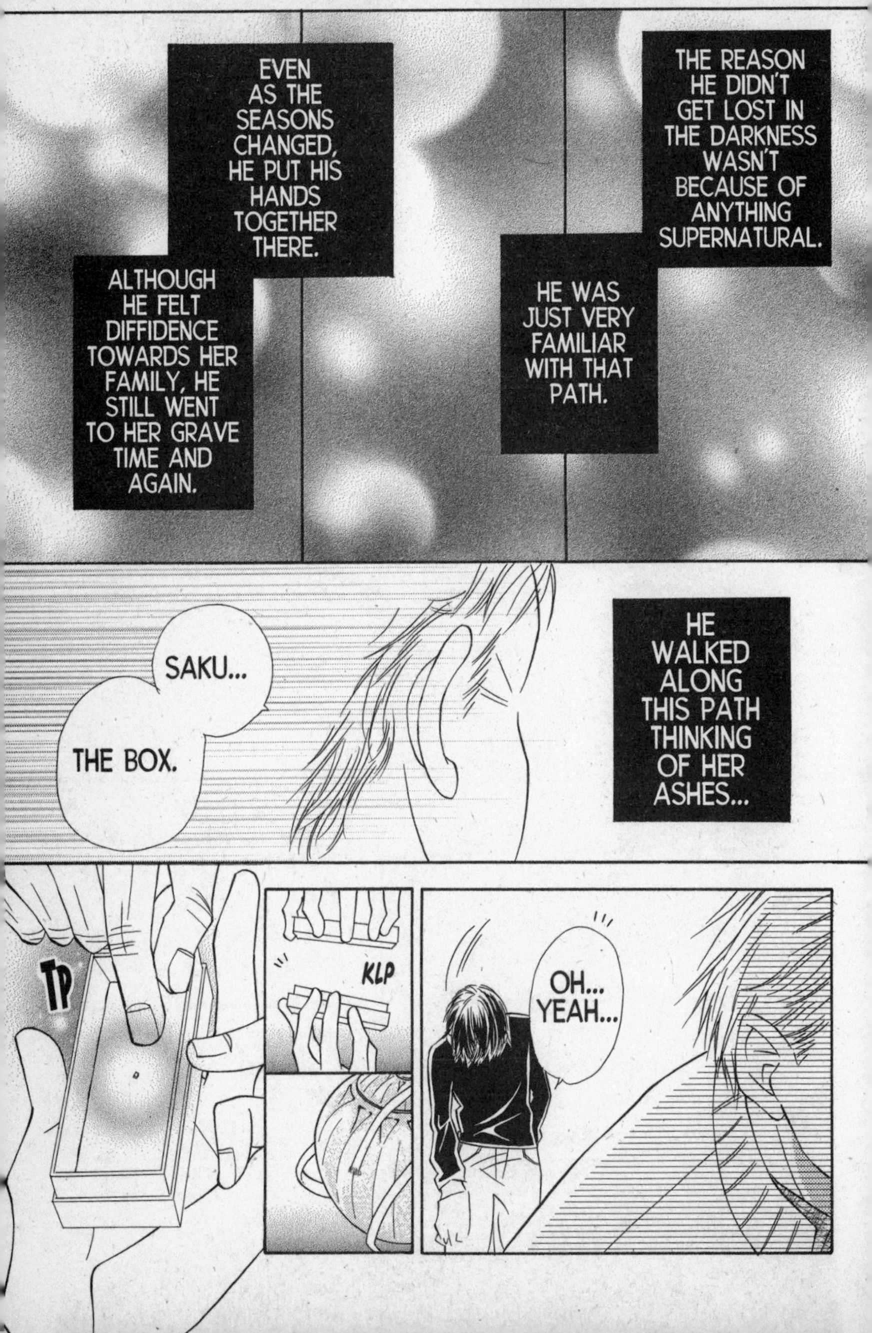
THE REASON HE DIDN'T GET LOST IN THE DARKNESS WASN'T BECAUSE OF ANYTHING SUPERNATURAL.
HE WAS JUST VERY FAMILIAR WITH THAT PATH.
EVEN AS THE SEASONS CHANGED, HE PUT HIS HANDS TOGETHER THERE.
ALTHOUGH HE FELT DIFFIDENCE TOWARDS HER FAMILY, HE STILL WENT TO HER GRAVE TIME AND AGAIN.
HE WALKED ALONG THIS PATH THINKING OF HER ASHES...
SAKU...
THE BOX.
OH... YEAH...
KLP
TP

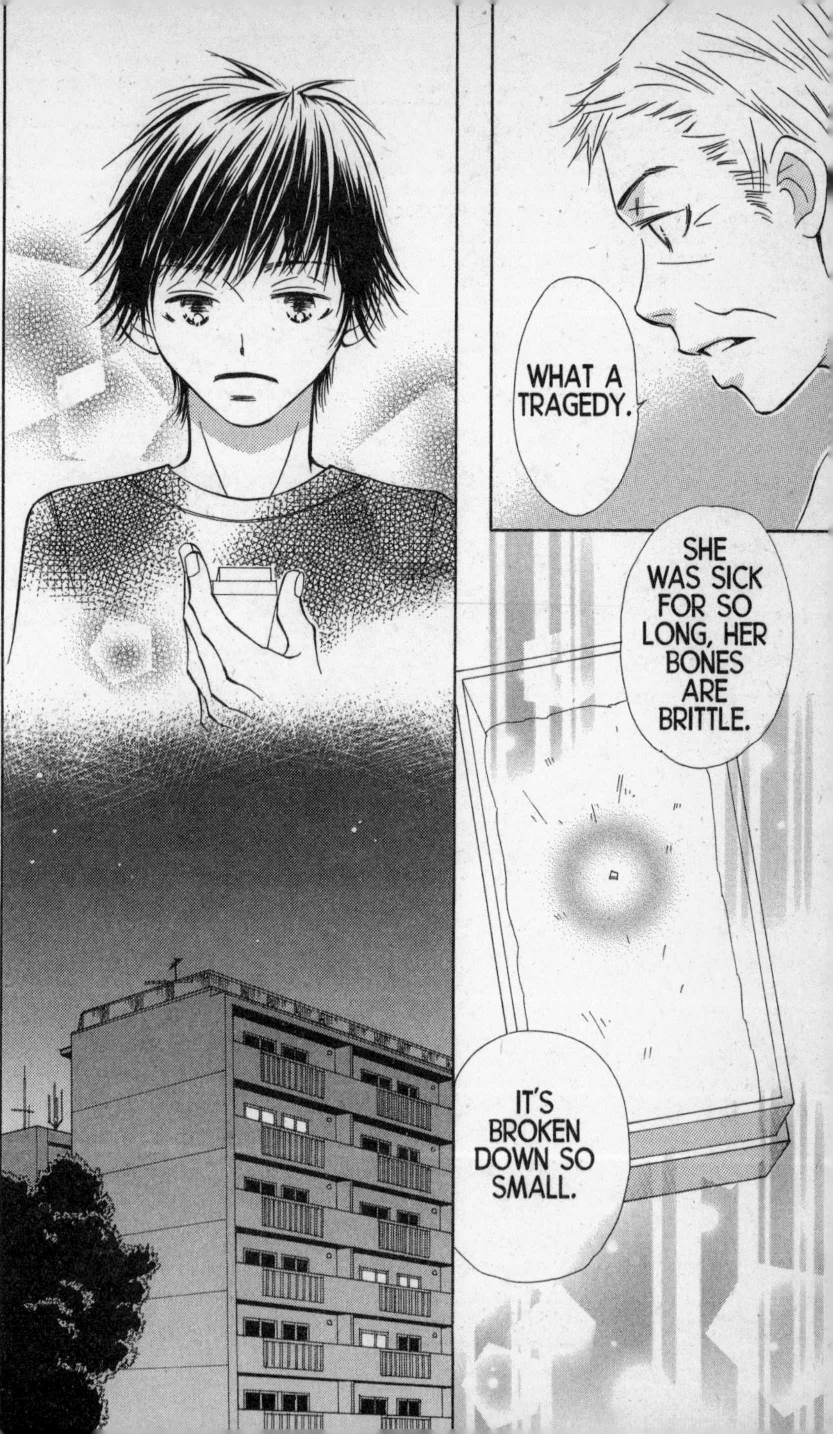
WHAT A TRAGEDY.
SHE WAS SICK FOR SO LONG, HER BONES ARE BRITTLE.
IT'S BROKEN DOWN SO SMALL.

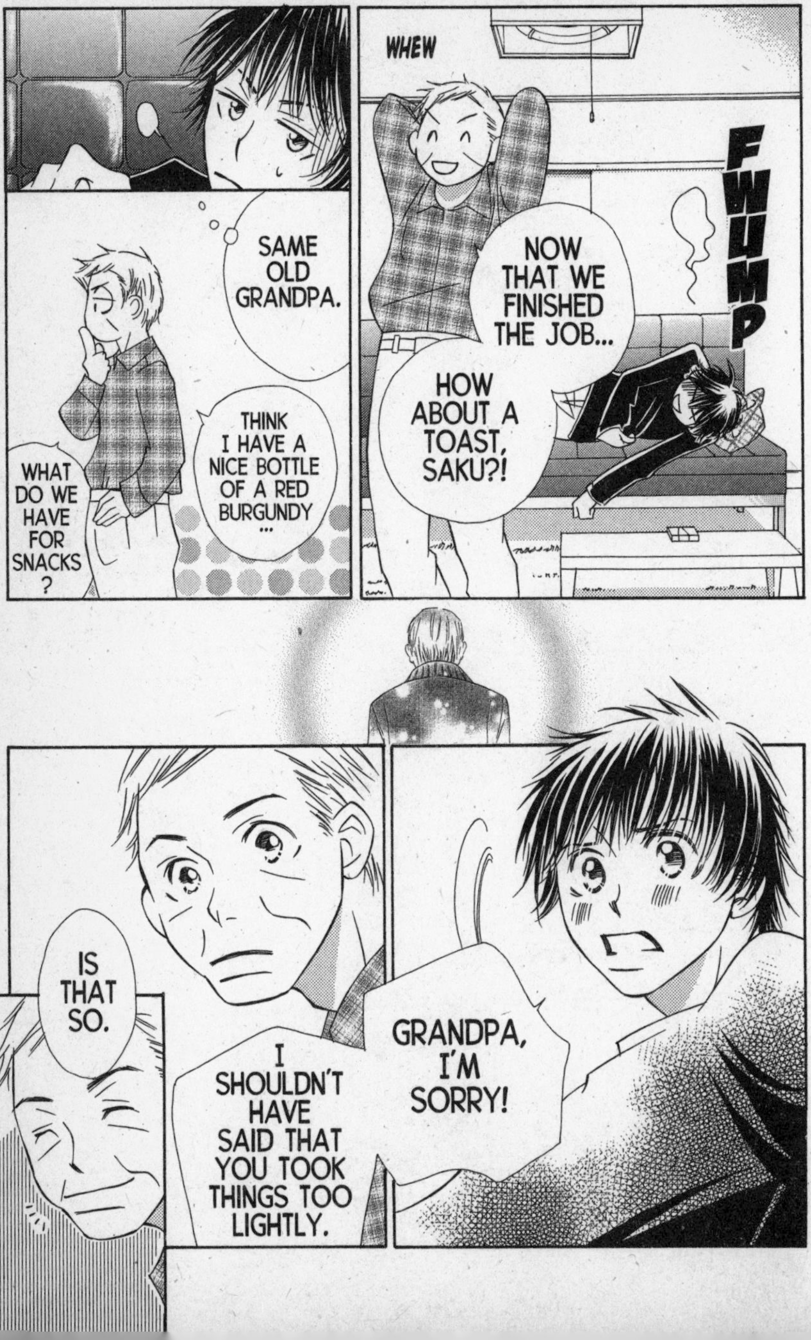
WHEW
FWUMP
NOW THAT WE FINISHED THE JOB...
HOW ABOUT A TOAST, SAKU?!
SAME OLD GRANDPA.
THINK I HAVE A NICE BOTTLE OF A RED BURGUNDY...
WHAT DO WE HAVE FOR SNACKS?
GRANDPA, I'M SORRY!
I SHOULDN'T HAVE SAID THAT YOU TOOK THINGS TOO LIGHTLY.
IS THAT SO.

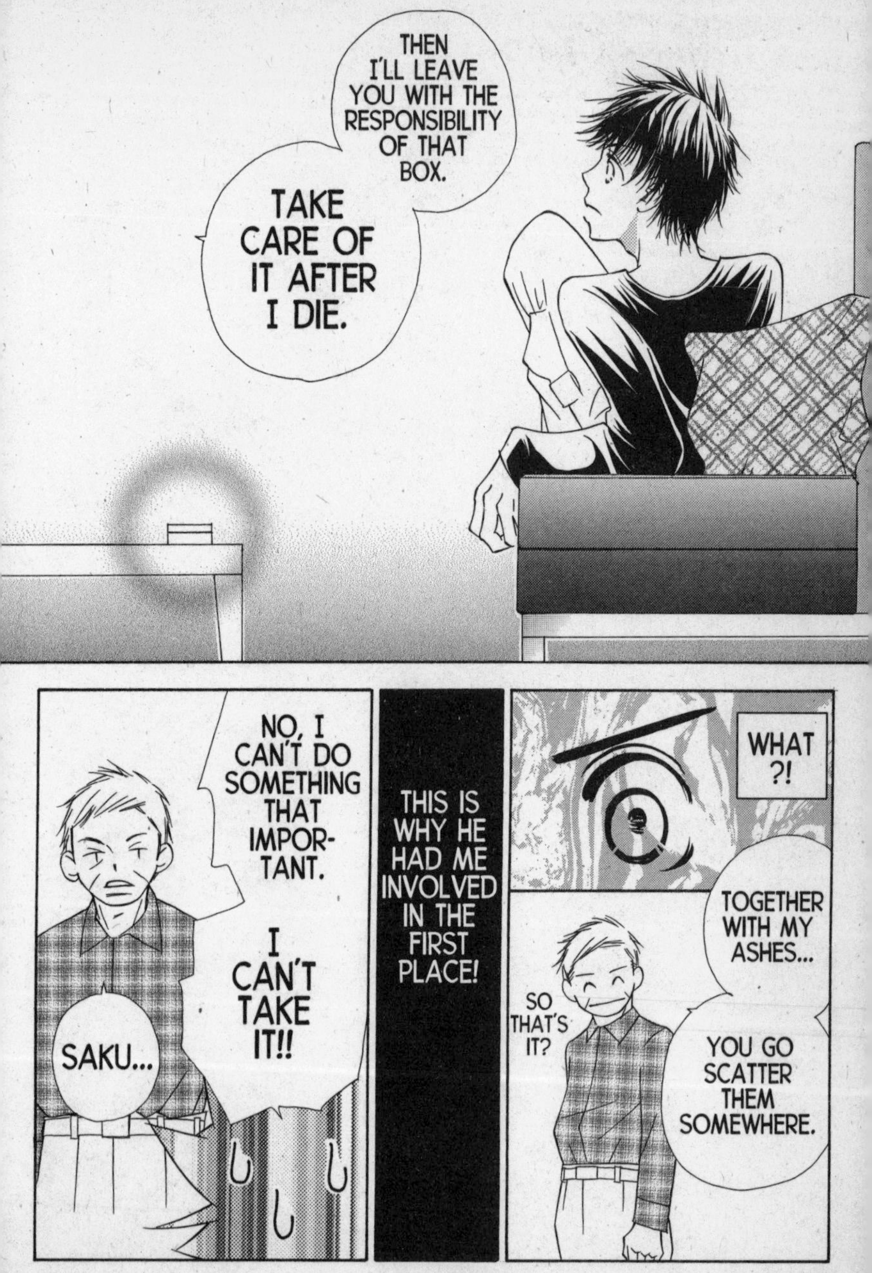
THEN I'LL LEAVE YOU WITH THE RESPONSIBILITY OF THAT BOX.
TAKE CARE OF IT AFTER I DIE.
WHAT?!
TOGETHER WITH MY ASHES...
YOU GO SCATTER THEM SOMEWHERE.
SO THAT'S IT?
THIS IS WHY HE HAD ME INVOLVED IN THE FIRST PLACE!
NO, I CAN'T DO SOMETHING THAT IMPOR-TANT.
I CAN'T TAKE IT!!
SAKU...

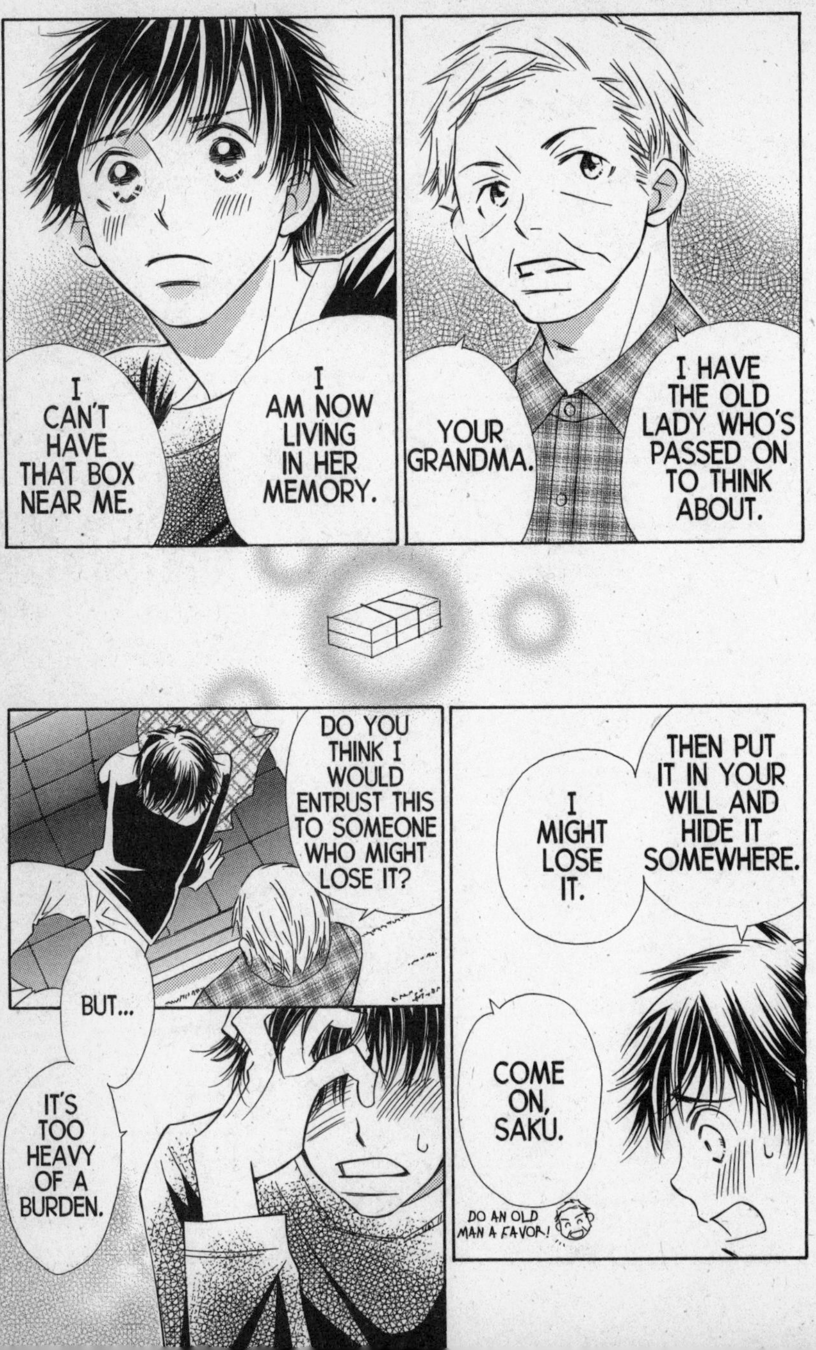
I HAVE THE OLD LADY WHO'S PASSED ON TO THINK ABOUT.
YOUR GRANDMA.
I AM NOW LIVING IN HER MEMORY.
I CAN'T HAVE THAT BOX NEAR ME.
THEN PUT IT IN YOUR WILL AND HIDE IT SOMEWHERE.
I MIGHT LOSE IT.
COME ON, SAKU.
DO AN OLD MAN A FAVOR!
DO YOU THINK I WOULD ENTRUST THIS TO SOMEONE WHO MIGHT LOSE IT?
BUT...
IT'S TOO HEAVY OF A BURDEN.

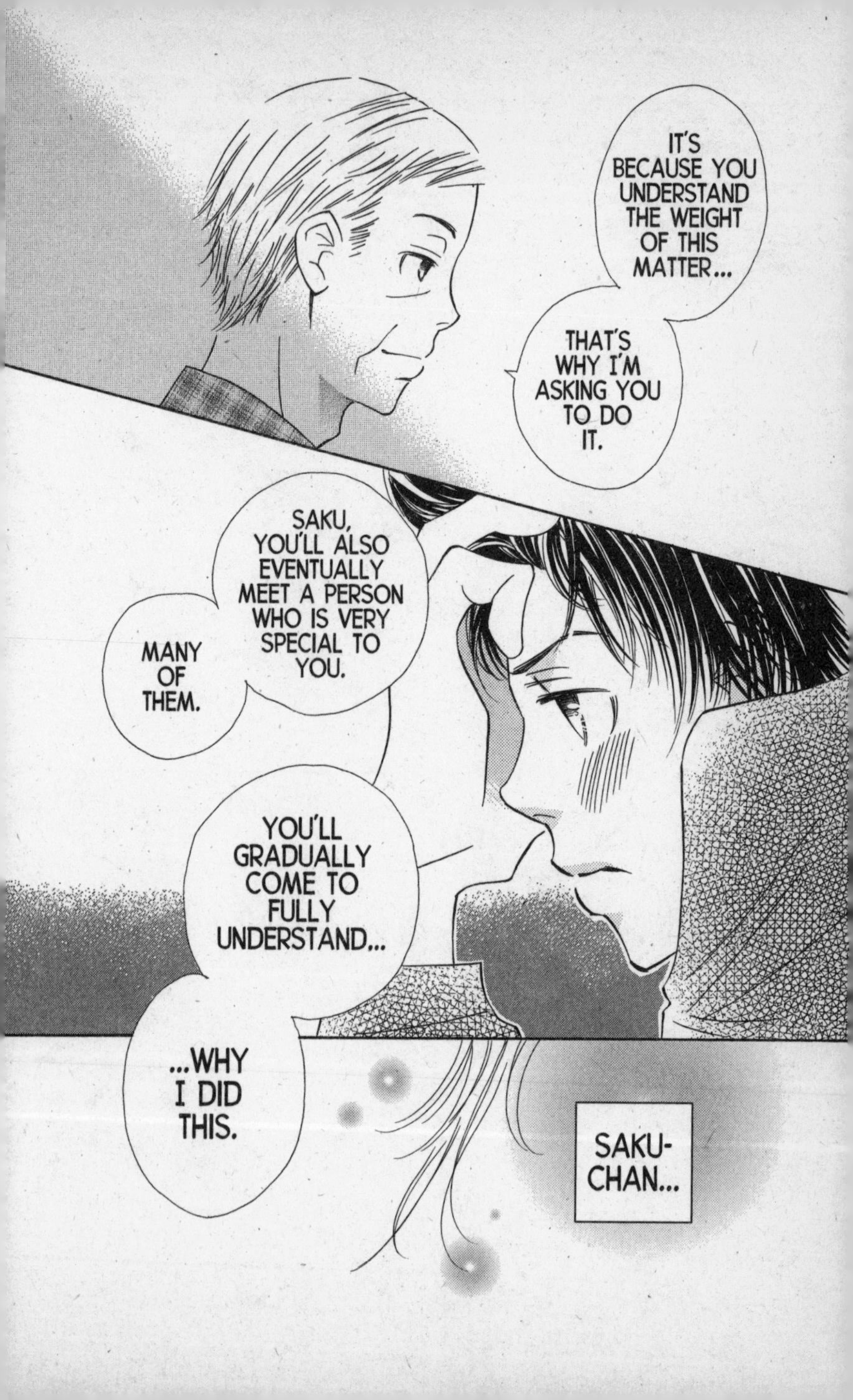
IT'S BECAUSE YOU UNDERSTAND THE WEIGHT OF THIS MATTER...
THAT'S WHY I'M ASKING YOU TO DO IT.
SAKU, YOU'LL ALSO EVENTUALLY MEET A PERSON WHO IS VERY SPECIAL TO YOU.
MANY OF THEM.
YOU'LL GRADUALLY COME TO FULLY UNDERSTAND...
...WHY I DID THIS.
SAKU-CHAN...

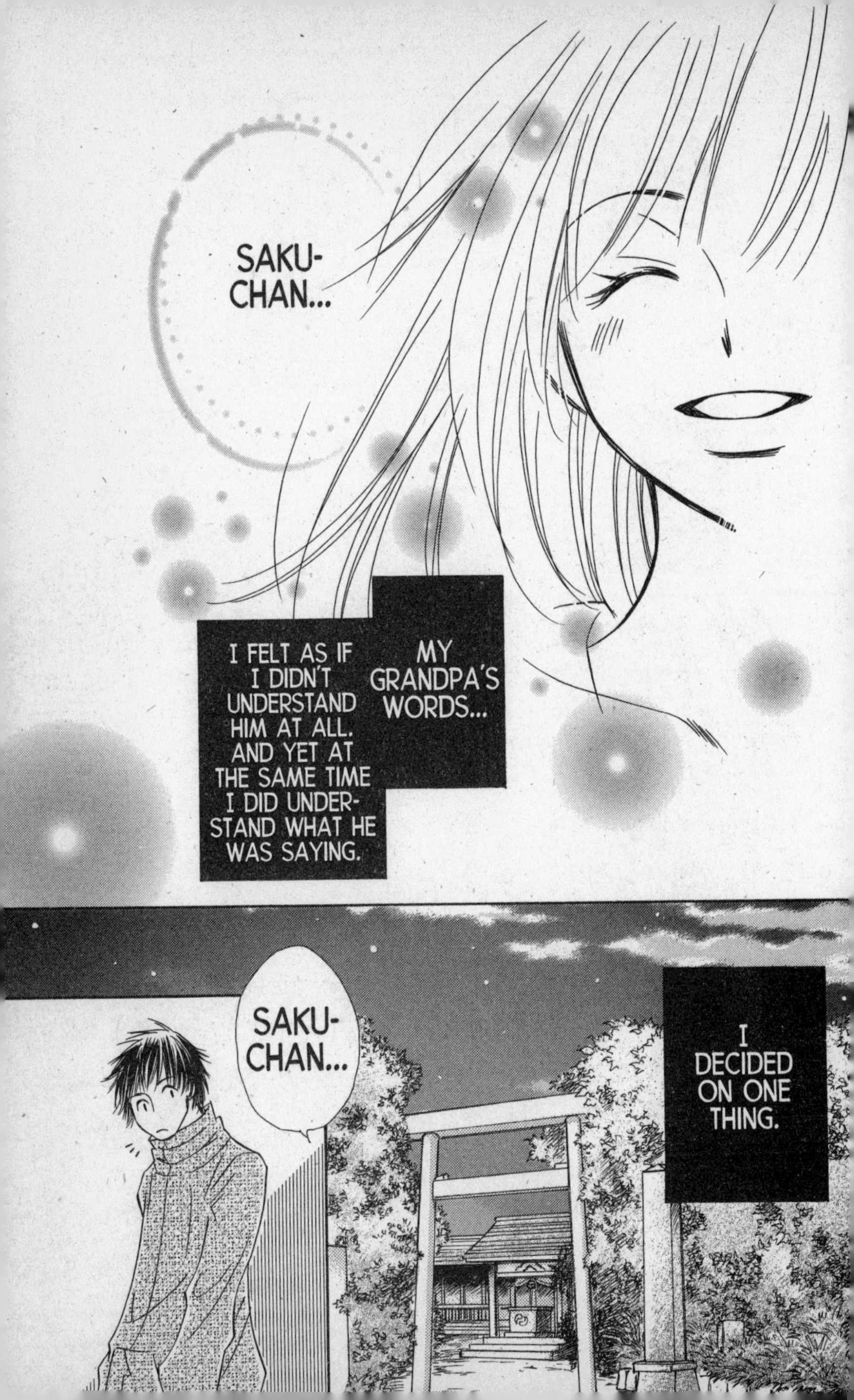
SAKU-CHAN...
MY GRANDPA'S WORDS...
I FELT AS IF I DIDN'T UNDERSTAND HIM AT ALL. AND YET AT THE SAME TIME I DID UNDERSTAND WHAT HE WAS SAYING.
I DECIDED ON ONE THING.
SAKU-CHAN...

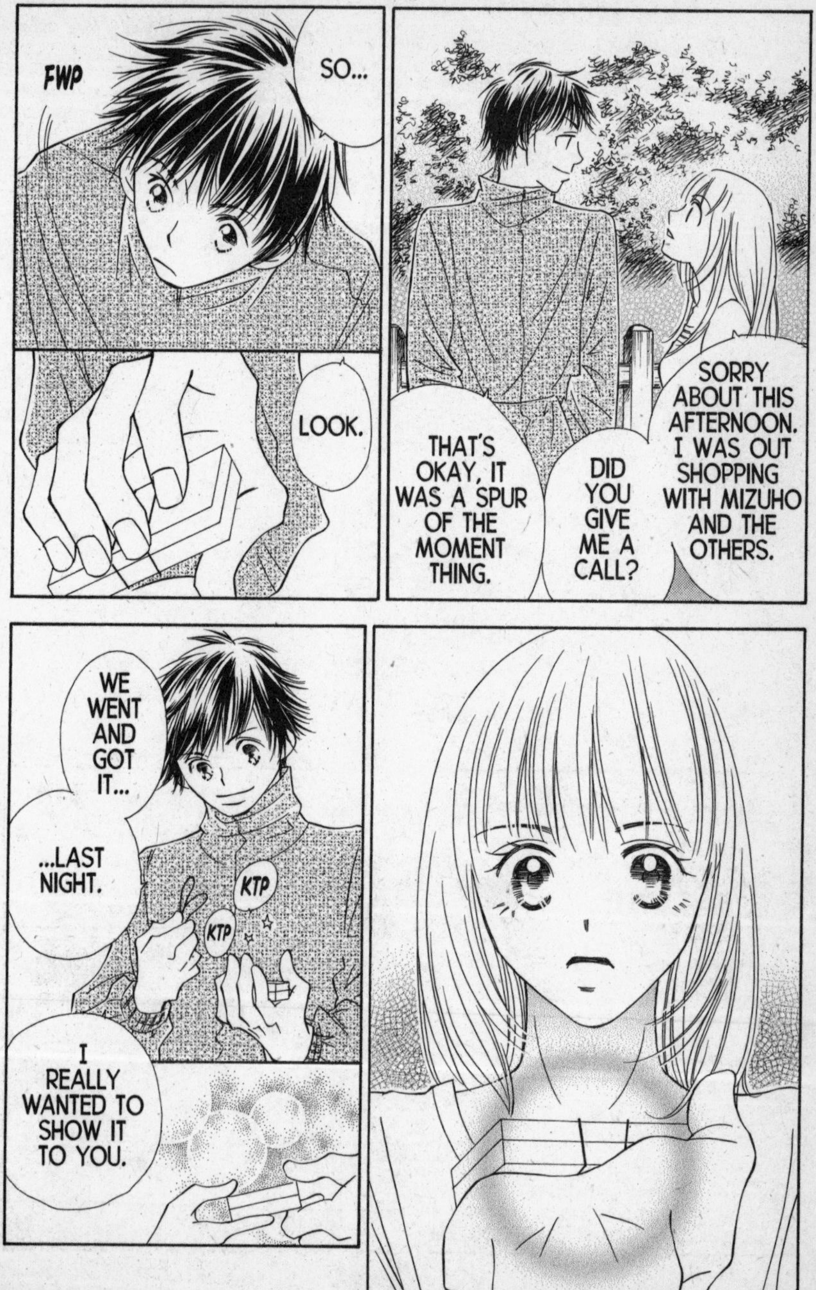
SORRY ABOUT THIS AFTERNOON. I WAS OUT SHOPPING WITH MIZUHO AND THE OTHERS.
DID YOU GIVE ME A CALL?
THAT'S OKAY, IT WAS A SPUR OF THE MOMENT THING.
FWP
SO...
LOOK.
WE WENT AND GOT IT...
...LAST NIGHT.
KTP
KTP
I REALLY WANTED TO SHOW IT TO YOU.

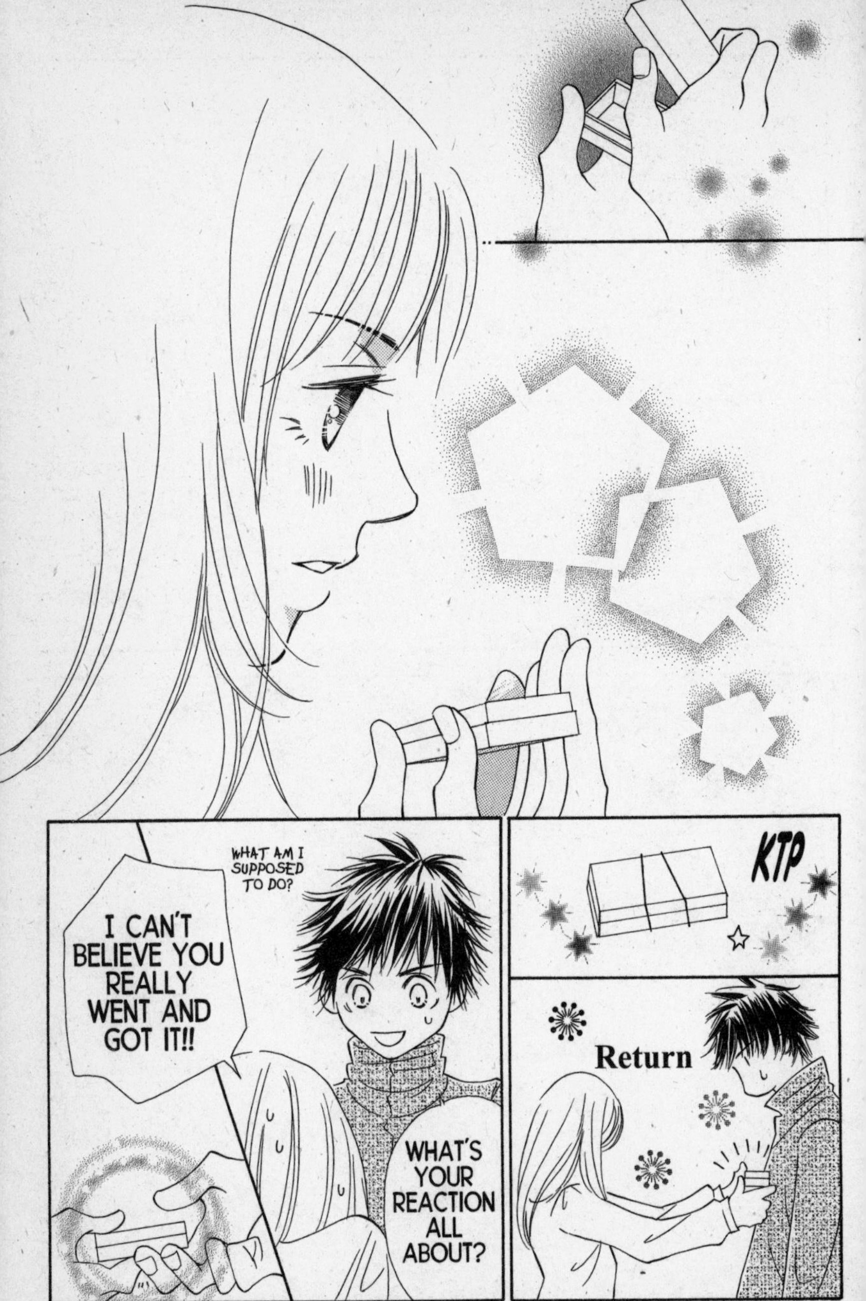
KTP
Return
WHAT AM I SUPPOSED TO DO?
I CAN'T BELIEVE YOU REALLY WENT AND GOT IT!!
WHAT'S YOUR REACTION ALL ABOUT?

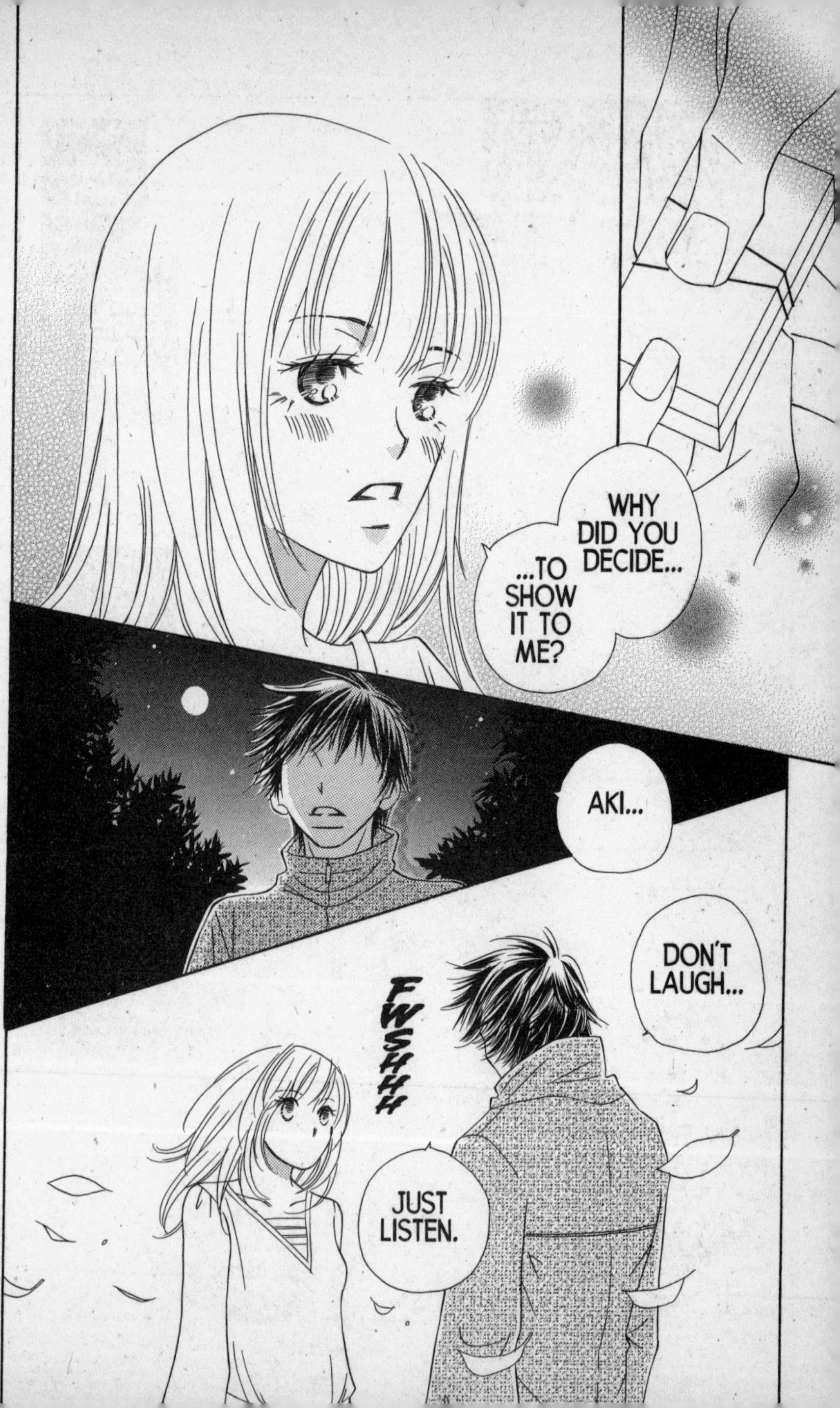
WHY DID YOU DECIDE...
...TO SHOW IT TO ME?
AKI...
DON'T LAUGH...
FWSHHH
JUST LISTEN.

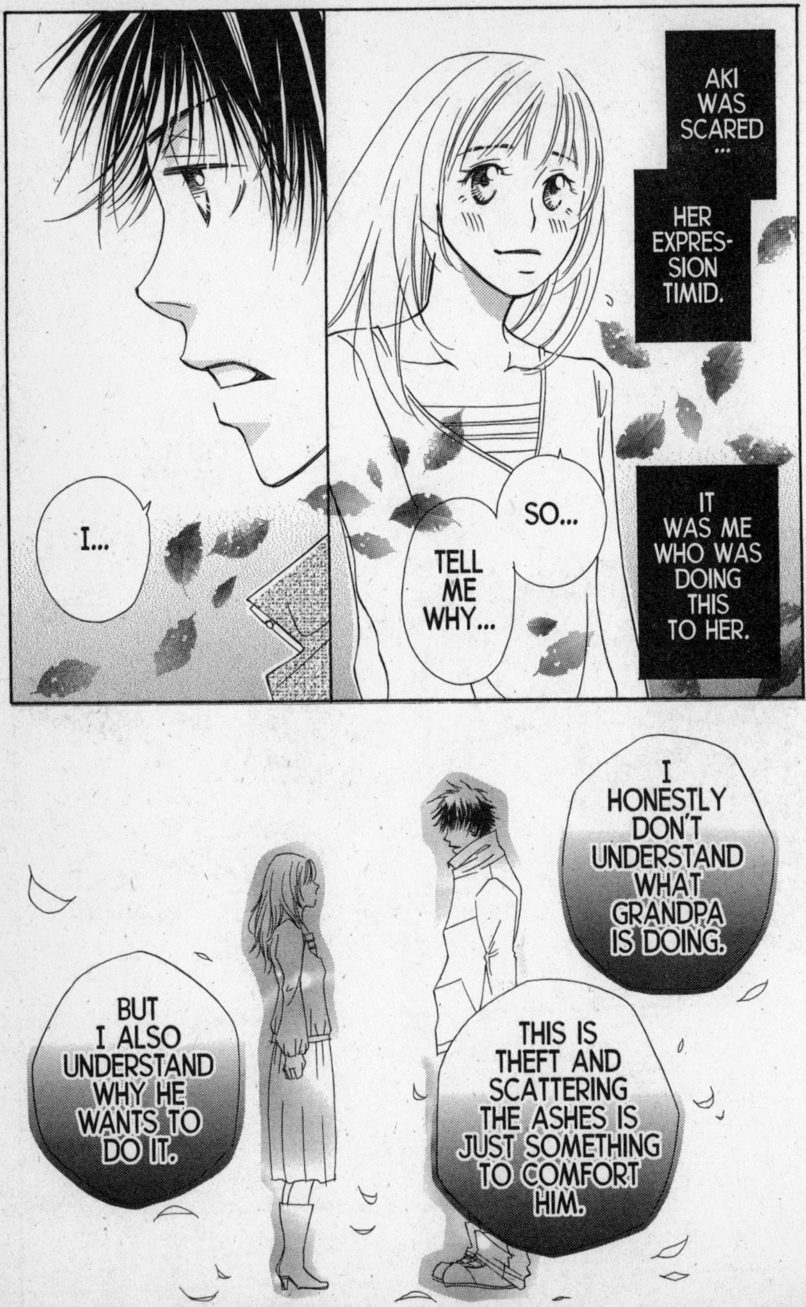
AKI WAS SCARED...
HER EXPRES-SION TIMID.
SO...
TELL ME WHY...
IT WAS ME WHO WAS DOING THIS TO HER.
I...
I HONESTLY DON'T UNDERSTAND WHAT GRANDPA IS DOING.
THIS IS THEFT AND SCATTERING THE ASHES IS JUST SOMETHING TO COMFORT HIM.
BUT I ALSO UNDERSTAND WHY HE WANTS TO DO IT.

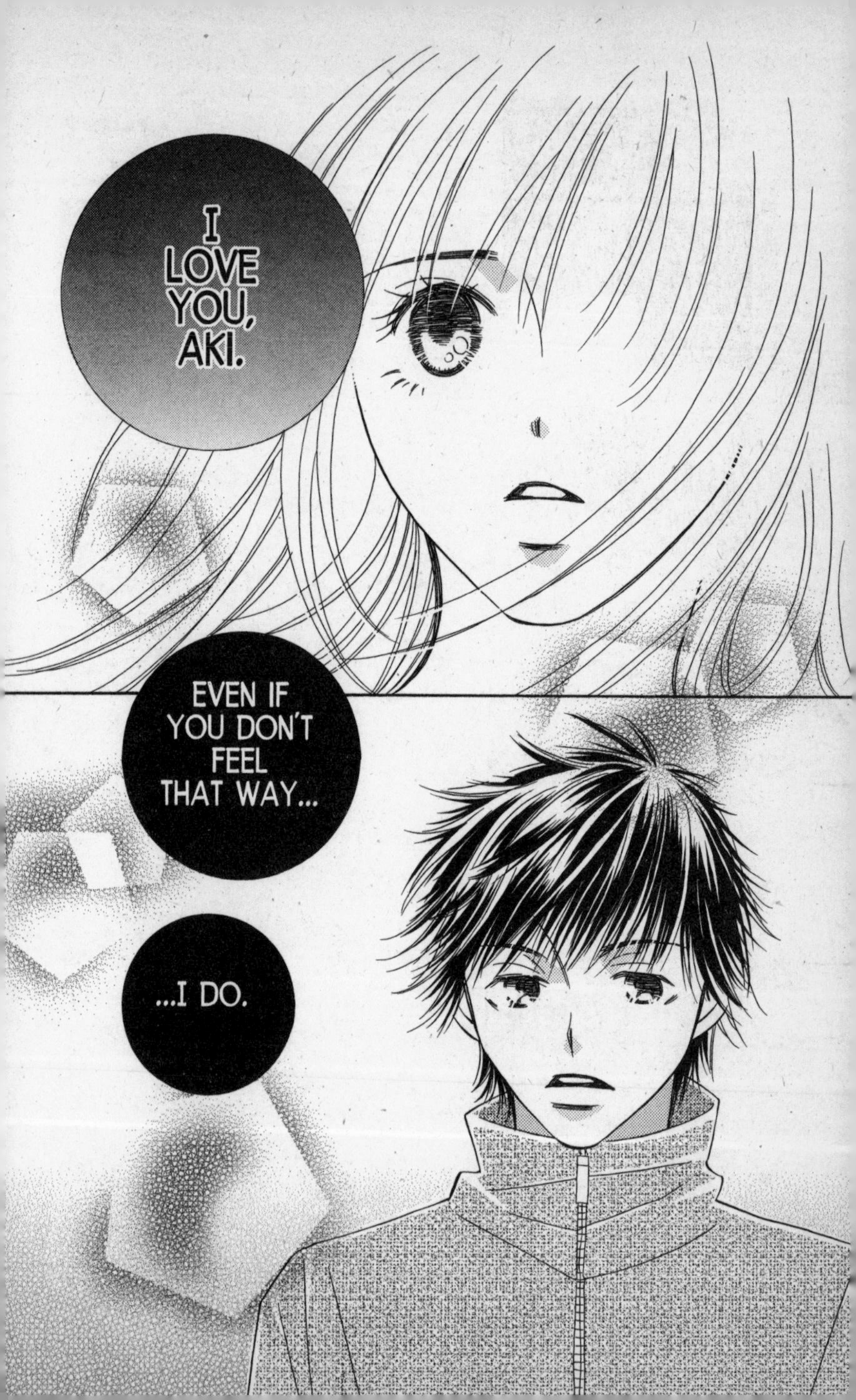
I LOVE YOU, AKI.
EVEN IF YOU DON'T FEEL THAT WAY...
...I DO.

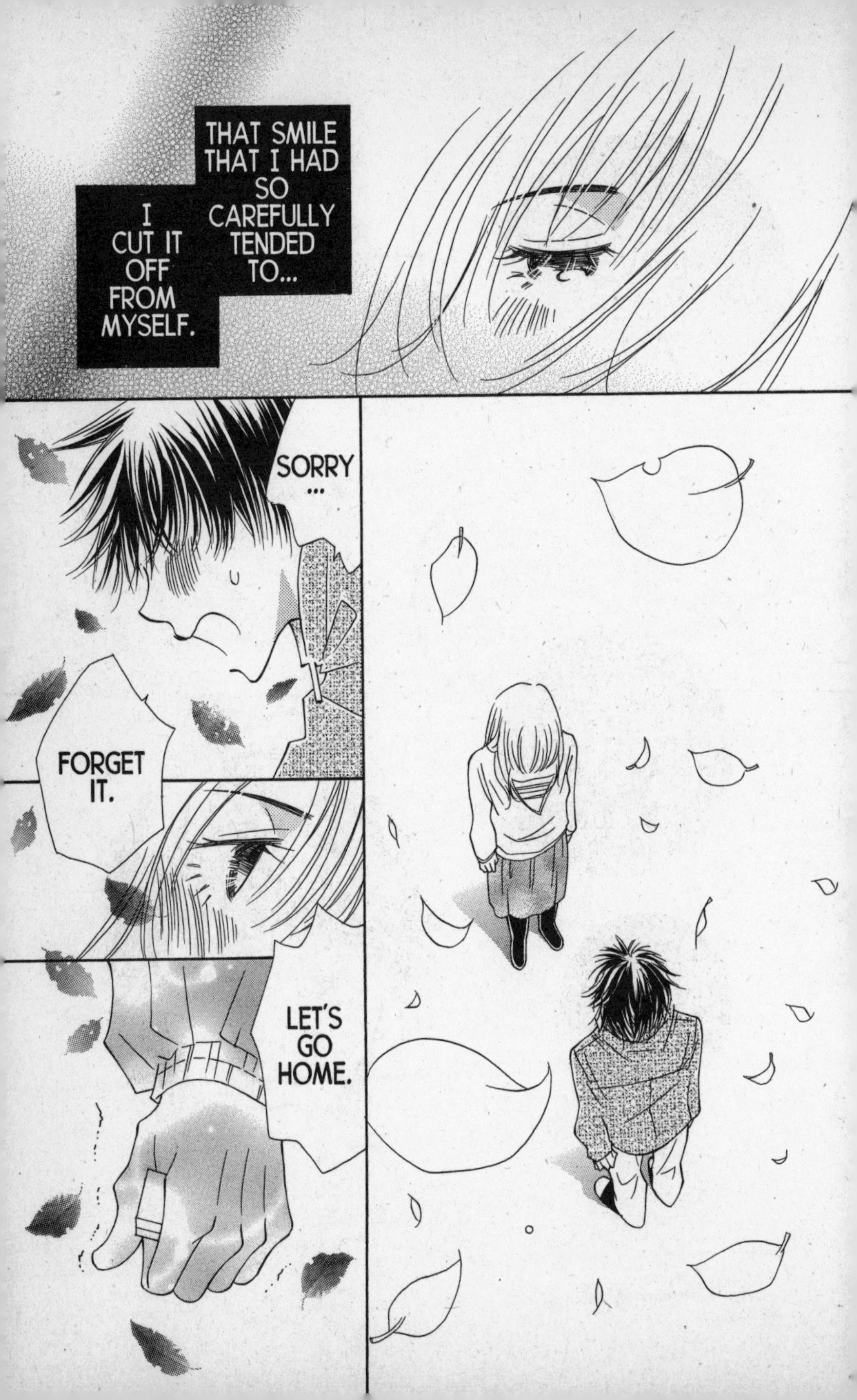
THAT SMILE THAT I HAD SO CAREFULLY TENDED TO...
I CUT IT OFF FROM MYSELF.
SORRY...
FORGET IT.
LET'S GO HOME.

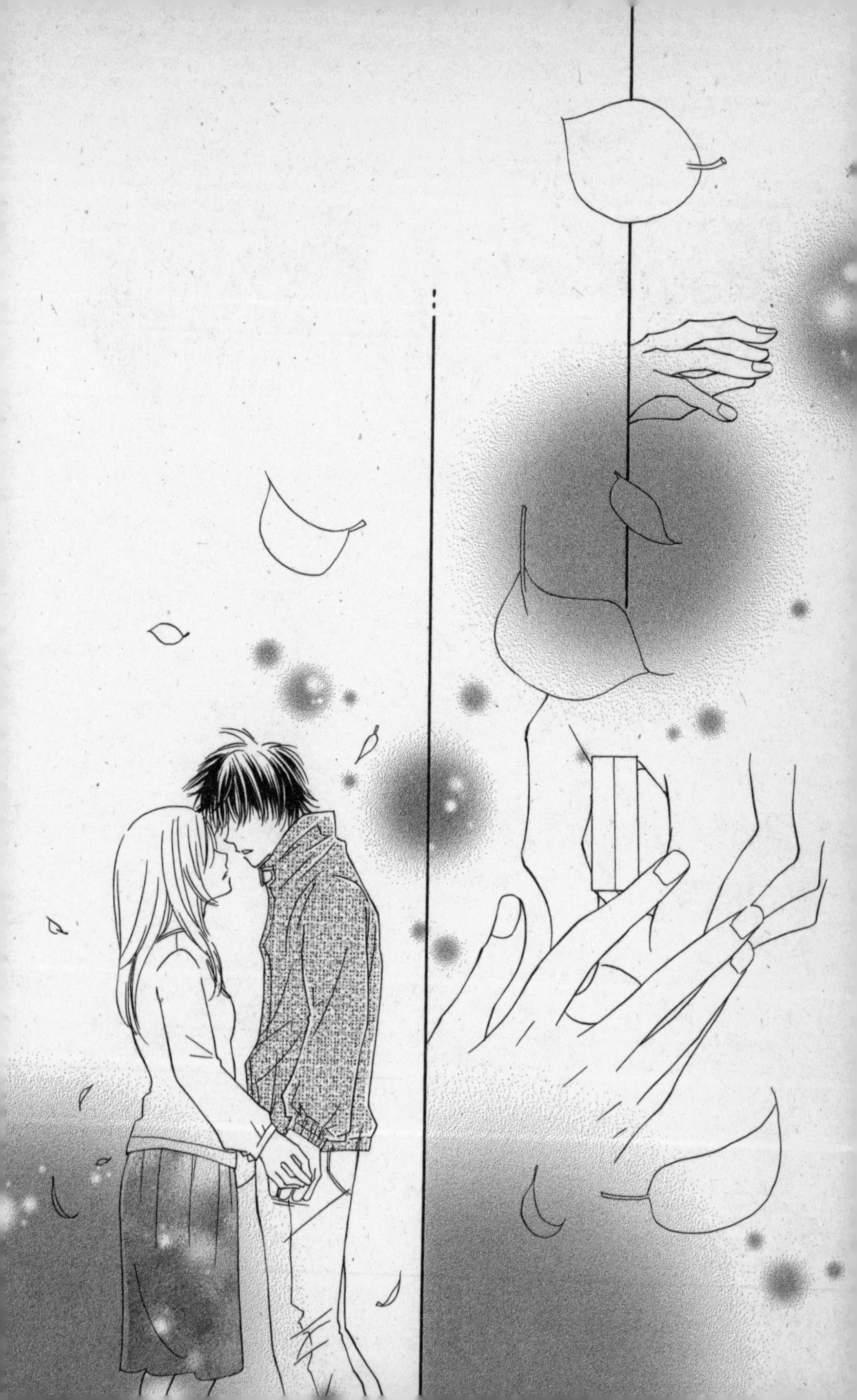

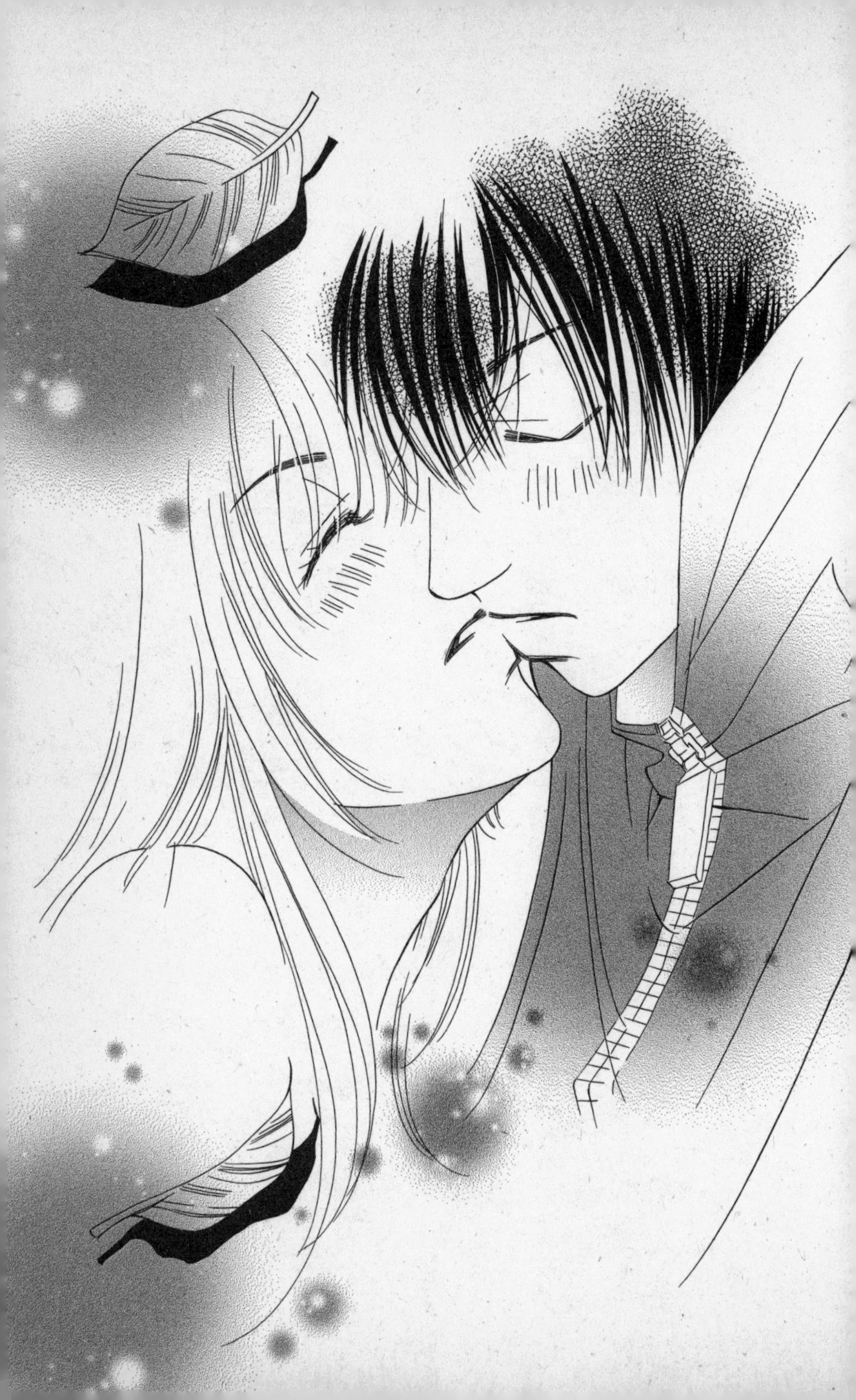

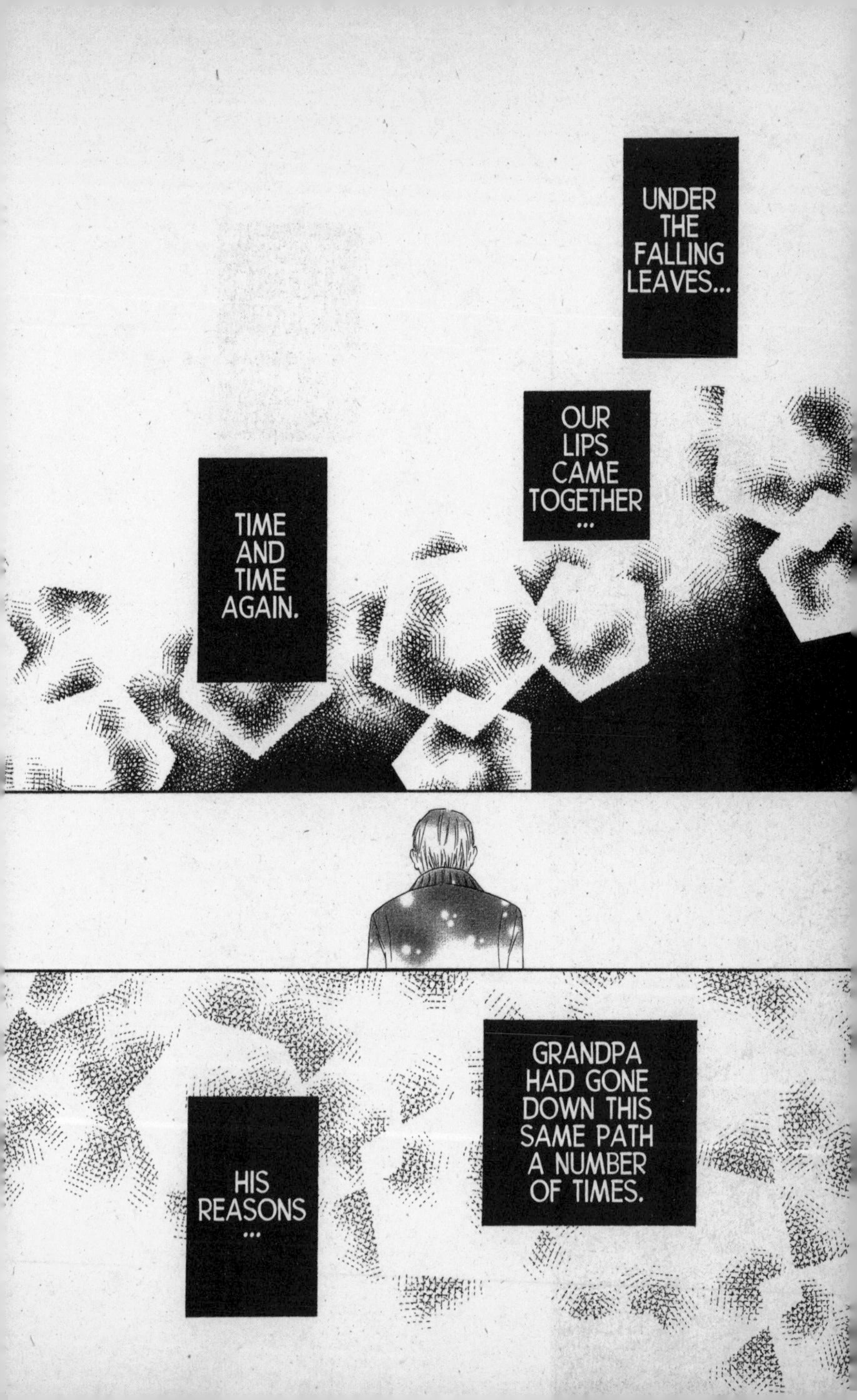
UNDER THE FALLING LEAVES...
OUR LIPS CAME TOGETHER...
TIME AND TIME AGAIN.
GRANDPA HAD GONE DOWN THIS SAME PATH A NUMBER OF TIMES.
HIS REASONS...

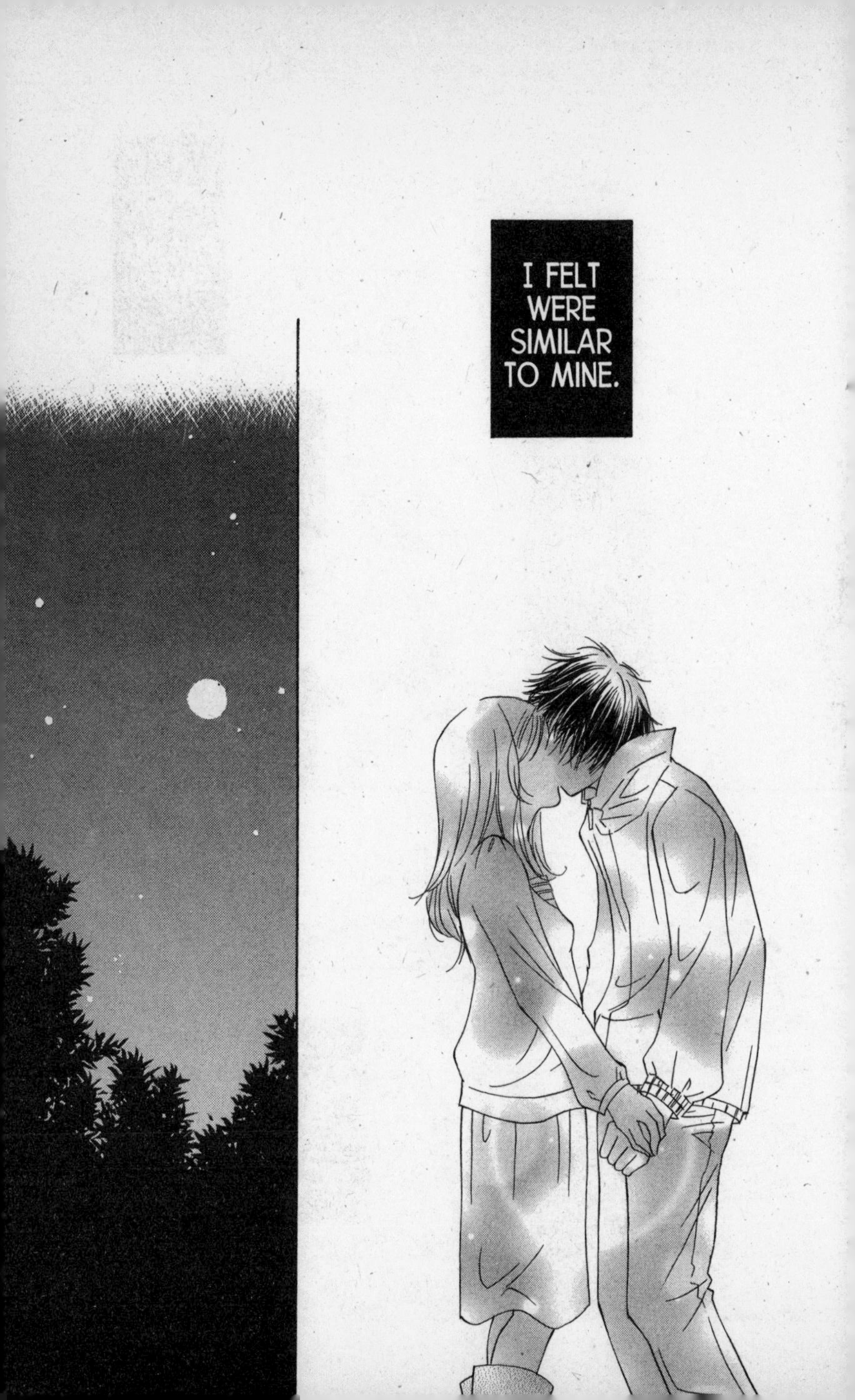
I FELT WERE SIMILAR TO MINE.

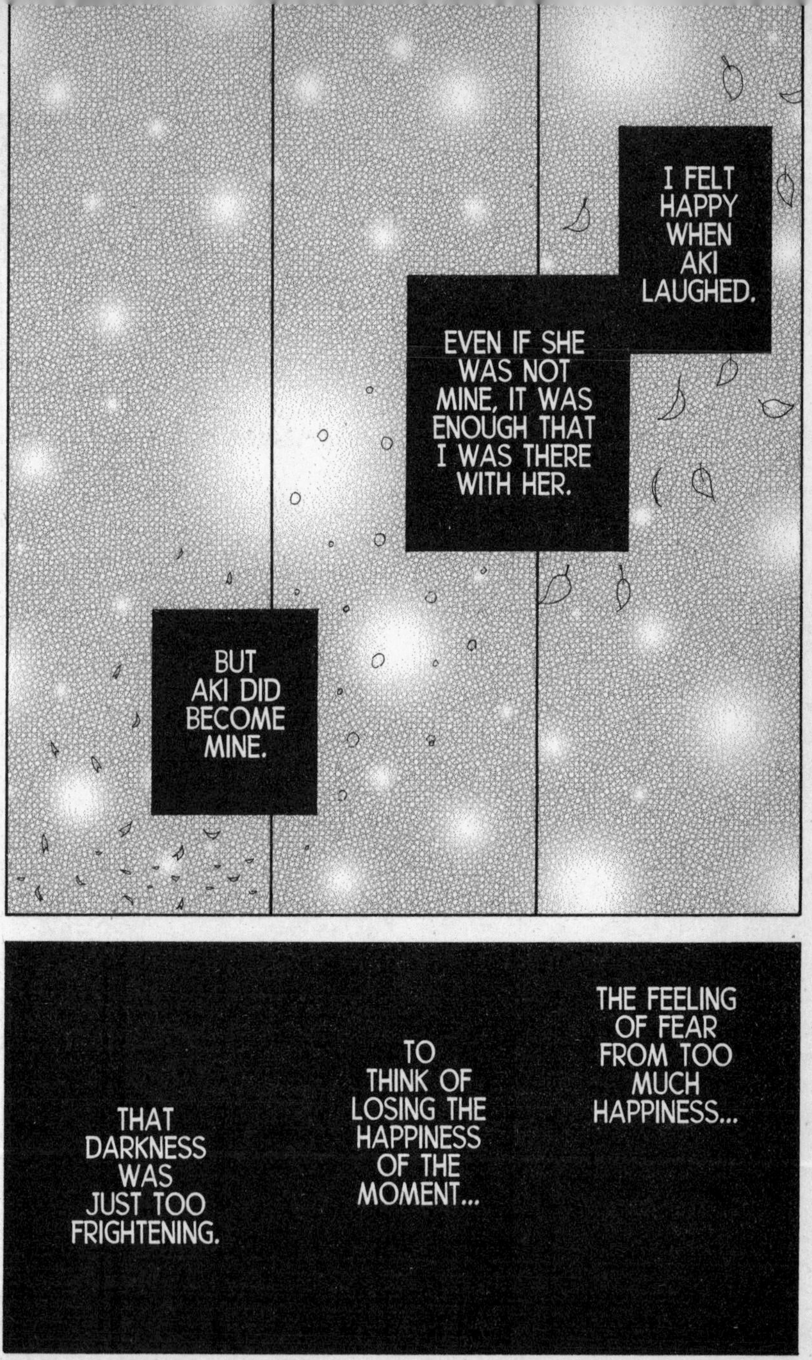
I FELT HAPPY WHEN AKI LAUGHED.
EVEN IF SHE WAS NOT MINE, IT WAS ENOUGH THAT I WAS THERE WITH HER.
BUT AKI DID BECOME MINE.
THE FEELING OF FEAR FROM TOO MUCH HAPPINESS...
TO THINK OF LOSING THE HAPPINESS OF THE MOMENT...
THAT DARKNESS WAS JUST TOO FRIGHTENING.

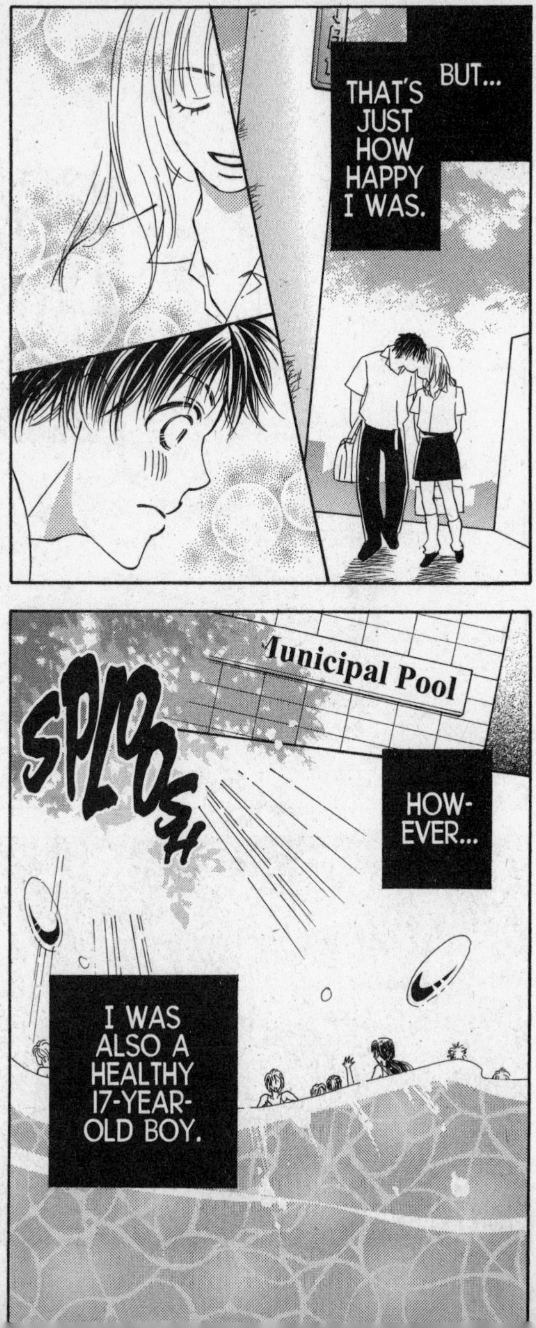
BUT...
THAT'S JUST HOW HAPPY I WAS.
Municipal Pool
SPLOOSH
HOW-EVER...
I WAS ALSO A HEALTHY 17-YEAR-OLD BOY.

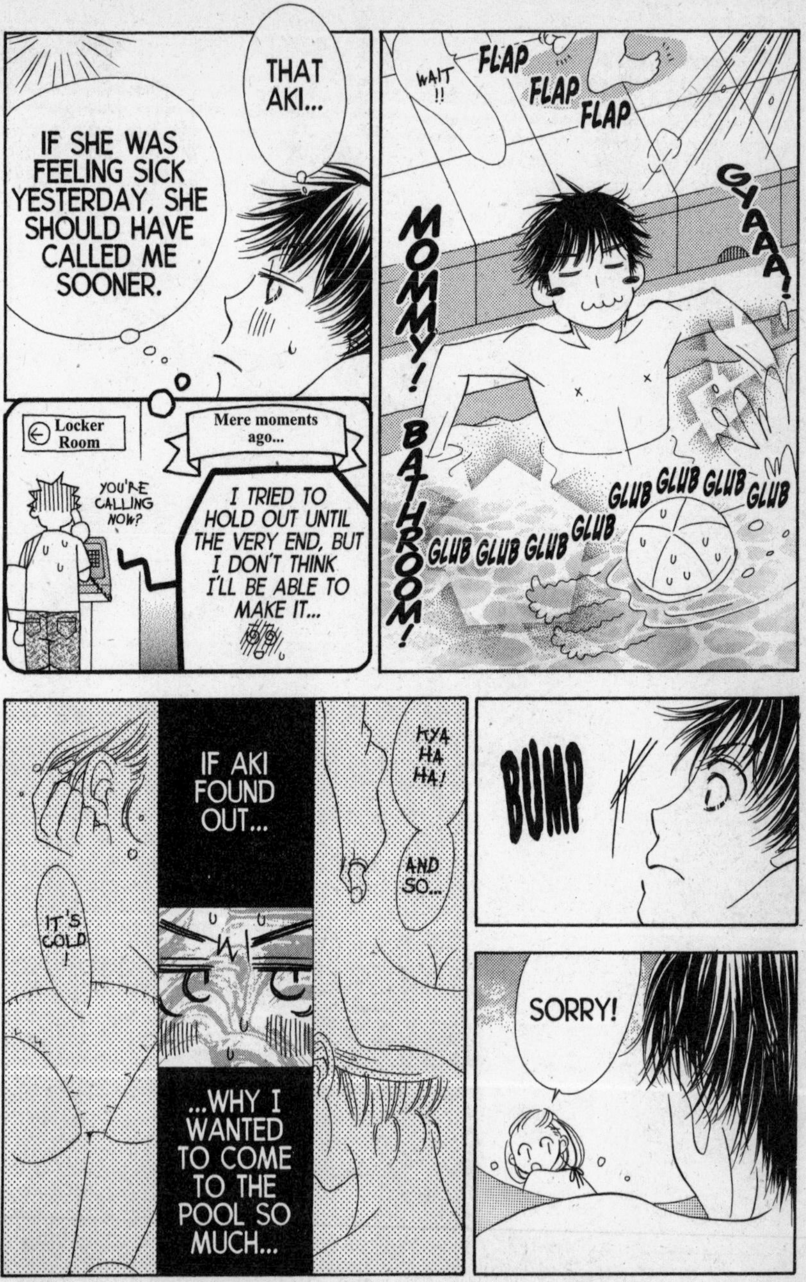
FLAP
FLAP
FLAP
WAIT !!
GYAAAA!
MOMMY! BATHROOM!
GLUB GLUB GLUB GLUB
GLUB GLUB GLUB GLUB
THAT AKI...
IF SHE WAS FEELING SICK YESTERDAY, SHE SHOULD HAVE CALLED ME SOONER.
Mere moments ago...
I TRIED TO HOLD OUT UNTIL THE VERY END, BUT I DON'T THINK I'LL BE ABLE TO MAKE IT...
YOU'RE CALLING NOW?
Locker Room
BUMP
SORRY!
KYA HA HA!
AND SO...
IF AKI FOUND OUT...
...WHY I WANTED TO COME TO THE POOL SO MUCH...
IT'S COLD!

SHE'D
BE
MAD.

GLUG

GLUG

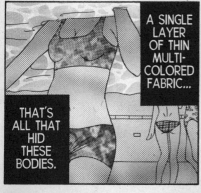

A SINGLE
LAYER
OF THIN
MULTI-
COLORED
FABRIC...

THAT'S
ALL THAT
HID
THESE
BODIES.

GLUG
GLUG

GRAB

CALM
DOWN!!

THE
GUY
DOWN
THERE!

OH,
NO!!

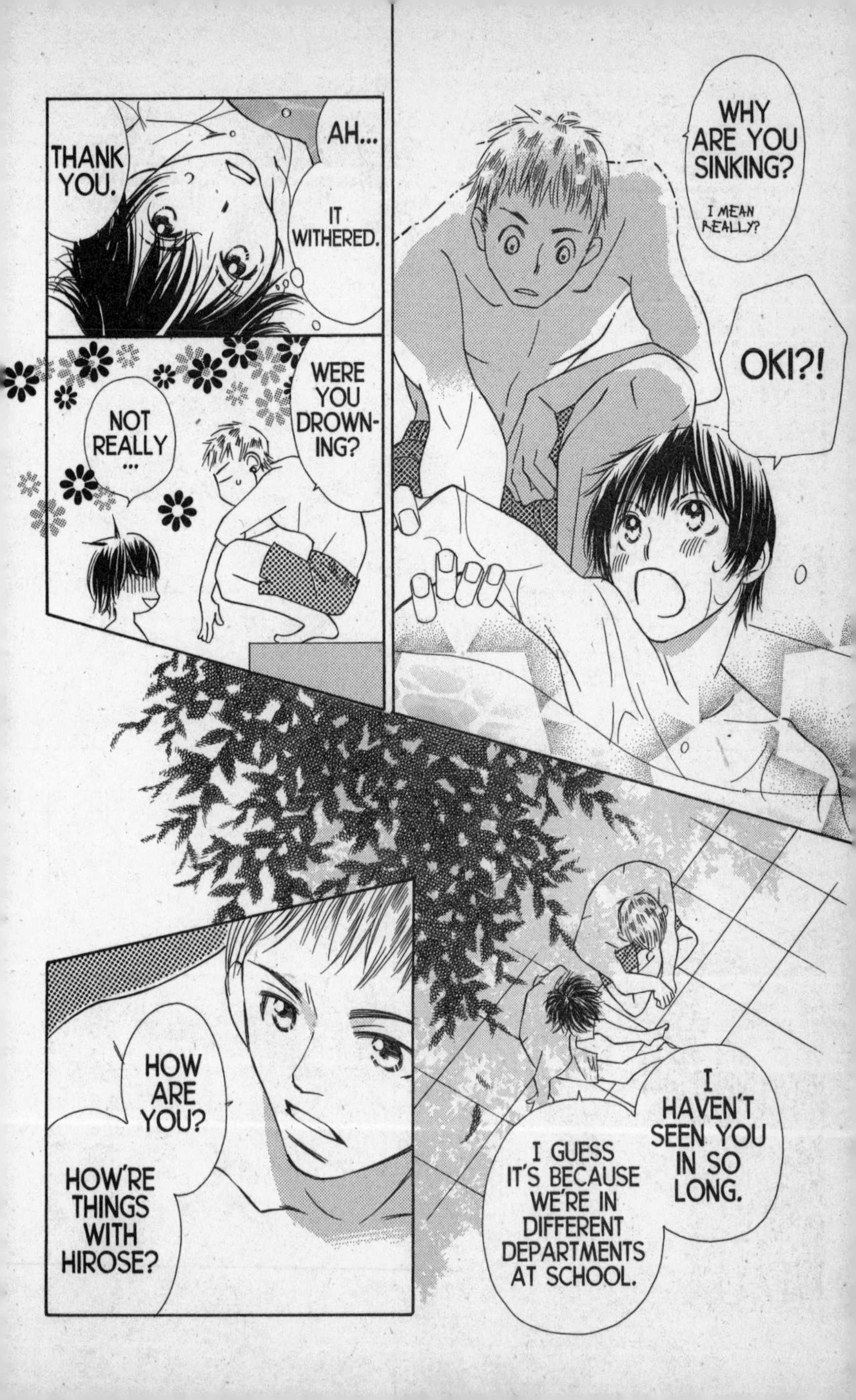
WHY ARE YOU SINKING?
I MEAN REALLY?
OKI?!
AH...
IT WITHERED.
THANK YOU.
WERE YOU DROWNING?
NOT REALLY ...
I HAVEN'T SEEN YOU IN SO LONG.
I GUESS IT'S BECAUSE WE'RE IN DIFFERENT DEPARTMENTS AT SCHOOL.
HOW ARE YOU?
HOW'RE THINGS WITH HIROSE?

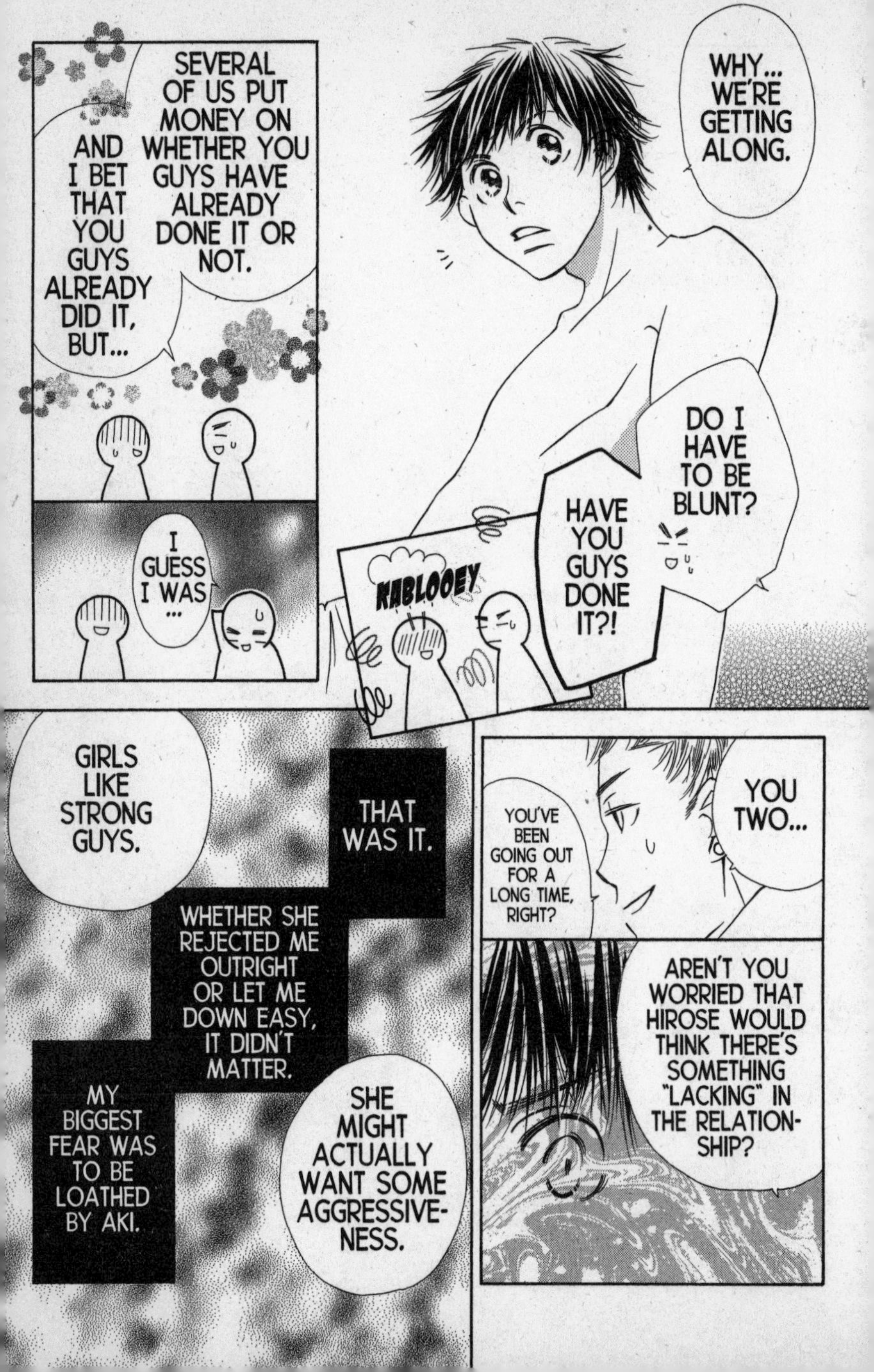
WHY... WE'RE GETTING ALONG.
DO I HAVE TO BE BLUNT?
HAVE YOU GUYS DONE IT?!
KABLOOEY
SEVERAL OF US PUT MONEY ON WHETHER YOU GUYS HAVE ALREADY DONE IT OR NOT.
AND I BET THAT YOU GUYS ALREADY DID IT, BUT...
I GUESS I WAS...
YOU TWO...
YOU'VE BEEN GOING OUT FOR A LONG TIME, RIGHT?
AREN'T YOU WORRIED THAT HIROSE WOULD THINK THERE'S SOMETHING "LACKING" IN THE RELATION-SHIP?
THAT WAS IT.
GIRLS LIKE STRONG GUYS.
WHETHER SHE REJECTED ME OUTRIGHT OR LET ME DOWN EASY, IT DIDN'T MATTER.
SHE MIGHT ACTUALLY WANT SOME AGGRESSIVE-NESS.
MY BIGGEST FEAR WAS TO BE LOATHED BY AKI.

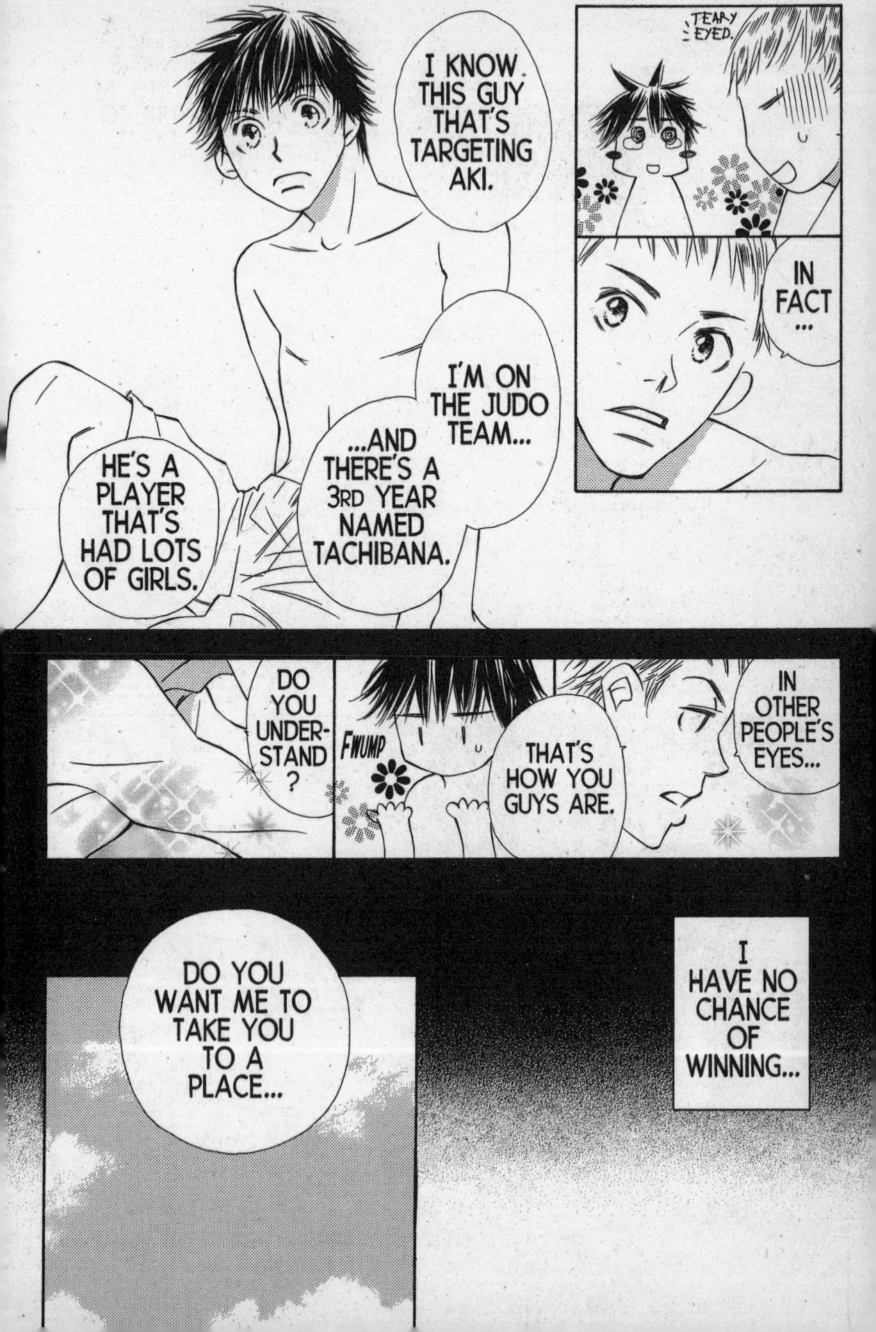
TEARY EYED.
IN FACT...
I KNOW. THIS GUY THAT'S TARGETING AKI.
I'M ON THE JUDO TEAM...
...AND THERE'S A 3RD YEAR NAMED TACHIBANA.
HE'S A PLAYER THAT'S HAD LOTS OF GIRLS.
IN OTHER PEOPLE'S EYES...
THAT'S HOW YOU GUYS ARE.
FWUMP
DO YOU UNDER-STAND?
I HAVE NO CHANCE OF WINNING...
DO YOU WANT ME TO TAKE YOU TO A PLACE...

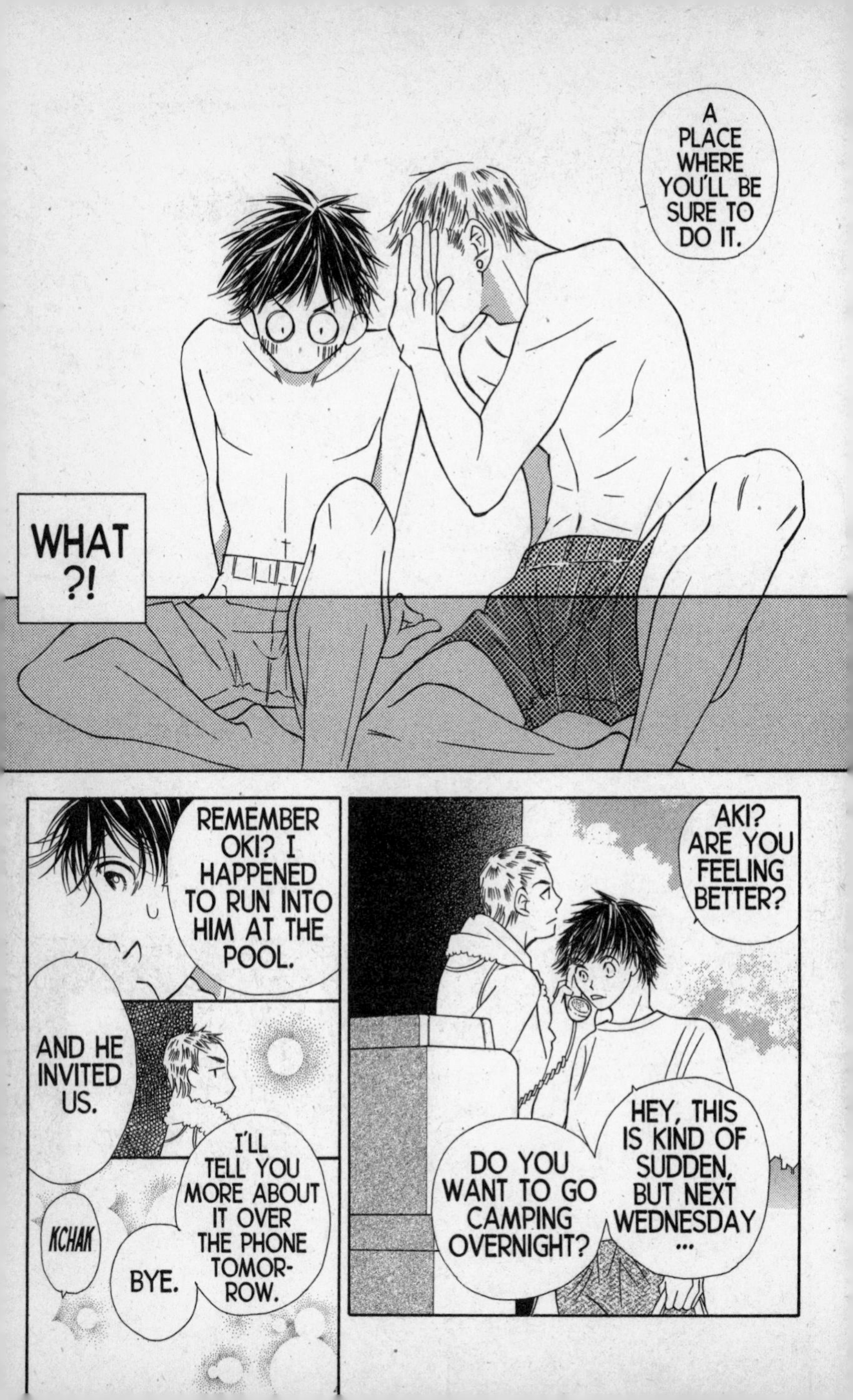
A PLACE WHERE YOU'LL BE SURE TO DO IT.
WHAT?!
AKI? ARE YOU FEELING BETTER?
HEY, THIS IS KIND OF SUDDEN, BUT NEXT WEDNESDAY...
DO YOU WANT TO GO CAMPING OVERNIGHT?
REMEMBER OKI? I HAPPENED TO RUN INTO HIM AT THE POOL.
AND HE INVITED US.
I'LL TELL YOU MORE ABOUT IT OVER THE PHONE TOMOR-ROW.
BYE.
KCHAK

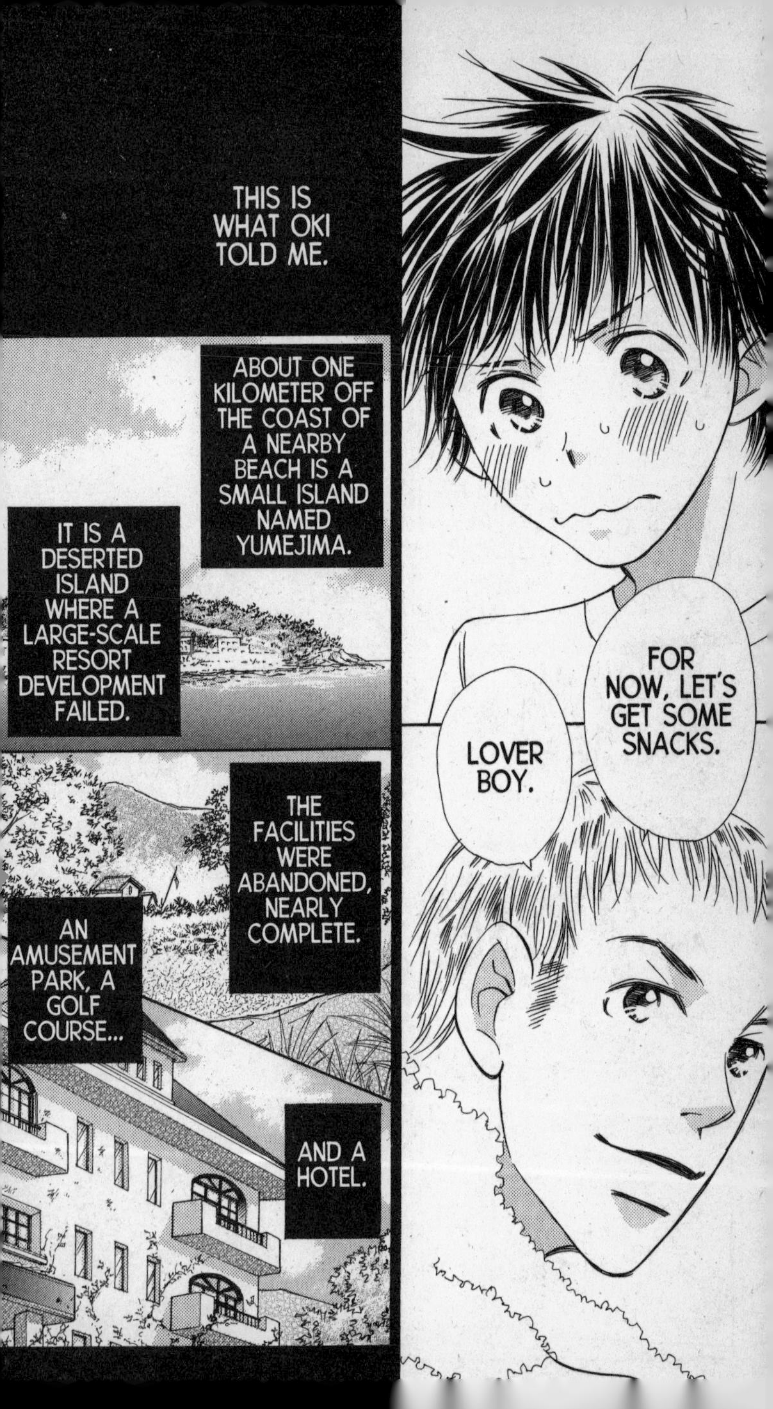
FOR NOW, LET'S GET SOME SNACKS.
LOVER BOY.
THIS IS WHAT OKI TOLD ME.
ABOUT ONE KILOMETER OFF THE COAST OF A NEARBY BEACH IS A SMALL ISLAND NAMED YUMEJIMA.
IT IS A DESERTED ISLAND WHERE A LARGE-SCALE RESORT DEVELOPMENT FAILED.
THE FACILITIES WERE ABANDONED, NEARLY COMPLETE.
AN AMUSEMENT PARK, A GOLF COURSE...
AND A HOTEL.

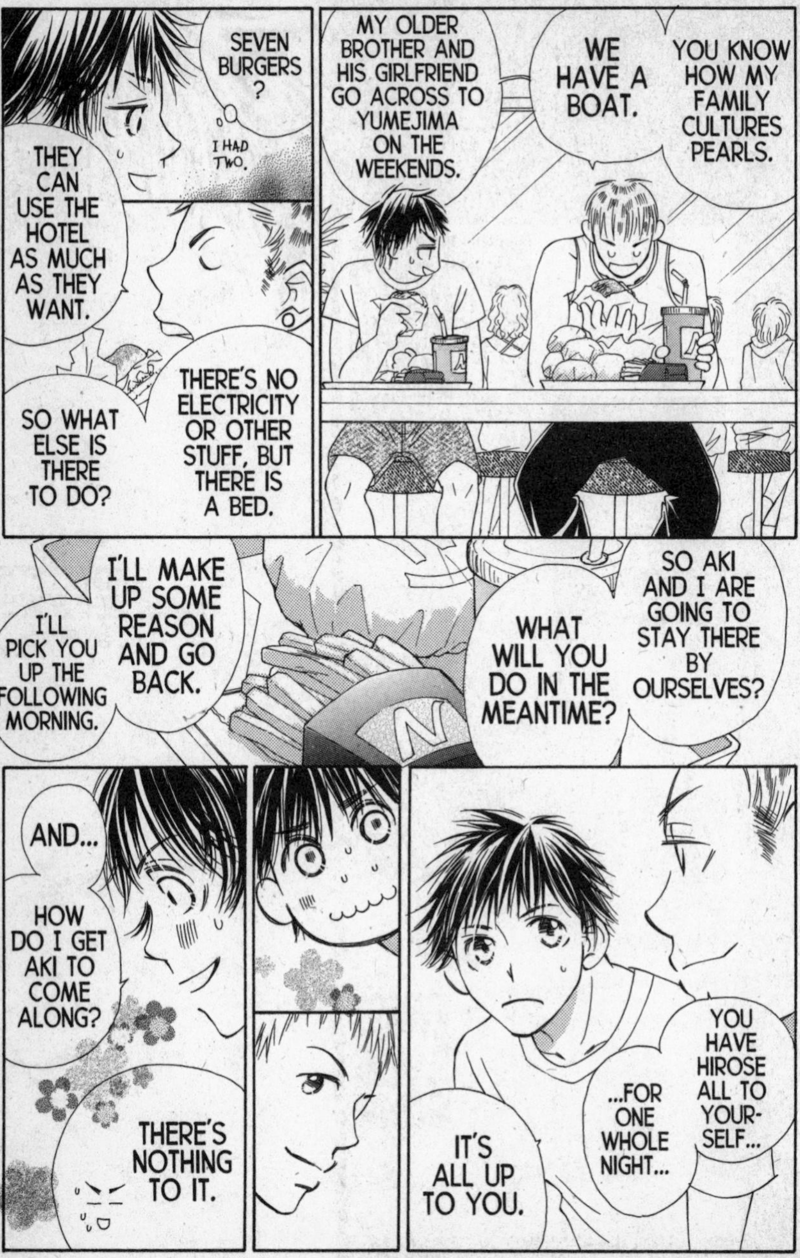
YOU KNOW HOW MY FAMILY CULTURES PEARLS.
WE HAVE A BOAT.
MY OLDER BROTHER AND HIS GIRLFRIEND GO ACROSS TO YUMEJIMA ON THE WEEKENDS.
SEVEN BURGERS?
I HAD TWO.
THEY CAN USE THE HOTEL AS MUCH AS THEY WANT.
THERE'S NO ELECTRICITY OR OTHER STUFF, BUT THERE IS A BED.
SO WHAT ELSE IS THERE TO DO?
SO AKI AND I ARE GOING TO STAY THERE BY OURSELVES?
WHAT WILL YOU DO IN THE MEANTIME?
I'LL MAKE UP SOME REASON AND GO BACK.
I'LL PICK YOU UP THE FOLLOWING MORNING.
YOU HAVE HIROSE ALL TO YOURSELF...
...FOR ONE WHOLE NIGHT...
IT'S ALL UP TO YOU.
AND...
HOW DO I GET AKI TO COME ALONG?
THERE'S NOTHING TO IT.

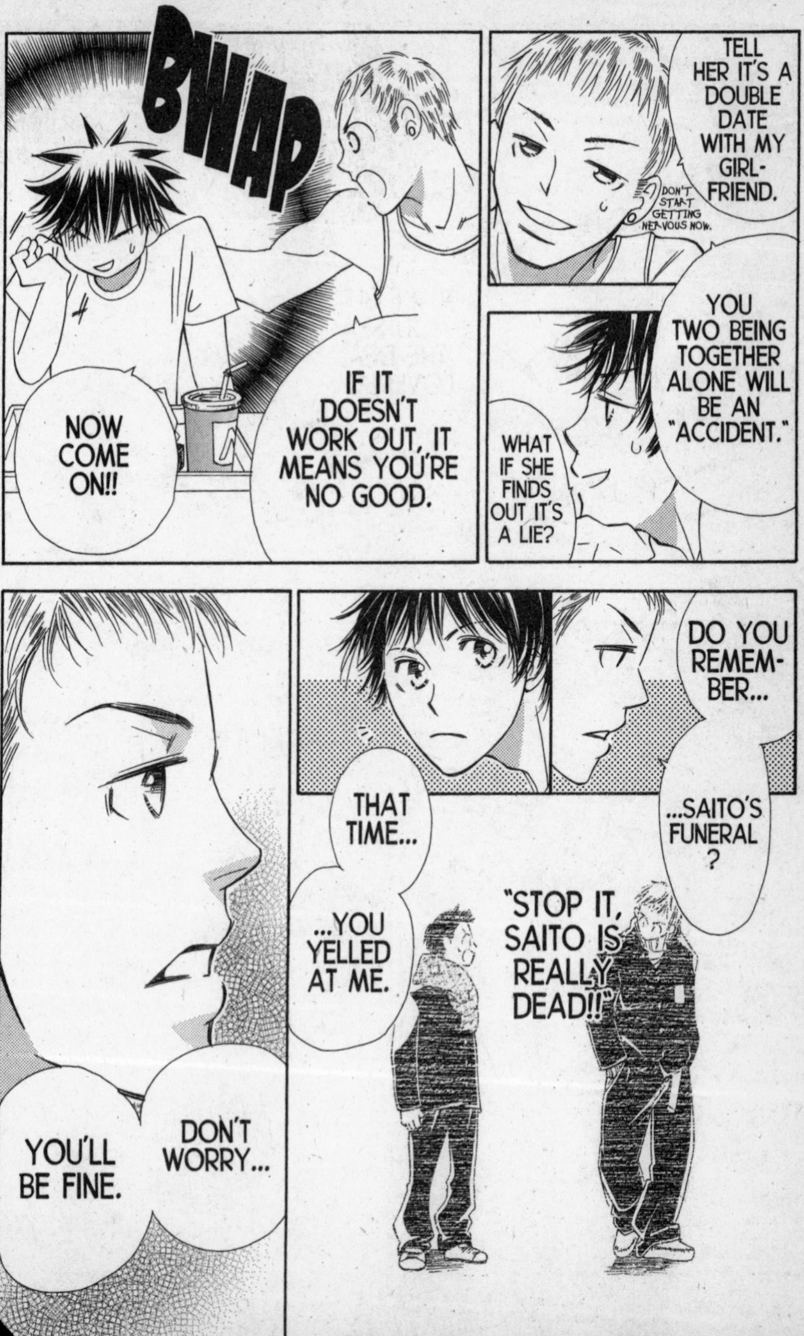
TELL HER IT'S A DOUBLE DATE WITH MY GIRL-FRIEND.
DON'T START GETTING NERVOUS NOW.
YOU TWO BEING TOGETHER ALONE WILL BE AN "ACCIDENT."
WHAT IF SHE FINDS OUT IT'S A LIE?
BWAP
IF IT DOESN'T WORK OUT, IT MEANS YOU'RE NO GOOD.
NOW COME ON!!
DO YOU REMEM-BER...
...SAITO'S FUNERAL ?
"STOP IT, SAITO IS REALLY DEAD!!"
THAT TIME...
...YOU YELLED AT ME.
DON'T WORRY...
YOU'LL BE FINE.

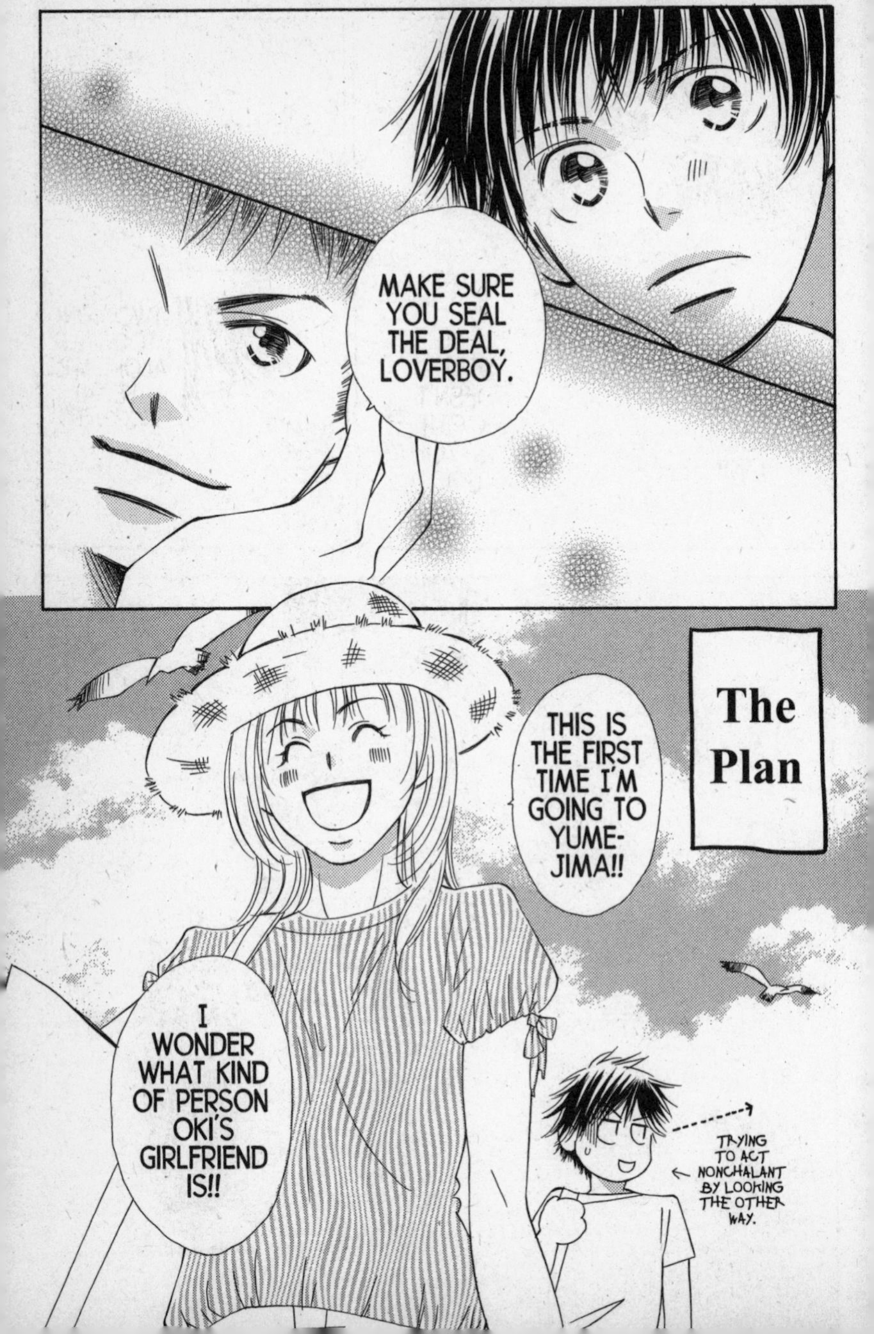
MAKE SURE YOU SEAL THE DEAL, LOVERBOY.
The Plan
THIS IS THE FIRST TIME I'M GOING TO YUME-JIMA!!
I WONDER WHAT KIND OF PERSON OKI'S GIRLFRIEND IS!!
TRYING TO ACT NONCHALANT BY LOOKING THE OTHER WAY.

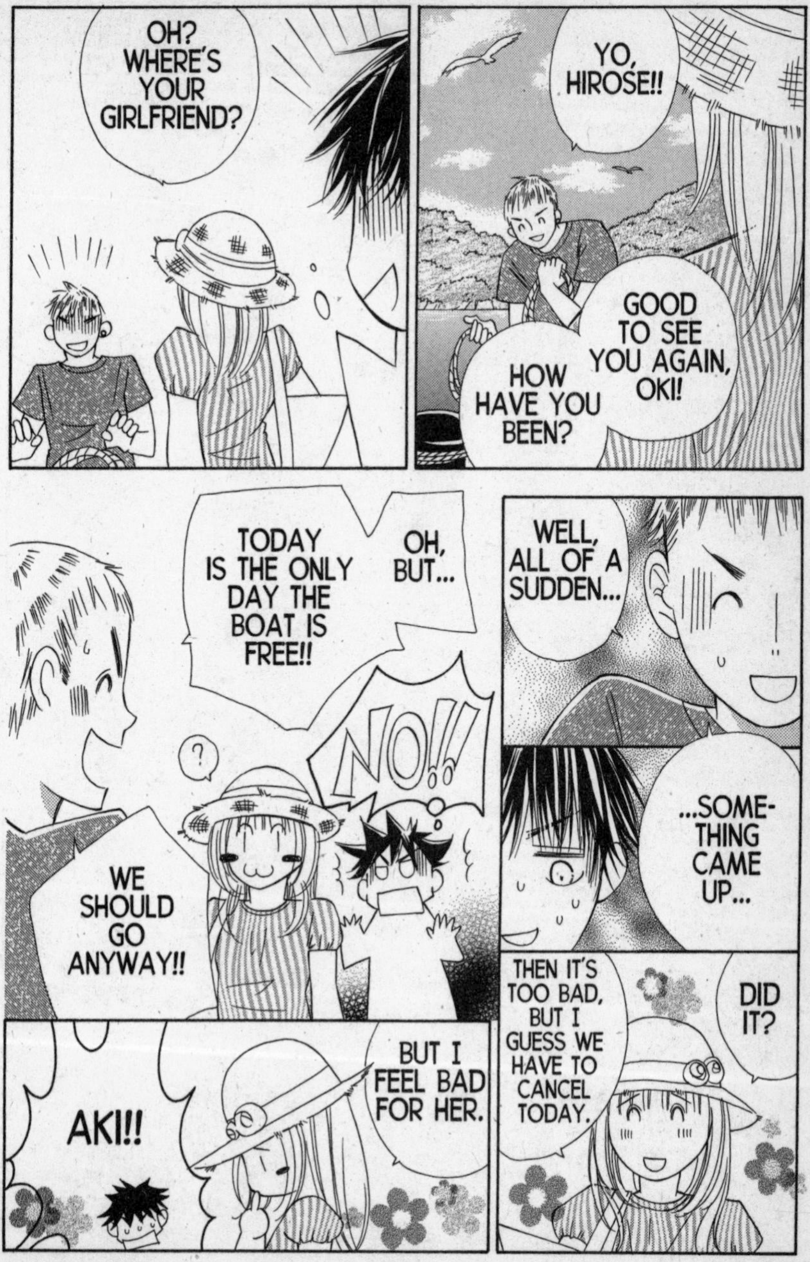
YO, HIROSE!!
GOOD TO SEE YOU AGAIN, OKI!
HOW HAVE YOU BEEN?
OH? WHERE'S YOUR GIRLFRIEND?
WELL, ALL OF A SUDDEN...
...SOME-THING CAME UP...
DID IT?
THEN IT'S TOO BAD, BUT I GUESS WE HAVE TO CANCEL TODAY.
OH, BUT...
TODAY IS THE ONLY DAY THE BOAT IS FREE!!
NO!!
?
WE SHOULD GO ANYWAY!!
BUT I FEEL BAD FOR HER.
AKI!!

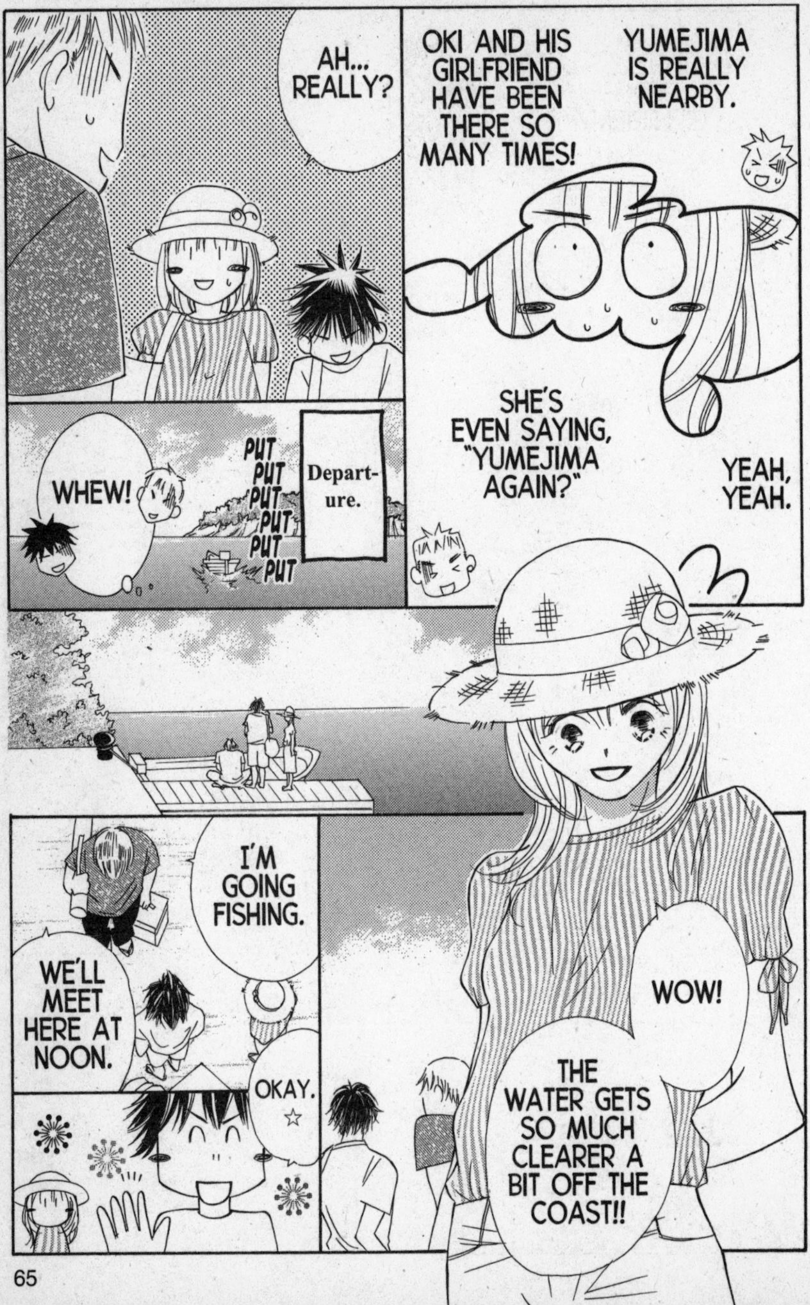
YUMEJIMA IS REALLY NEARBY.
OKI AND HIS GIRLFRIEND HAVE BEEN THERE SO MANY TIMES!
YEAH, YEAH.
SHE'S EVEN SAYING, "YUMEJIMA AGAIN?"
AH... REALLY?
Departure.
PUT PUT PUT PUT PUT PUT
WHEW!
WOW!
THE WATER GETS SO MUCH CLEARER A BIT OFF THE COAST!!
I'M GOING FISHING.
WE'LL MEET HERE AT NOON.
OKAY. ☆

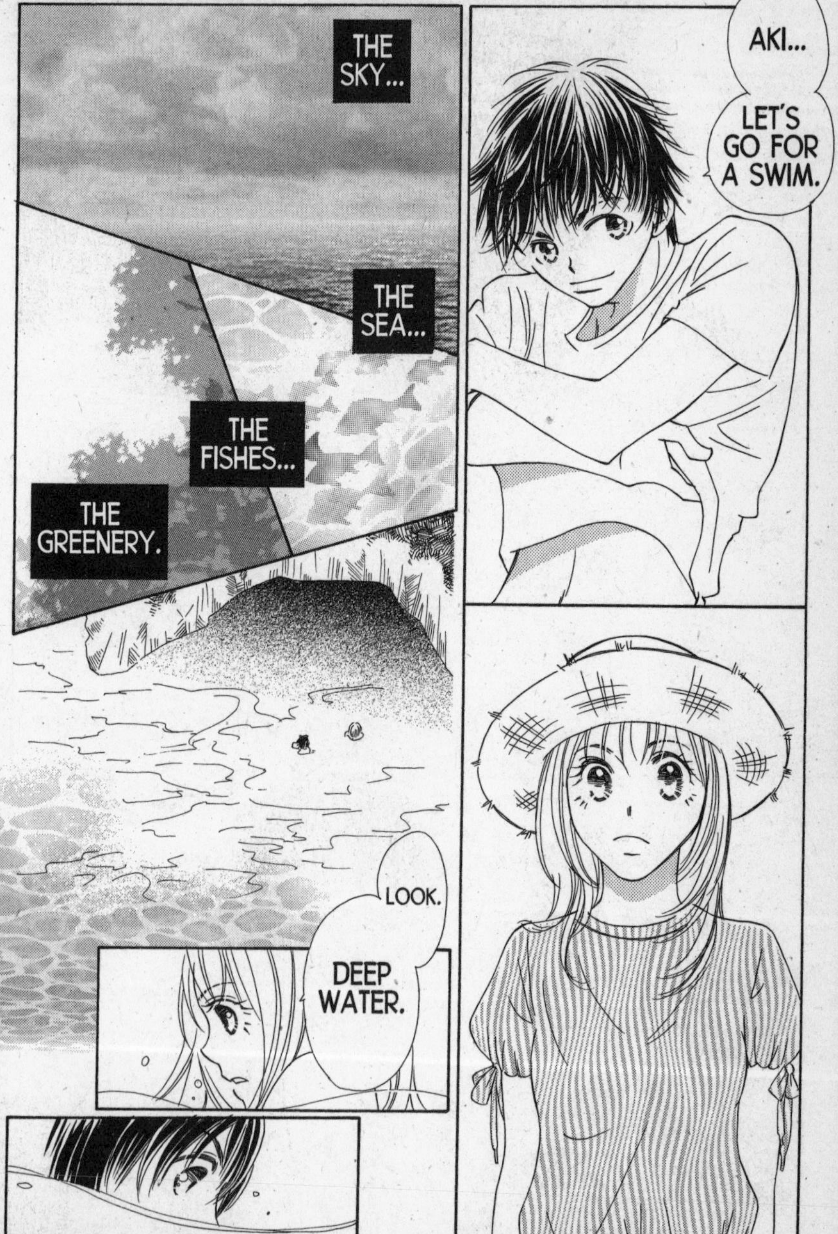
AKI...
LET'S GO FOR A SWIM.
THE SKY...
THE SEA...
THE FISHES...
THE GREENERY.
LOOK.
DEEP WATER.

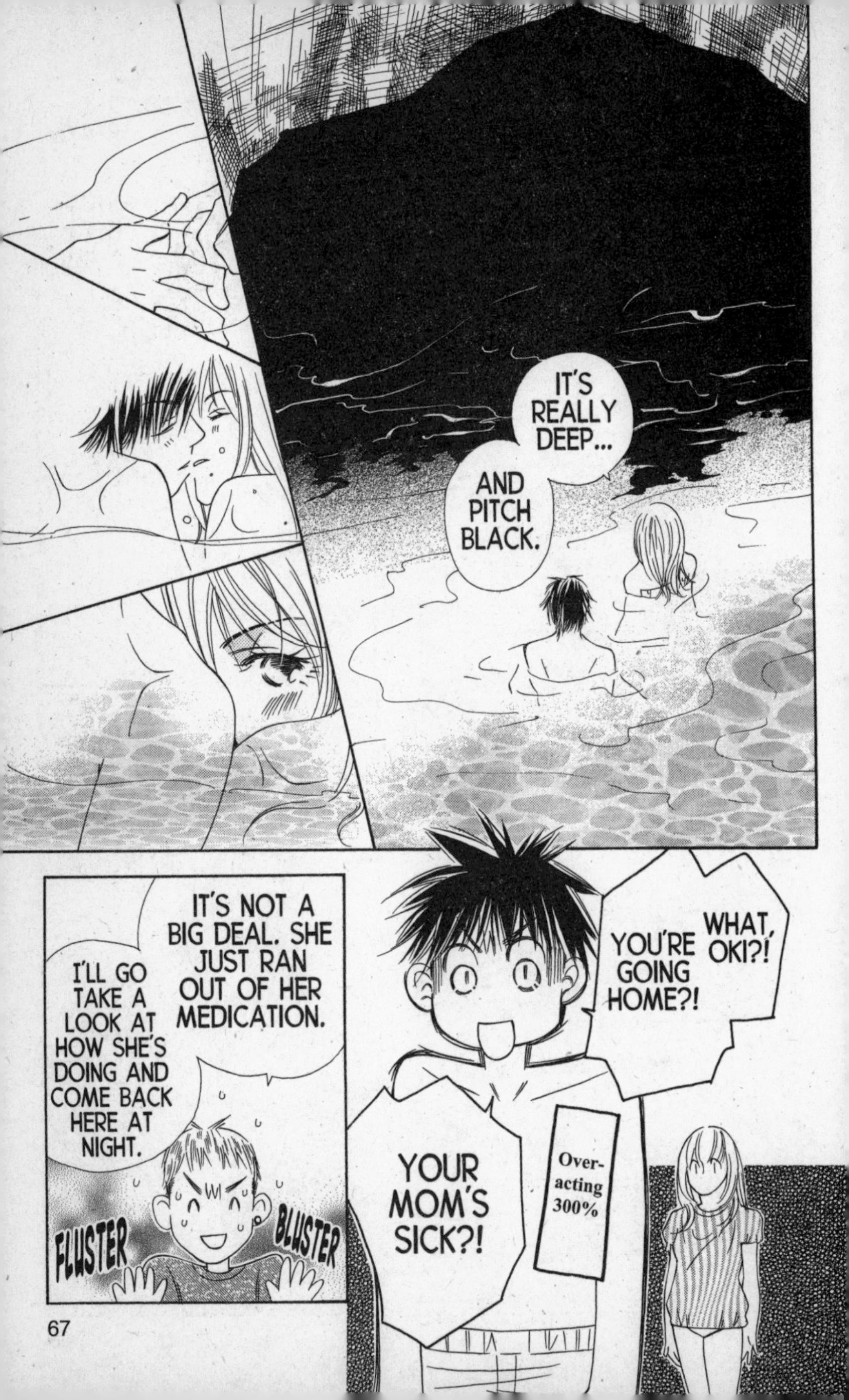
IT'S REALLY DEEP...
AND PITCH BLACK.
WHAT, OKI?! YOU'RE GOING HOME?!
YOUR MOM'S SICK?!
Over-acting 300%
IT'S NOT A BIG DEAL. SHE JUST RAN OUT OF HER MEDICATION.
I'LL GO TAKE A LOOK AT HOW SHE'S DOING AND COME BACK HERE AT NIGHT.
BLUSTER
FLUSTER

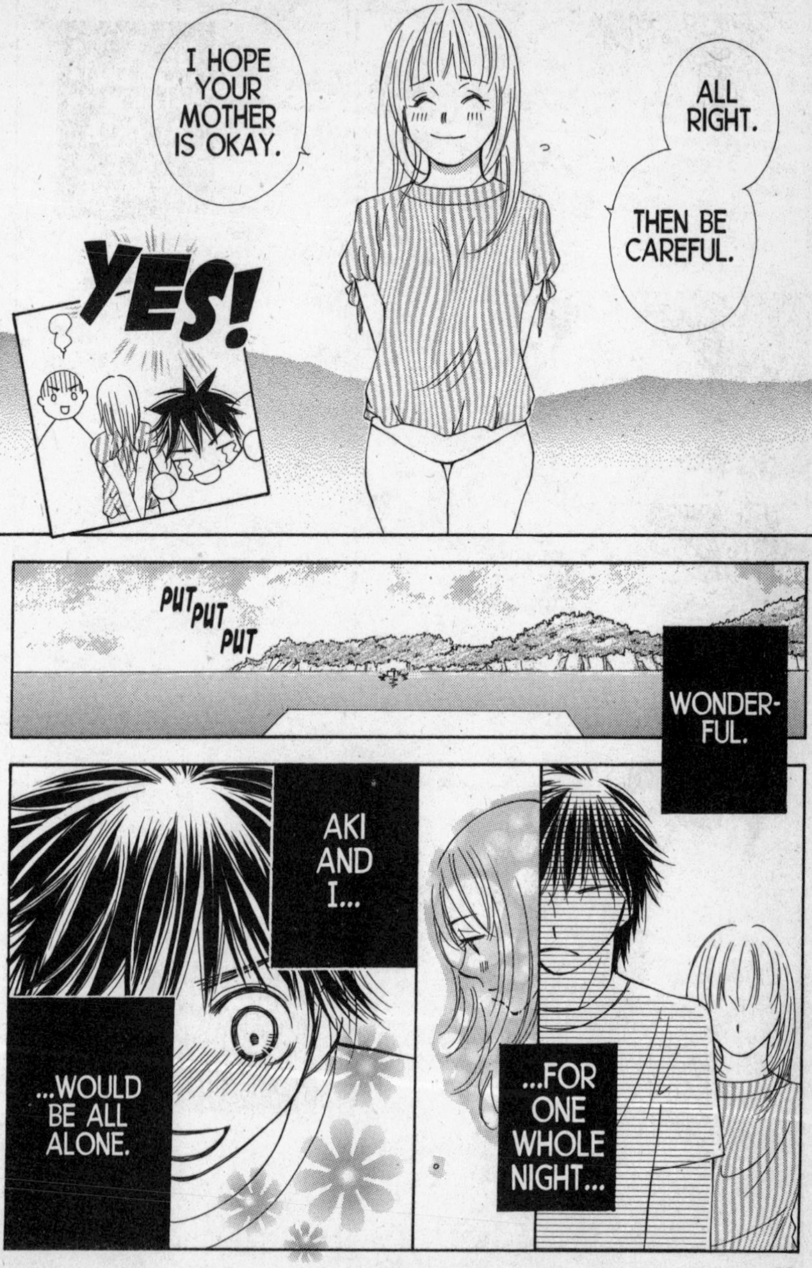
ALL RIGHT.
THEN BE CAREFUL.
I HOPE YOUR MOTHER IS OKAY.
YES!
PUT PUT PUT
WONDERFUL.
...FOR ONE WHOLE NIGHT...
AKI AND I...
...WOULD BE ALL ALONE.

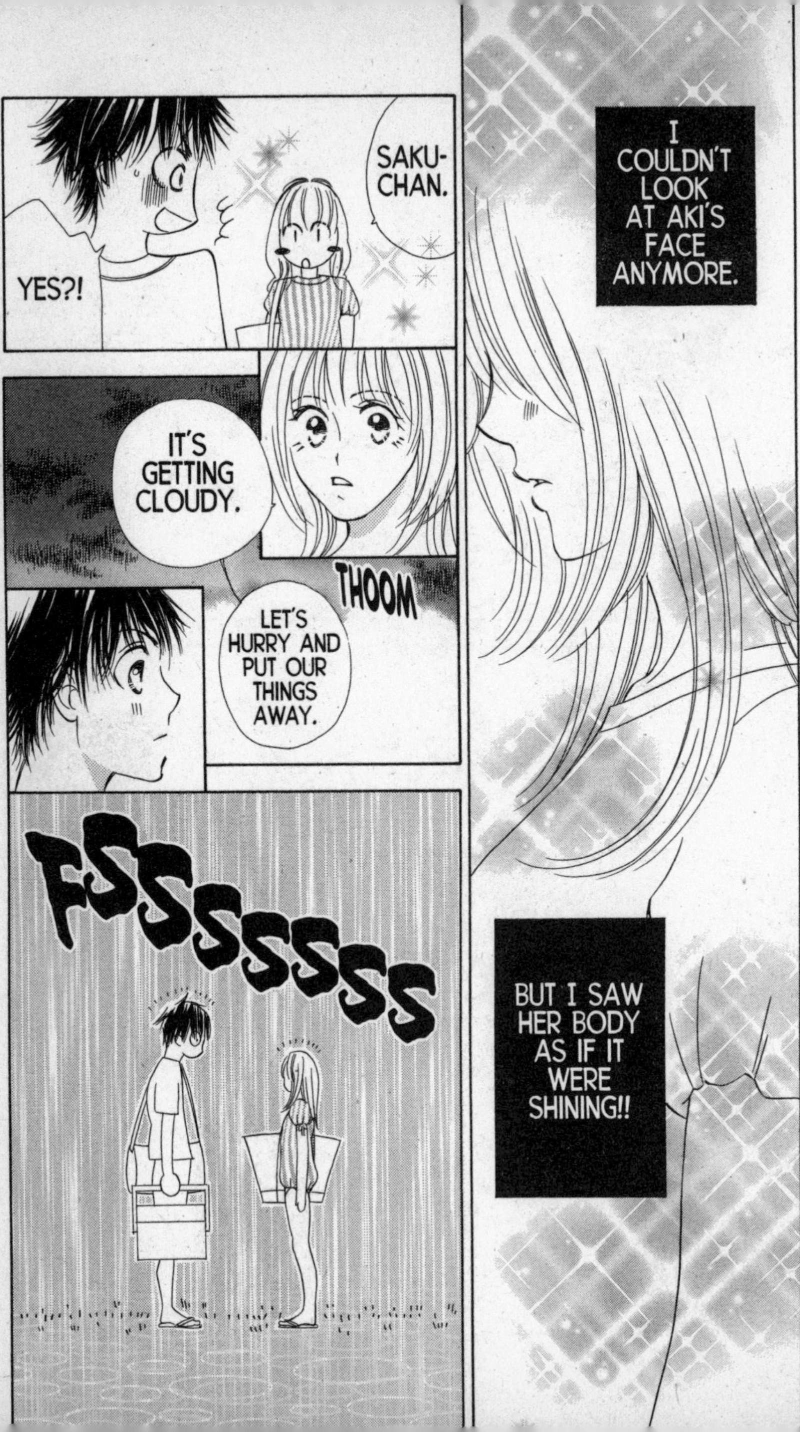
I COULDN'T LOOK AT AKI'S FACE ANYMORE.
BUT I SAW HER BODY AS IF IT WERE SHINING!!
SAKU-CHAN.
YES?!
IT'S GETTING CLOUDY.
THOOM
LET'S HURRY AND PUT OUR THINGS AWAY.
FSSSSSSSS

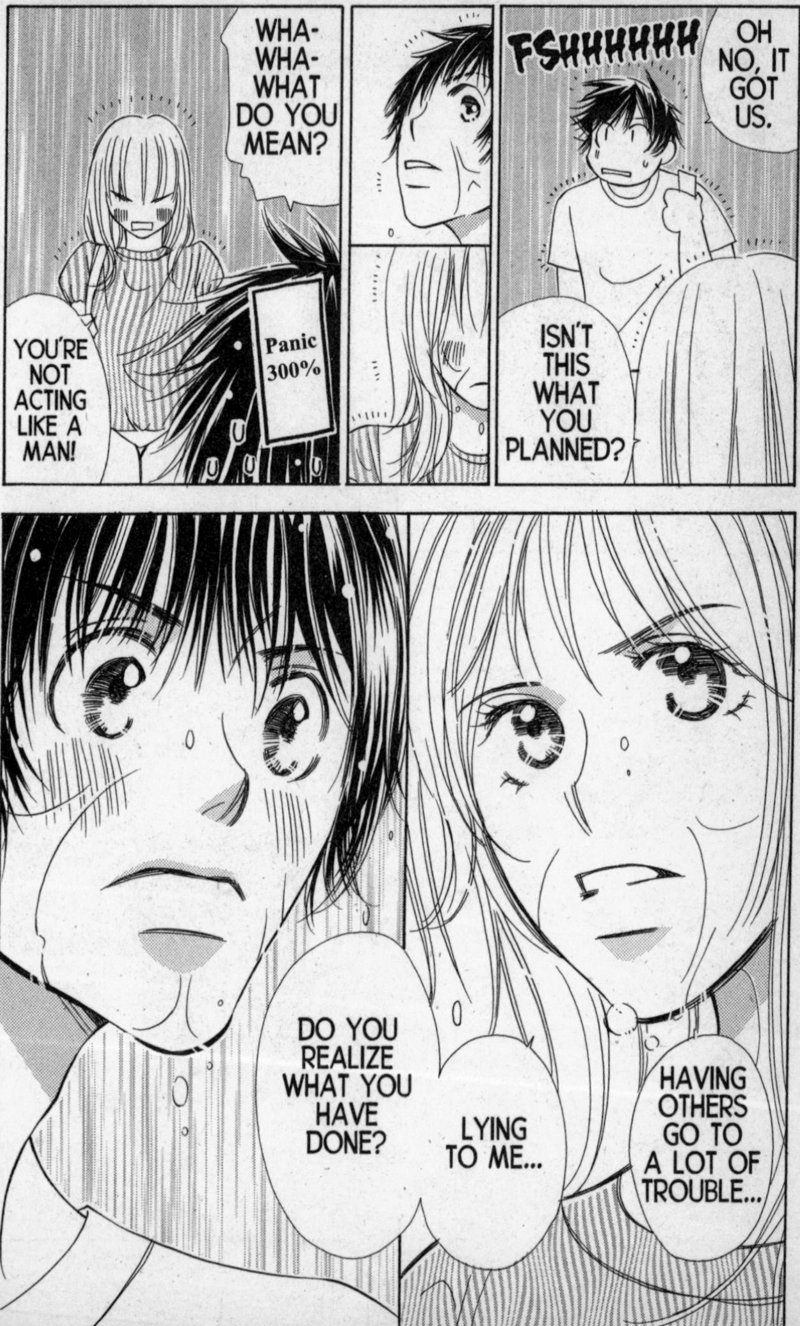
FSHHHHHH
OH NO, IT GOT US.
ISN'T THIS WHAT YOU PLANNED?
WHA-WHA-WHAT DO YOU MEAN?
Panic 300%
YOU'RE NOT ACTING LIKE A MAN!
HAVING OTHERS GO TO A LOT OF TROUBLE...
LYING TO ME...
DO YOU REALIZE WHAT YOU HAVE DONE?

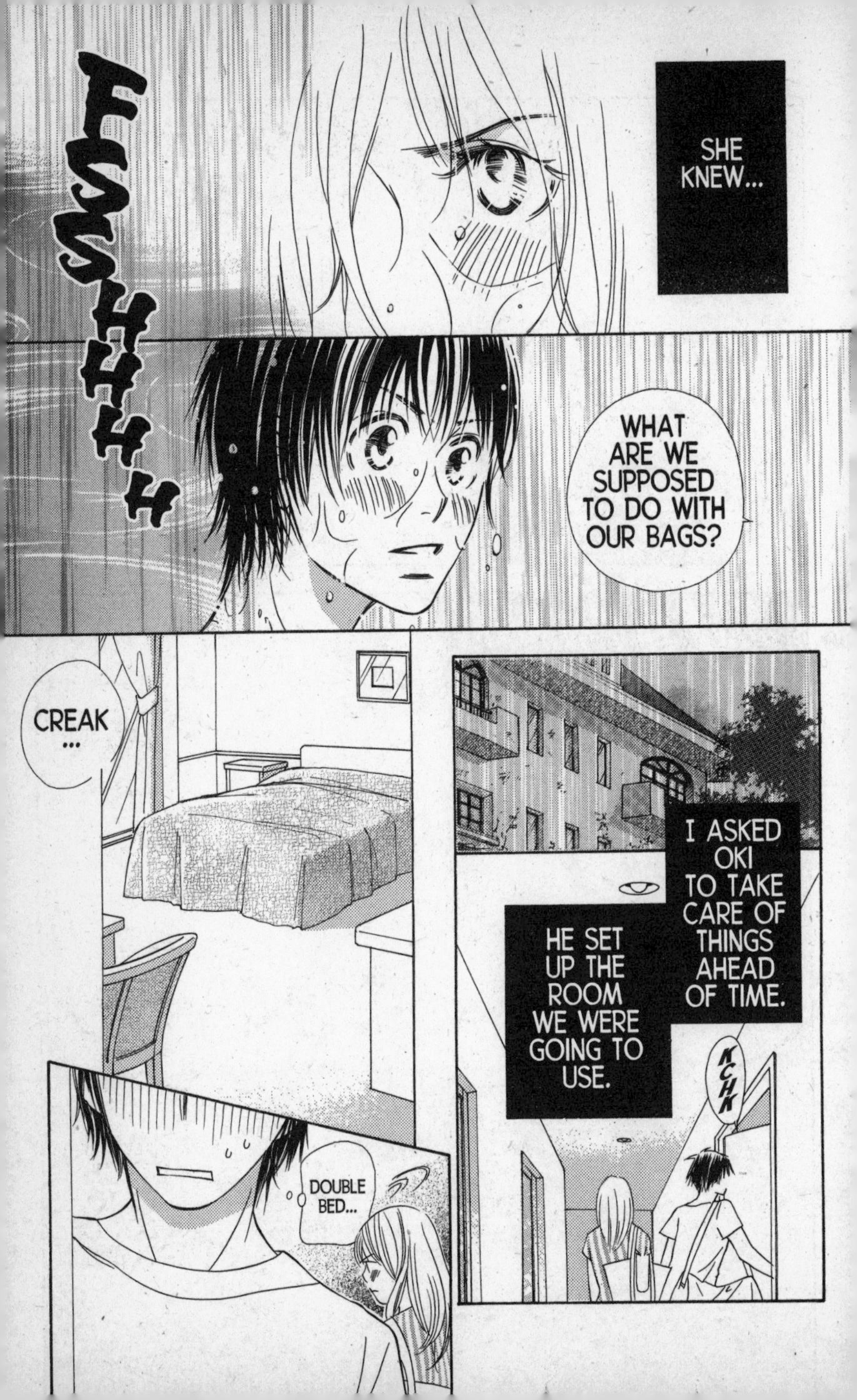
SHE KNEW...
FSSHHHHH
WHAT ARE WE SUPPOSED TO DO WITH OUR BAGS?
I ASKED OKI TO TAKE CARE OF THINGS AHEAD OF TIME.
HE SET UP THE ROOM WE WERE GOING TO USE.
KCHK
CREAK...
DOUBLE BED...

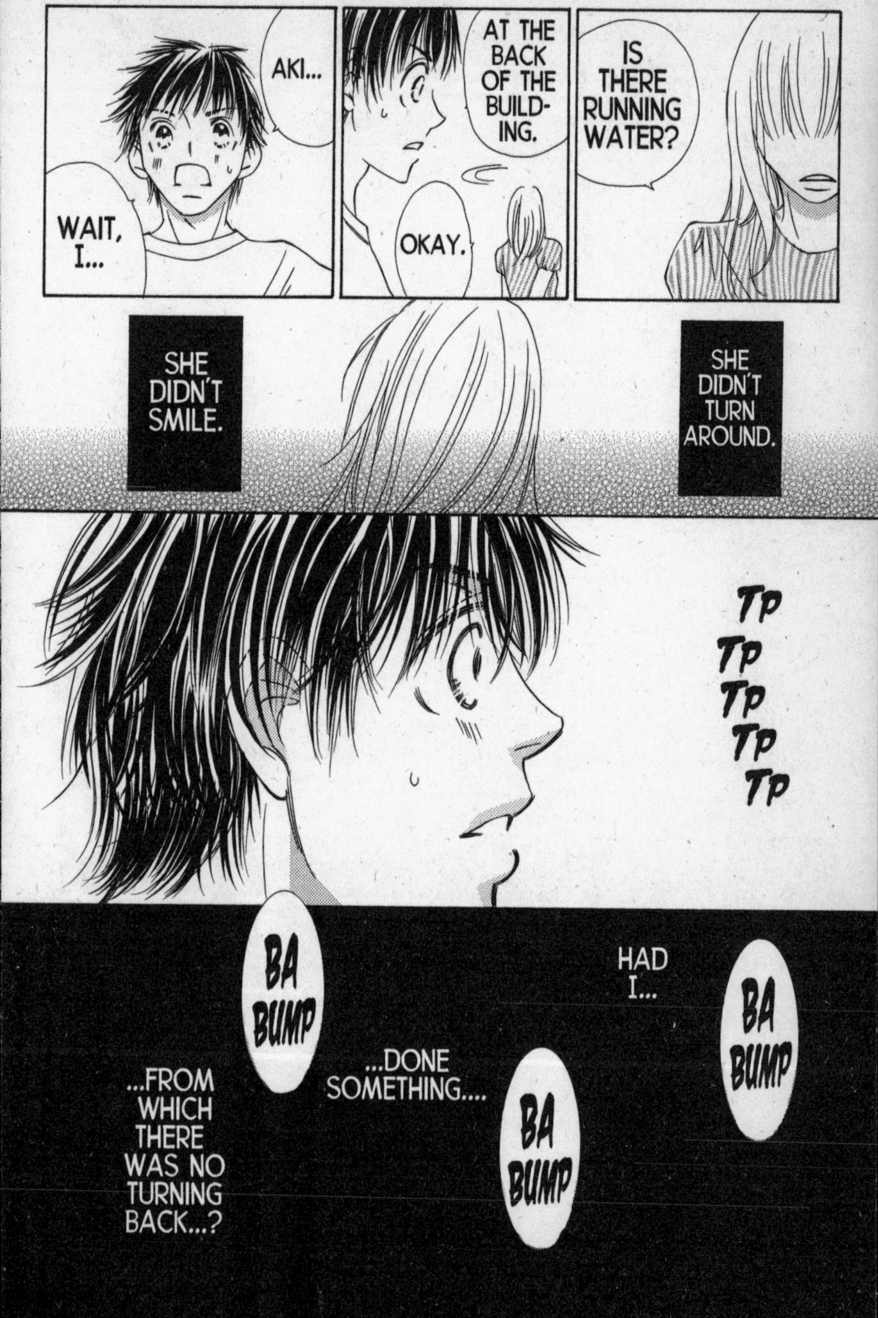
IS THERE RUNNING WATER?
AT THE BACK OF THE BUILD-ING.
OKAY.
AKI...
WAIT, I...
SHE DIDN'T TURN AROUND.
SHE DIDN'T SMILE.
TP TP TP TP TP
HAD I...
BA BUMP
...DONE SOMETHING....
BA BUMP
BA BUMP
...FROM WHICH THERE WAS NO TURNING BACK...?

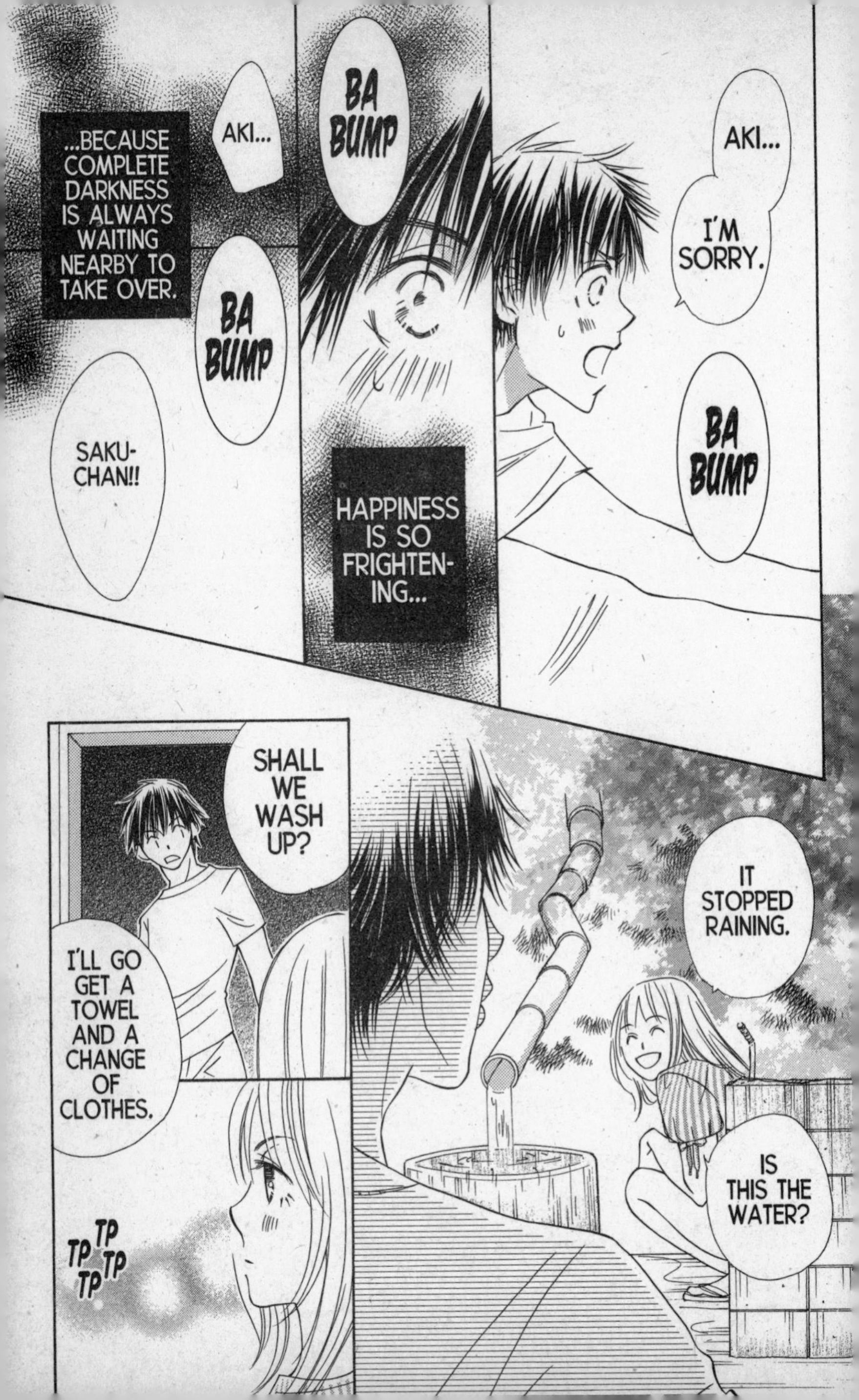
AKI...
I'M SORRY.
BA BUMP
BA BUMP
HAPPINESS IS SO FRIGHTEN-ING...
AKI...
...BECAUSE COMPLETE DARKNESS IS ALWAYS WAITING NEARBY TO TAKE OVER.
BA BUMP
SAKU-CHAN!!
IT STOPPED RAINING.
IS THIS THE WATER?
SHALL WE WASH UP?
I'LL GO GET A TOWEL AND A CHANGE OF CLOTHES.
TP TP TP TP TP

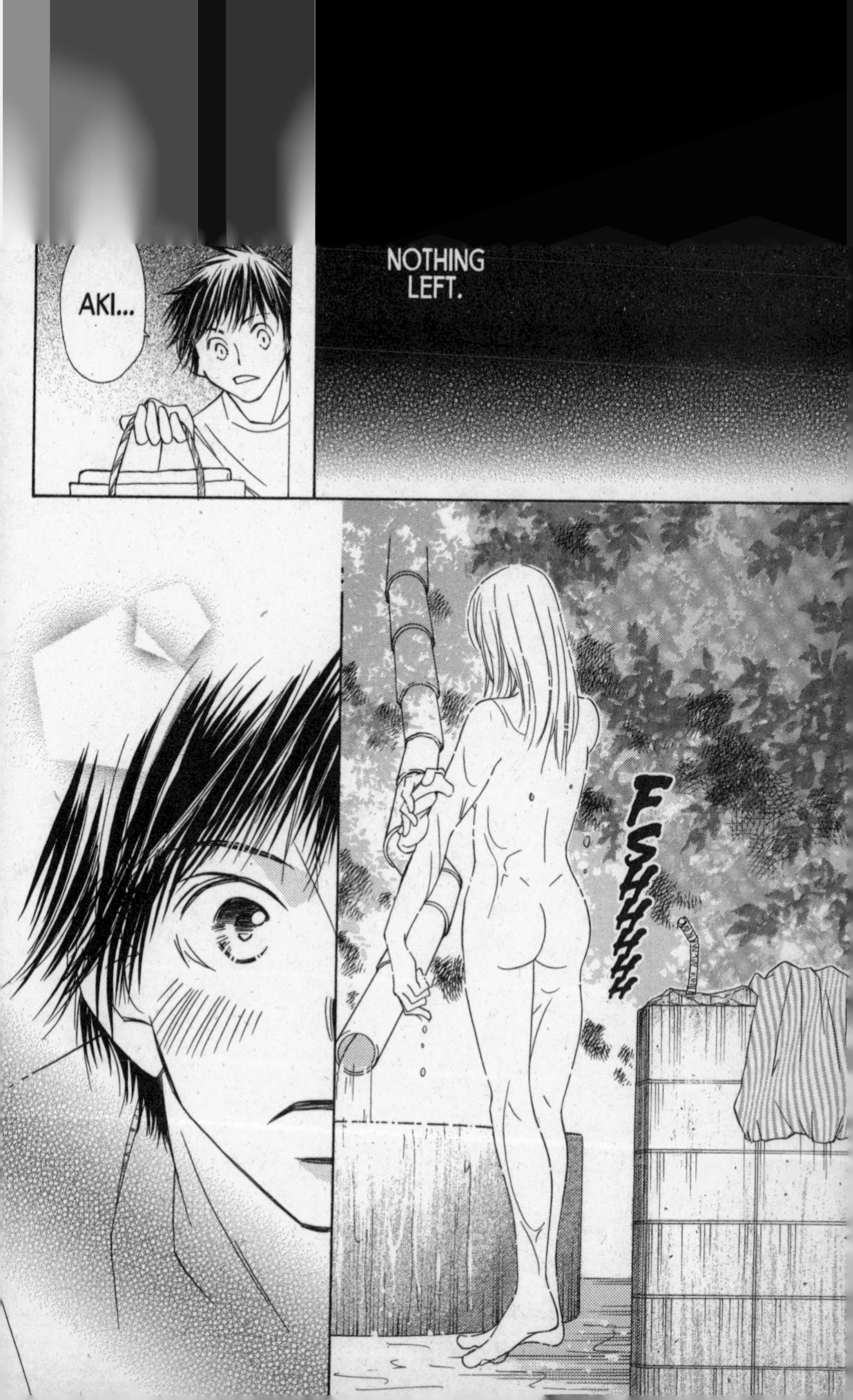
NOTHING LEFT.
AKI...
FSHHHHH

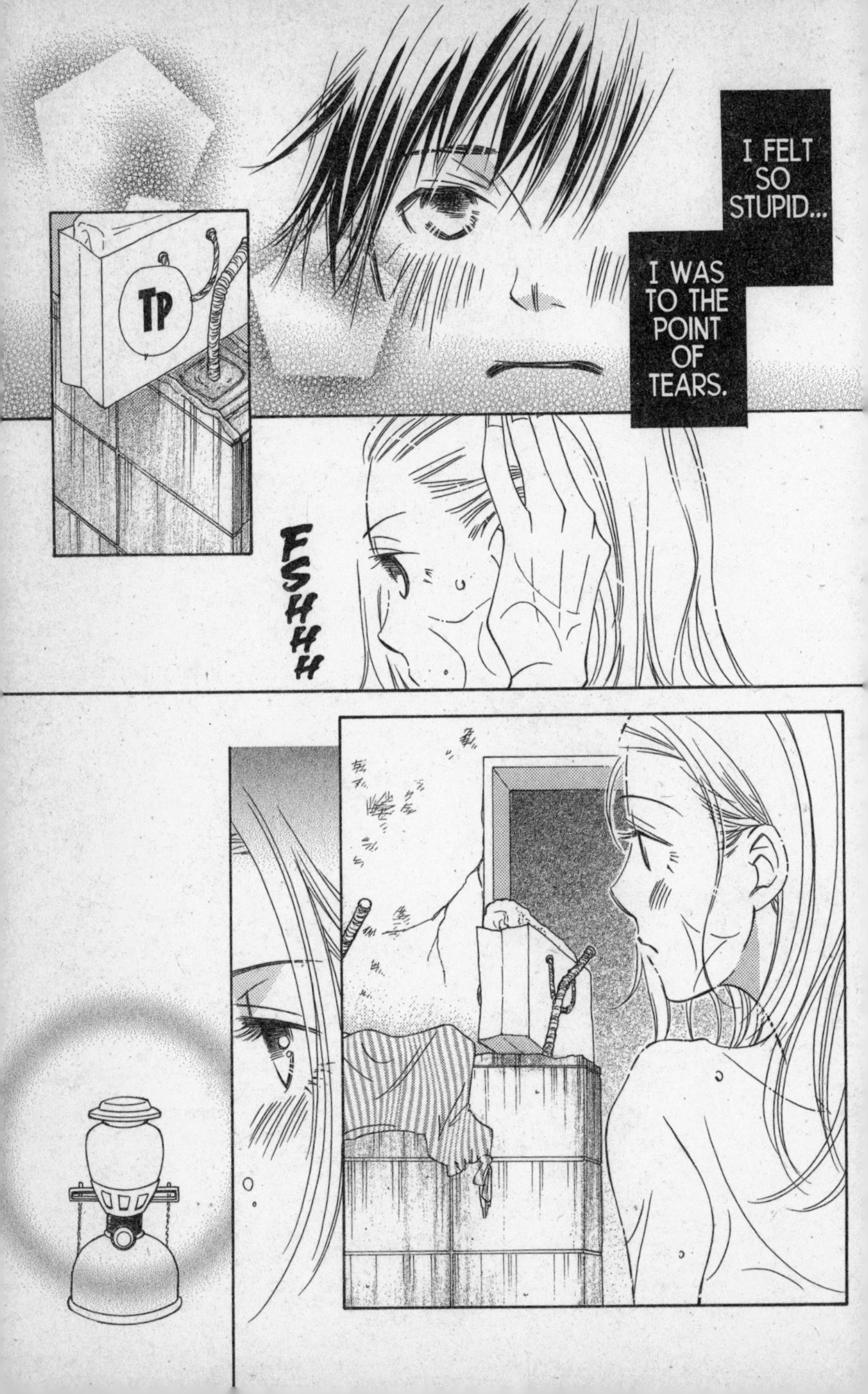
I FELT SO STUPID...
I WAS TO THE POINT OF TEARS.
FSHHH

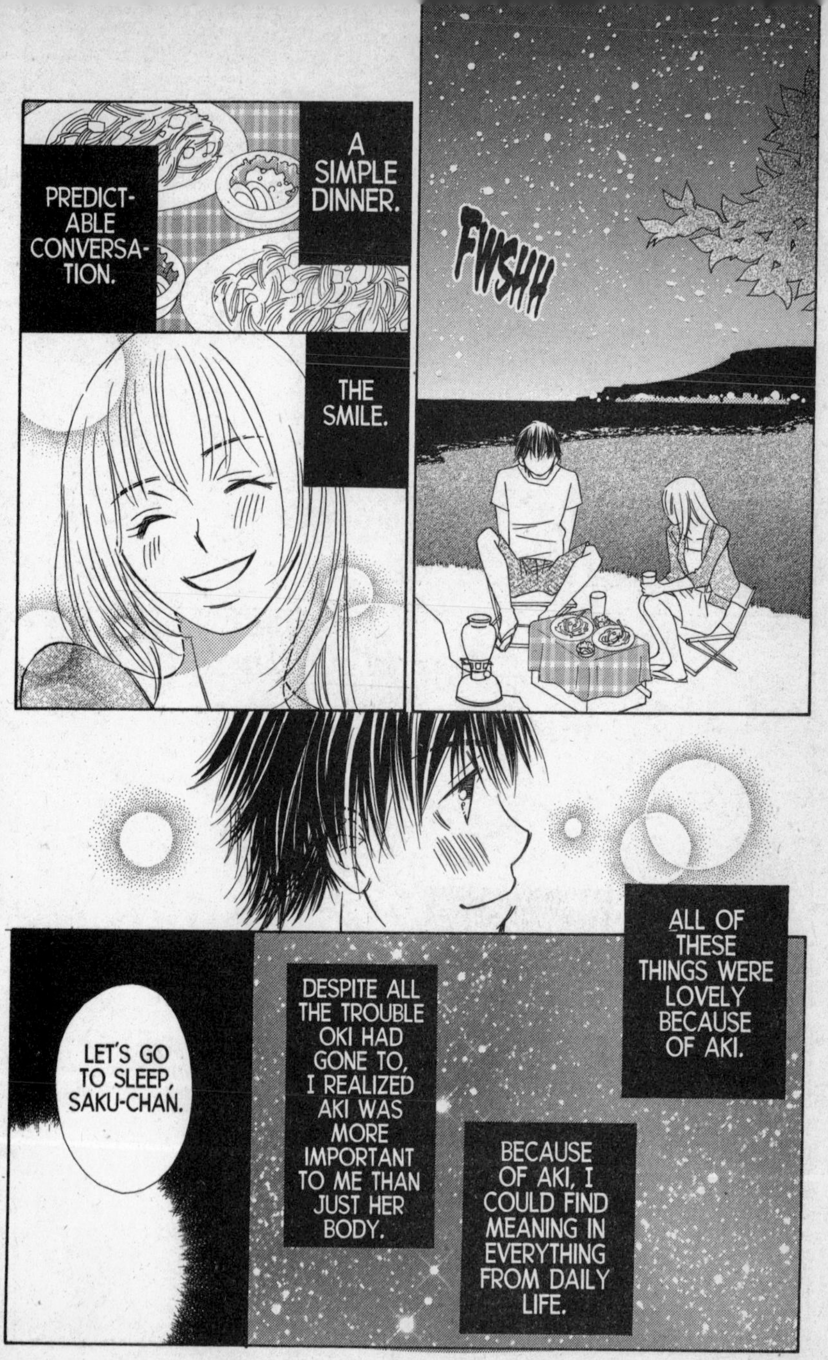
FWSHH
A SIMPLE DINNER.
PREDICT-ABLE CONVERSA-TION.
THE SMILE.
ALL OF THESE THINGS WERE LOVELY BECAUSE OF AKI.
DESPITE ALL THE TROUBLE OKI HAD GONE TO, I REALIZED AKI WAS MORE IMPORTANT TO ME THAN JUST HER BODY.
BECAUSE OF AKI, I COULD FIND MEANING IN EVERYTHING FROM DAILY LIFE.
LET'S GO TO SLEEP, SAKU-CHAN.

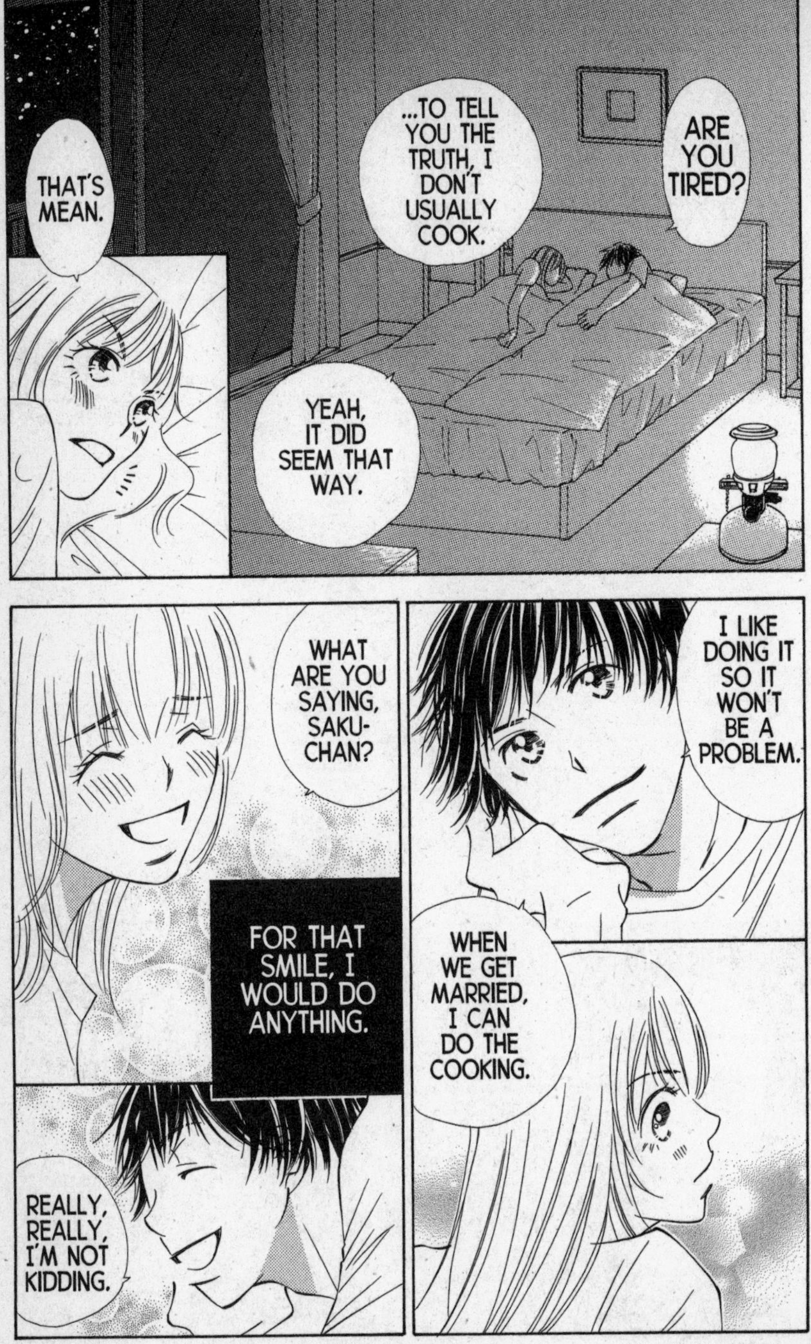
ARE YOU TIRED?
...TO TELL YOU THE TRUTH, I DON'T USUALLY COOK.
YEAH, IT DID SEEM THAT WAY.
THAT'S MEAN.
I LIKE DOING IT SO IT WON'T BE A PROBLEM.
WHEN WE GET MARRIED, I CAN DO THE COOKING.
WHAT ARE YOU SAYING, SAKU-CHAN?
FOR THAT SMILE, I WOULD DO ANYTHING.
REALLY, REALLY, I'M NOT KIDDING.

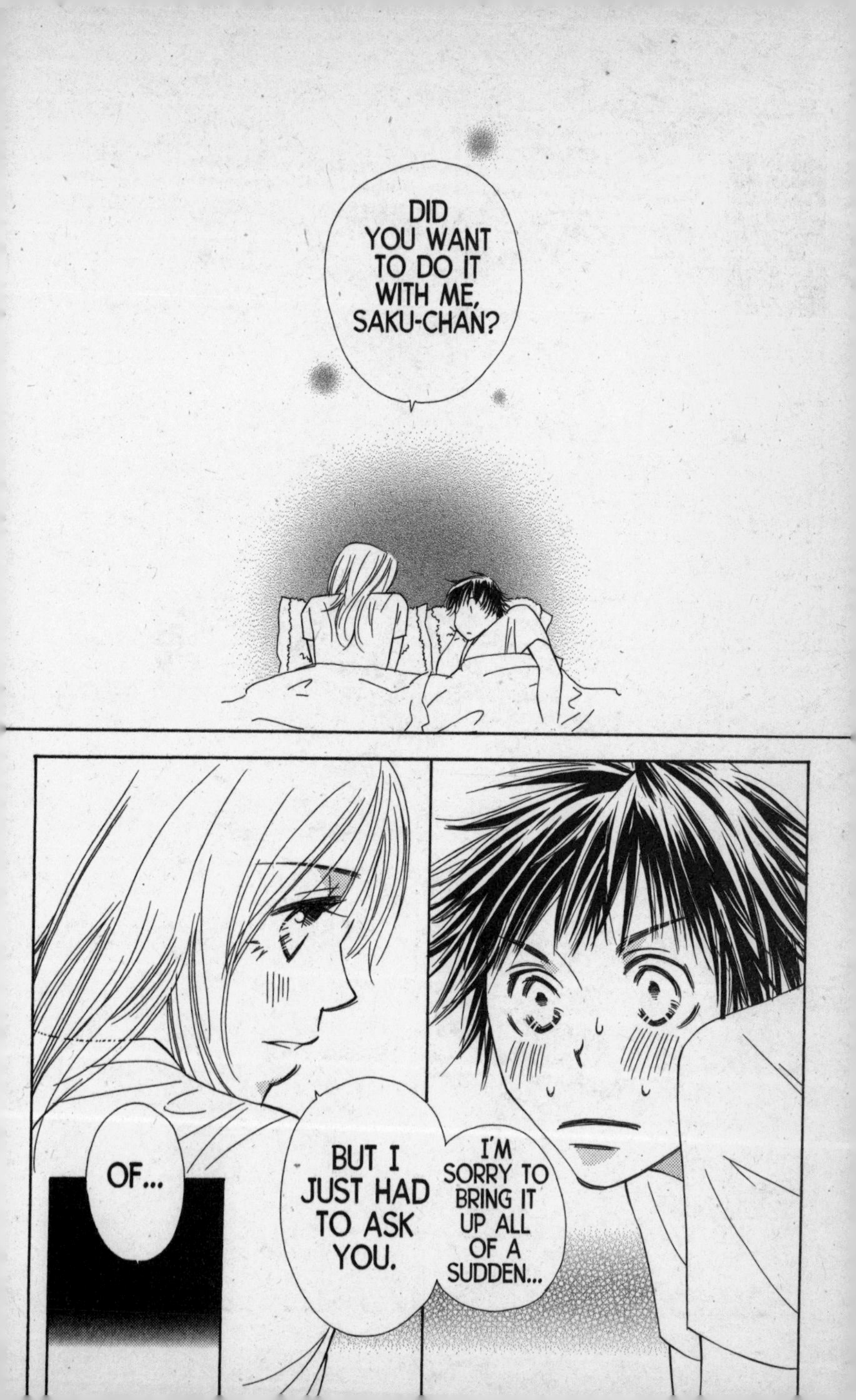
DID YOU WANT TO DO IT WITH ME, SAKU-CHAN?
I'M SORRY TO BRING IT UP ALL OF A SUDDEN...
BUT I JUST HAD TO ASK YOU.
OF...

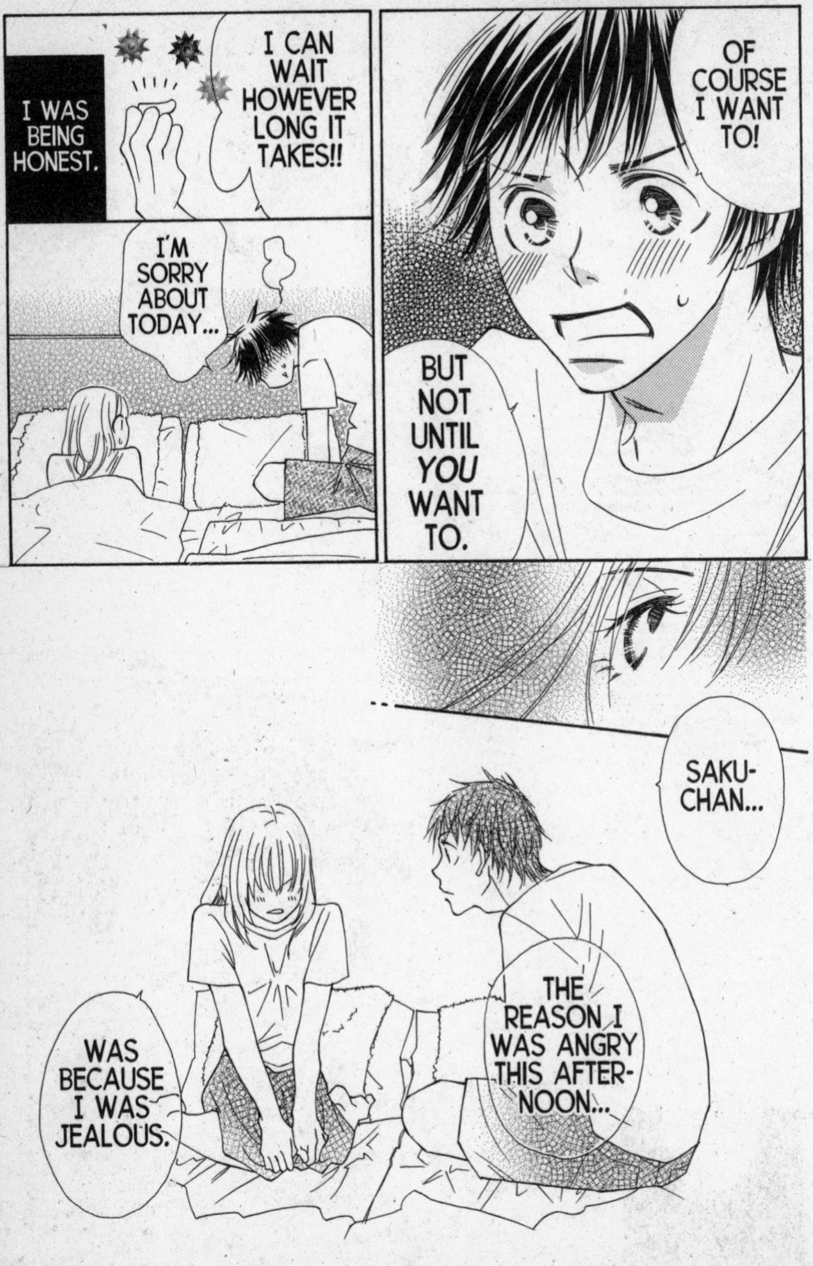
OF COURSE I WANT TO!
BUT NOT UNTIL *YOU* WANT TO.
I CAN WAIT HOWEVER LONG IT TAKES!!
I WAS BEING HONEST.
I'M SORRY ABOUT TODAY...
SAKU-CHAN...
THE REASON I WAS ANGRY THIS AFTER-NOON...
WAS BECAUSE I WAS JEALOUS.

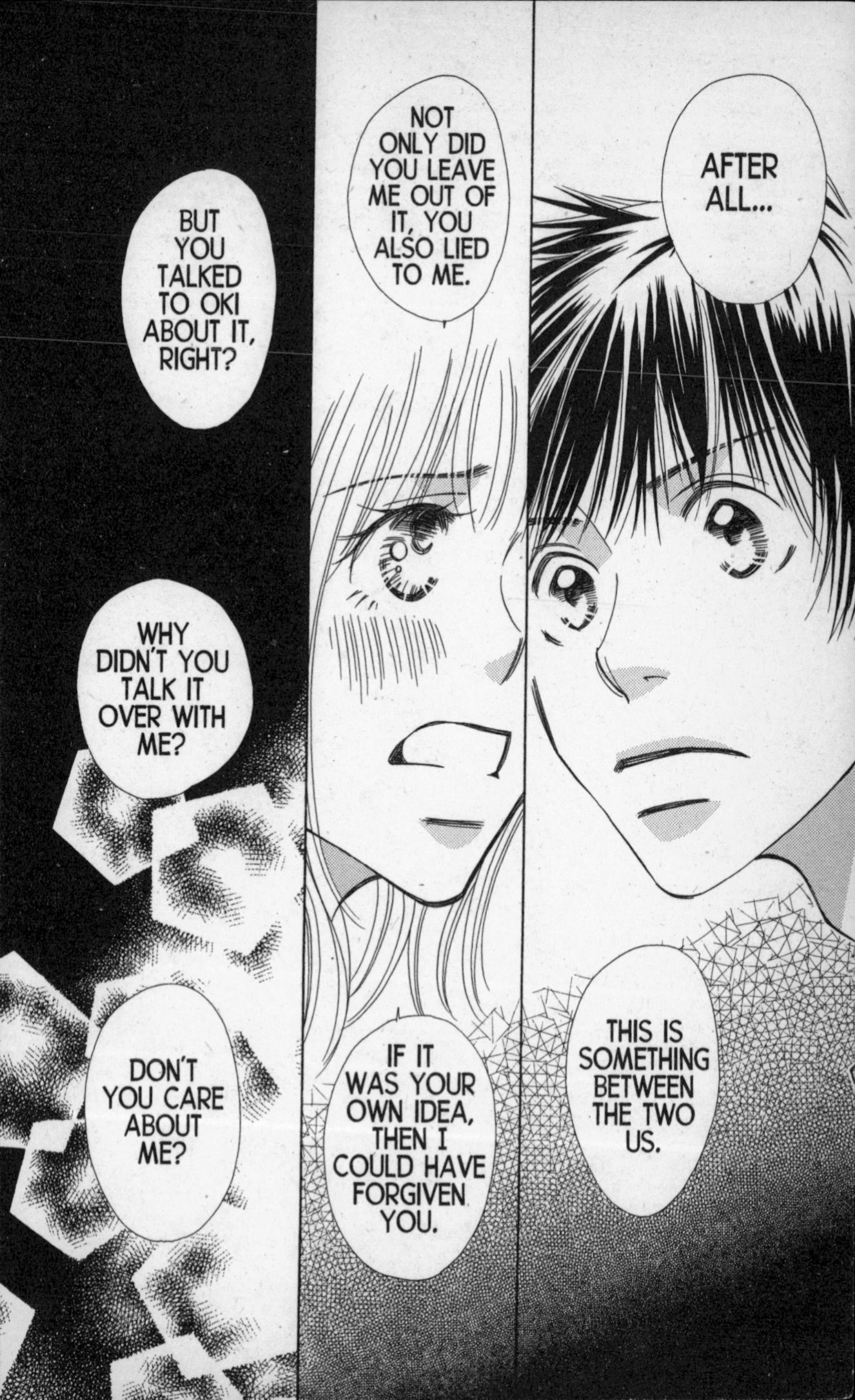
AFTER ALL...
THIS IS SOMETHING BETWEEN THE TWO US.
NOT ONLY DID YOU LEAVE ME OUT OF IT, YOU ALSO LIED TO ME.
IF IT WAS YOUR OWN IDEA, THEN I COULD HAVE FORGIVEN YOU.
BUT YOU TALKED TO OKI ABOUT IT, RIGHT?
WHY DIDN'T YOU TALK IT OVER WITH ME?
DON'T YOU CARE ABOUT ME?

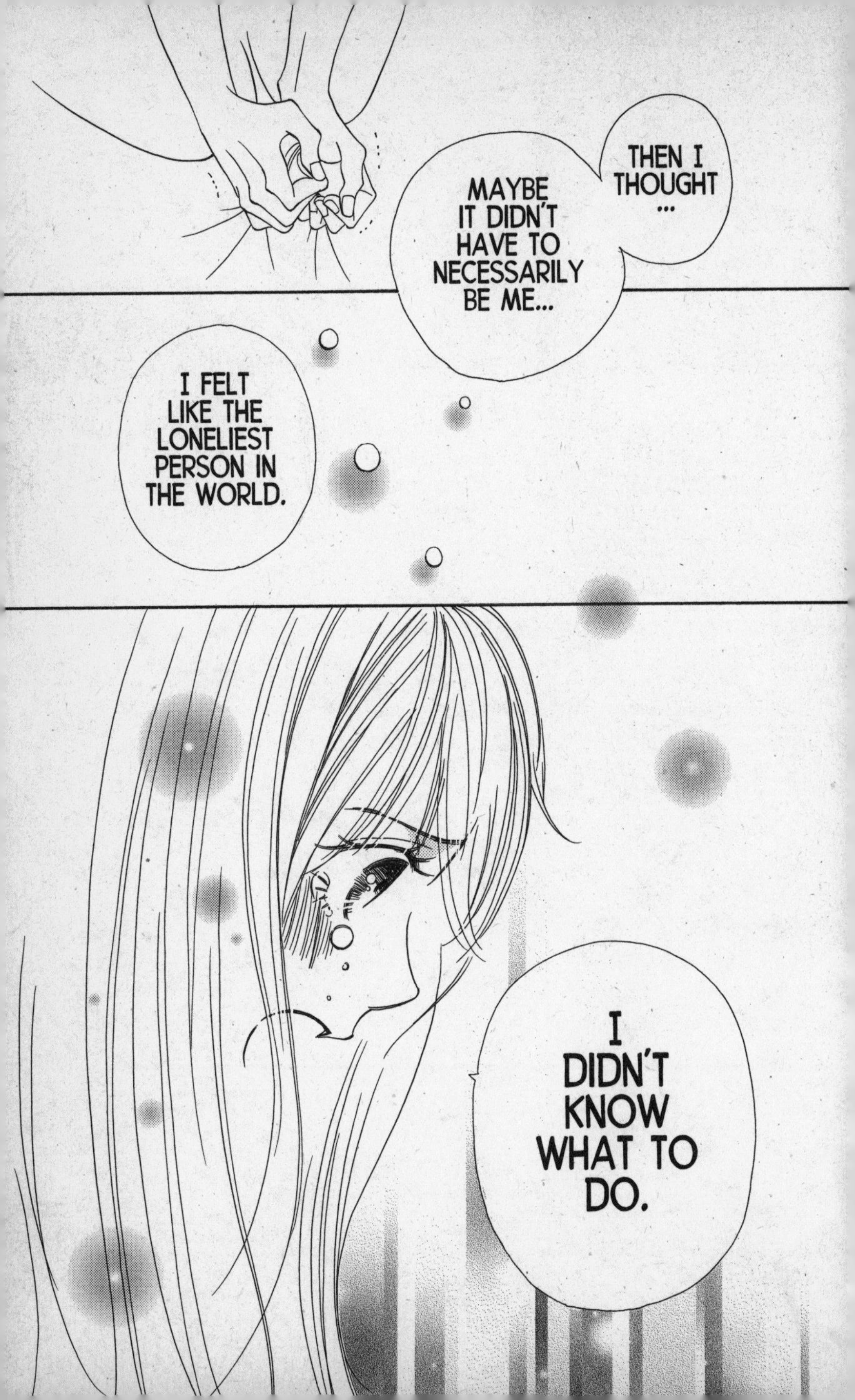
THEN I THOUGHT ...
MAYBE IT DIDN'T HAVE TO NECESSARILY BE ME...
I FELT LIKE THE LONELIEST PERSON IN THE WORLD.
I DIDN'T KNOW WHAT TO DO.

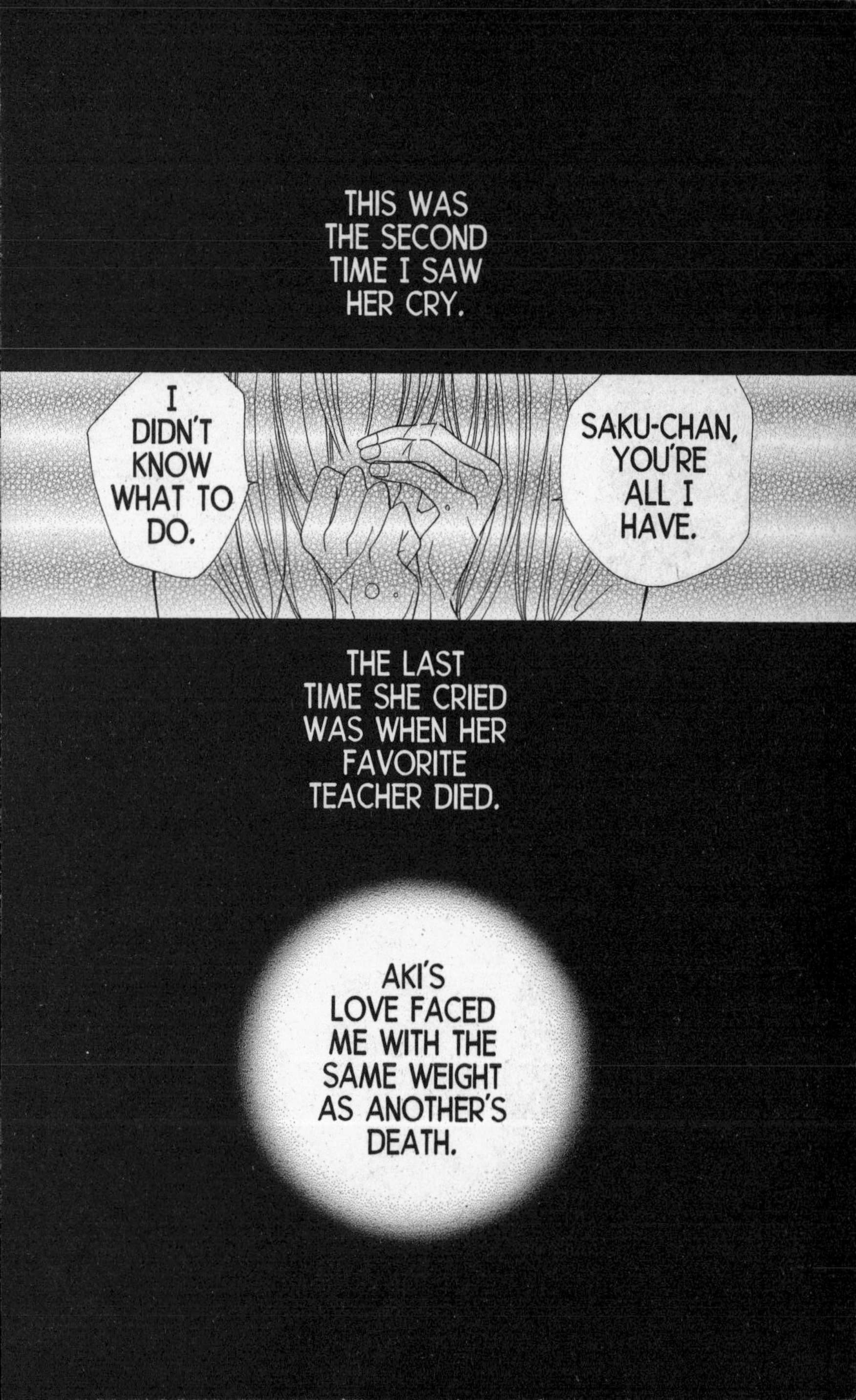
THIS WAS THE SECOND TIME I SAW HER CRY.
SAKU-CHAN, YOU'RE ALL I HAVE.
I DIDN'T KNOW WHAT TO DO.
THE LAST TIME SHE CRIED WAS WHEN HER FAVORITE TEACHER DIED.
AKI'S LOVE FACED ME WITH THE SAME WEIGHT AS ANOTHER'S DEATH.

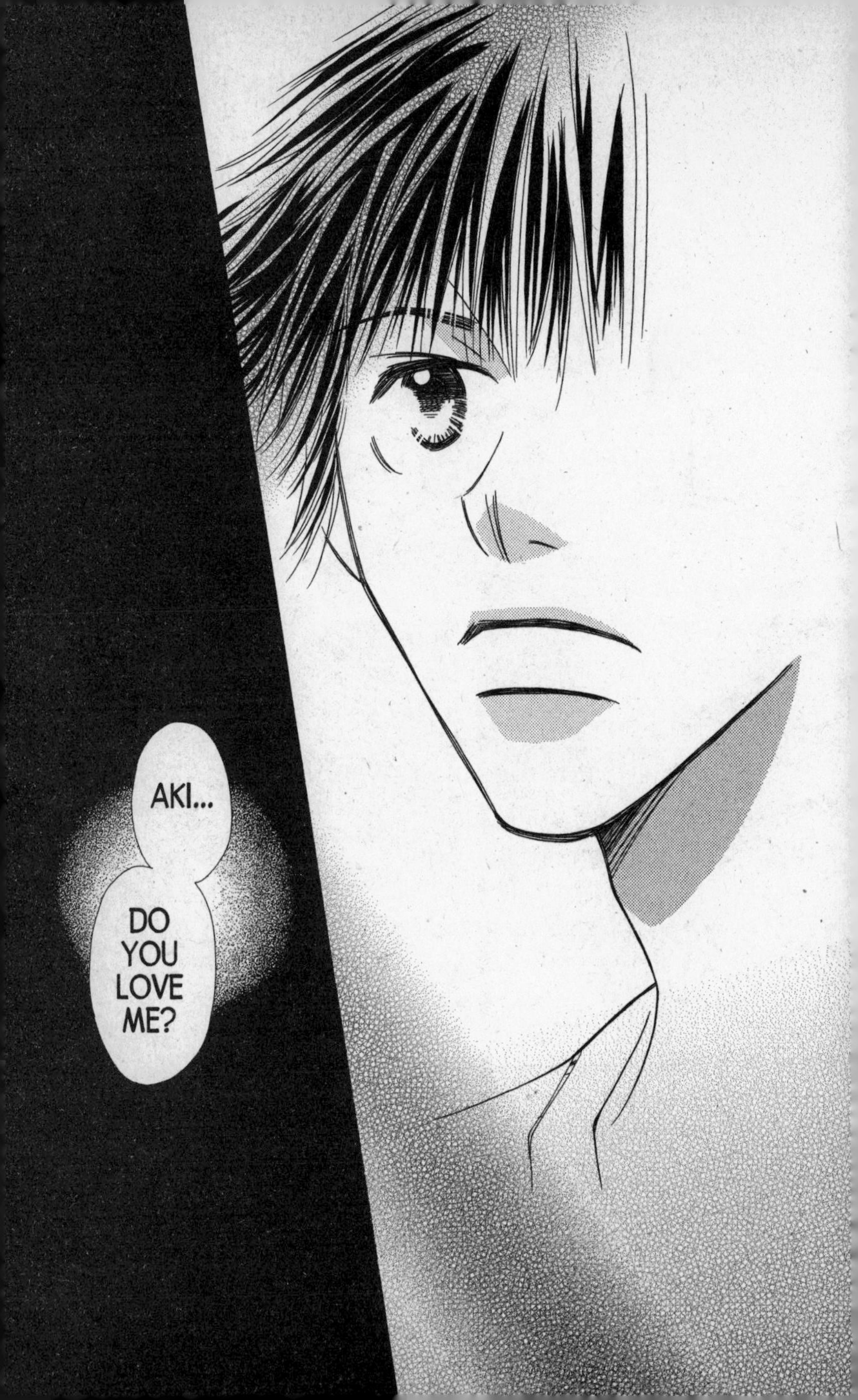
AKI...
DO YOU LOVE ME?

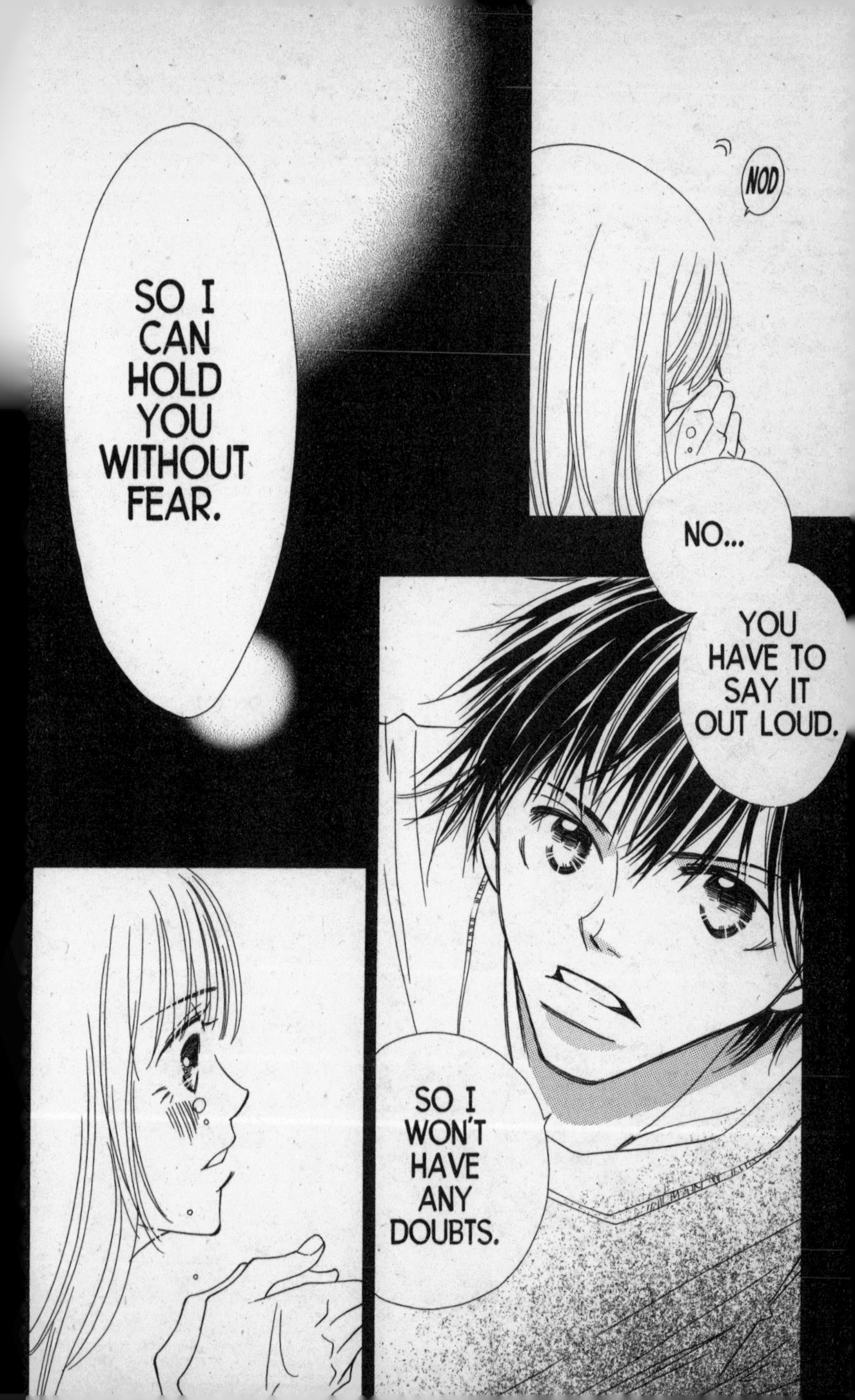
NOD
NO...
YOU HAVE TO SAY IT OUT LOUD.
SO I WON'T HAVE ANY DOUBTS.
SO I CAN HOLD YOU WITHOUT FEAR.

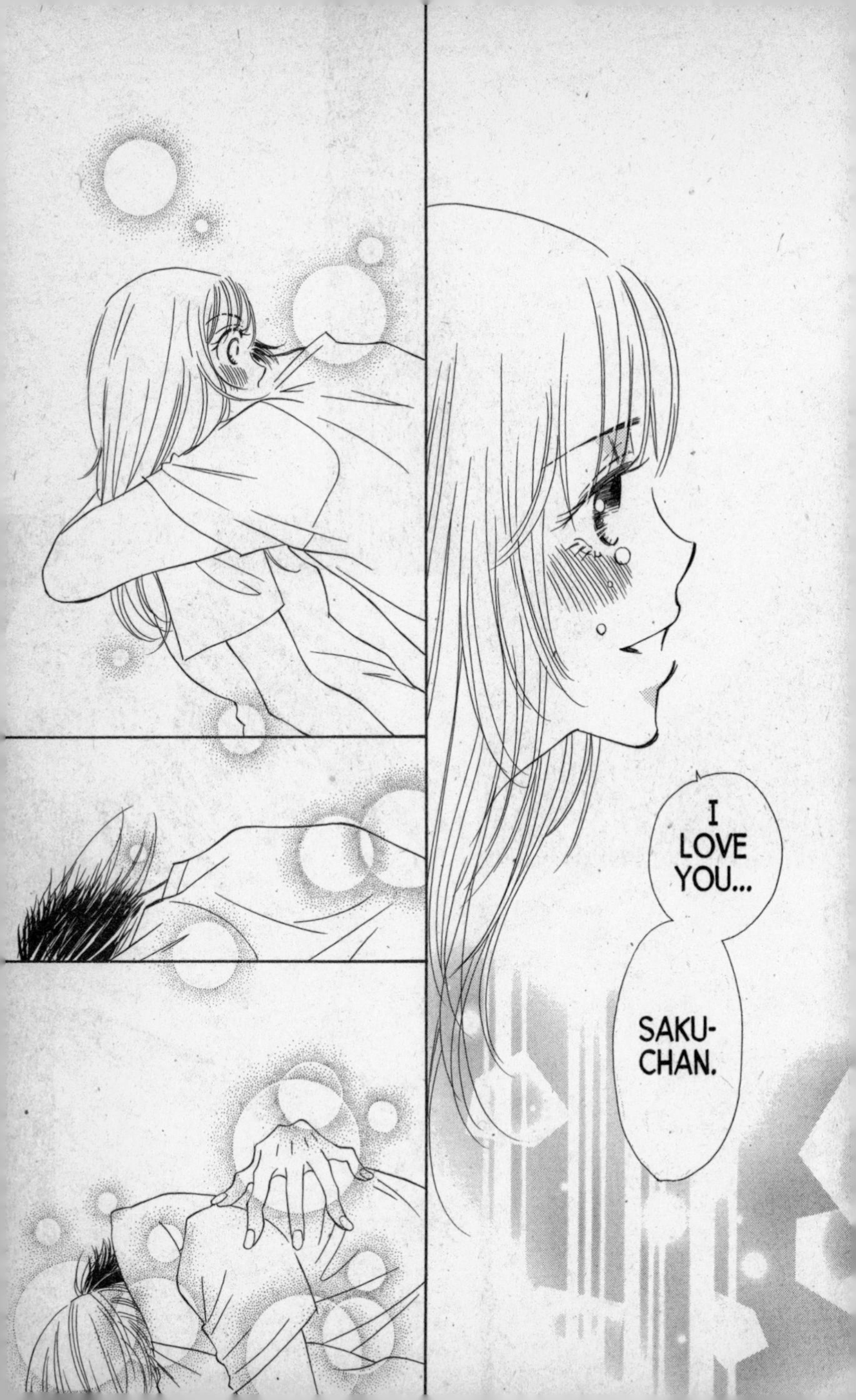
I LOVE YOU...
SAKU-CHAN.

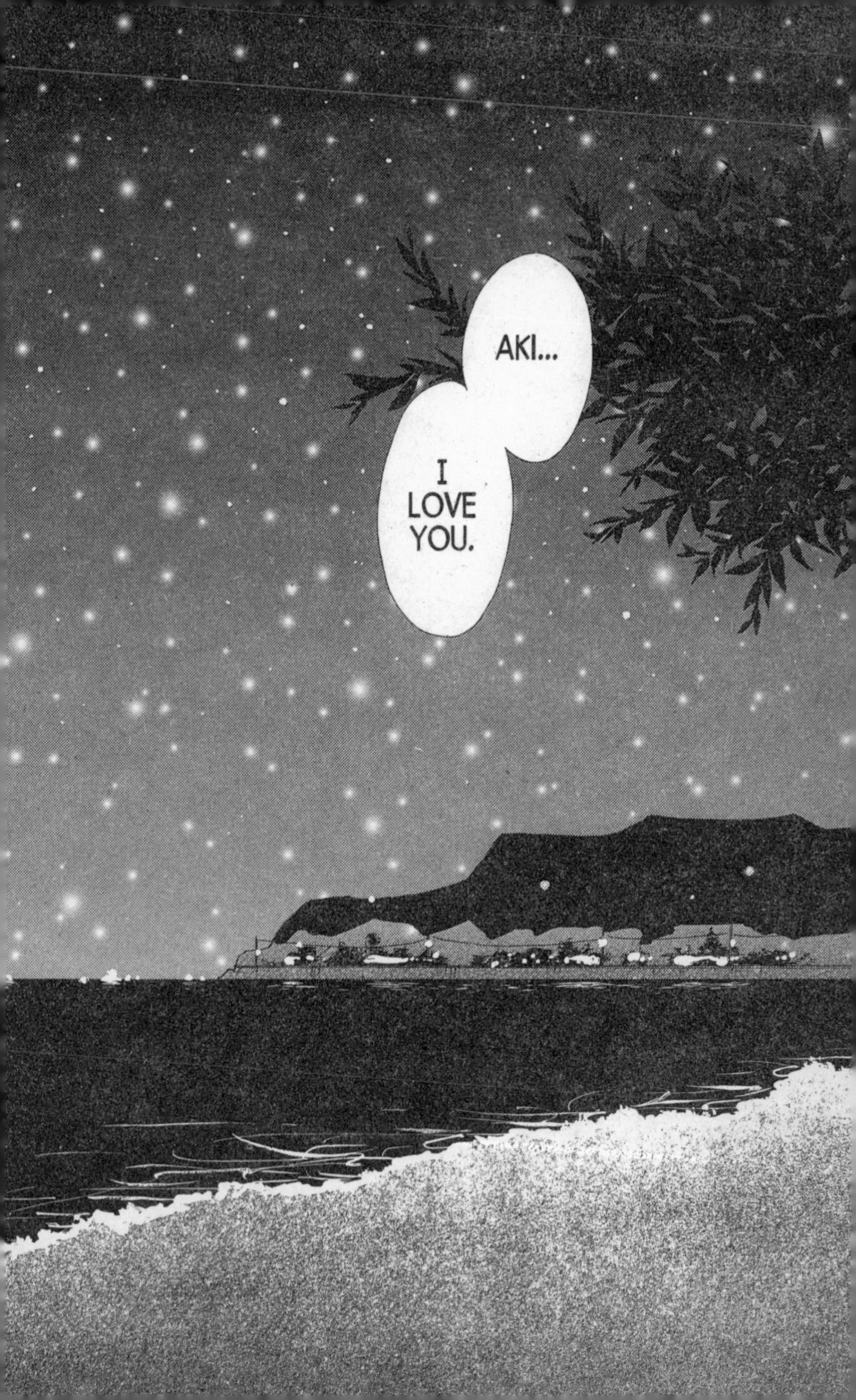
AKI...
I LOVE YOU.

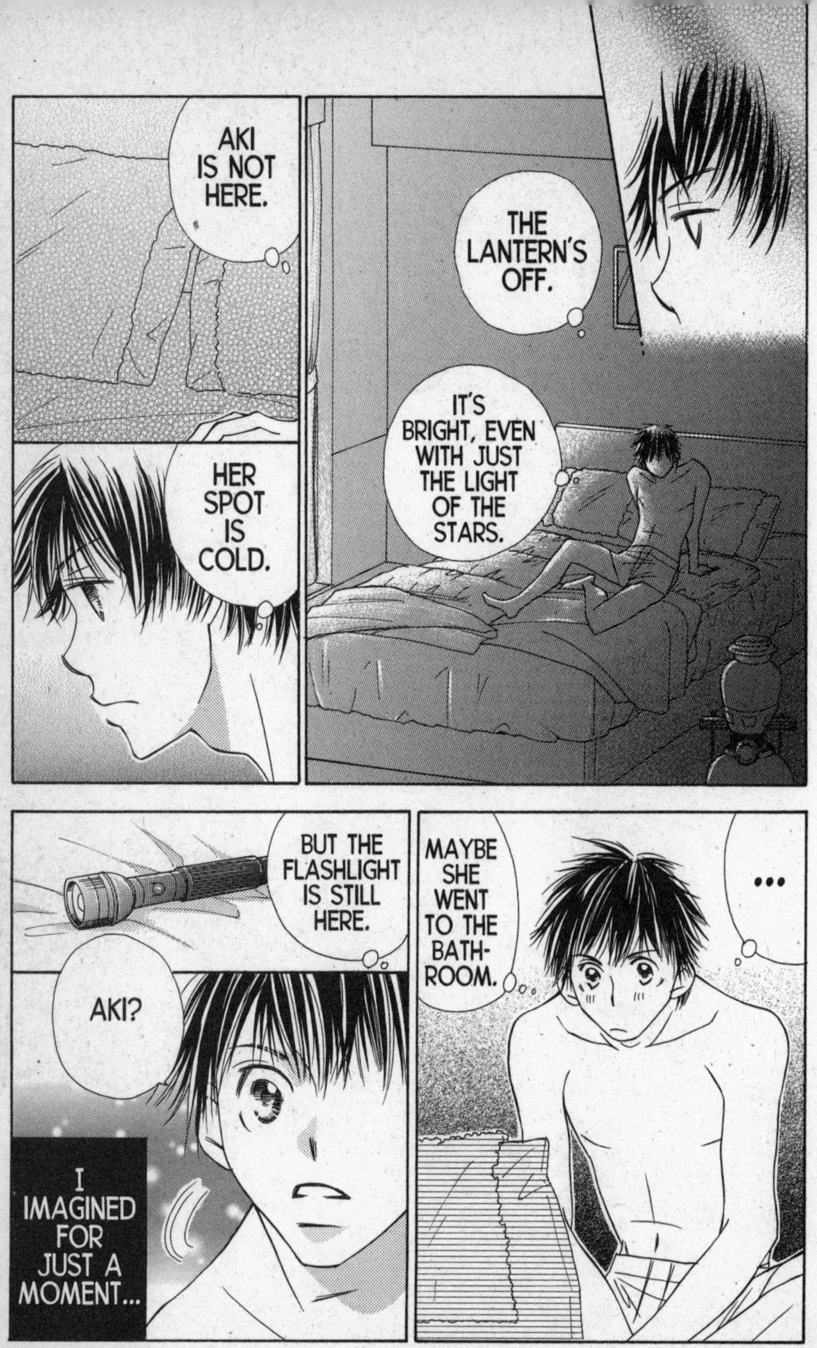
THE LANTERN'S OFF.
IT'S BRIGHT, EVEN WITH JUST THE LIGHT OF THE STARS.
AKI IS NOT HERE.
HER SPOT IS COLD.
...
MAYBE SHE WENT TO THE BATH-ROOM.
BUT THE FLASHLIGHT IS STILL HERE.
AKI?
I IMAGINED FOR JUST A MOMENT...

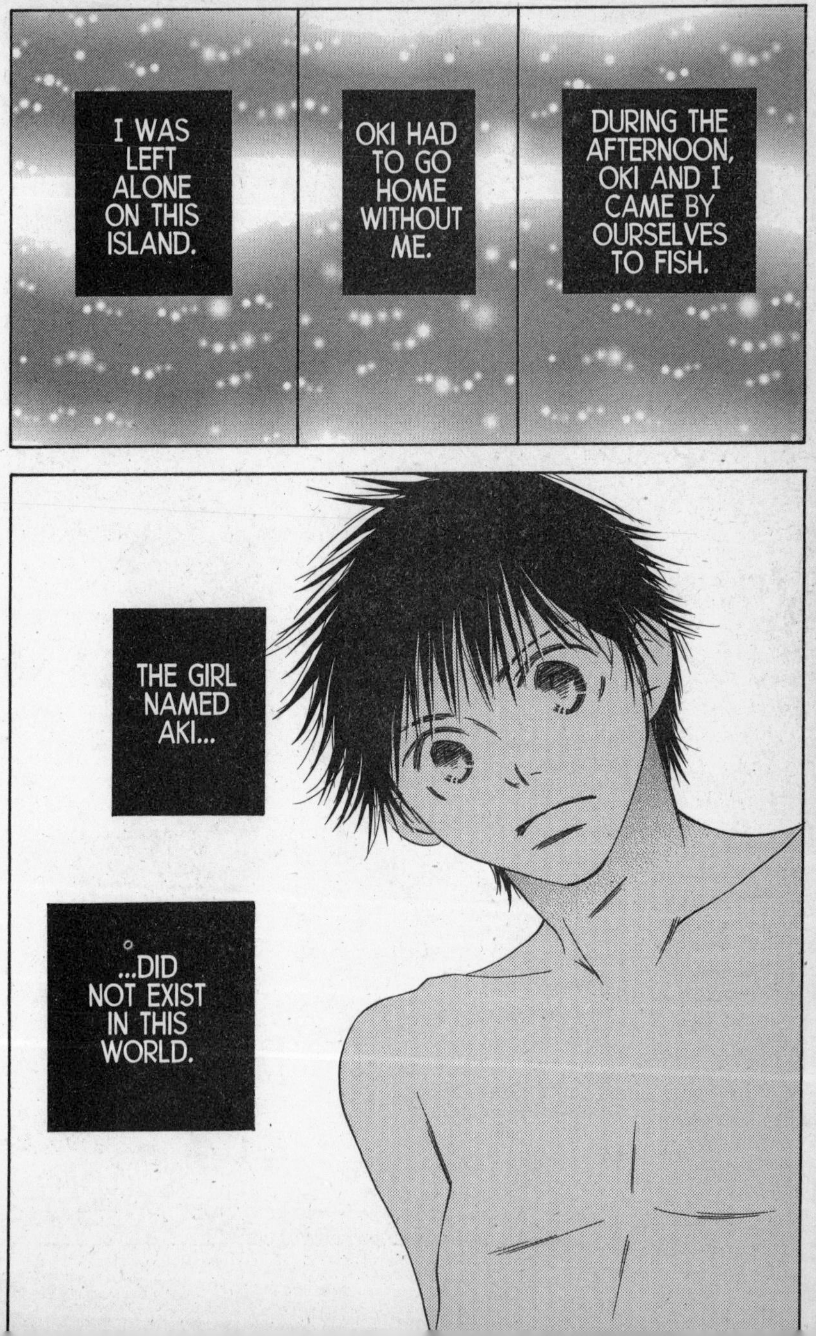
DURING THE AFTERNOON, OKI AND I CAME BY OURSELVES TO FISH.
OKI HAD TO GO HOME WITHOUT ME.
I WAS LEFT ALONE ON THIS ISLAND.
THE GIRL NAMED AKI...
...DID NOT EXIST IN THIS WORLD.

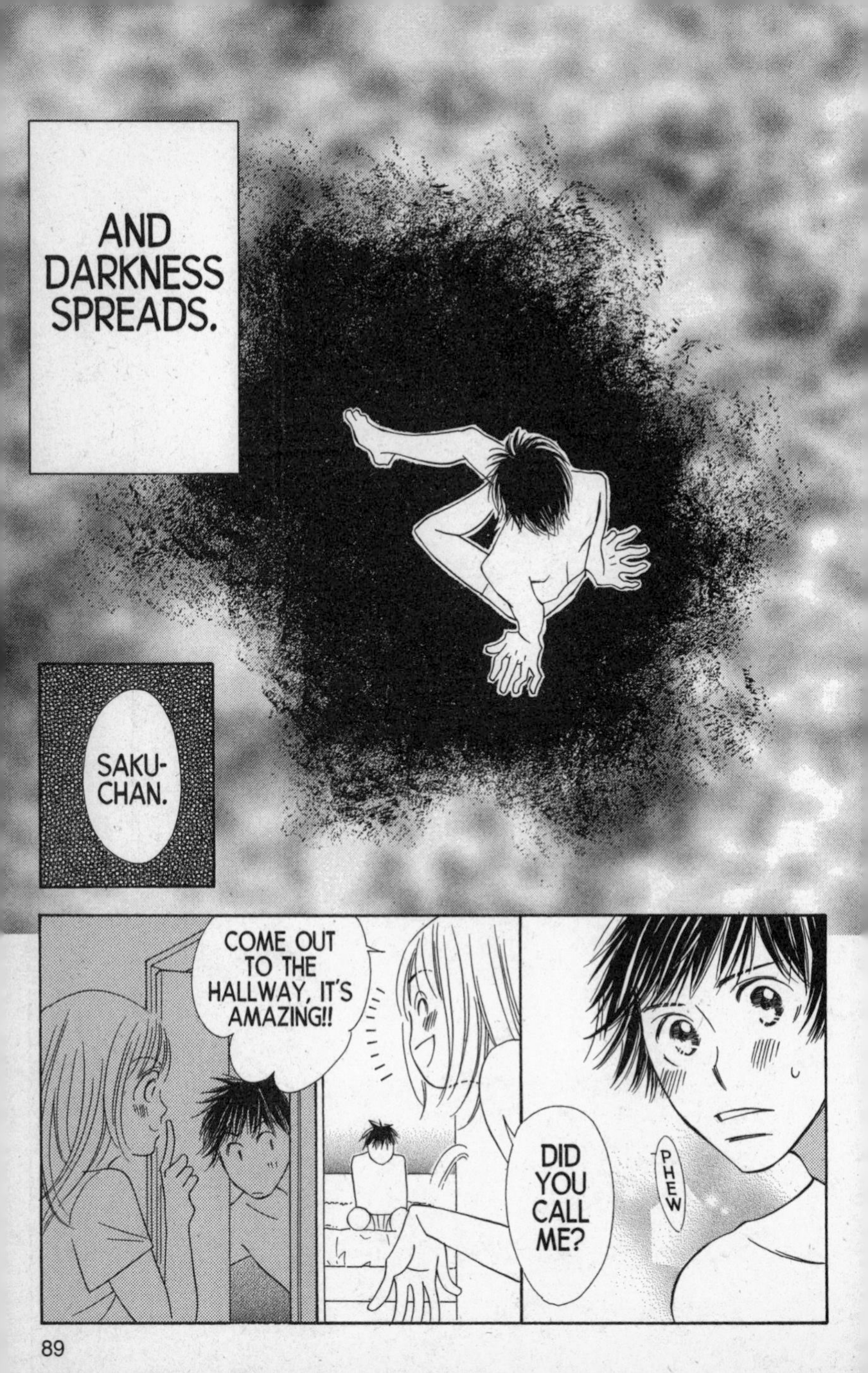
AND DARKNESS SPREADS.
SAKU-CHAN.
DID YOU CALL ME?
PHEW
COME OUT TO THE HALLWAY, IT'S AMAZING!!

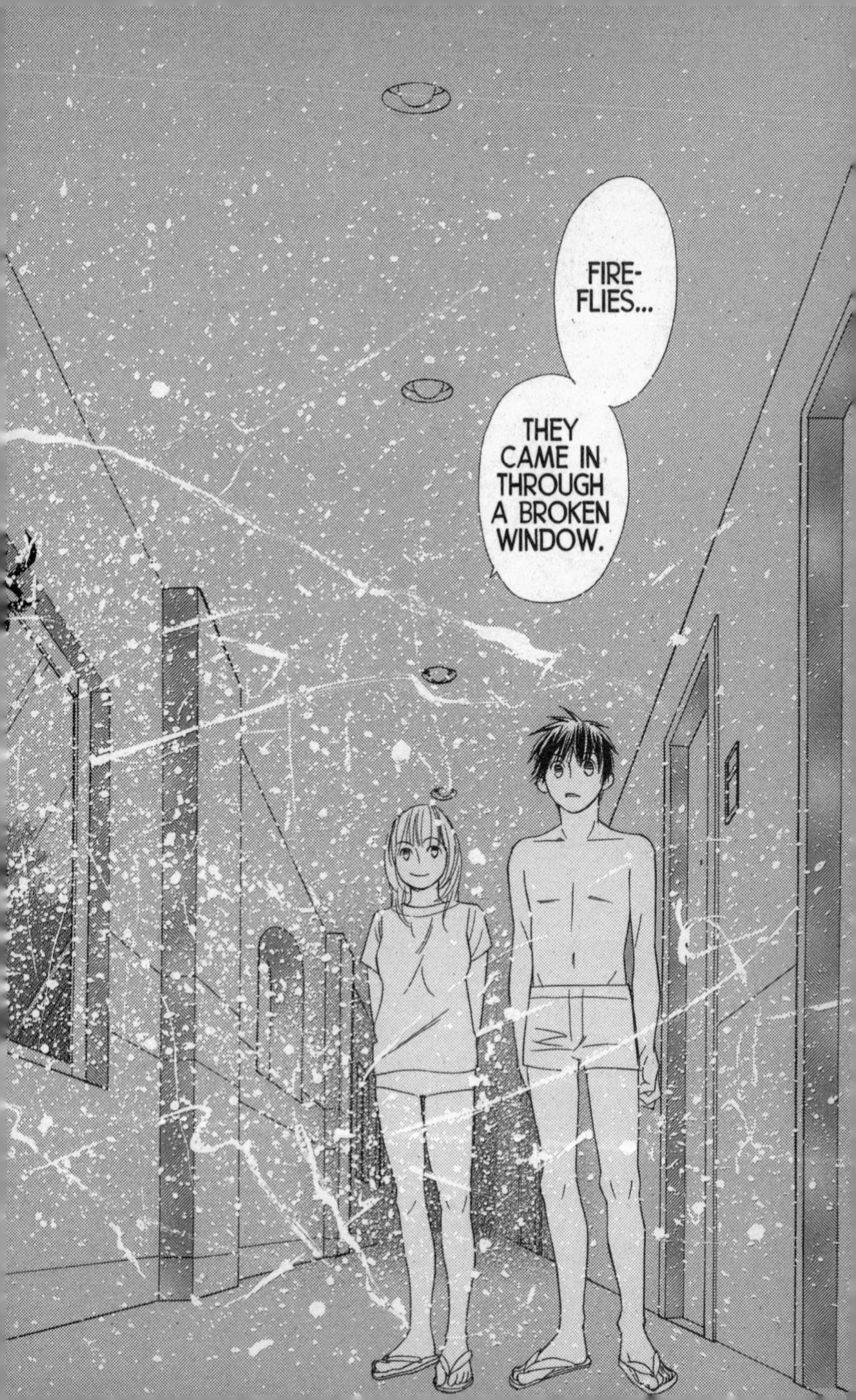
FIRE-FLIES...
THEY CAME IN THROUGH A BROKEN WINDOW.

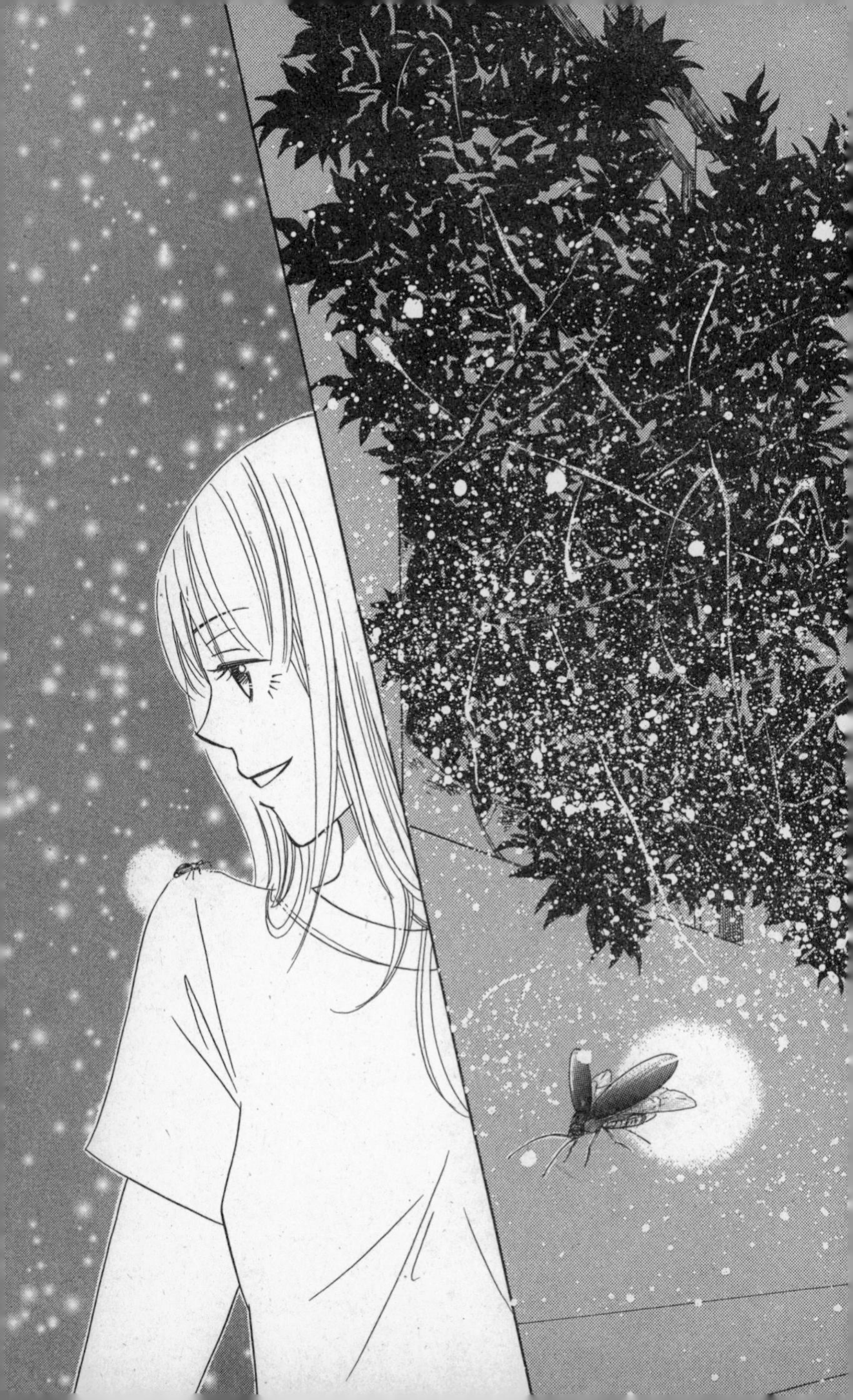

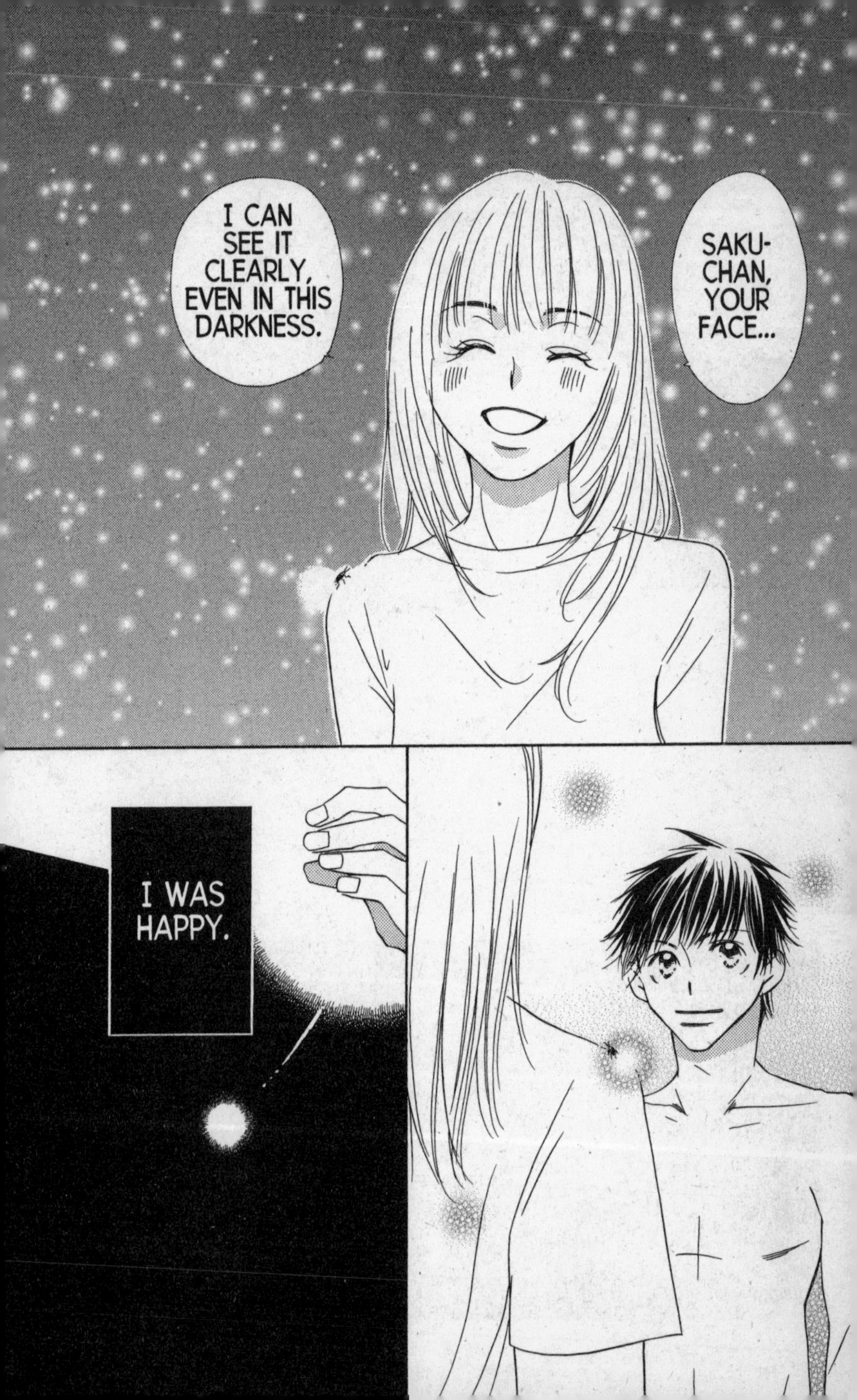
SAKU-CHAN, YOUR FACE...
I CAN SEE IT CLEARLY, EVEN IN THIS DARKNESS.
I WAS HAPPY.

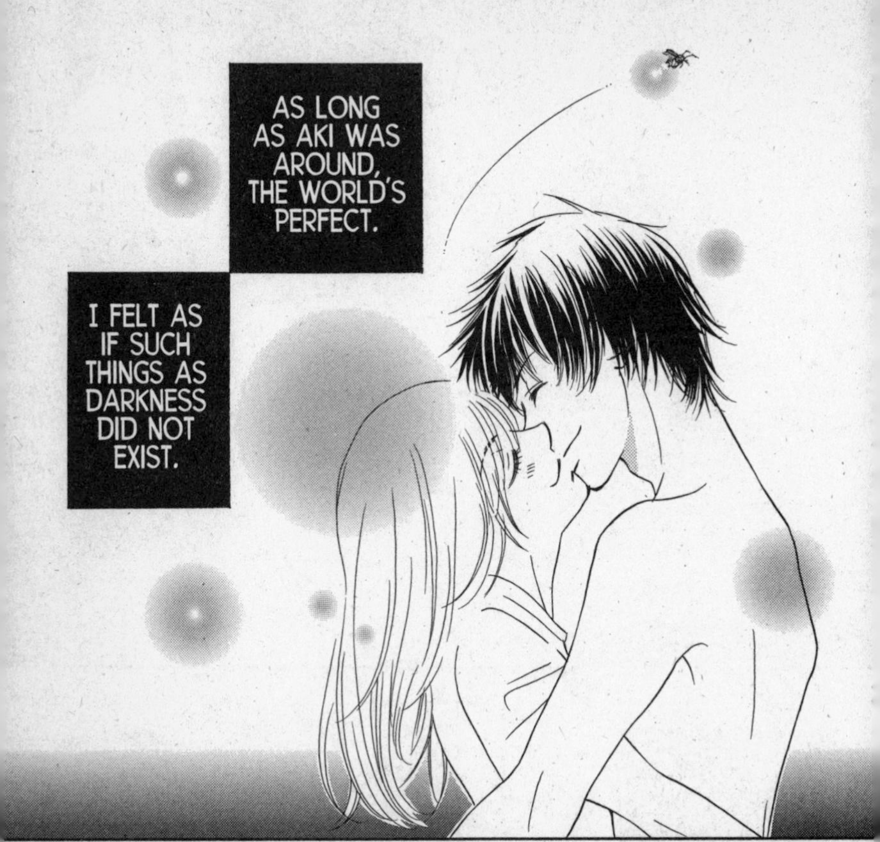
AS LONG AS AKI WAS AROUND, THE WORLD'S PERFECT.
I FELT AS IF SUCH THINGS AS DARKNESS DID NOT EXIST.

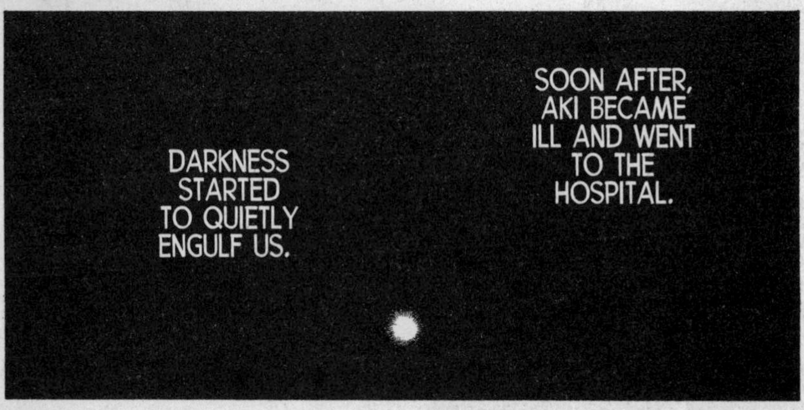
SOON AFTER, AKI BECAME ILL AND WENT TO THE HOSPITAL.
DARKNESS STARTED TO QUIETLY ENGULF US.

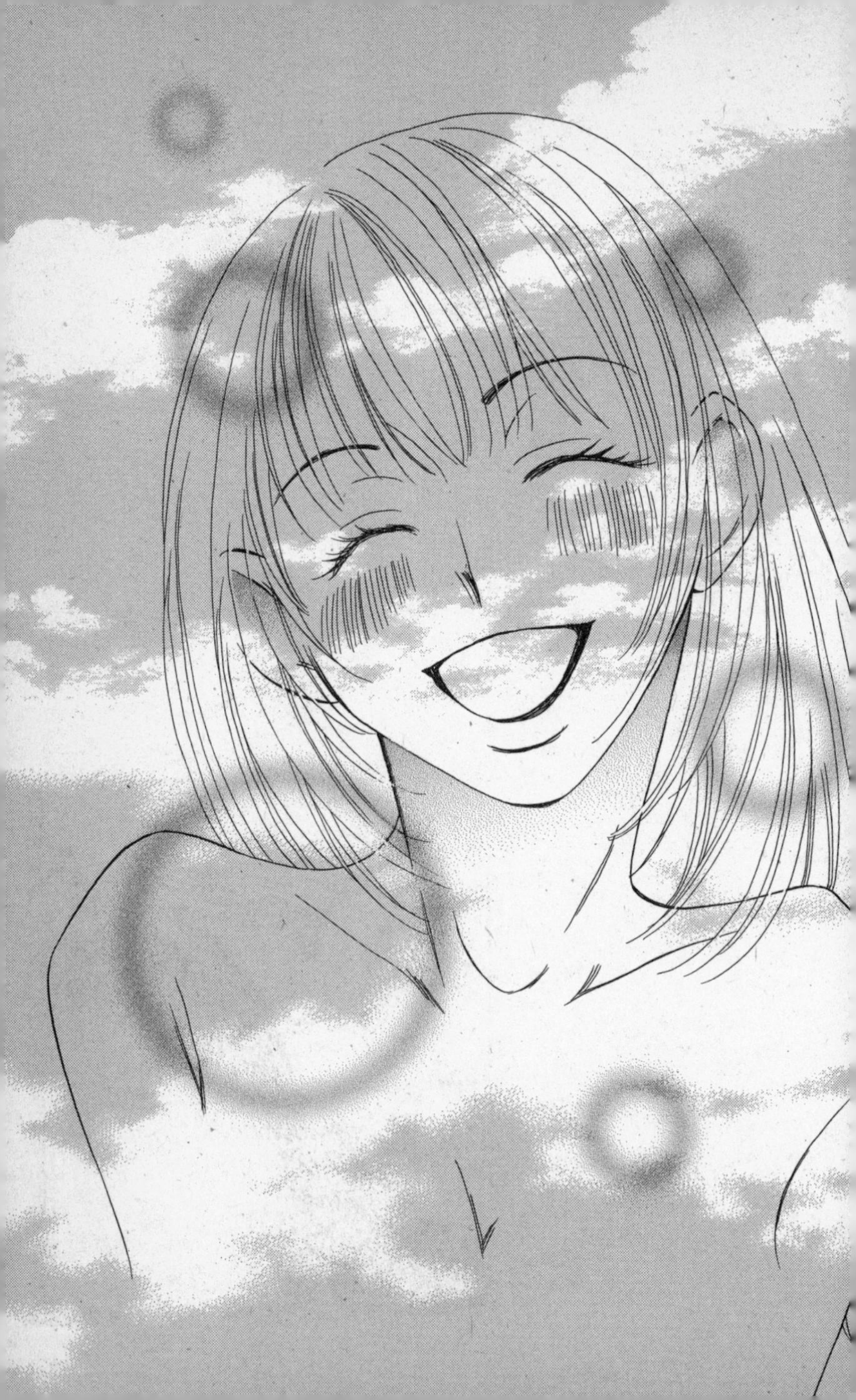

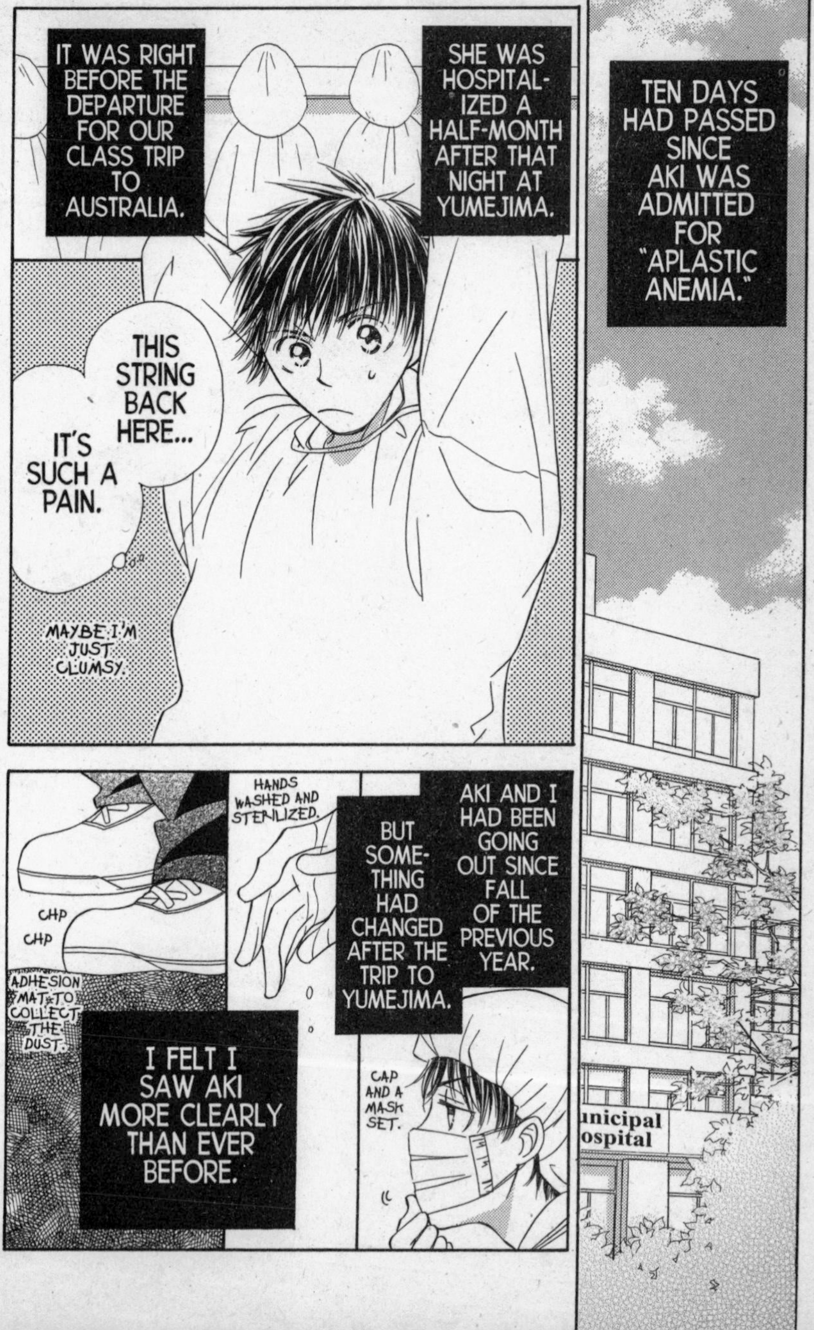
TEN DAYS HAD PASSED SINCE AKI WAS ADMITTED FOR "APLASTIC ANEMIA."
unicipal
ospital
SHE WAS HOSPITAL-IZED A HALF-MONTH AFTER THAT NIGHT AT YUMEJIMA.
IT WAS RIGHT BEFORE THE DEPARTURE FOR OUR CLASS TRIP TO AUSTRALIA.
THIS STRING BACK HERE...
IT'S SUCH A PAIN.
MAYBE I'M JUST CLUMSY.
AKI AND I HAD BEEN GOING OUT SINCE FALL OF THE PREVIOUS YEAR.
BUT SOME-THING HAD CHANGED AFTER THE TRIP TO YUMEJIMA.
CAP AND A MASK SET.
HANDS WASHED AND STERILIZED.
CHP
CHP
ADHESION MAT TO COLLECT THE DUST.
I FELT I SAW AKI MORE CLEARLY THAN EVER BEFORE.

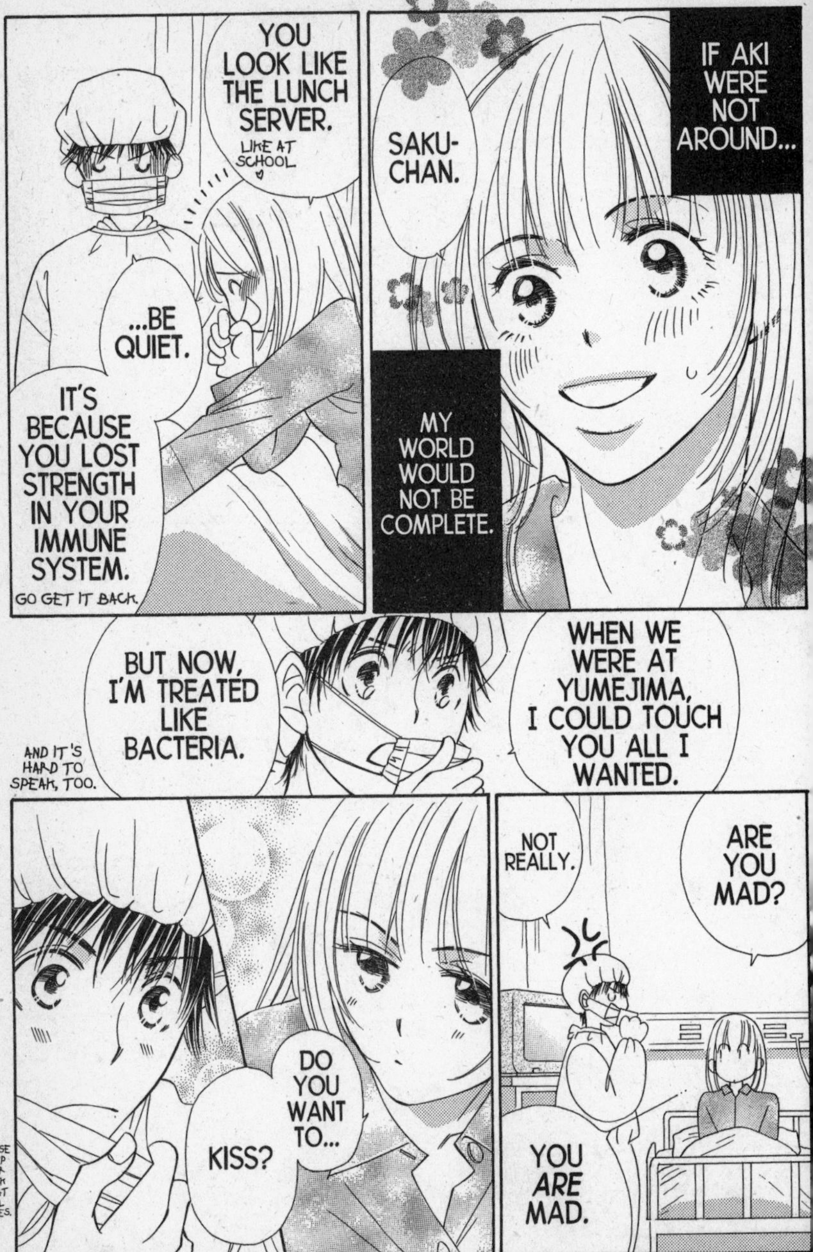
IF AKI WERE NOT AROUND...
SAKU-CHAN.
MY WORLD WOULD NOT BE COMPLETE.
YOU LOOK LIKE THE LUNCH SERVER.
LIKE AT SCHOOL
...BE QUIET.
IT'S BECAUSE YOU LOST STRENGTH IN YOUR IMMUNE SYSTEM.
GO GET IT BACK.
WHEN WE WERE AT YUMEJIMA, I COULD TOUCH YOU ALL I WANTED.
BUT NOW, I'M TREATED LIKE BACTERIA.
AND IT'S HARD TO SPEAK, TOO.
ARE YOU MAD?
NOT REALLY.
YOU *ARE* MAD.
DO YOU WANT TO...
KISS?
PLEASE KEEP YOUR MASK ON AT ALL TIMES.

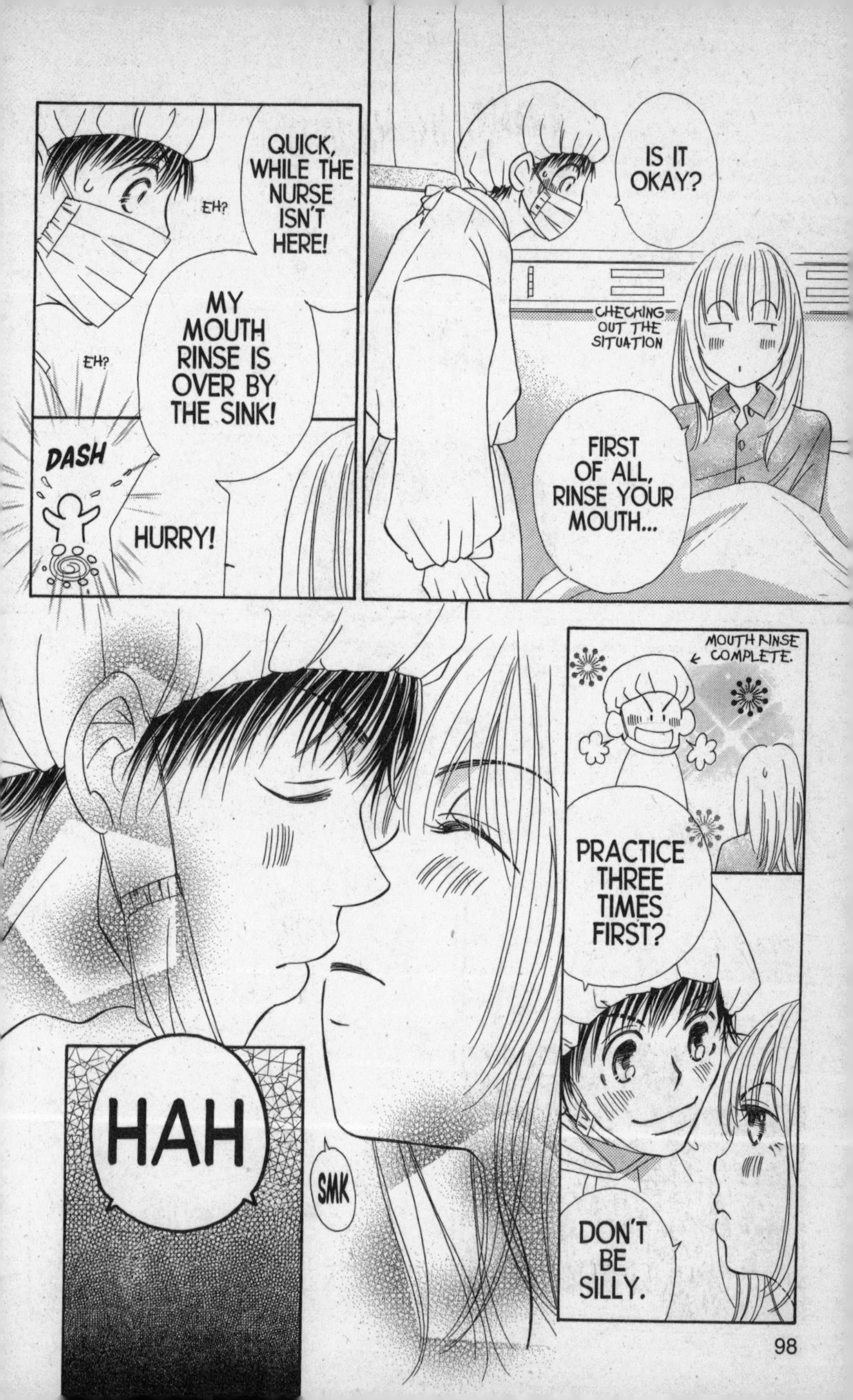
IS IT OKAY?
CHECKING OUT THE SITUATION
FIRST OF ALL, RINSE YOUR MOUTH...
QUICK, WHILE THE NURSE ISN'T HERE!
EH?
MY MOUTH RINSE IS OVER BY THE SINK!
EH?
DASH
HURRY!
MOUTH RINSE COMPLETE.
PRACTICE THREE TIMES FIRST?
DON'T BE SILLY.
SMK
HAH

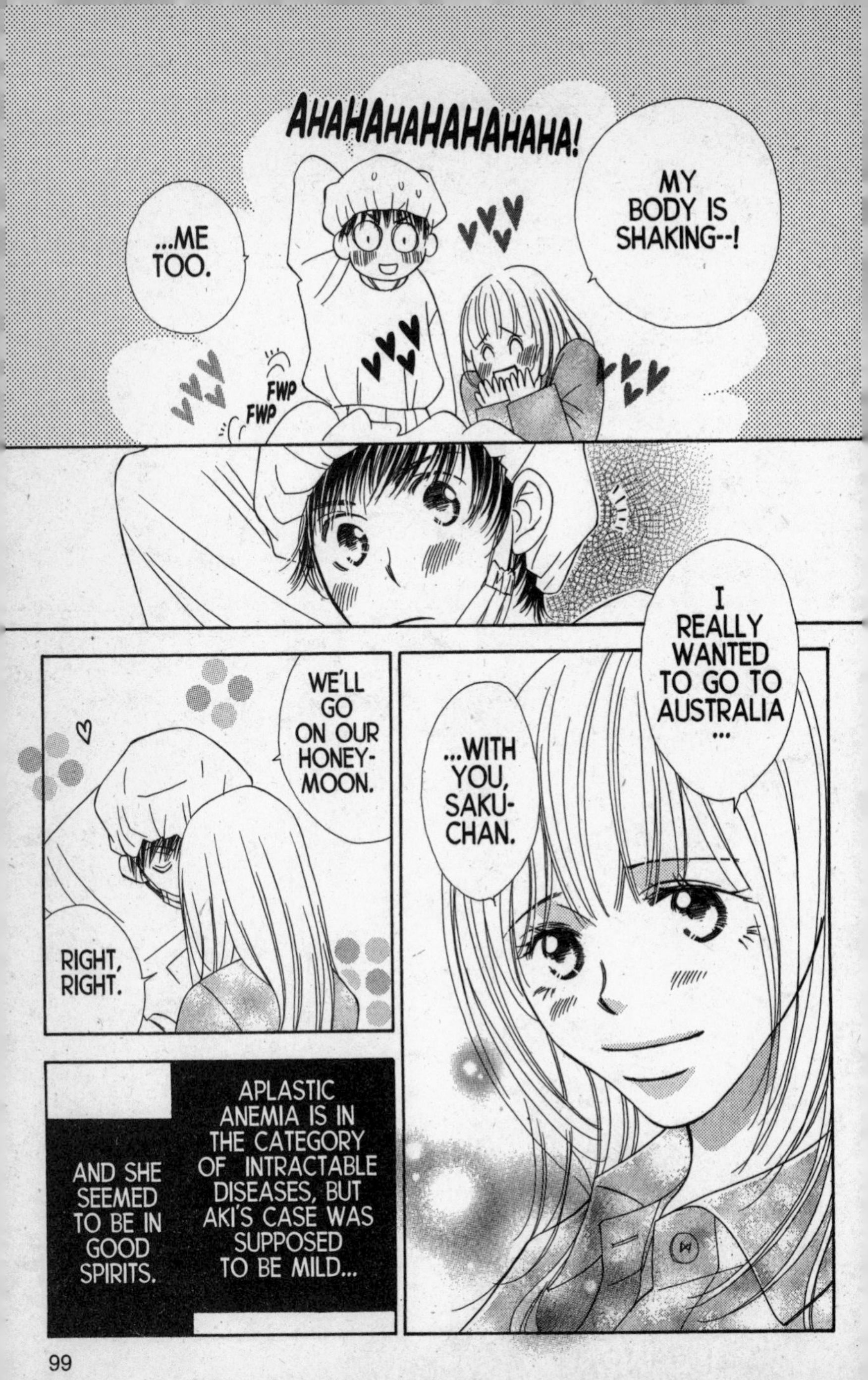
AHAHAHAHAHAHAHA!
MY BODY IS SHAKING--!
...ME TOO.
FWP
FWP
I REALLY WANTED TO GO TO AUSTRALIA...
...WITH YOU, SAKU-CHAN.
WE'LL GO ON OUR HONEY-MOON.
RIGHT, RIGHT.
APLASTIC ANEMIA IS IN THE CATEGORY OF INTRACTABLE DISEASES, BUT AKI'S CASE WAS SUPPOSED TO BE MILD...
AND SHE SEEMED TO BE IN GOOD SPIRITS.

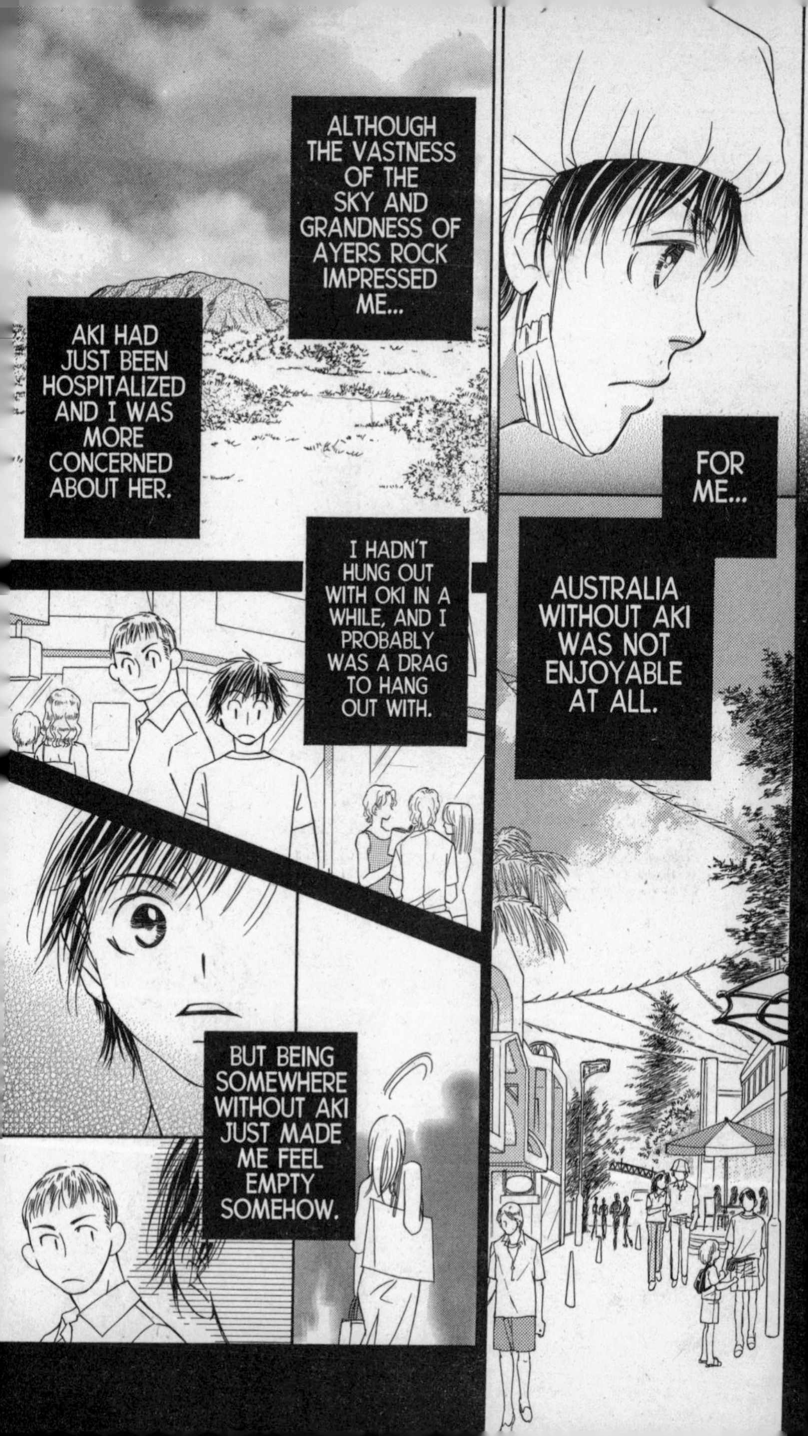
FOR ME...
AUSTRALIA WITHOUT AKI WAS NOT ENJOYABLE AT ALL.
ALTHOUGH THE VASTNESS OF THE SKY AND GRANDNESS OF AYERS ROCK IMPRESSED ME...
AKI HAD JUST BEEN HOSPITALIZED AND I WAS MORE CONCERNED ABOUT HER.
I HADN'T HUNG OUT WITH OKI IN A WHILE, AND I PROBABLY WAS A DRAG TO HANG OUT WITH.
BUT BEING SOMEWHERE WITHOUT AKI JUST MADE ME FEEL EMPTY SOMEHOW.

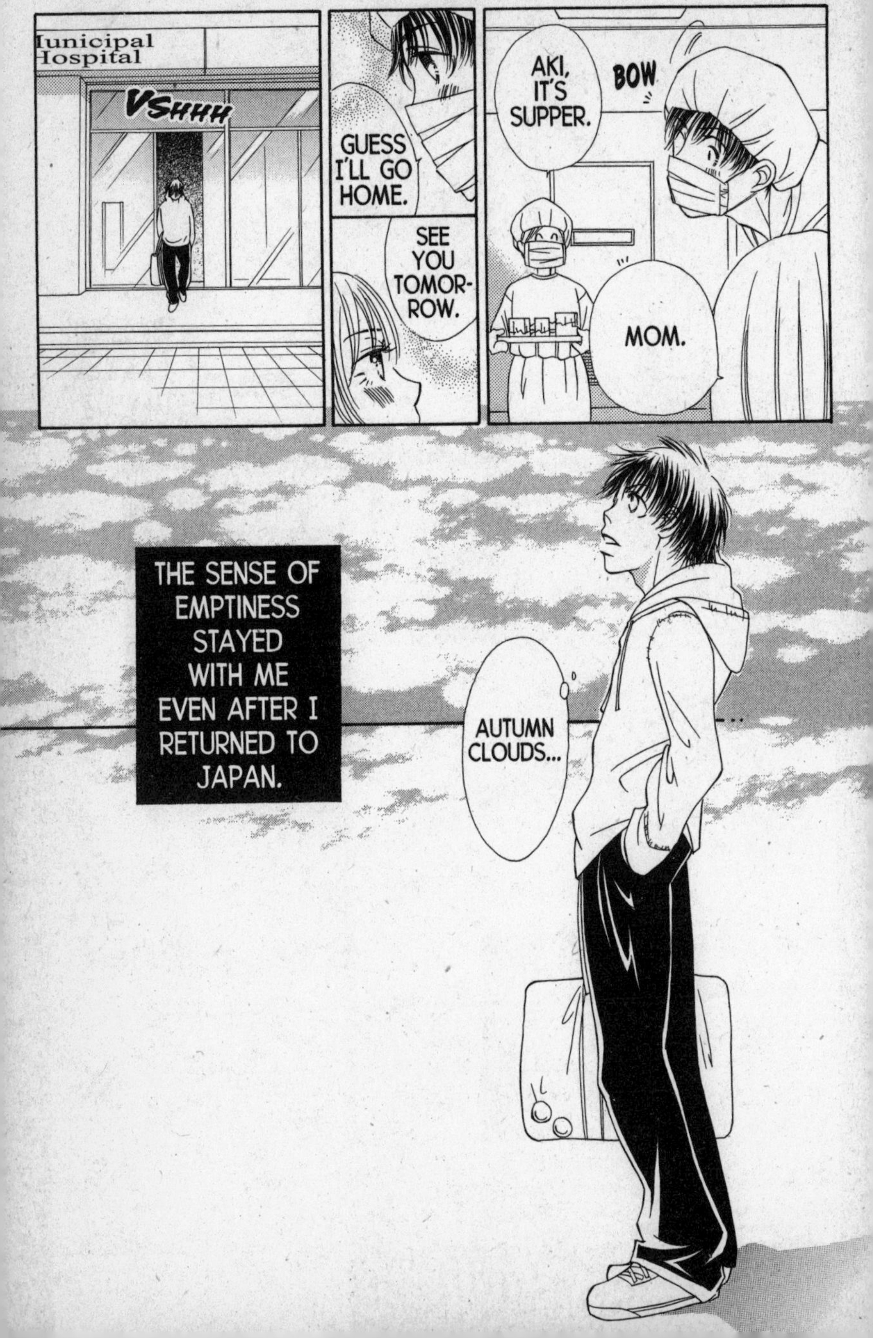
AKI, IT'S SUPPER.
BOW
MOM.
GUESS I'LL GO HOME.
SEE YOU TOMORROW.
unicipal Hospital
VSHHH
THE SENSE OF EMPTINESS STAYED WITH ME EVEN AFTER I RETURNED TO JAPAN.
AUTUMN CLOUDS...

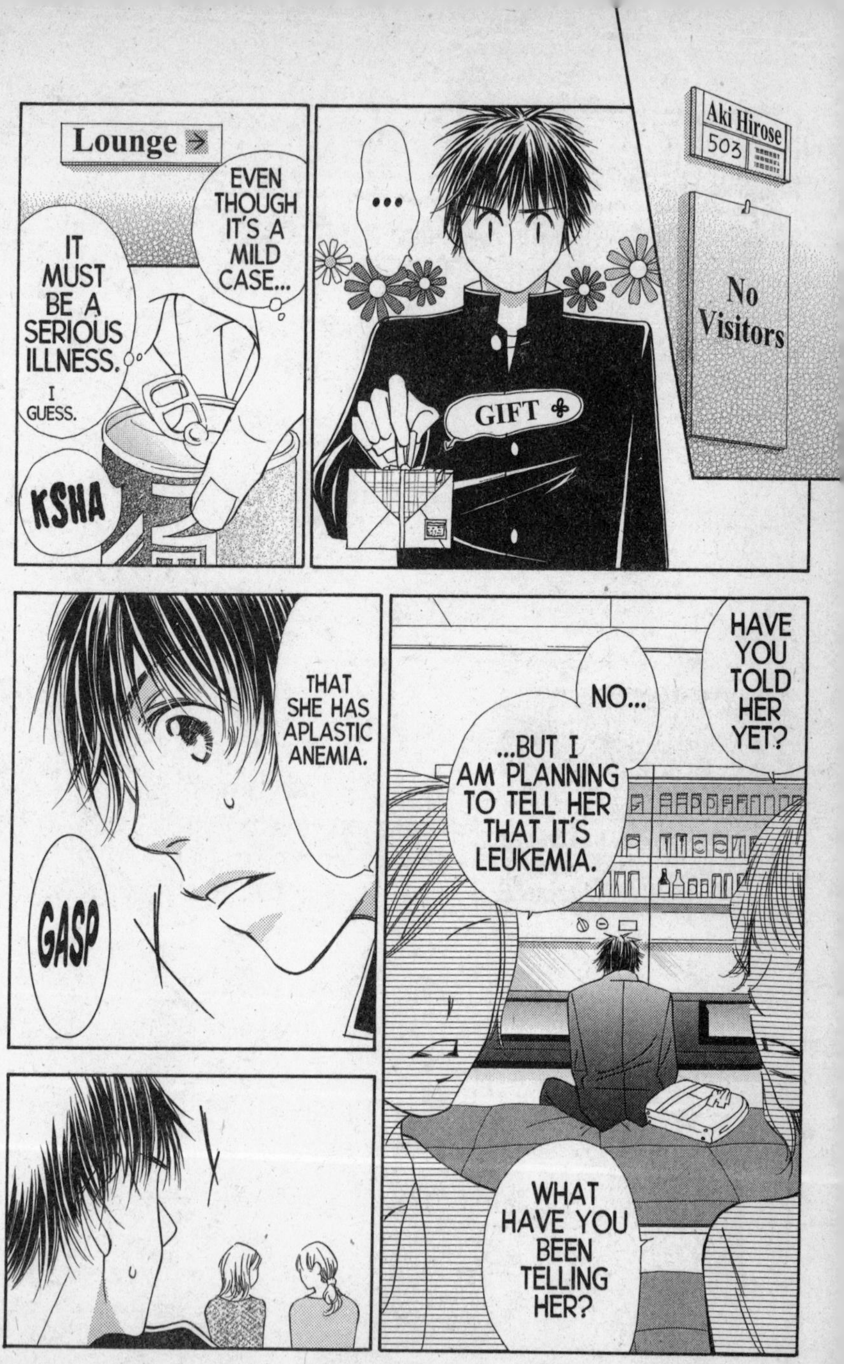
Aki Hirose
503
No Visitors
...
GIFT
Lounge
EVEN THOUGH IT'S A MILD CASE...
IT MUST BE A SERIOUS ILLNESS.
I GUESS.
KSHA
HAVE YOU TOLD HER YET?
NO...
...BUT I AM PLANNING TO TELL HER THAT IT'S LEUKEMIA.
WHAT HAVE YOU BEEN TELLING HER?
THAT SHE HAS APLASTIC ANEMIA.
GASP

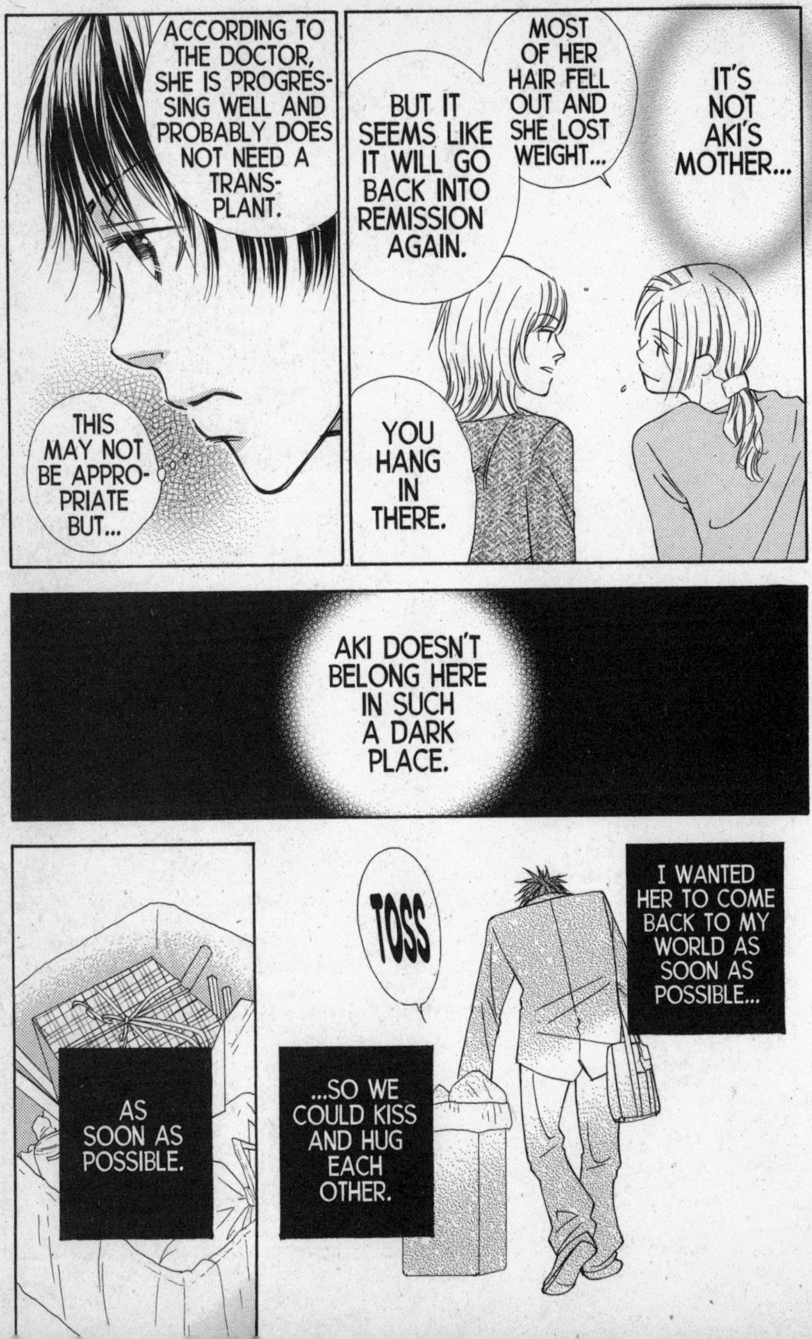
IT'S NOT AKI'S MOTHER...
MOST OF HER HAIR FELL OUT AND SHE LOST WEIGHT...
BUT IT SEEMS LIKE IT WILL GO BACK INTO REMISSION AGAIN.
YOU HANG IN THERE.
ACCORDING TO THE DOCTOR, SHE IS PROGRES-SING WELL AND PROBABLY DOES NOT NEED A TRANS-PLANT.
THIS MAY NOT BE APPRO-PRIATE BUT...
AKI DOESN'T BELONG HERE IN SUCH A DARK PLACE.
I WANTED HER TO COME BACK TO MY WORLD AS SOON AS POSSIBLE...
TOSS
...SO WE COULD KISS AND HUG EACH OTHER.
AS SOON AS POSSIBLE.

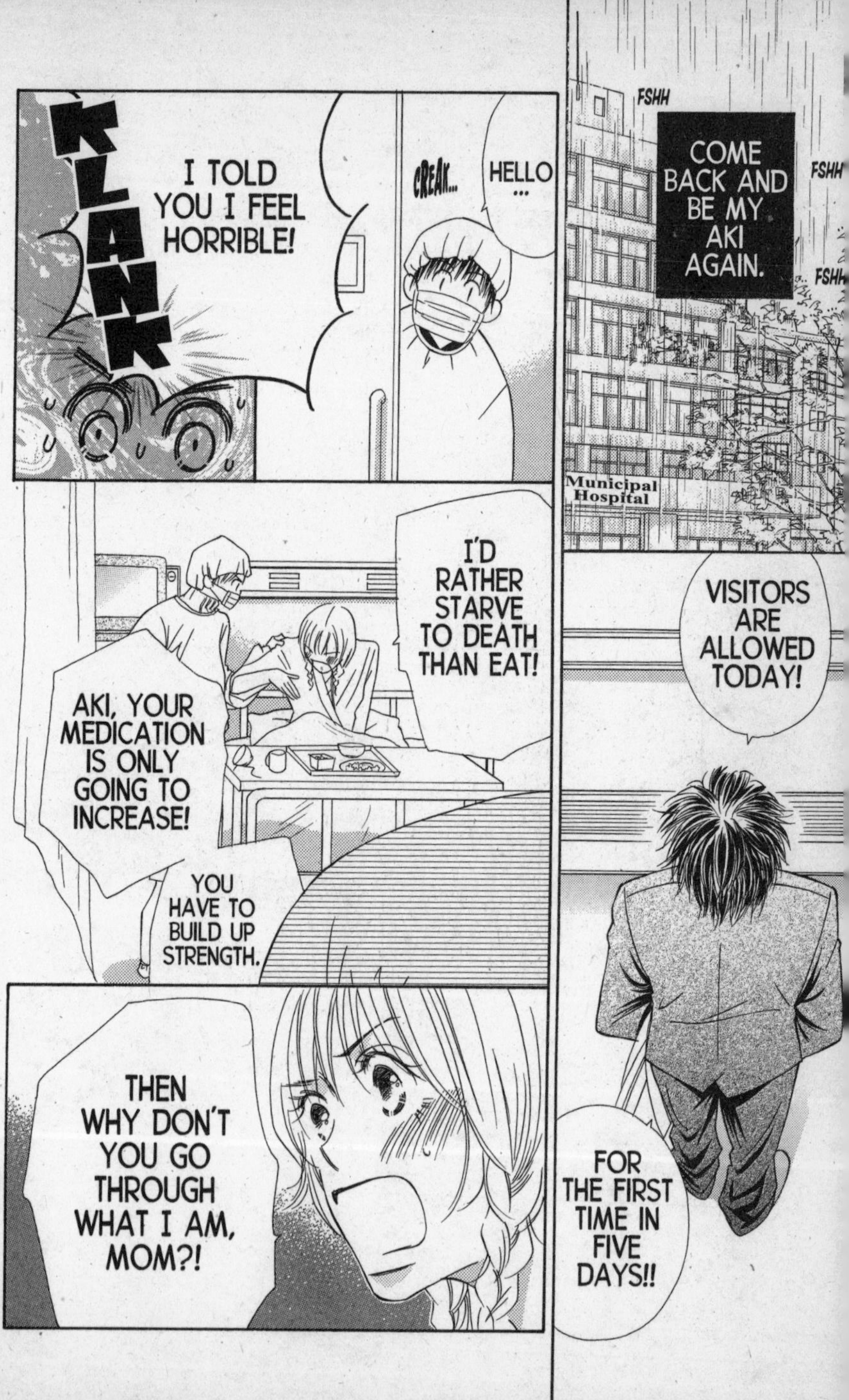
FSHH
COME BACK AND BE MY AKI AGAIN.
FSHH
FSHH
Municipal Hospital
VISITORS ARE ALLOWED TODAY!
FOR THE FIRST TIME IN FIVE DAYS!!
HELLO ...
CREAK...
I TOLD YOU I FEEL HORRIBLE!
KLANK
I'D RATHER STARVE TO DEATH THAN EAT!
AKI, YOUR MEDICATION IS ONLY GOING TO INCREASE!
YOU HAVE TO BUILD UP STRENGTH.
THEN WHY DON'T YOU GO THROUGH WHAT I AM, MOM?!

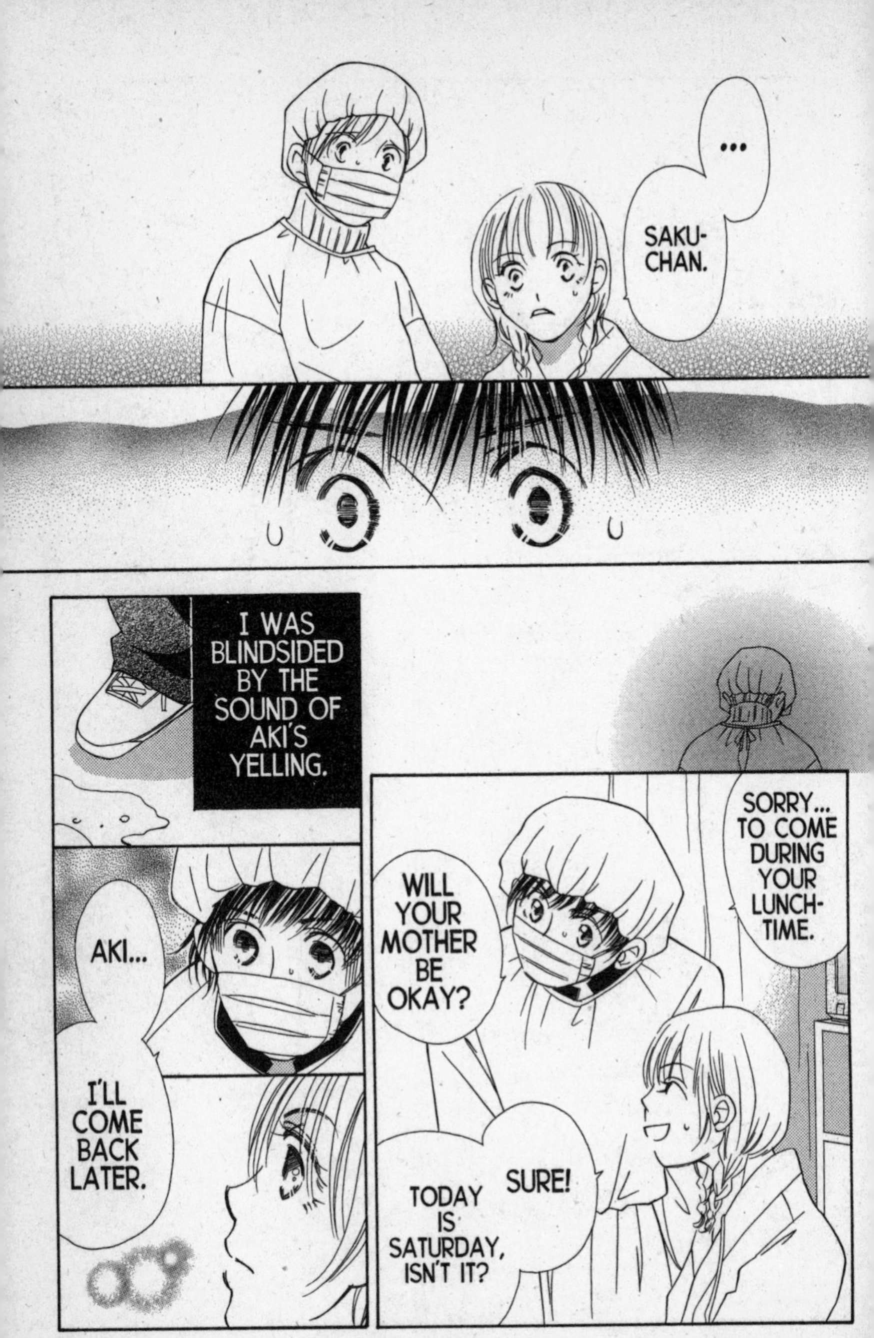
...
SAKU-CHAN.
SORRY... TO COME DURING YOUR LUNCHTIME.
WILL YOUR MOTHER BE OKAY?
SURE!
TODAY IS SATURDAY, ISN'T IT?
I WAS BLINDSIDED BY THE SOUND OF AKI'S YELLING.
AKI...
I'LL COME BACK LATER.

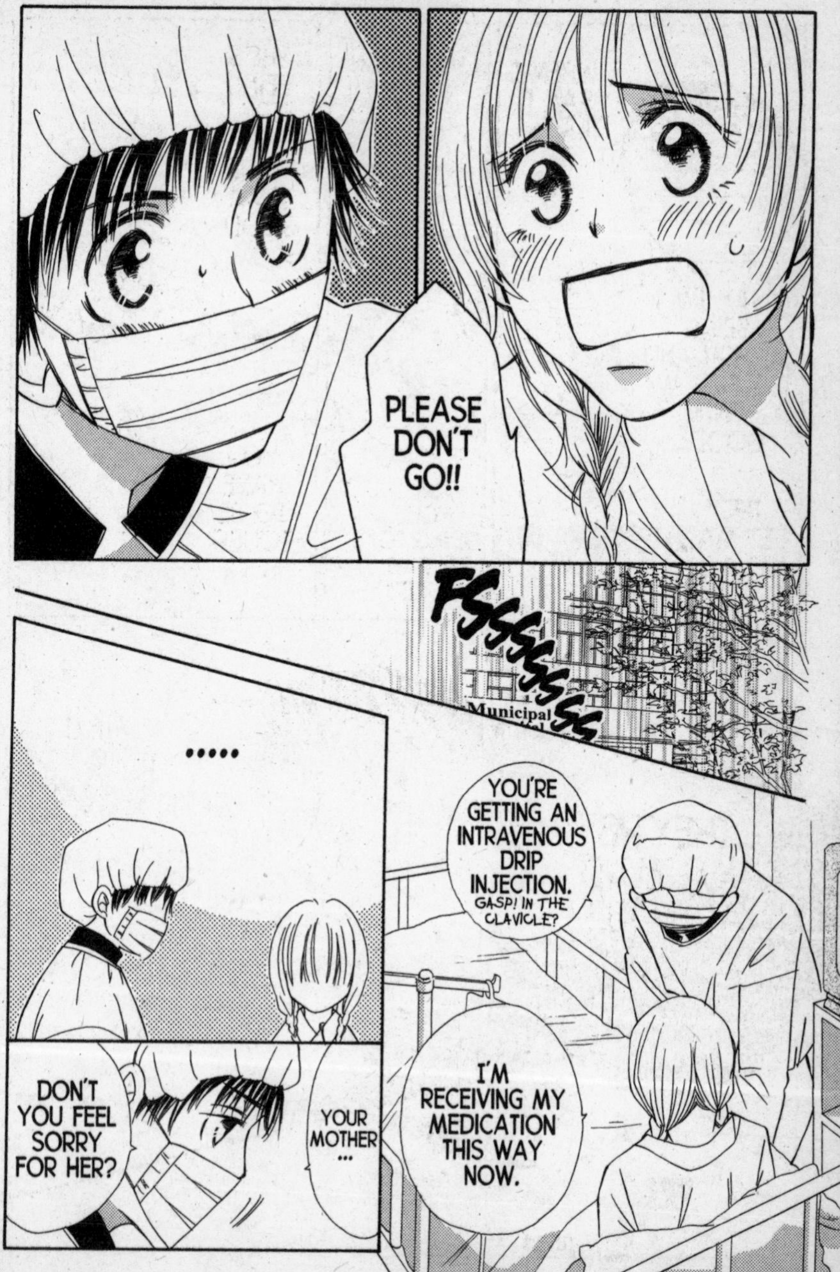
PLEASE DON'T GO!!
FSSSSSSS
Municipal
YOU'RE GETTING AN INTRAVENOUS DRIP INJECTION.
GASP! IN THE CLAVICLE?
I'M RECEIVING MY MEDICATION THIS WAY NOW.
.....
YOUR MOTHER...
DON'T YOU FEEL SORRY FOR HER?

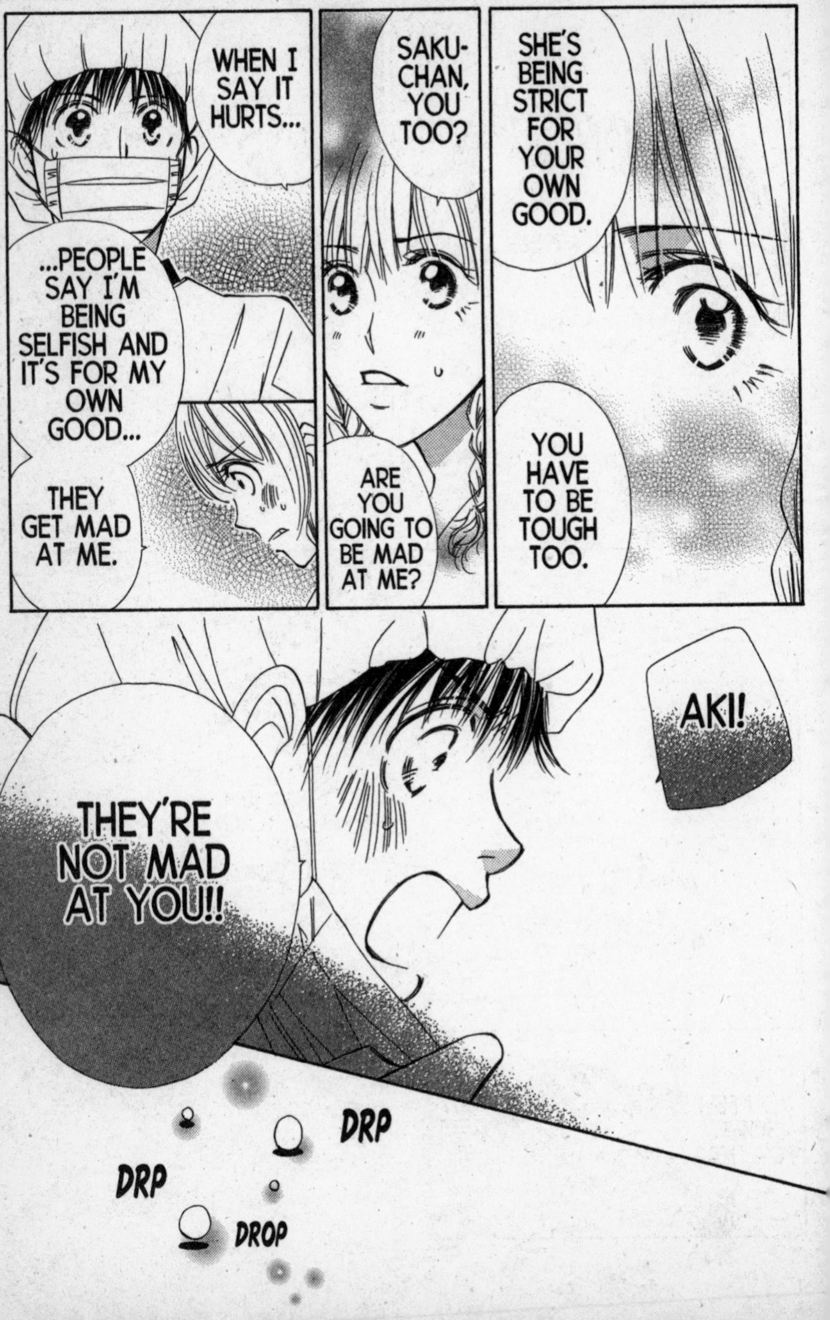
WHEN I SAY IT HURTS...
...PEOPLE SAY I'M BEING SELFISH AND IT'S FOR MY OWN GOOD...
THEY GET MAD AT ME.
SAKU-CHAN, YOU TOO?
ARE YOU GOING TO BE MAD AT ME?
SHE'S BEING STRICT FOR YOUR OWN GOOD.
YOU HAVE TO BE TOUGH TOO.
AKI!
THEY'RE NOT MAD AT YOU!!
DRP
DRP
DROP

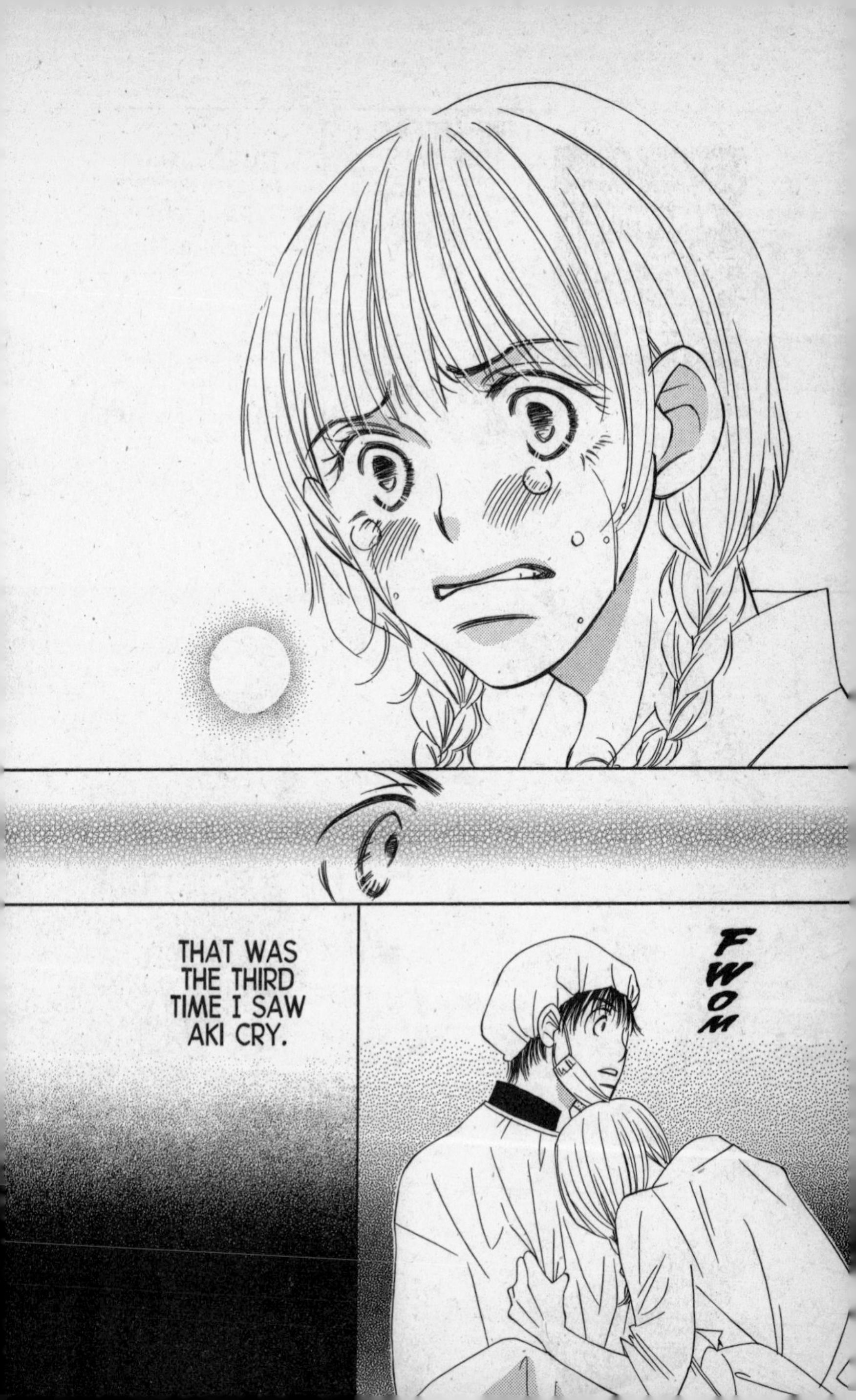
FWOM
THAT WAS THE THIRD TIME I SAW AKI CRY.

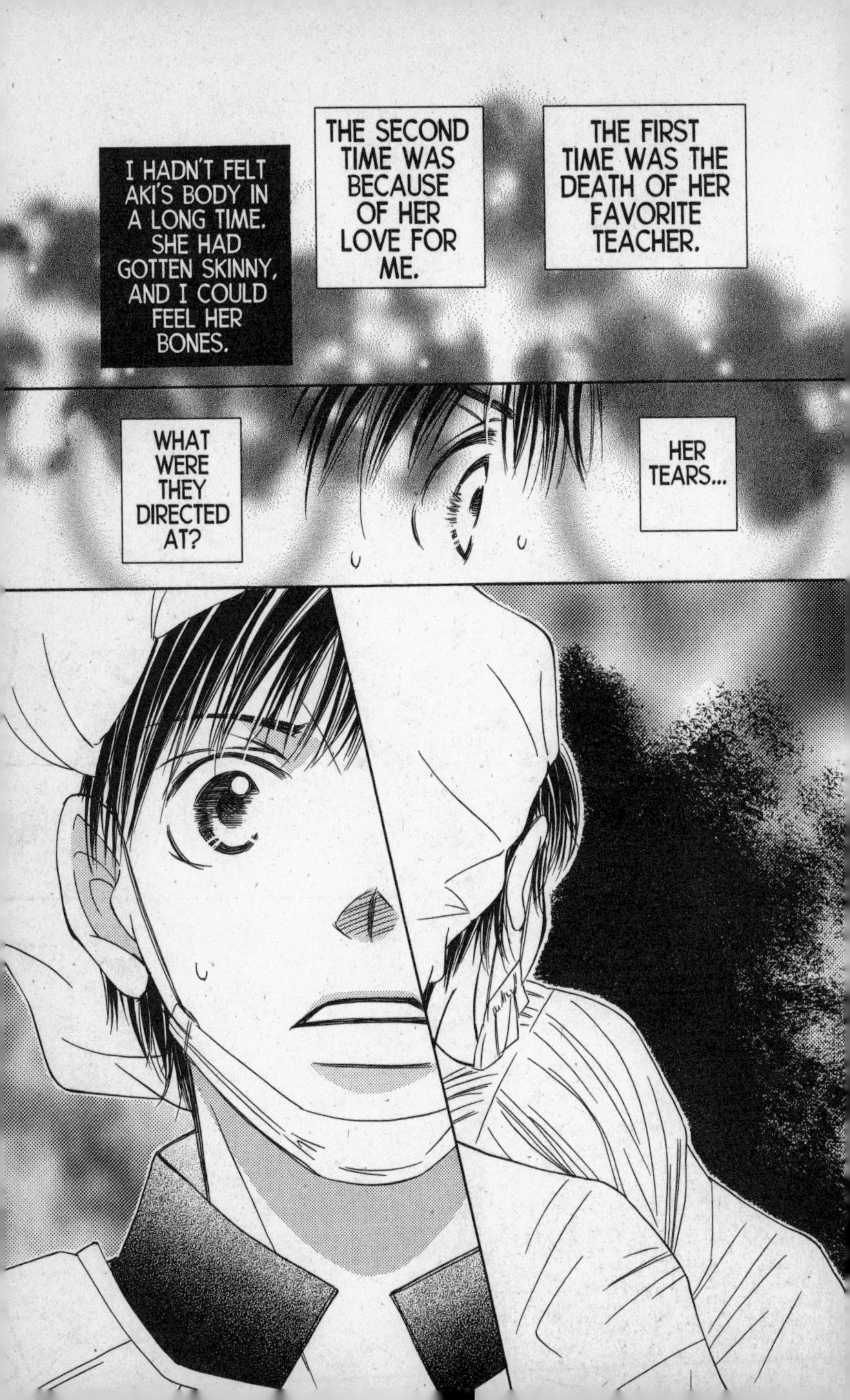
THE FIRST TIME WAS THE DEATH OF HER FAVORITE TEACHER.
THE SECOND TIME WAS BECAUSE OF HER LOVE FOR ME.
I HADN'T FELT AKI'S BODY IN A LONG TIME. SHE HAD GOTTEN SKINNY, AND I COULD FEEL HER BONES.
HER TEARS...
WHAT WERE THEY DIRECTED AT?

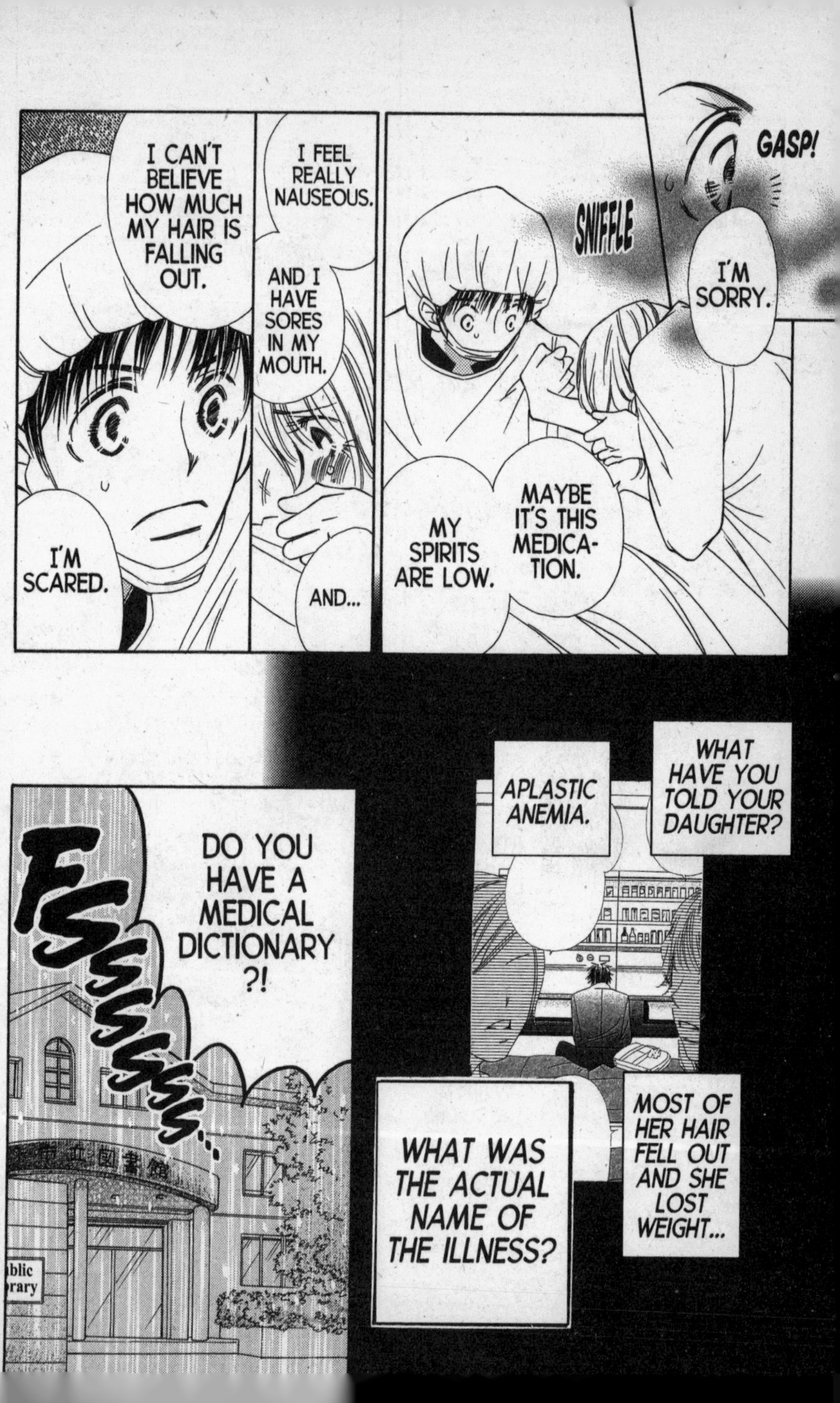
GASP!
I'M SORRY.
SNIFFLE
MAYBE IT'S THIS MEDICA-TION.
MY SPIRITS ARE LOW.
I FEEL REALLY NAUSEOUS.
AND I HAVE SORES IN MY MOUTH.
AND...
I CAN'T BELIEVE HOW MUCH MY HAIR IS FALLING OUT.
I'M SCARED.
WHAT HAVE YOU TOLD YOUR DAUGHTER?
APLASTIC ANEMIA.
MOST OF HER HAIR FELL OUT AND SHE LOST WEIGHT...
WHAT WAS THE ACTUAL NAME OF THE ILLNESS?
DO YOU HAVE A MEDICAL DICTIONARY?!
FSSSSSS...

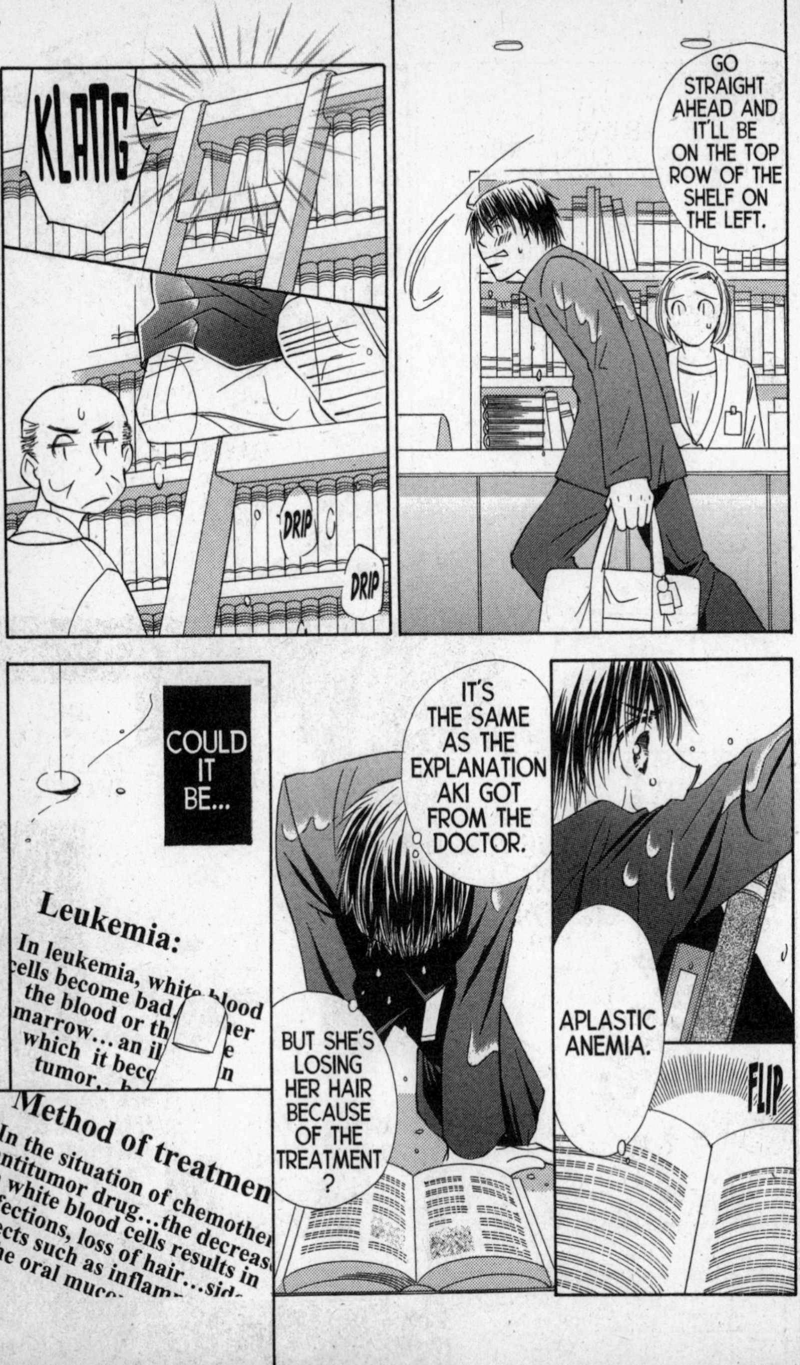
GO STRAIGHT AHEAD AND IT'LL BE ON THE TOP ROW OF THE SHELF ON THE LEFT.
KLANG
DRIP
DRIP
APLASTIC ANEMIA.
FLIP
IT'S THE SAME AS THE EXPLANATION AKI GOT FROM THE DOCTOR.
BUT SHE'S LOSING HER HAIR BECAUSE OF THE TREATMENT ?
COULD IT BE...
Leukemia:
In leukemia, white blood cells become bad the blood or th marrow…an il which it bec tumor..
Method of treatmen
In the situation of chemother antitumor drug…the decreas in white blood cells results in infections, loss of hair…side effects such as inflam of the oral muco

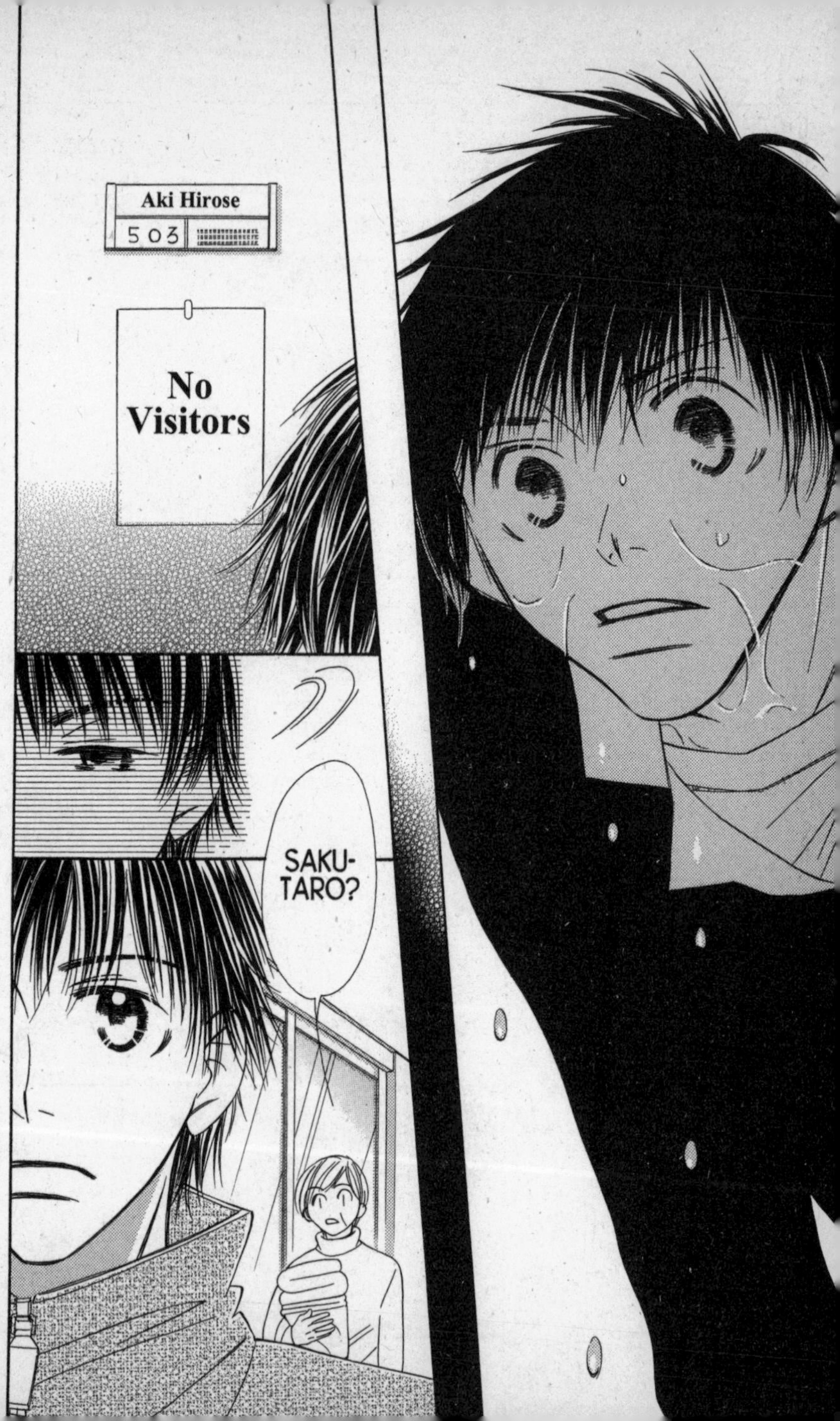
Aki Hirose
503
No Visitors
SAKU-TARO?

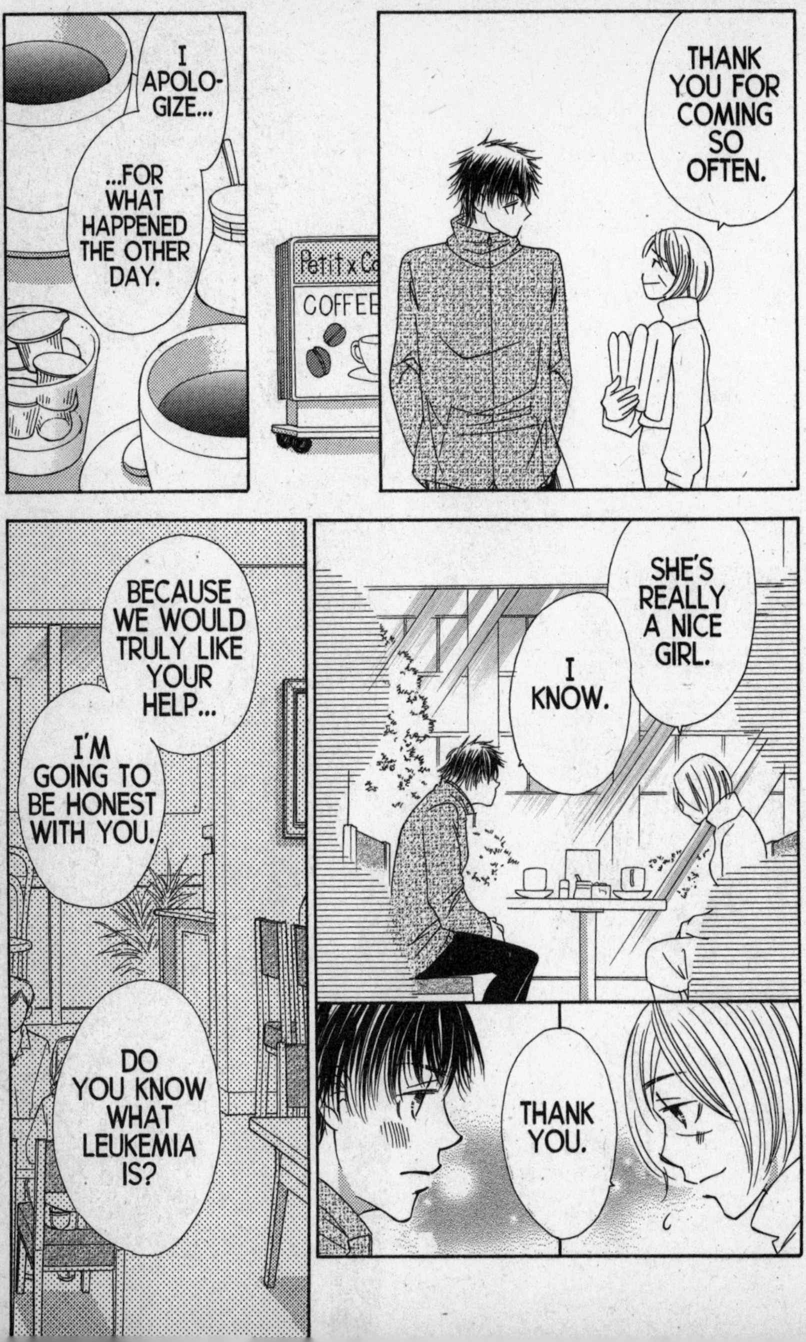
THANK YOU FOR COMING SO OFTEN.
I APOLOGIZE...
...FOR WHAT HAPPENED THE OTHER DAY.
SHE'S REALLY A NICE GIRL.
I KNOW.
THANK YOU.
BECAUSE WE WOULD TRULY LIKE YOUR HELP...
I'M GOING TO BE HONEST WITH YOU.
DO YOU KNOW WHAT LEUKEMIA IS?

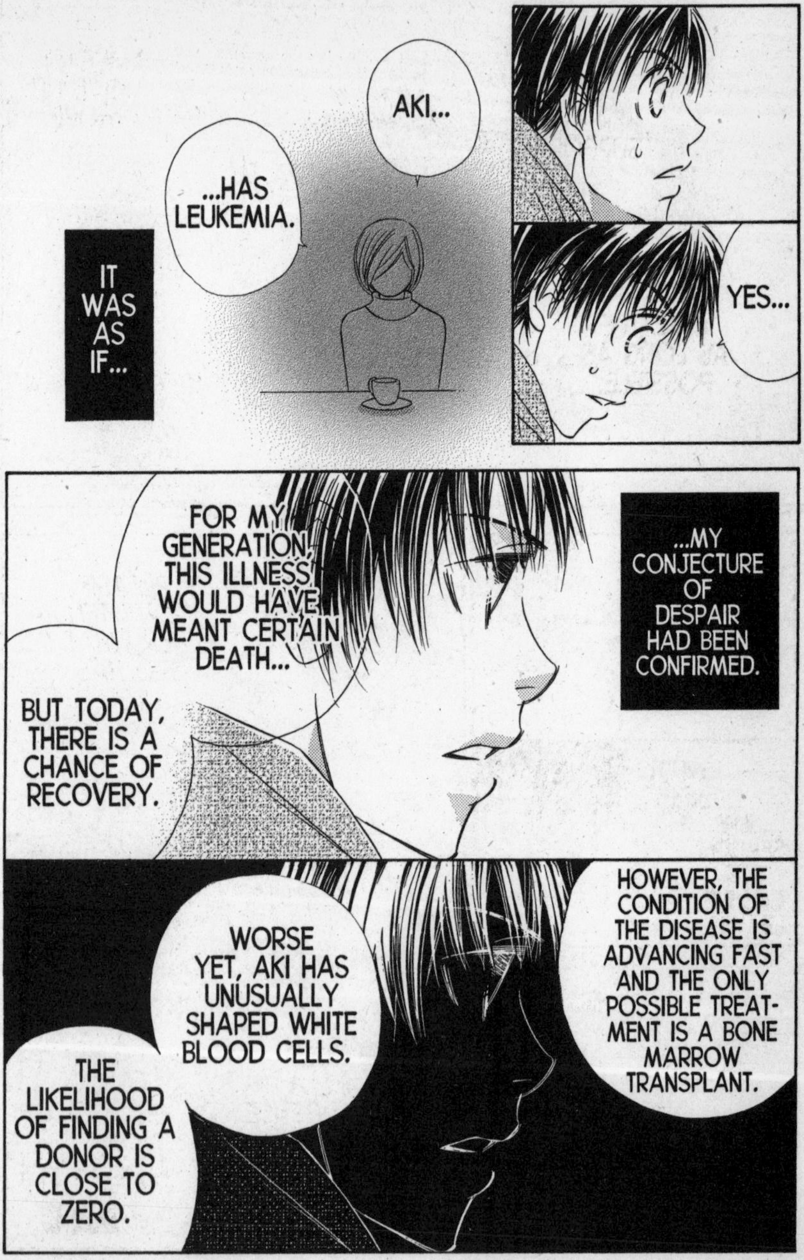
YES...
AKI...
...HAS LEUKEMIA.
IT WAS AS IF...
...MY CONJECTURE OF DESPAIR HAD BEEN CONFIRMED.
FOR MY GENERATION, THIS ILLNESS WOULD HAVE MEANT CERTAIN DEATH...
BUT TODAY, THERE IS A CHANCE OF RECOVERY.
HOWEVER, THE CONDITION OF THE DISEASE IS ADVANCING FAST AND THE ONLY POSSIBLE TREATMENT IS A BONE MARROW TRANSPLANT.
WORSE YET, AKI HAS UNUSUALLY SHAPED WHITE BLOOD CELLS.
THE LIKELIHOOD OF FINDING A DONOR IS CLOSE TO ZERO.

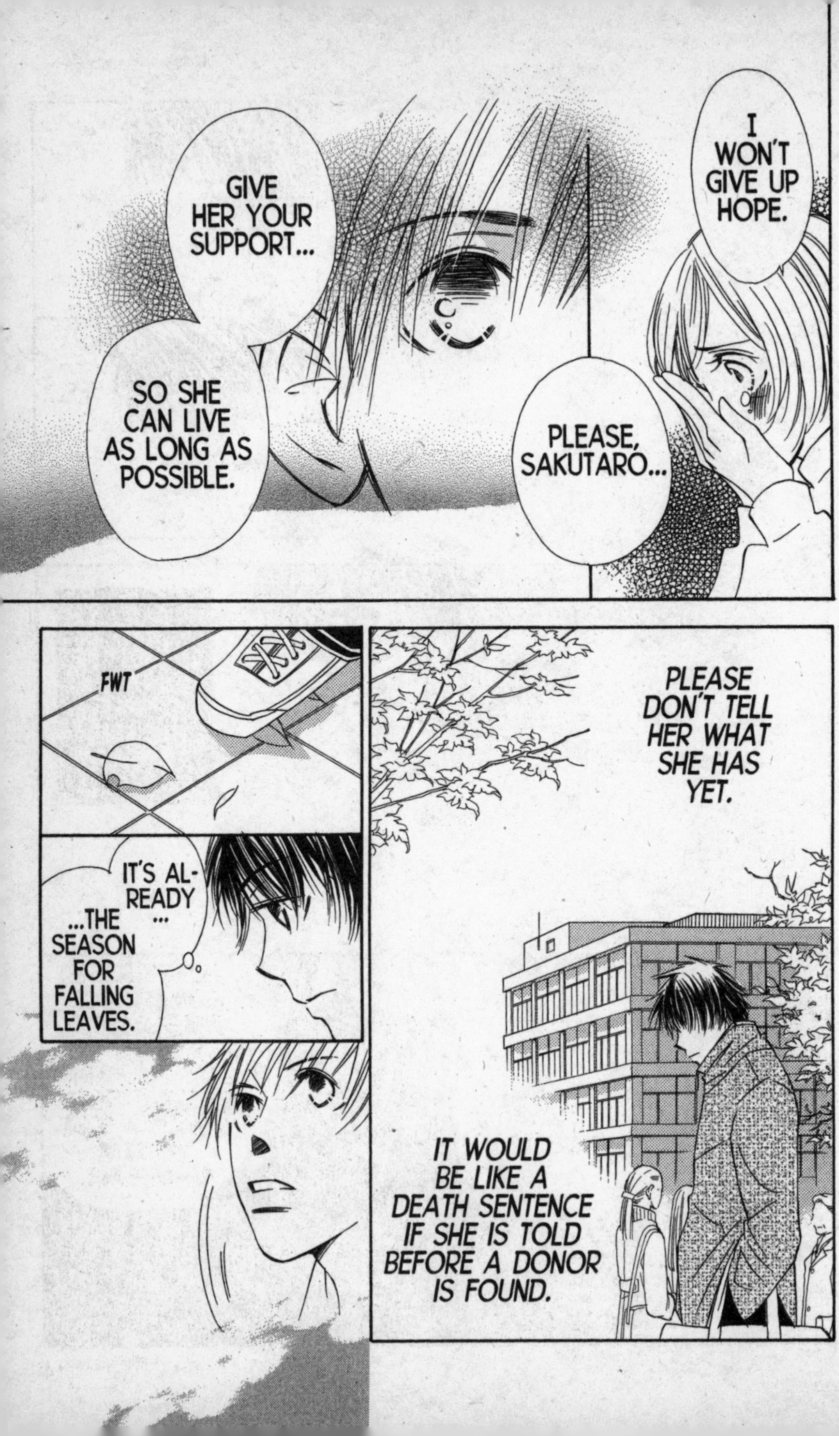
I WON'T GIVE UP HOPE.
PLEASE, SAKUTARO...
GIVE HER YOUR SUPPORT...
SO SHE CAN LIVE AS LONG AS POSSIBLE.
PLEASE DON'T TELL HER WHAT SHE HAS YET.
IT WOULD BE LIKE A DEATH SENTENCE IF SHE IS TOLD BEFORE A DONOR IS FOUND.
FWT
IT'S AL-READY ...
...THE SEASON FOR FALLING LEAVES.

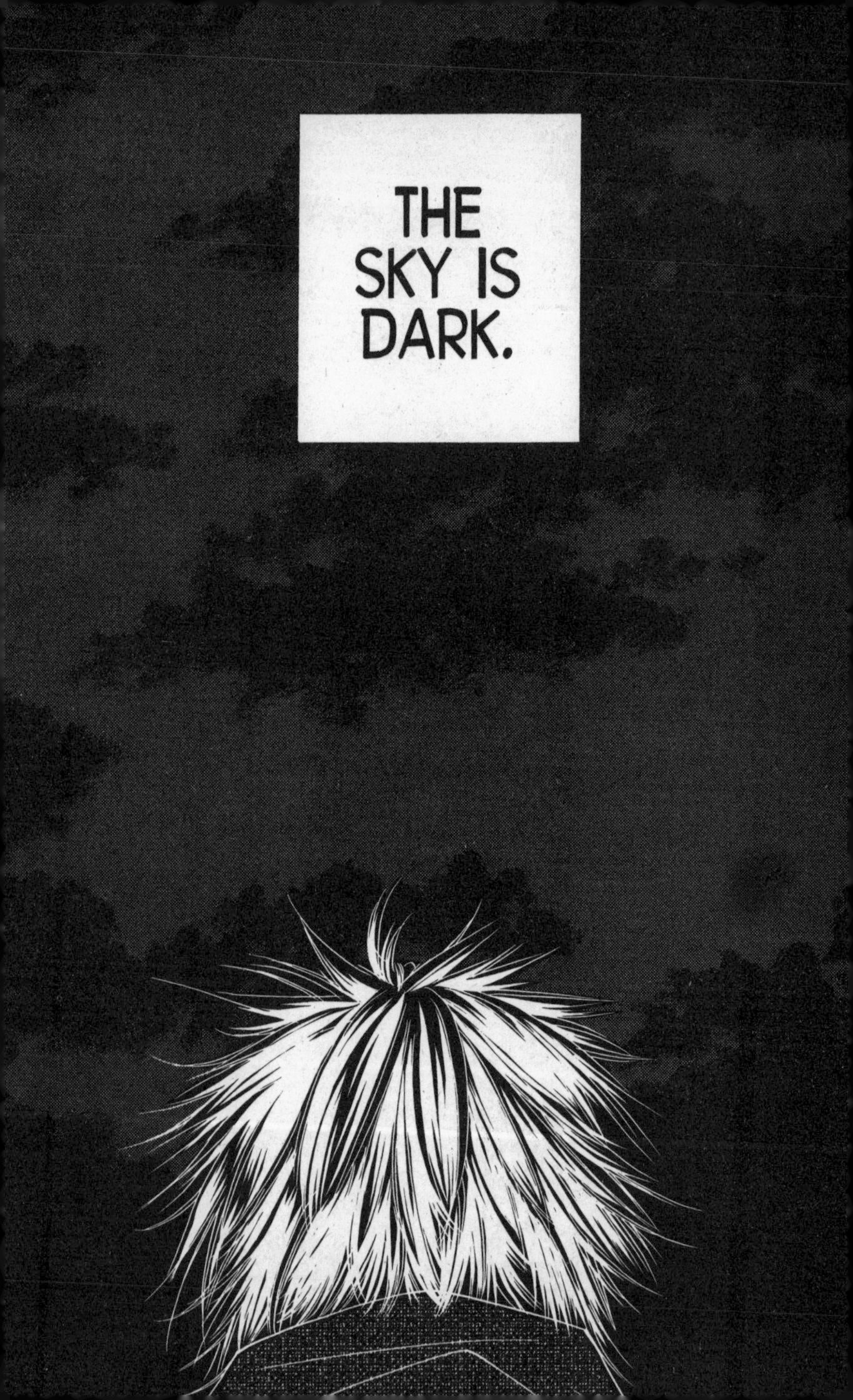
THE SKY IS DARK.

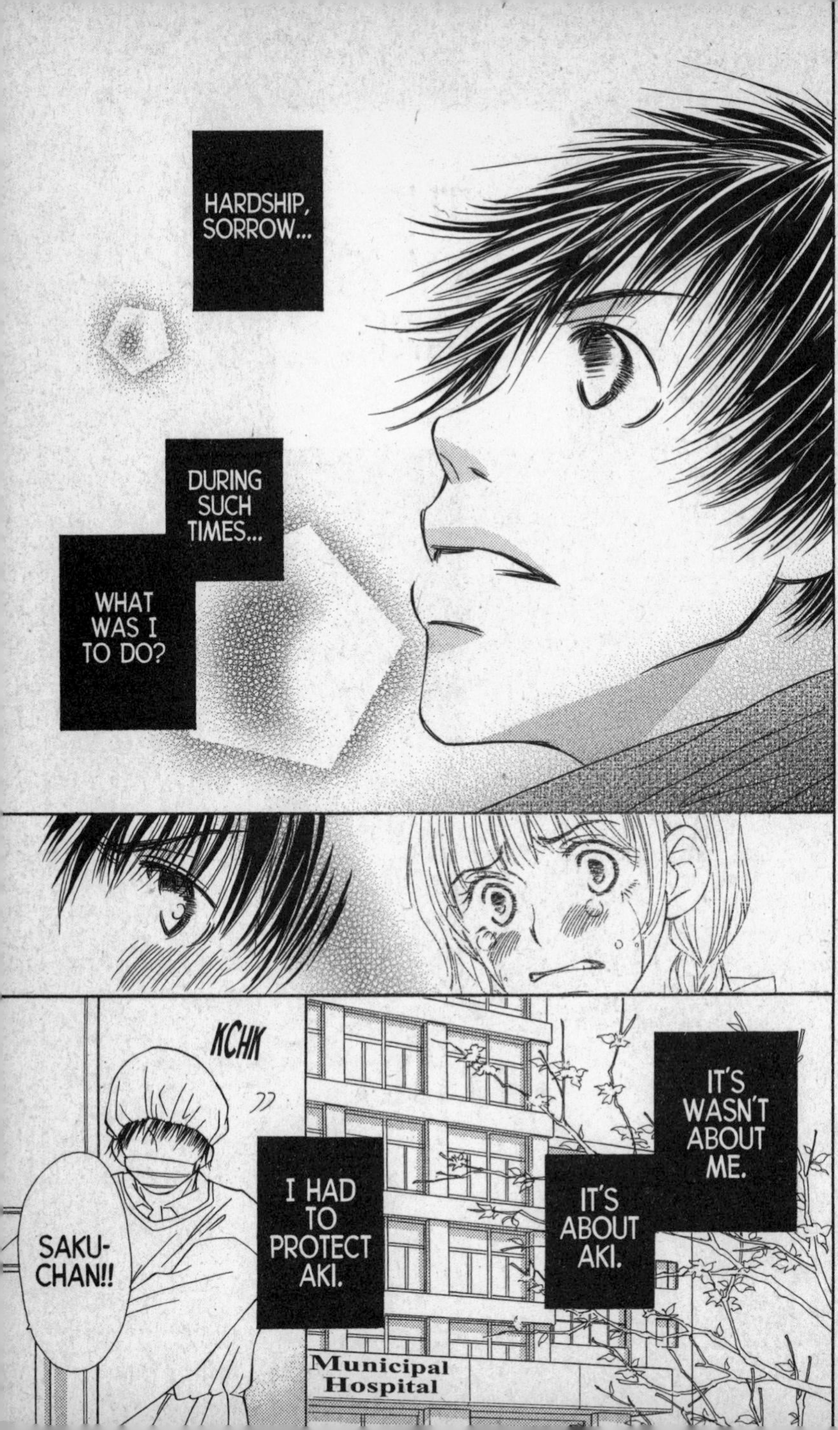
HARDSHIP, SORROW...
DURING SUCH TIMES...
WHAT WAS I TO DO?
IT'S WASN'T ABOUT ME.
IT'S ABOUT AKI.
KCHK
I HAD TO PROTECT AKI.
SAKU-CHAN!!
Municipal Hospital

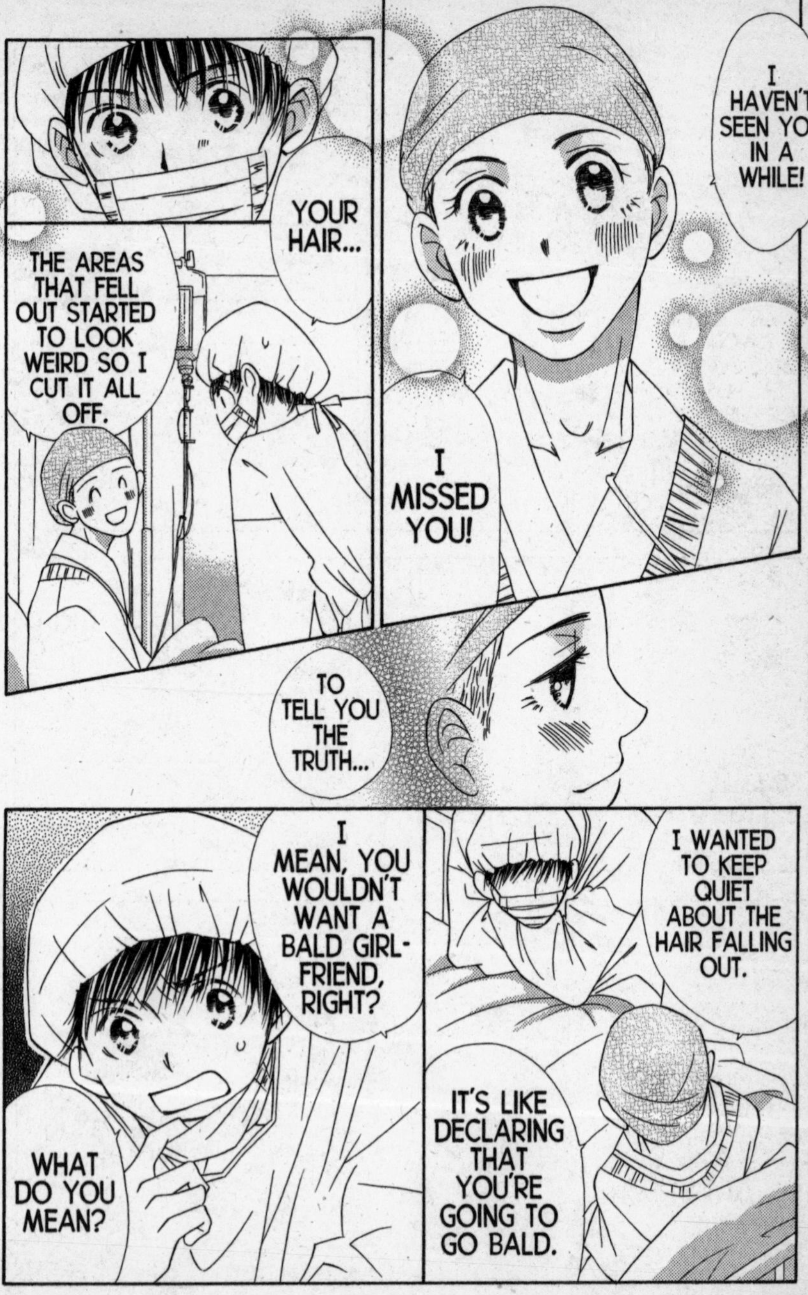
I HAVEN'T SEEN YOU IN A WHILE!
I MISSED YOU!
YOUR HAIR...
THE AREAS THAT FELL OUT STARTED TO LOOK WEIRD SO I CUT IT ALL OFF.
TO TELL YOU THE TRUTH...
I WANTED TO KEEP QUIET ABOUT THE HAIR FALLING OUT.
IT'S LIKE DECLARING THAT YOU'RE GOING TO GO BALD.
I MEAN, YOU WOULDN'T WANT A BALD GIRL-FRIEND, RIGHT?
WHAT DO YOU MEAN?

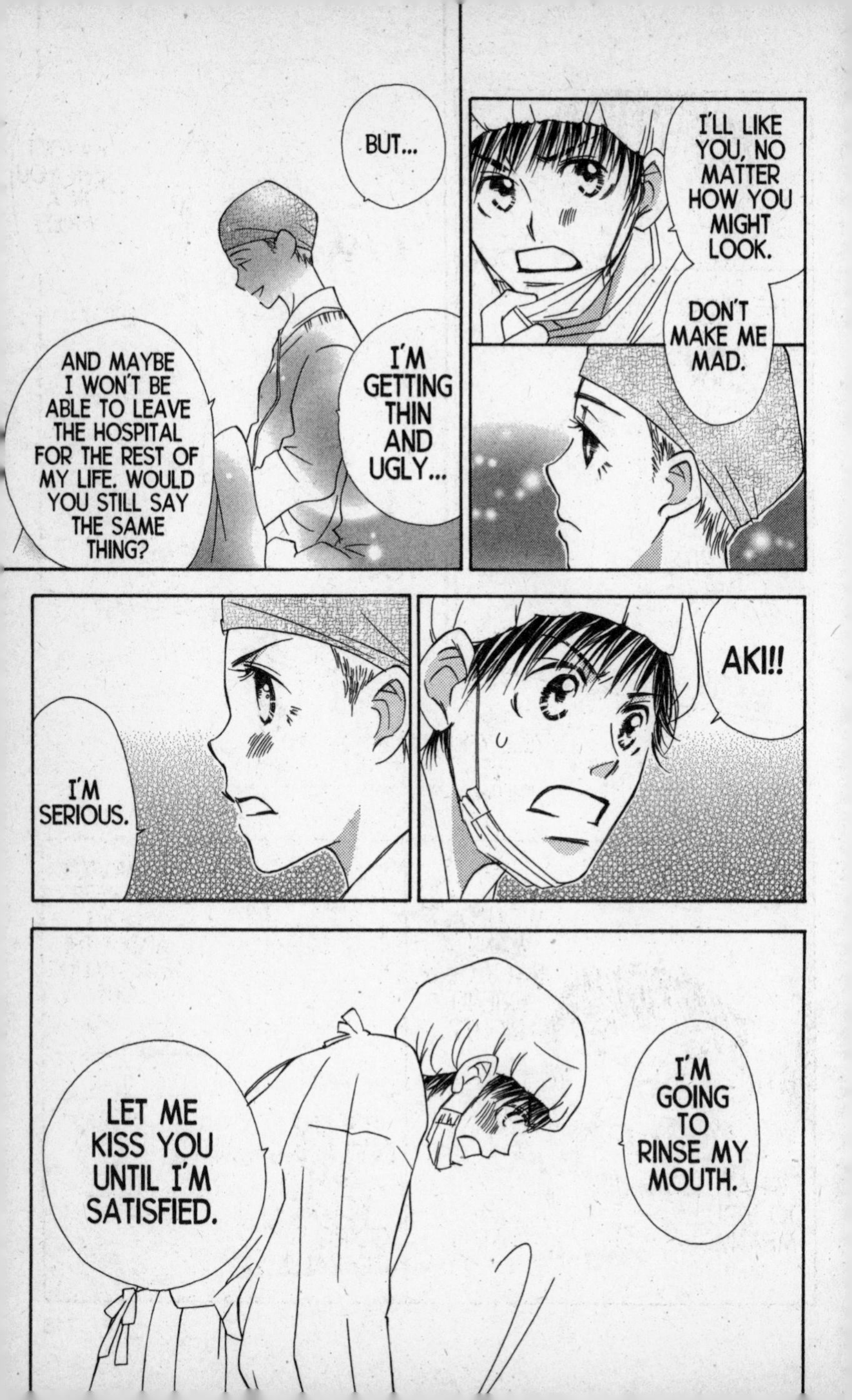
I'LL LIKE YOU, NO MATTER HOW YOU MIGHT LOOK.
DON'T MAKE ME MAD.
BUT...
I'M GETTING THIN AND UGLY...
AND MAYBE I WON'T BE ABLE TO LEAVE THE HOSPITAL FOR THE REST OF MY LIFE. WOULD YOU STILL SAY THE SAME THING?
AKI!!
I'M SERIOUS.
I'M GOING TO RINSE MY MOUTH.
LET ME KISS YOU UNTIL I'M SATISFIED.

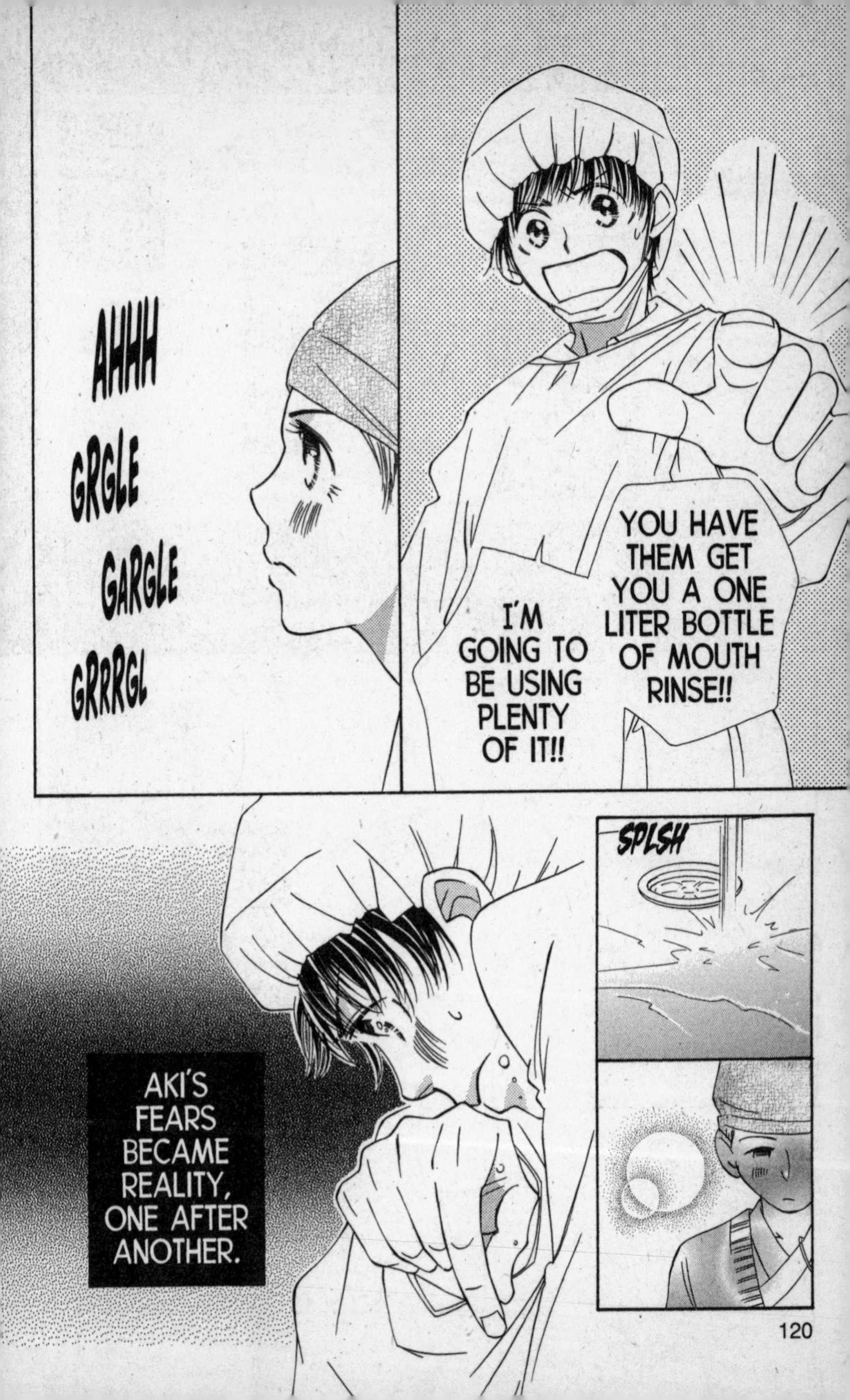
YOU HAVE THEM GET YOU A ONE LITER BOTTLE OF MOUTH RINSE!!
I'M GOING TO BE USING PLENTY OF IT!!
AHHH
GRGLE
GARGLE
GRRRGL
SPLSH
AKI'S FEARS BECAME REALITY, ONE AFTER ANOTHER.

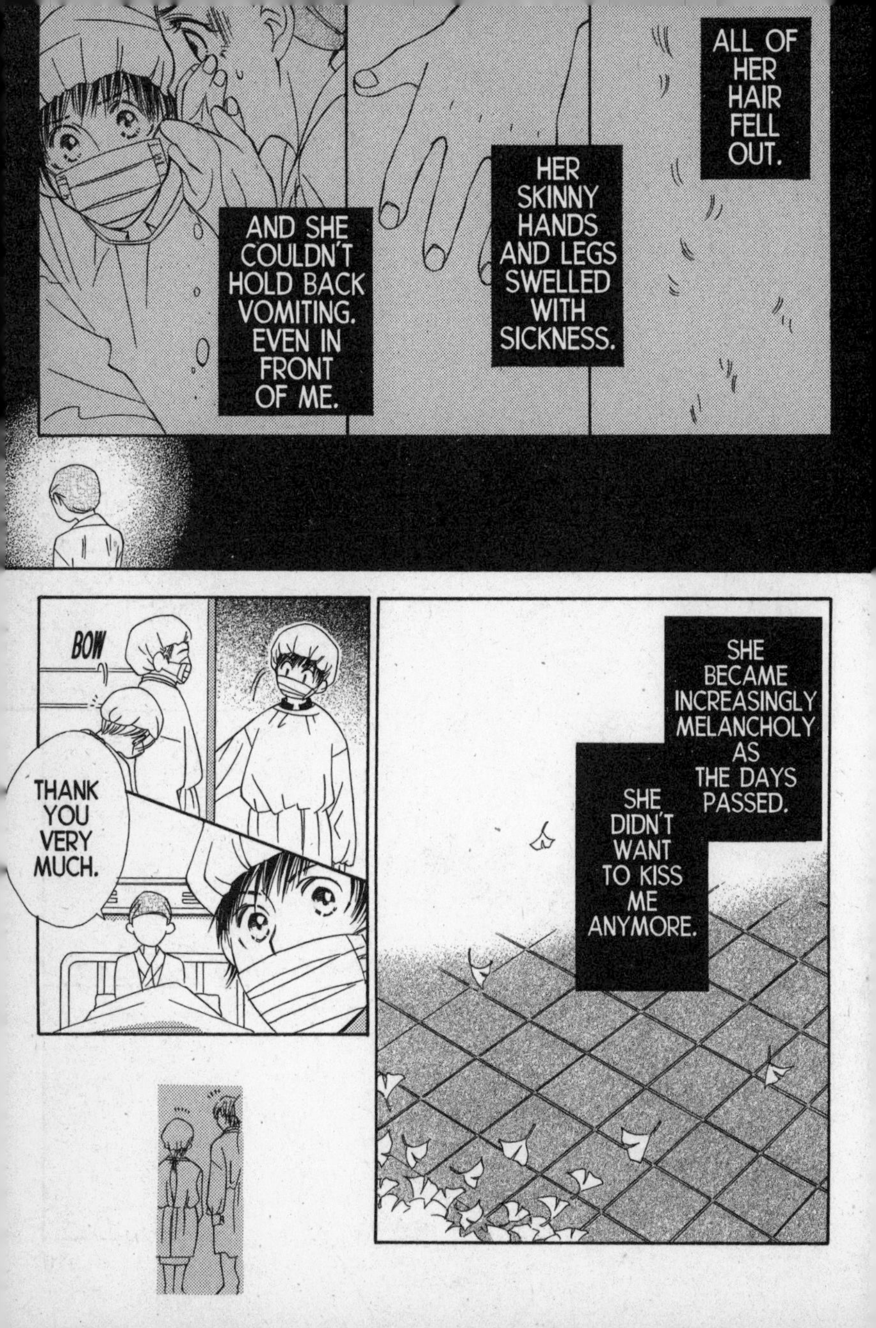
ALL OF HER HAIR FELL OUT.
HER SKINNY HANDS AND LEGS SWELLED WITH SICKNESS.
AND SHE COULDN'T HOLD BACK VOMITING. EVEN IN FRONT OF ME.
SHE BECAME INCREASINGLY MELANCHOLY AS THE DAYS PASSED.
SHE DIDN'T WANT TO KISS ME ANYMORE.
BOW
THANK YOU VERY MUCH.

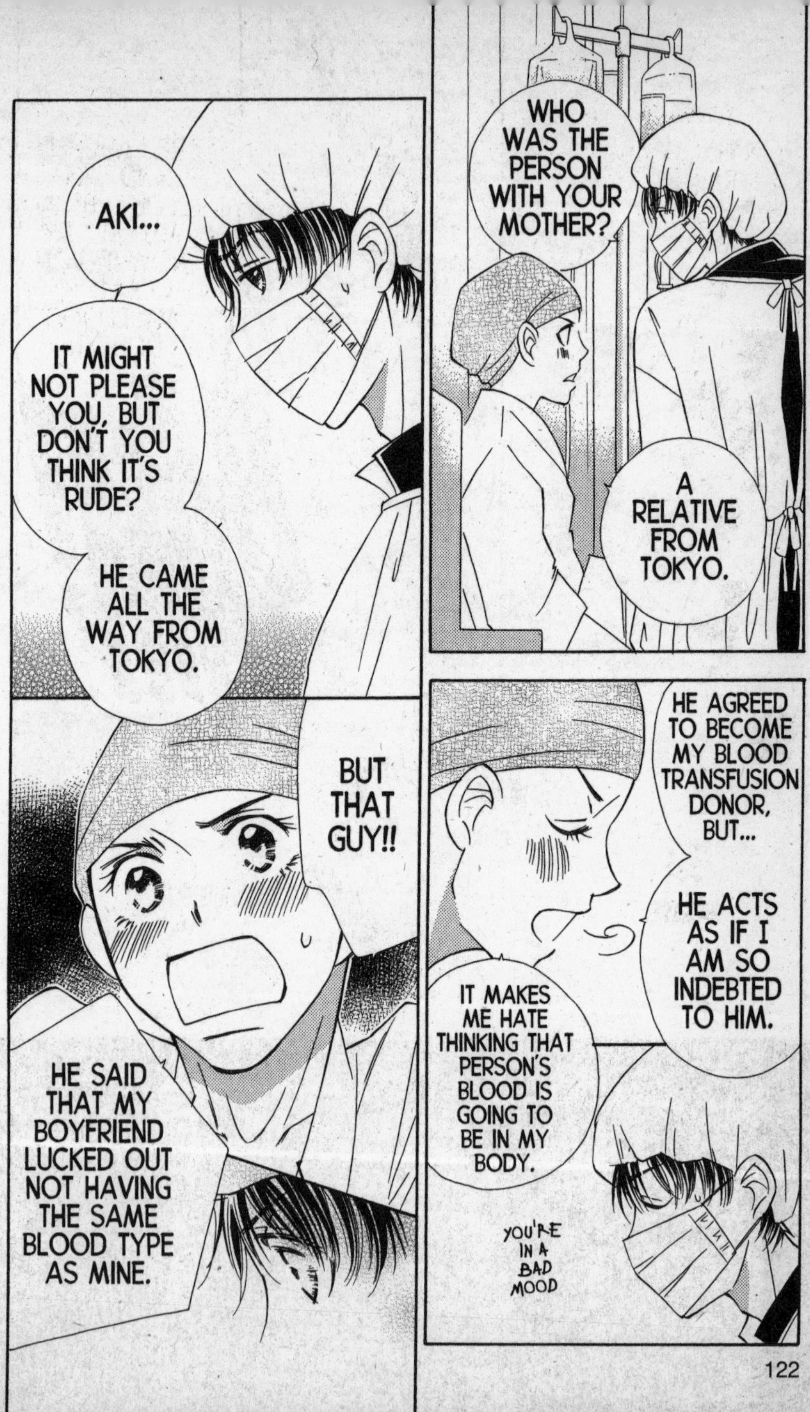
WHO WAS THE PERSON WITH YOUR MOTHER?
A RELATIVE FROM TOKYO.
AKI...
IT MIGHT NOT PLEASE YOU, BUT DON'T YOU THINK IT'S RUDE?
HE CAME ALL THE WAY FROM TOKYO.
HE AGREED TO BECOME MY BLOOD TRANSFUSION DONOR, BUT...
HE ACTS AS IF I AM SO INDEBTED TO HIM.
IT MAKES ME HATE THINKING THAT PERSON'S BLOOD IS GOING TO BE IN MY BODY.
YOU'RE IN A BAD MOOD
BUT THAT GUY!!
HE SAID THAT MY BOYFRIEND LUCKED OUT NOT HAVING THE SAME BLOOD TYPE AS MINE.

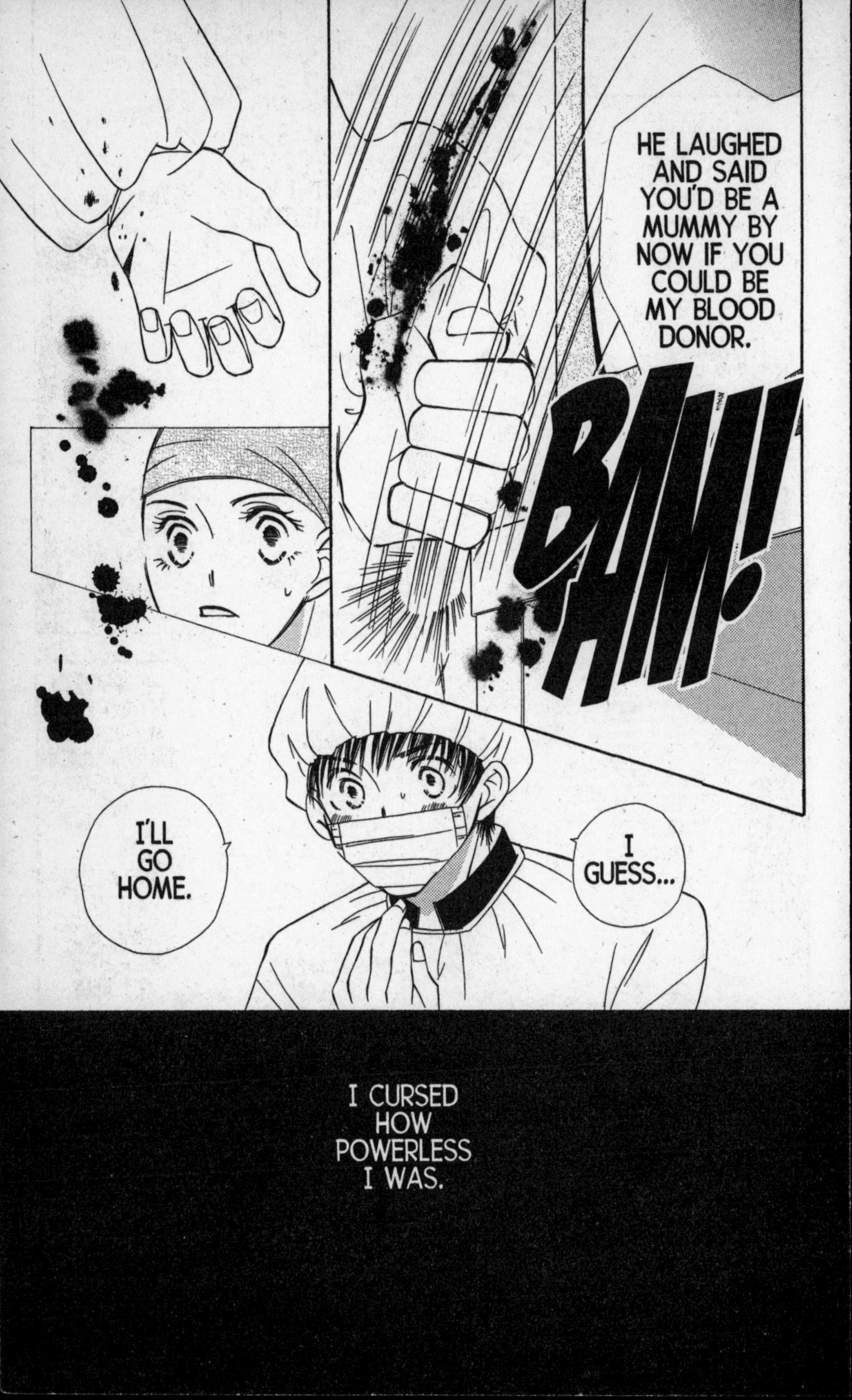
HE LAUGHED AND SAID YOU'D BE A MUMMY BY NOW IF YOU COULD BE MY BLOOD DONOR.
BAM!
I GUESS...
I'LL GO HOME.
I CURSED HOW POWERLESS I WAS.

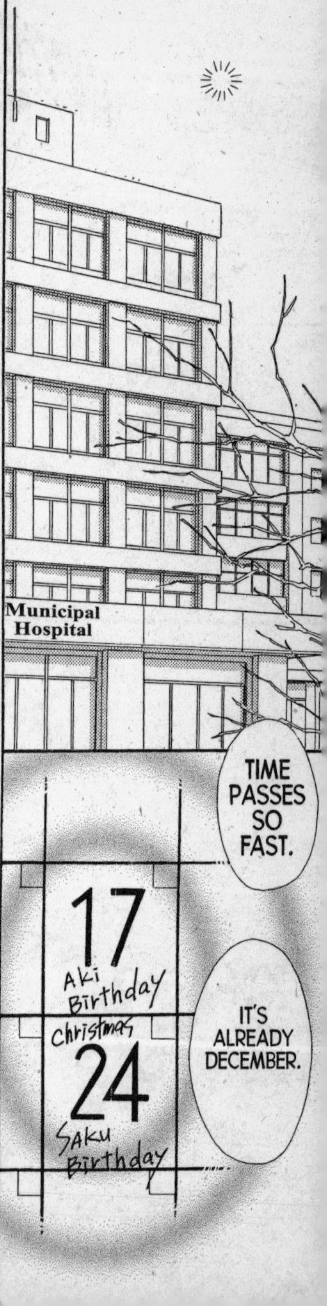
Municipal Hospital
TIME PASSES SO FAST.
17
Aki Birthday
Christmas
24
Saku Birthday
IT'S ALREADY DECEMBER.

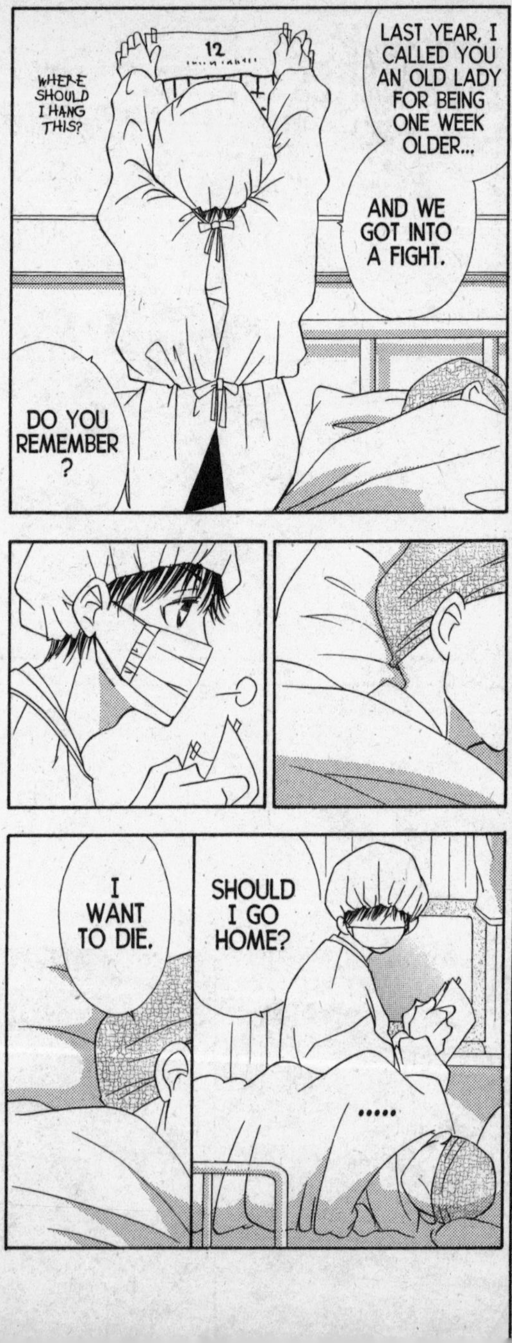
LAST YEAR, I CALLED YOU AN OLD LADY FOR BEING ONE WEEK OLDER...
AND WE GOT INTO A FIGHT.
12
WHERE SHOULD I HANG THIS?
DO YOU REMEMBER?
SHOULD I GO HOME?
......
I WANT TO DIE.

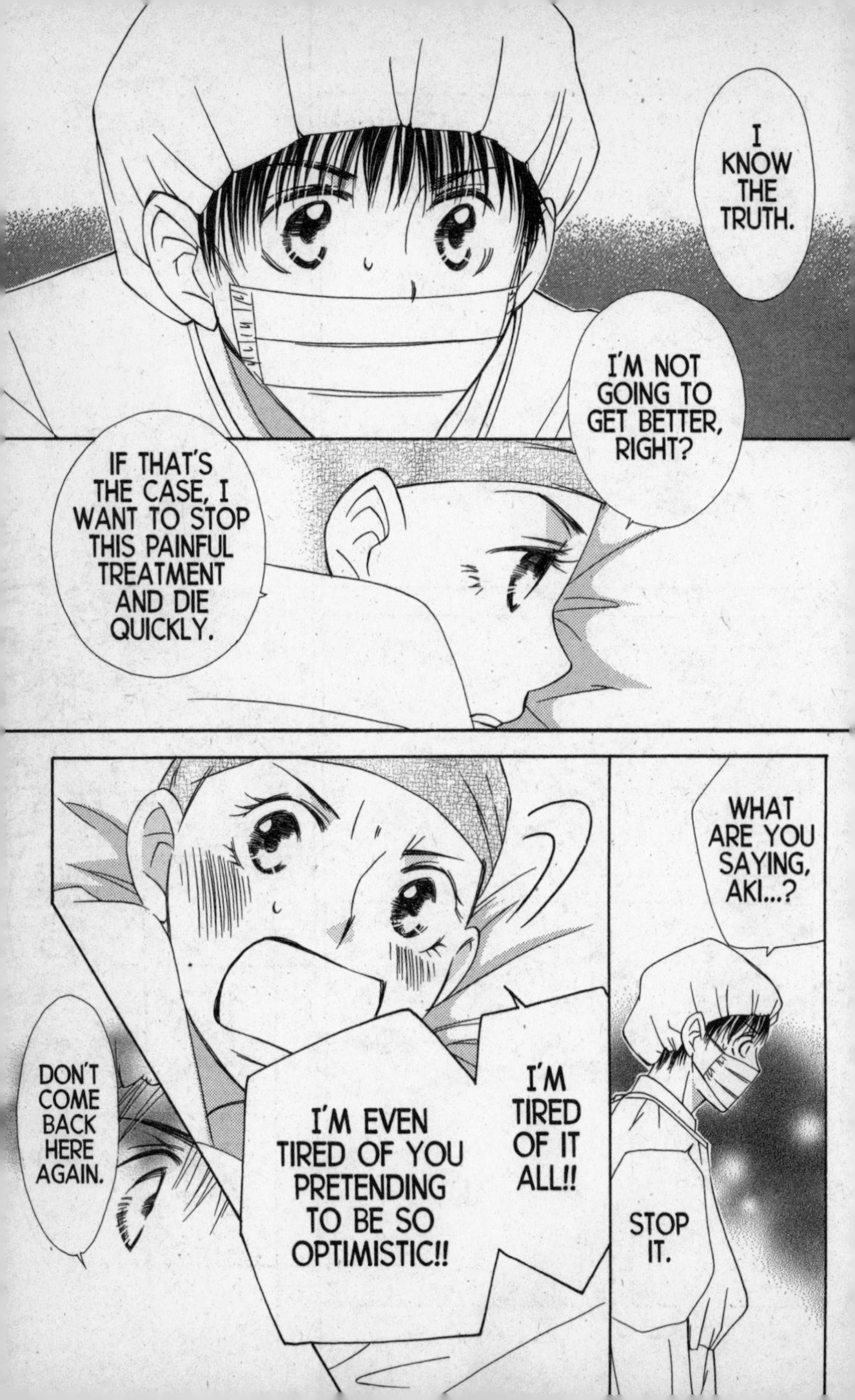
I KNOW THE TRUTH.
I'M NOT GOING TO GET BETTER, RIGHT?
IF THAT'S THE CASE, I WANT TO STOP THIS PAINFUL TREATMENT AND DIE QUICKLY.
WHAT ARE YOU SAYING, AKI...?
STOP IT.
I'M TIRED OF IT ALL!!
I'M EVEN TIRED OF YOU PRETENDING TO BE SO OPTIMISTIC!!
DON'T COME BACK HERE AGAIN.

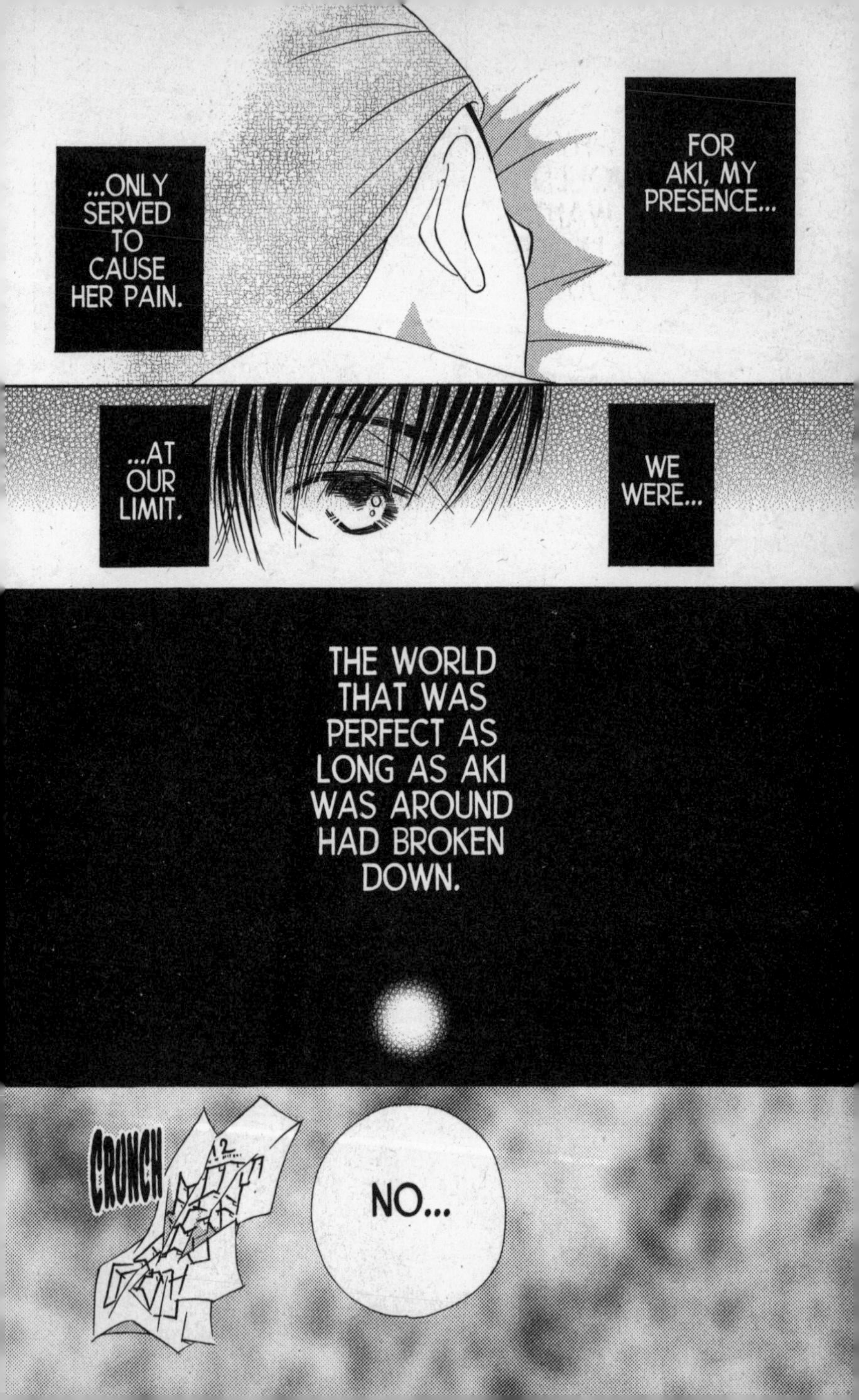
FOR AKI, MY PRESENCE...
...ONLY SERVED TO CAUSE HER PAIN.
WE WERE...
...AT OUR LIMIT.
THE WORLD THAT WAS PERFECT AS LONG AS AKI WAS AROUND HAD BROKEN DOWN.
NO...
CRUNCH

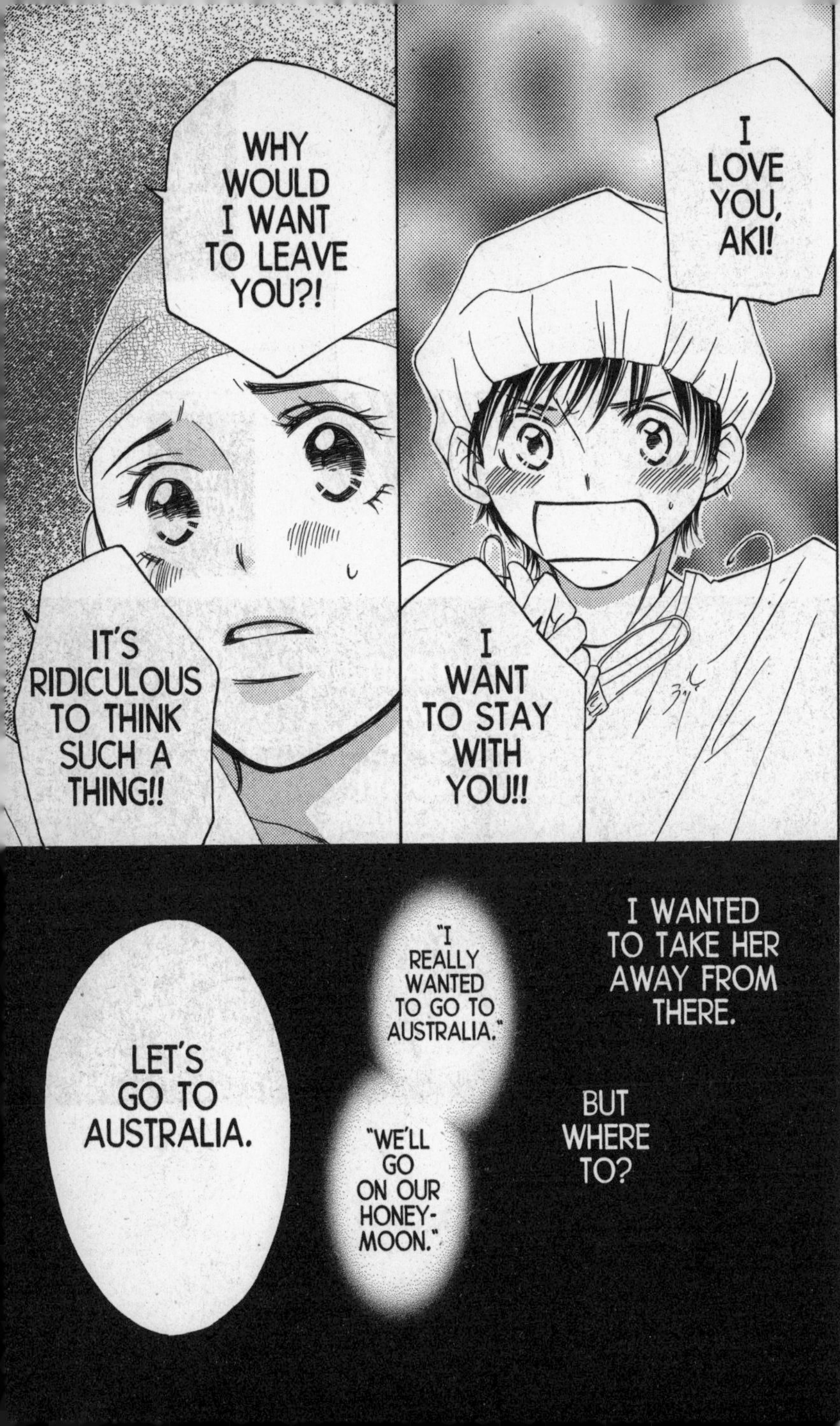
I LOVE YOU, AKI!
I WANT TO STAY WITH YOU!!
WHY WOULD I WANT TO LEAVE YOU?!
IT'S RIDICULOUS TO THINK SUCH A THING!!
I WANTED TO TAKE HER AWAY FROM THERE.
BUT WHERE TO?
"I REALLY WANTED TO GO TO AUSTRALIA."
"WE'LL GO ON OUR HONEYMOON."
LET'S GO TO AUSTRALIA.

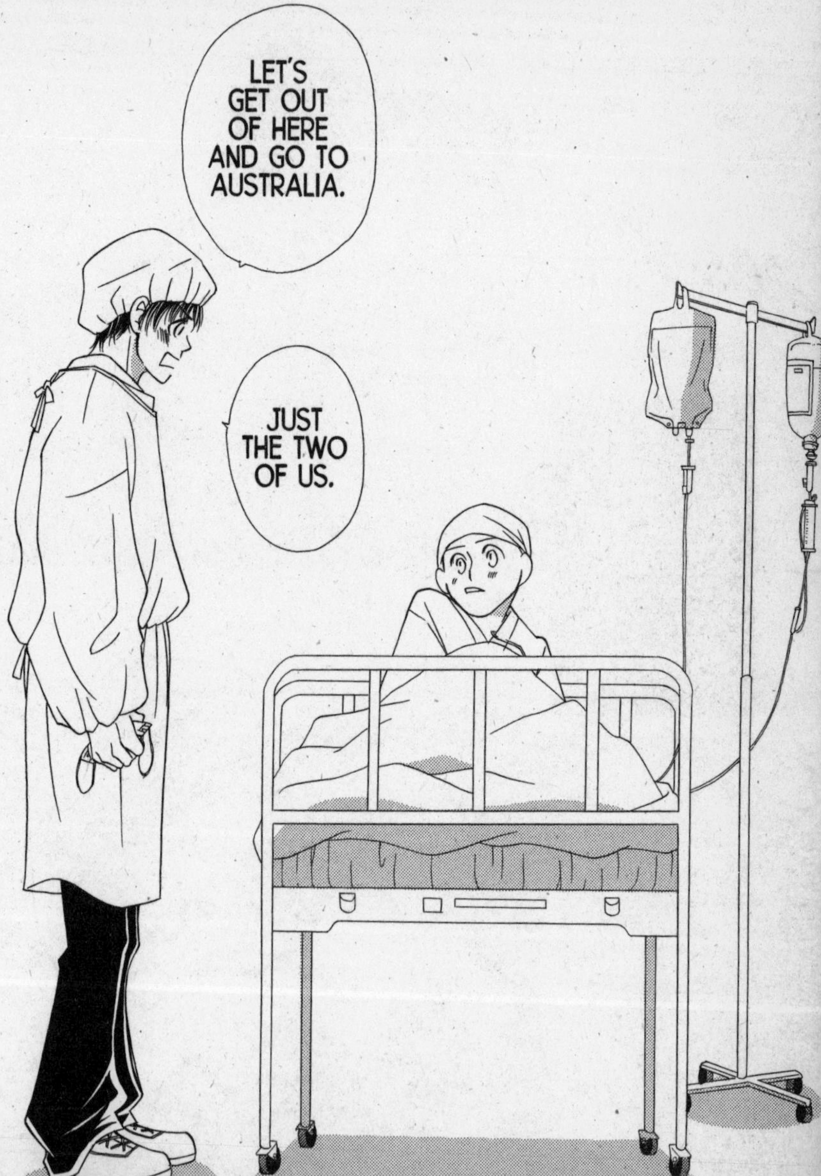
LET'S GET OUT OF HERE AND GO TO AUSTRALIA.
JUST THE TWO OF US.

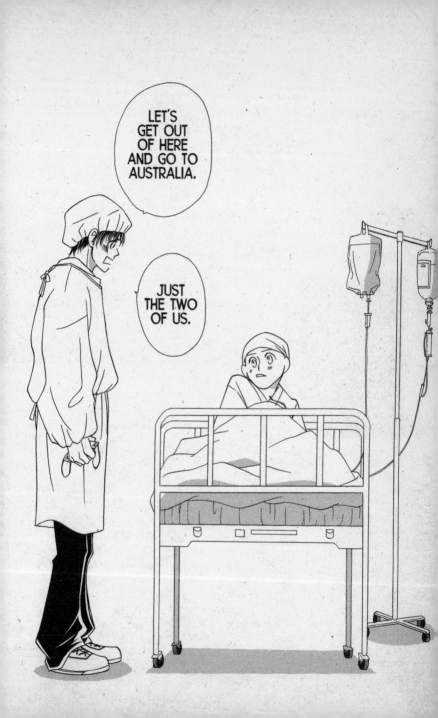

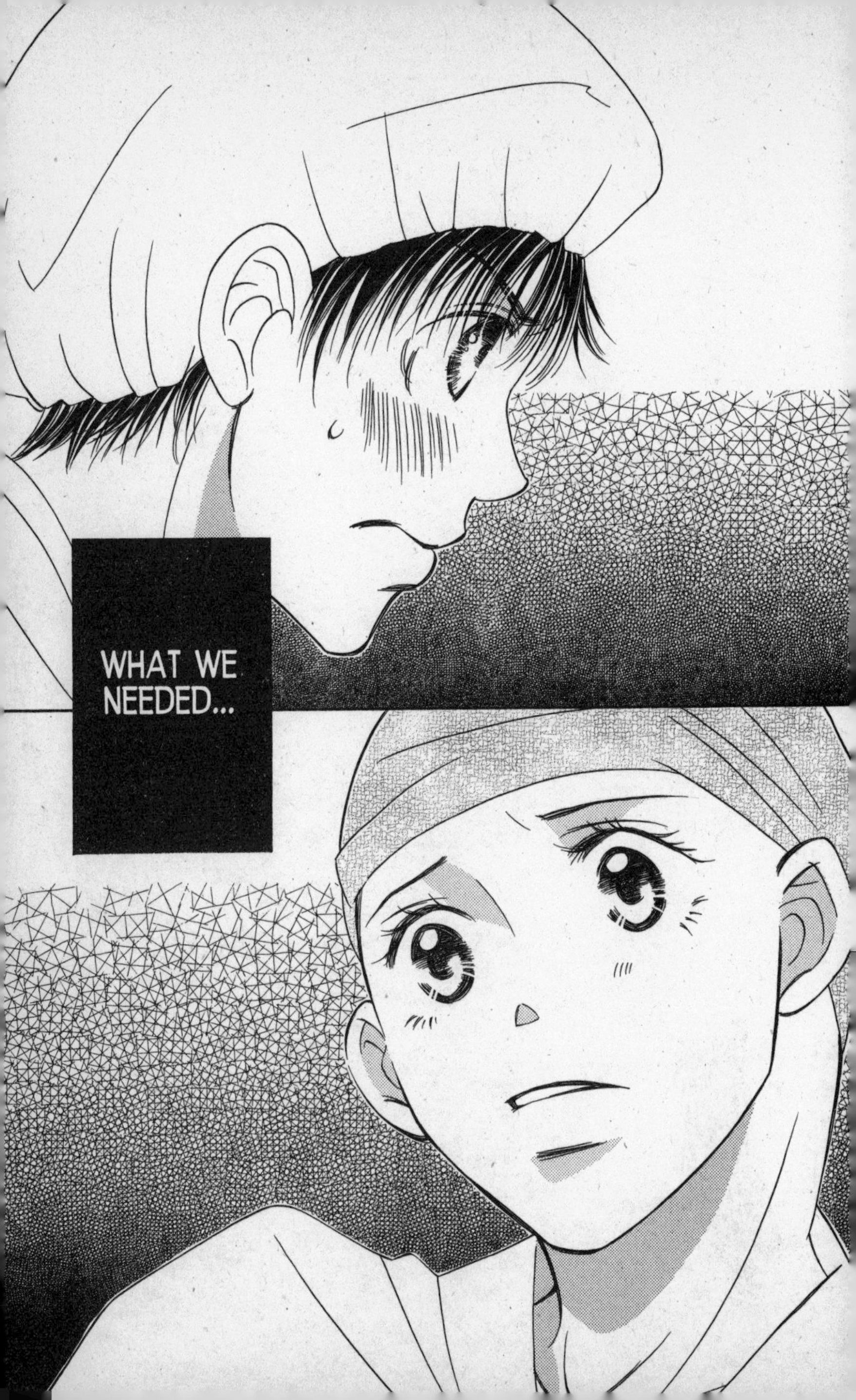
WHAT WE NEEDED...

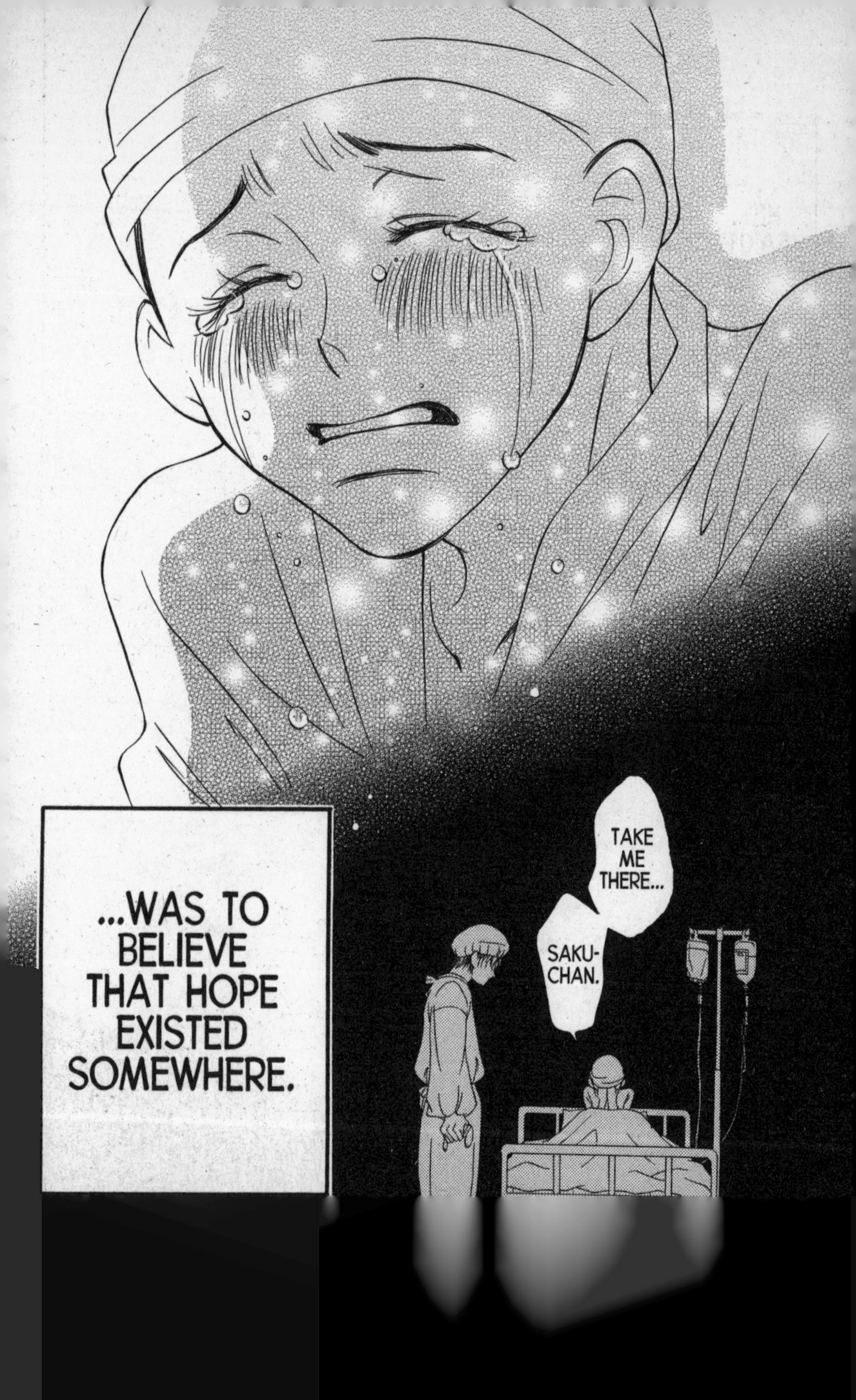
TAKE ME THERE...
SAKU-CHAN.
...WAS TO BELIEVE THAT HOPE EXISTED SOMEWHERE.

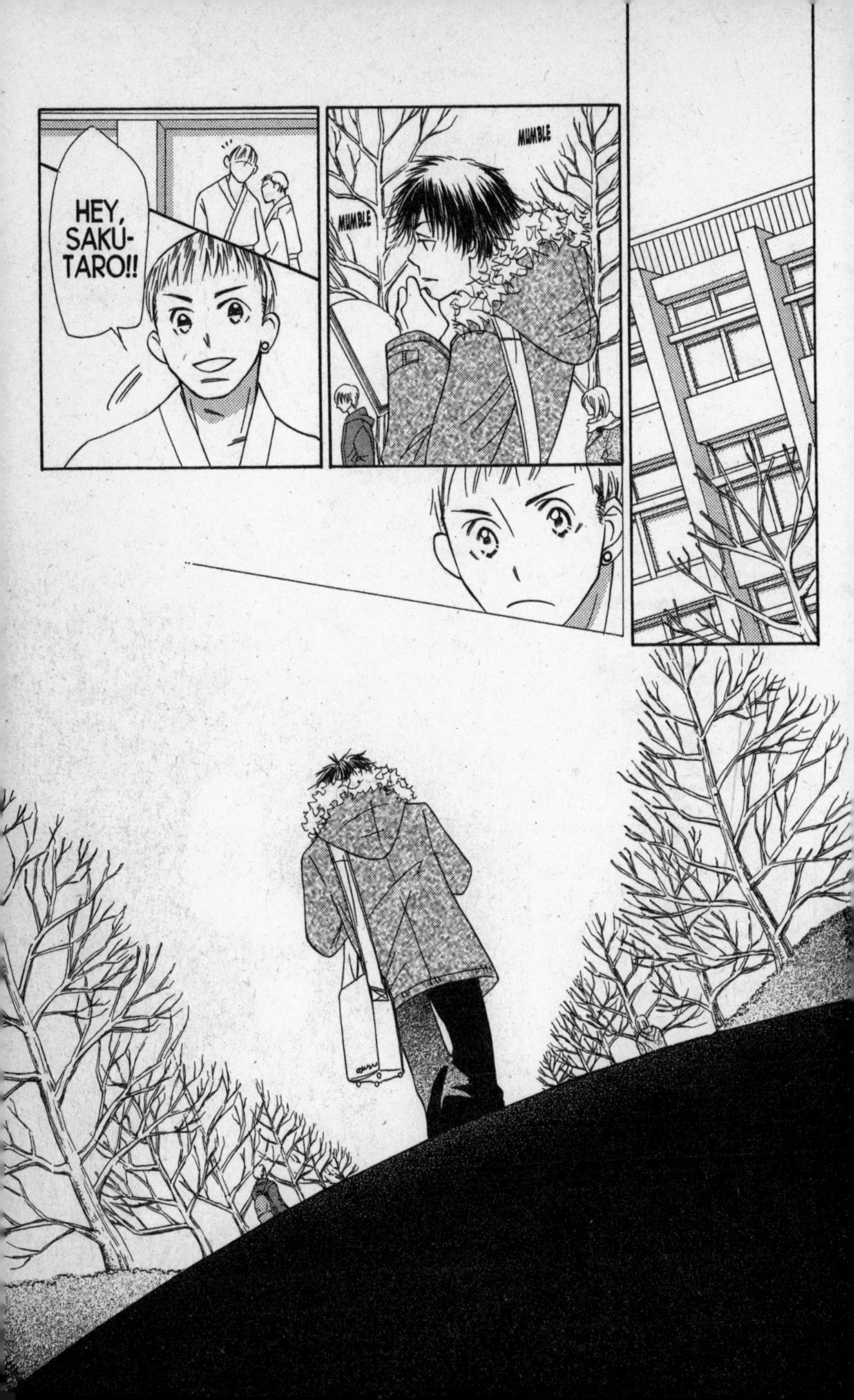
MUMBLE
MUMBLE
HEY, SAKU-TARO!!

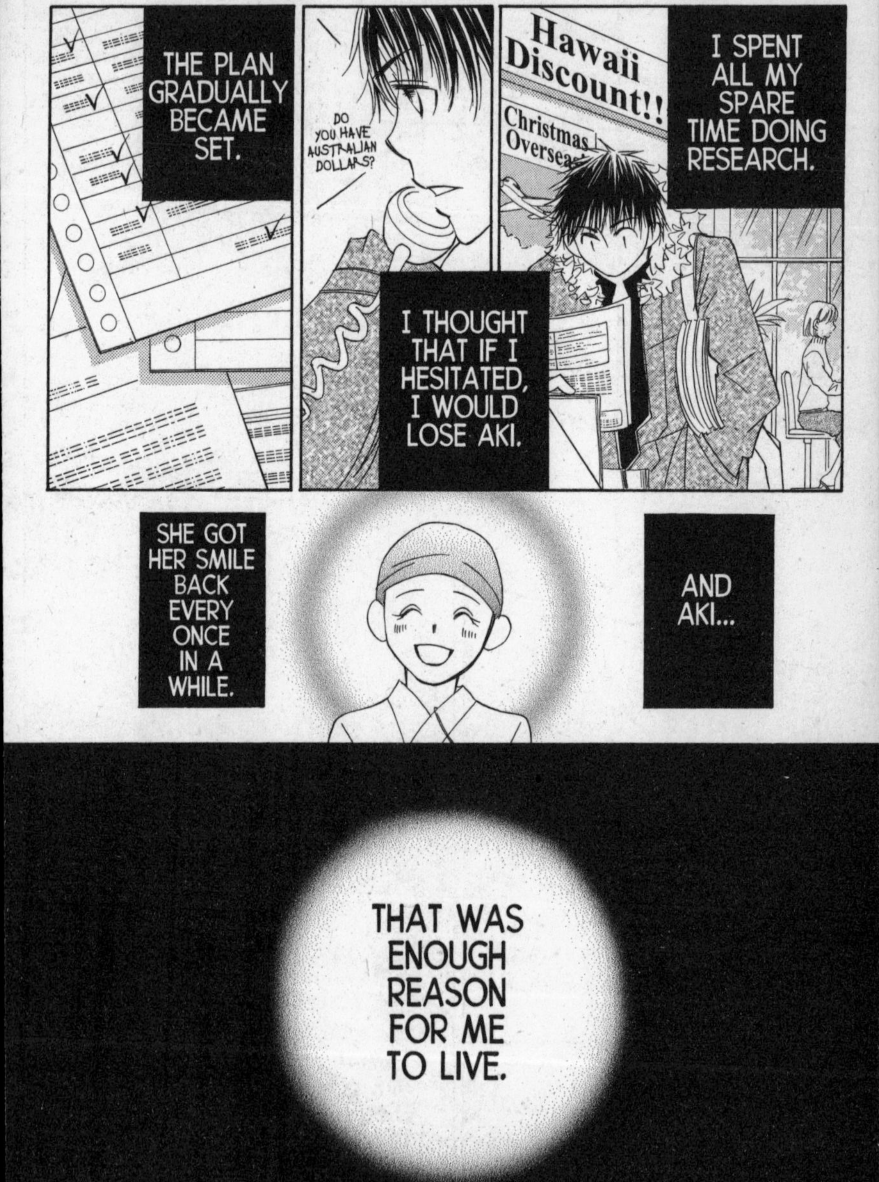
Hawaii Discount!!
Christmas
Oversea
I SPENT ALL MY SPARE TIME DOING RESEARCH.
DO YOU HAVE AUSTRALIAN DOLLARS?
I THOUGHT THAT IF I HESITATED, I WOULD LOSE AKI.
THE PLAN GRADUALLY BECAME SET.
AND AKI...
SHE GOT HER SMILE BACK EVERY ONCE IN A WHILE.
THAT WAS ENOUGH REASON FOR ME TO LIVE.

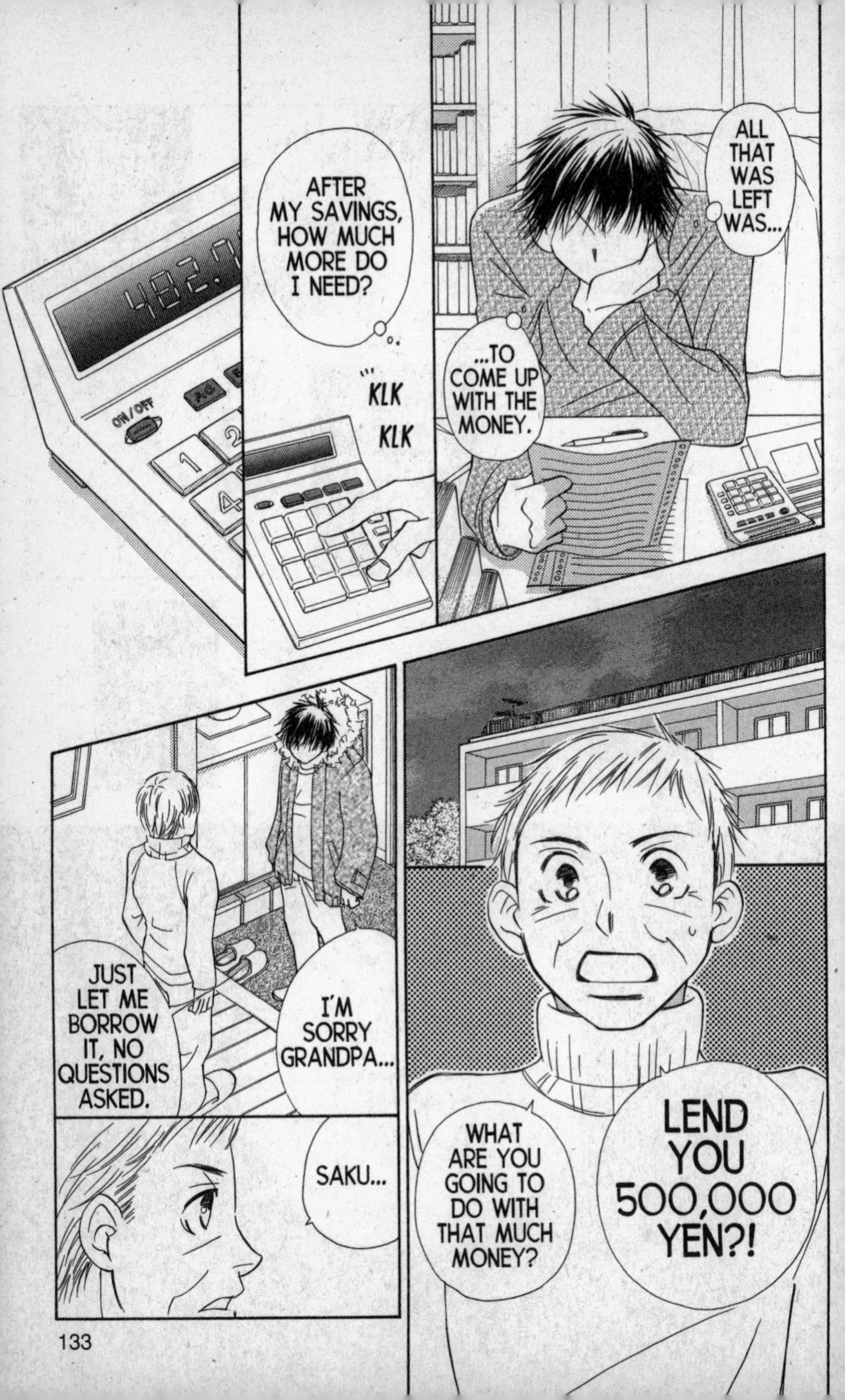
ALL THAT WAS LEFT WAS...
...TO COME UP WITH THE MONEY.
AFTER MY SAVINGS, HOW MUCH MORE DO I NEED?
KLK
KLK
ON/OFF
AC
LEND YOU 500,000 YEN?!
WHAT ARE YOU GOING TO DO WITH THAT MUCH MONEY?
I'M SORRY GRANDPA...
JUST LET ME BORROW IT, NO QUESTIONS ASKED.
SAKU...

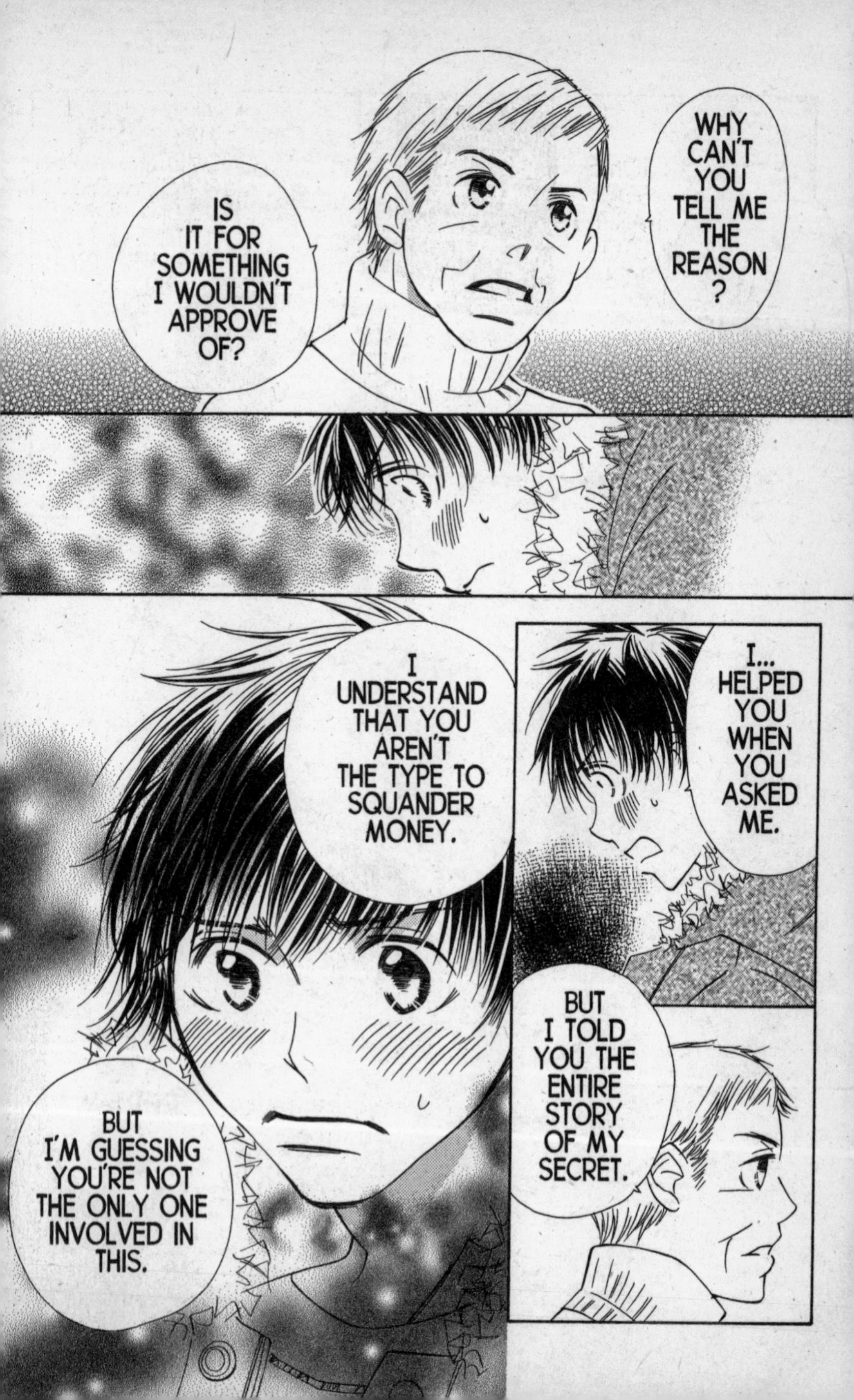
WHY CAN'T YOU TELL ME THE REASON?
IS IT FOR SOMETHING I WOULDN'T APPROVE OF?
I... HELPED YOU WHEN YOU ASKED ME.
BUT I TOLD YOU THE ENTIRE STORY OF MY SECRET.
I UNDERSTAND THAT YOU AREN'T THE TYPE TO SQUANDER MONEY.
BUT I'M GUESSING YOU'RE NOT THE ONLY ONE INVOLVED IN THIS.

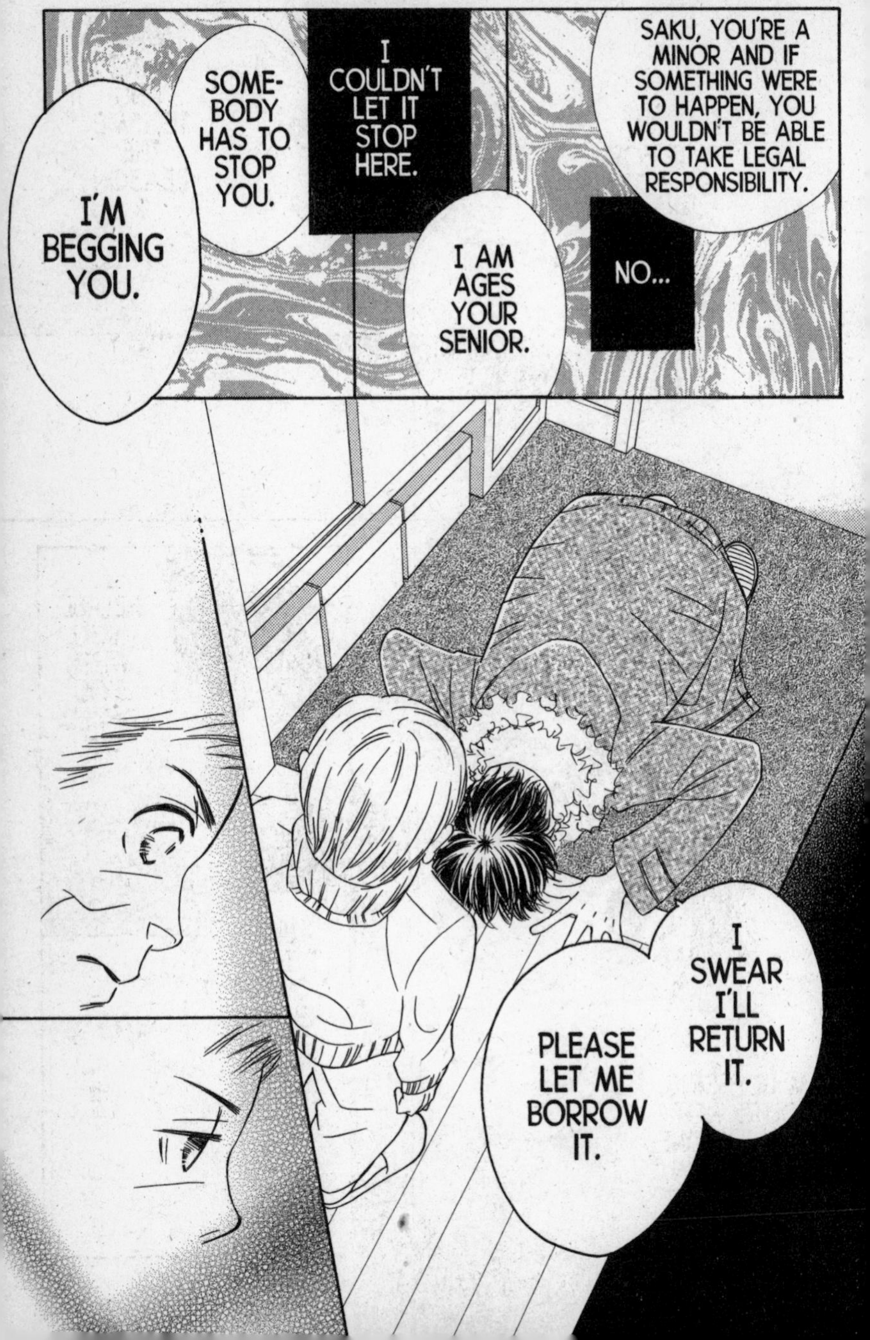
SAKU, YOU'RE A MINOR AND IF SOMETHING WERE TO HAPPEN, YOU WOULDN'T BE ABLE TO TAKE LEGAL RESPONSIBILITY.
NO...
I AM AGES YOUR SENIOR.
I COULDN'T LET IT STOP HERE.
SOME-BODY HAS TO STOP YOU.
I'M BEGGING YOU.
I SWEAR I'LL RETURN IT.
PLEASE LET ME BORROW IT.

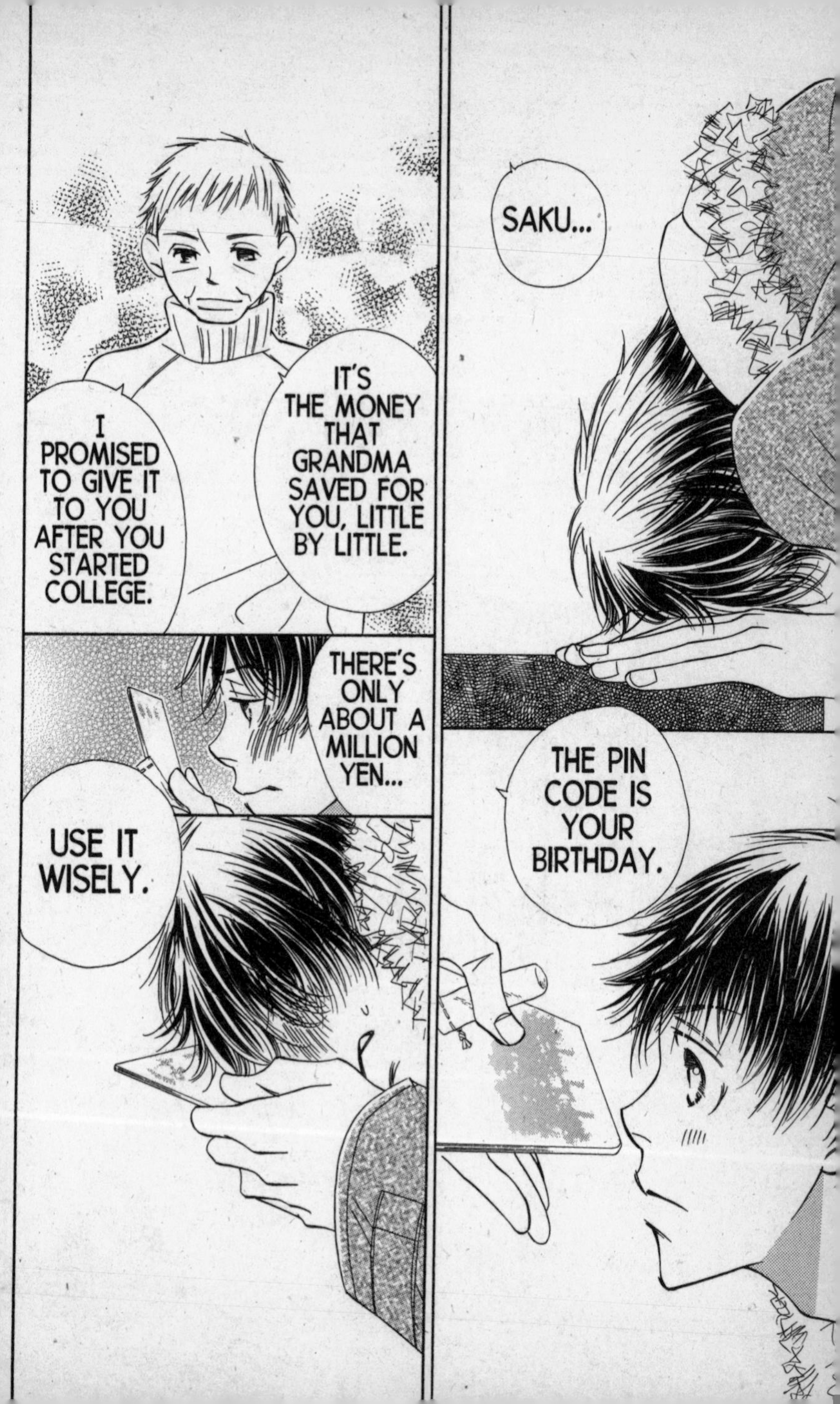
SAKU...
THE PIN CODE IS YOUR BIRTHDAY.
IT'S THE MONEY THAT GRANDMA SAVED FOR YOU, LITTLE BY LITTLE.
I PROMISED TO GIVE IT TO YOU AFTER YOU STARTED COLLEGE.
THERE'S ONLY ABOUT A MILLION YEN...
USE IT WISELY.

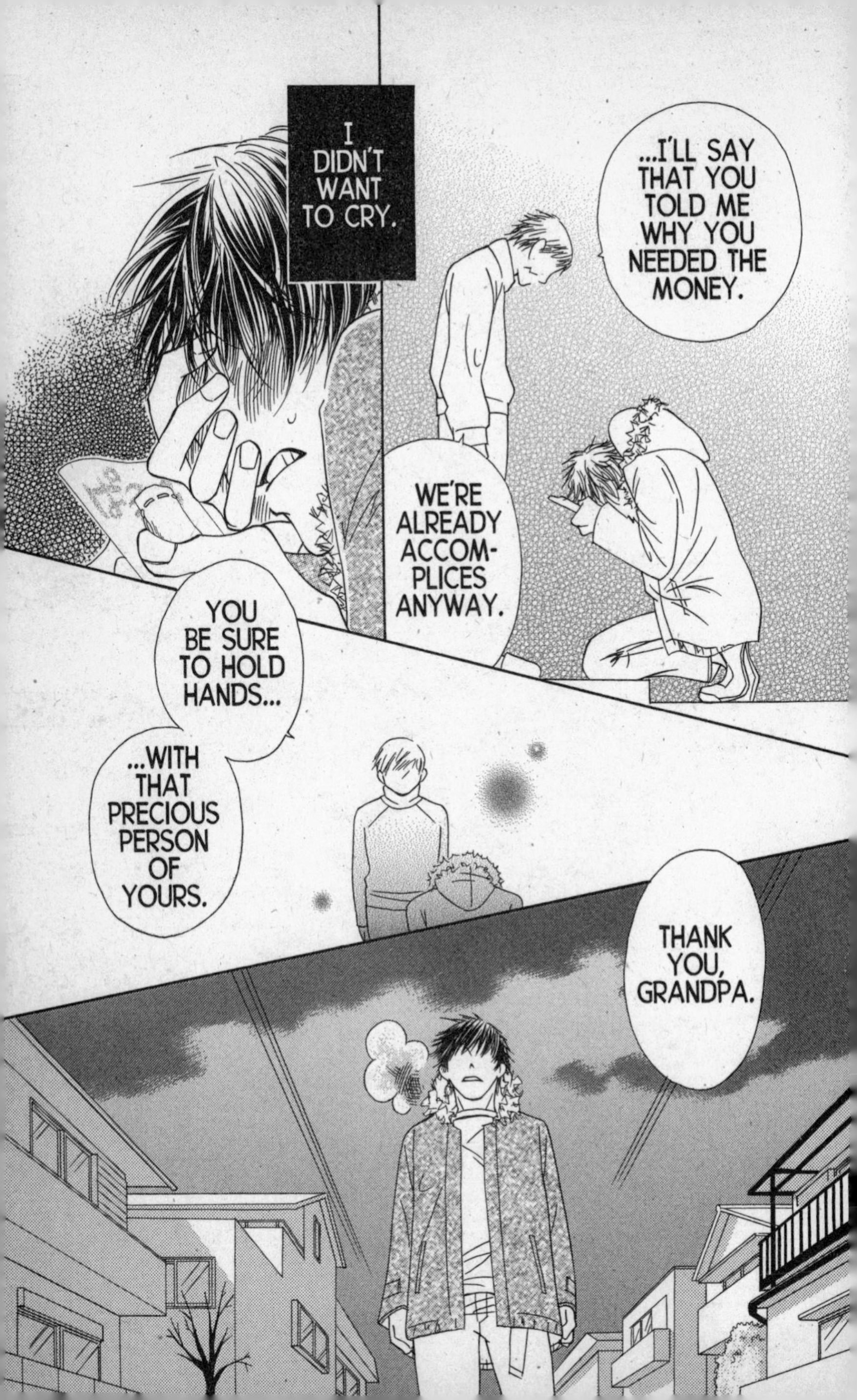
...I'LL SAY THAT YOU TOLD ME WHY YOU NEEDED THE MONEY.
WE'RE ALREADY ACCOMPLICES ANYWAY.
I DIDN'T WANT TO CRY.
YOU BE SURE TO HOLD HANDS...
...WITH THAT PRECIOUS PERSON OF YOURS.
THANK YOU, GRANDPA.

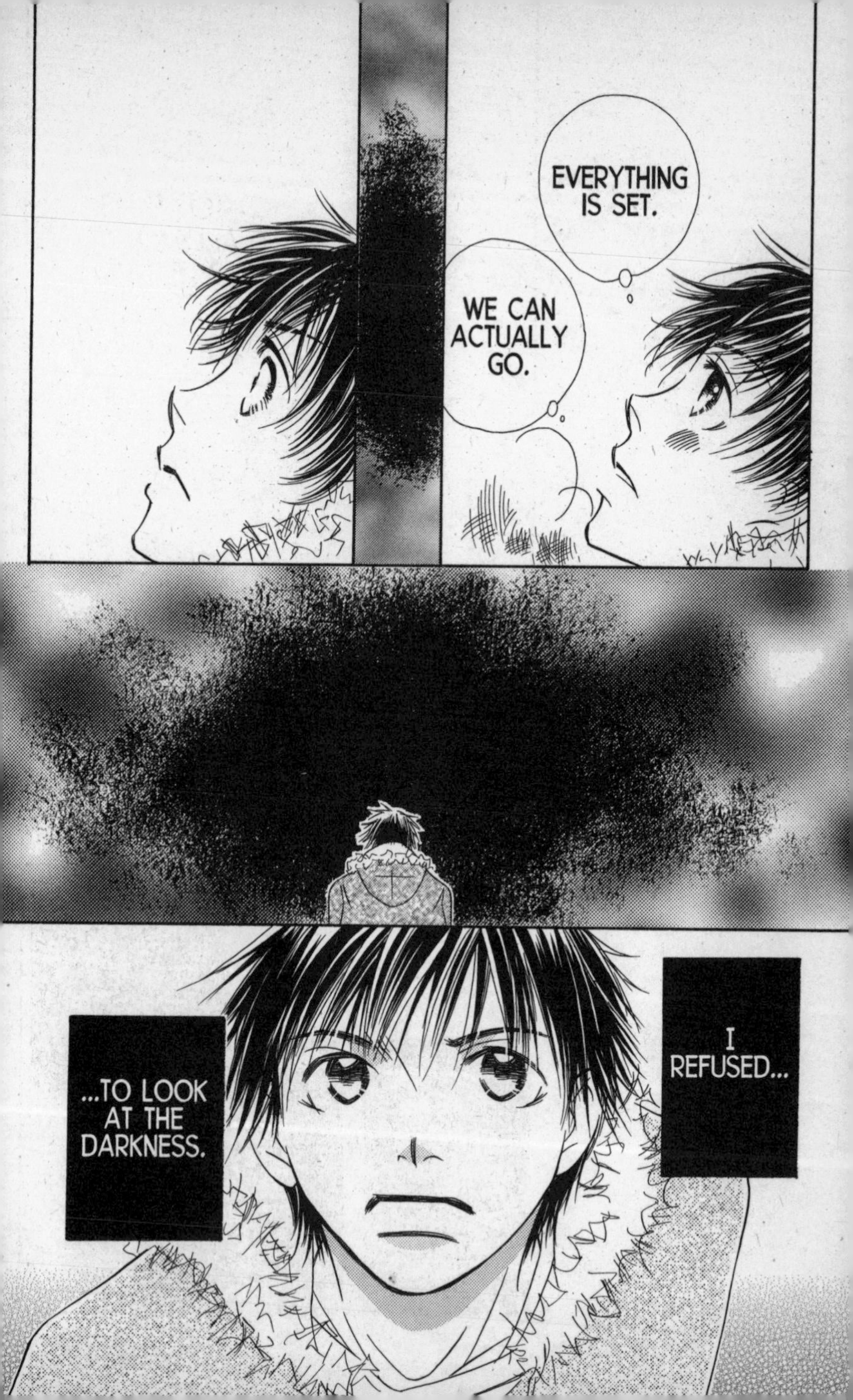
EVERYTHING IS SET.
WE CAN ACTUALLY GO.
I REFUSED...
...TO LOOK AT THE DARKNESS.

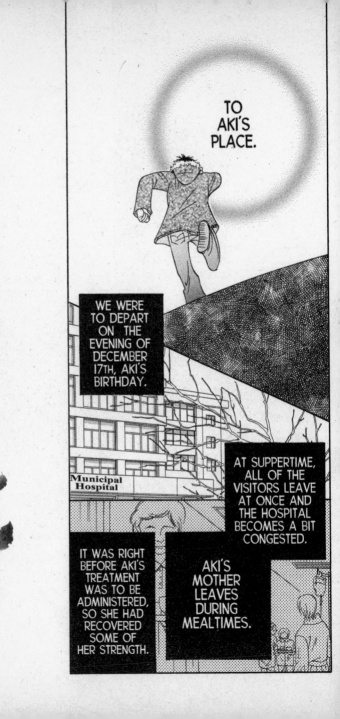

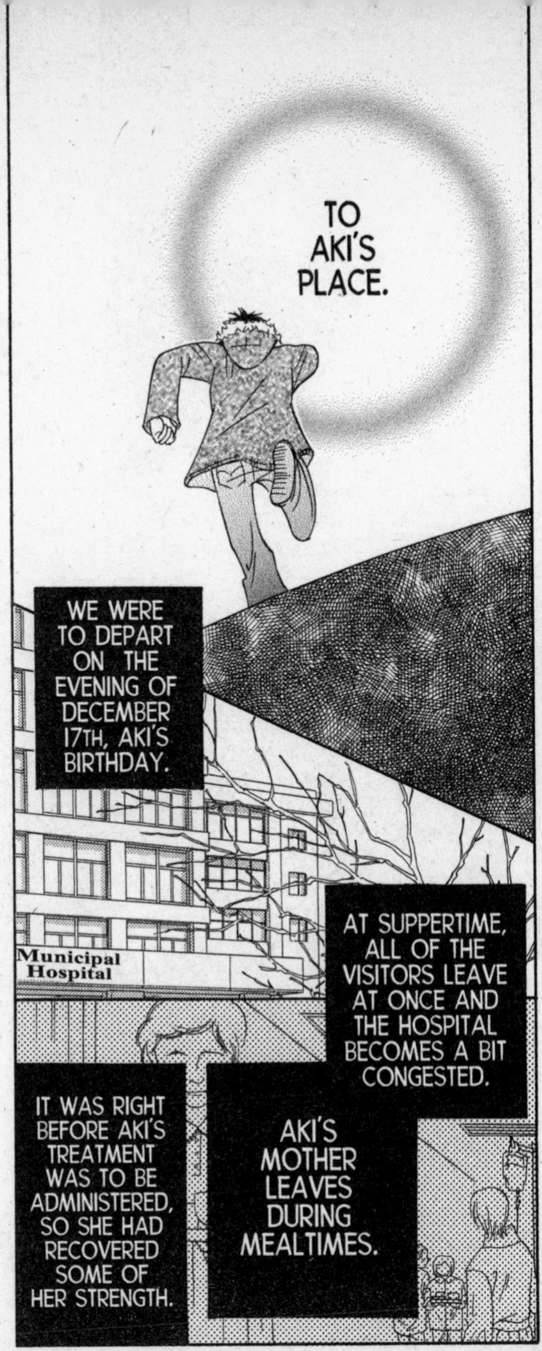
TO AKI'S PLACE.
WE WERE TO DEPART ON THE EVENING OF DECEMBER 17TH, AKI'S BIRTHDAY.
Municipal Hospital
AT SUPPERTIME, ALL OF THE VISITORS LEAVE AT ONCE AND THE HOSPITAL BECOMES A BIT CONGESTED.
AKI'S MOTHER LEAVES DURING MEALTIMES.
IT WAS RIGHT BEFORE AKI'S TREATMENT WAS TO BE ADMINISTERED, SO SHE HAD RECOVERED SOME OF HER STRENGTH.

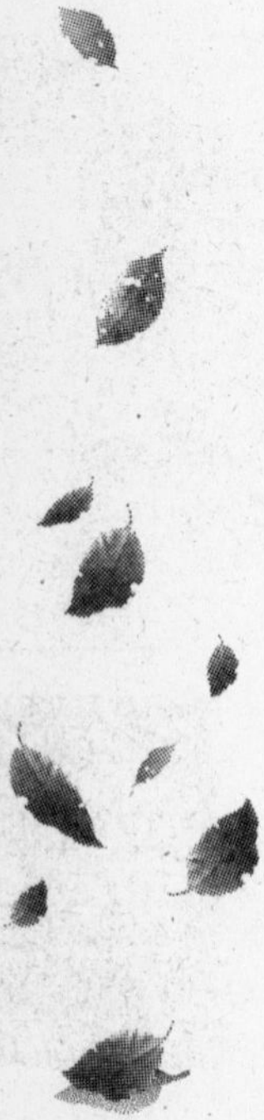

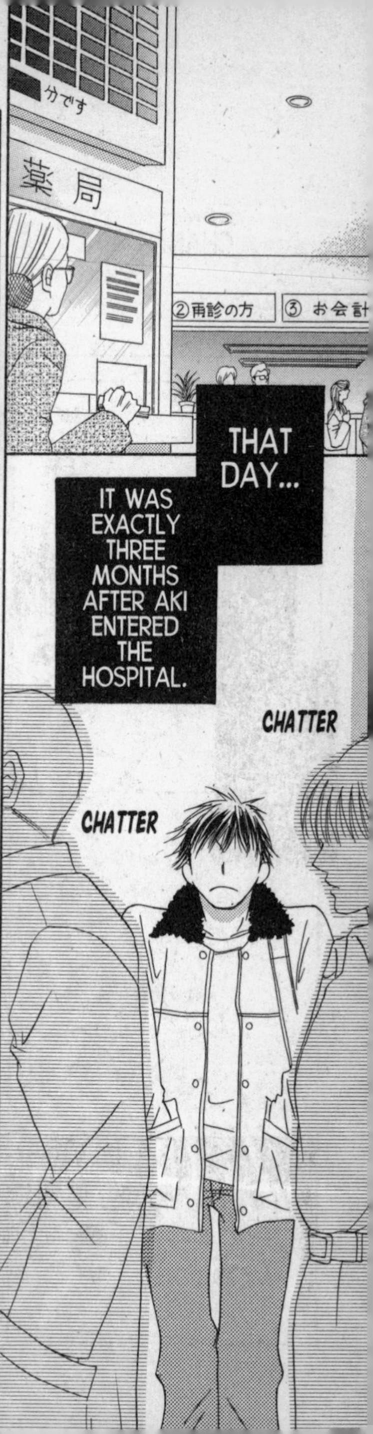
分です
薬局
②再診の方
③ お会計
THAT DAY...
IT WAS EXACTLY THREE MONTHS AFTER AKI ENTERED THE HOSPITAL.
CHATTER
CHATTER

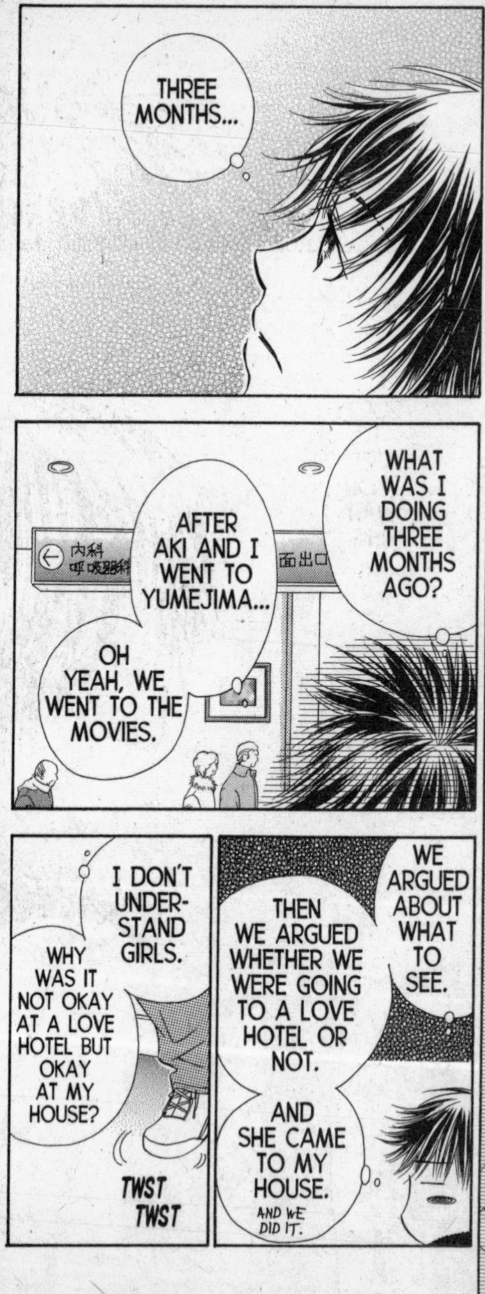
THREE MONTHS...
WHAT WAS I DOING THREE MONTHS AGO?
AFTER AKI AND I WENT TO YUMEJIMA...
OH YEAH, WE WENT TO THE MOVIES.
WE ARGUED ABOUT WHAT TO SEE.
THEN WE ARGUED WHETHER WE WERE GOING TO A LOVE HOTEL OR NOT.
AND SHE CAME TO MY HOUSE.
AND WE DID IT.
I DON'T UNDER-STAND GIRLS.
WHY WAS IT NOT OKAY AT A LOVE HOTEL BUT OKAY AT MY HOUSE?
TWST TWST

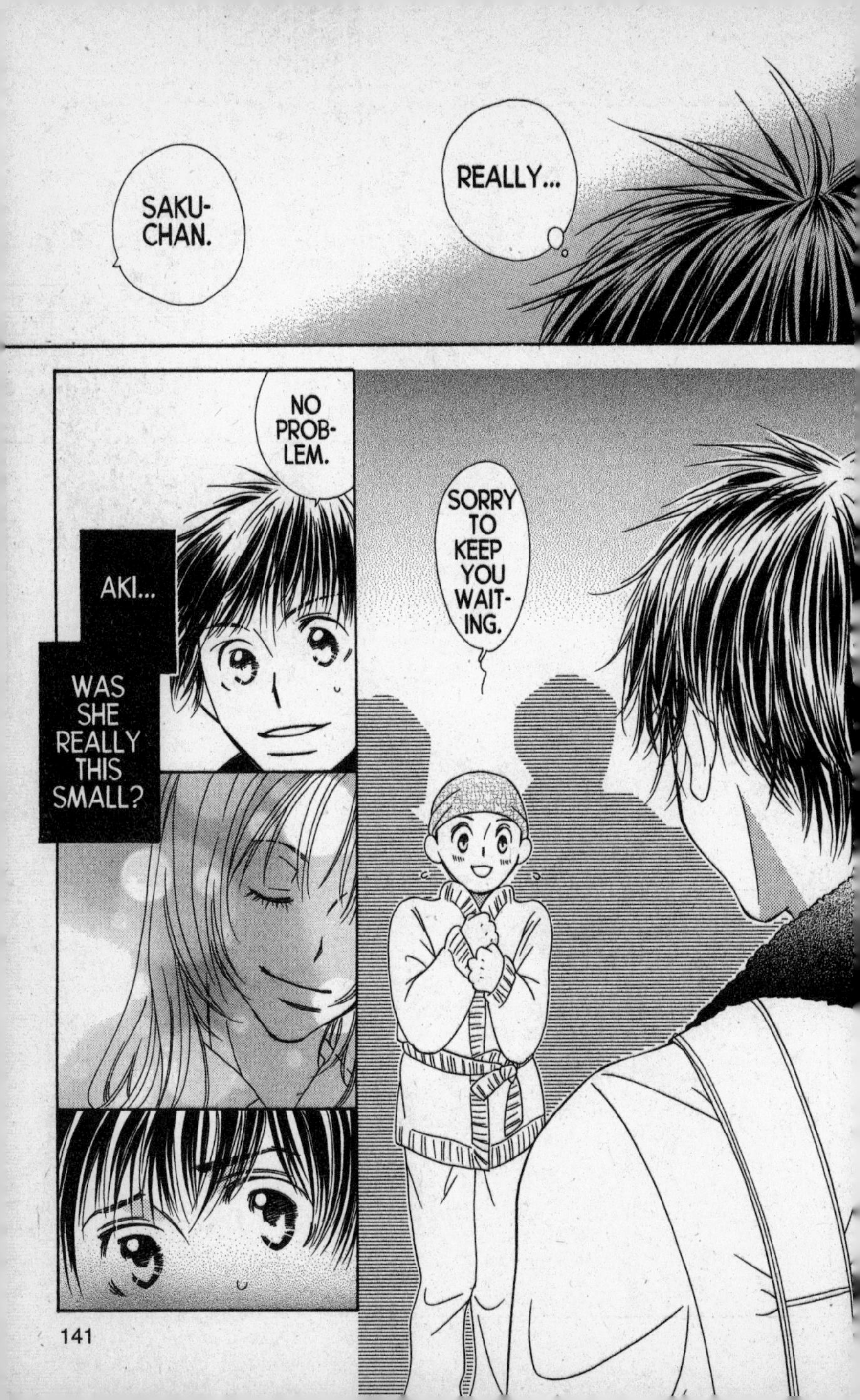
REALLY...
SAKU-CHAN.
SORRY TO KEEP YOU WAIT-ING.
NO PROB-LEM.
AKI...
WAS SHE REALLY THIS SMALL?

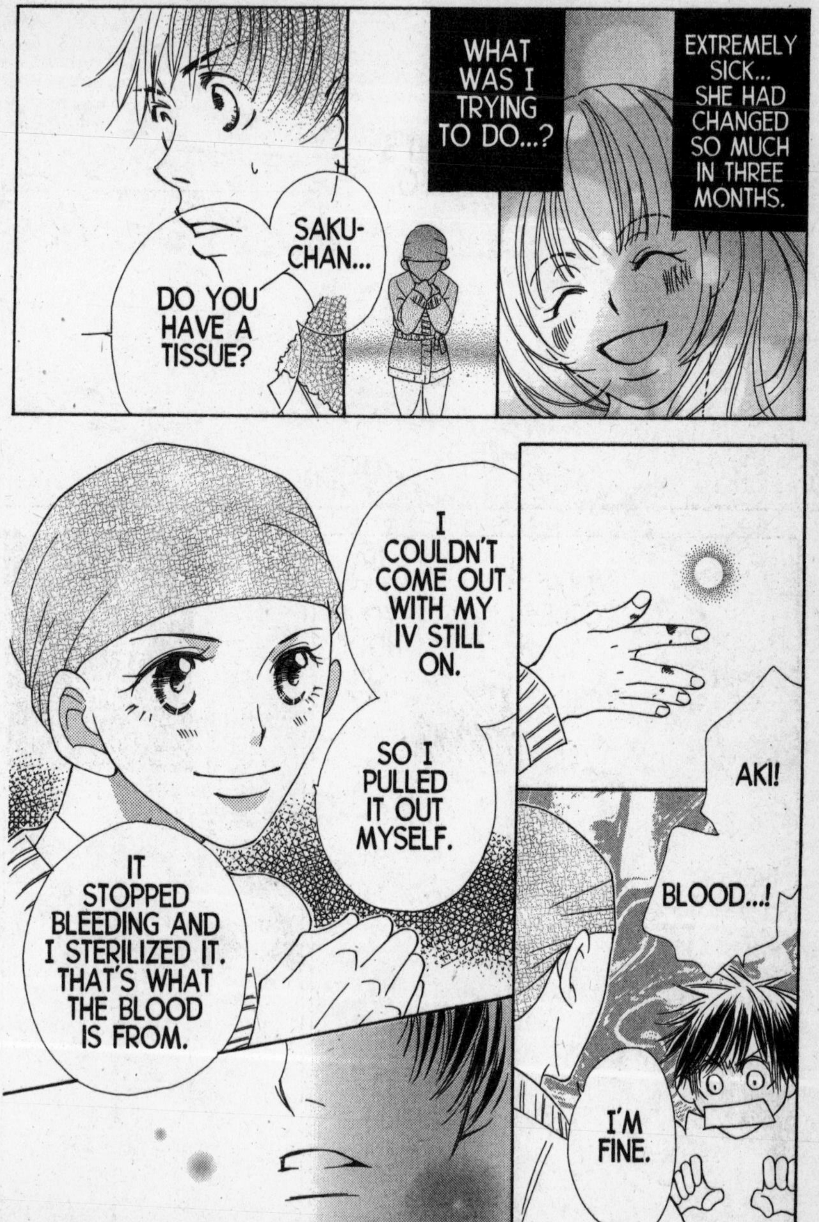
EXTREMELY SICK... SHE HAD CHANGED SO MUCH IN THREE MONTHS.
WHAT WAS I TRYING TO DO...?
SAKU-CHAN...
DO YOU HAVE A TISSUE?
AKI!
BLOOD...!
I'M FINE.
I COULDN'T COME OUT WITH MY IV STILL ON.
SO I PULLED IT OUT MYSELF.
IT STOPPED BLEEDING AND I STERILIZED IT. THAT'S WHAT THE BLOOD IS FROM.

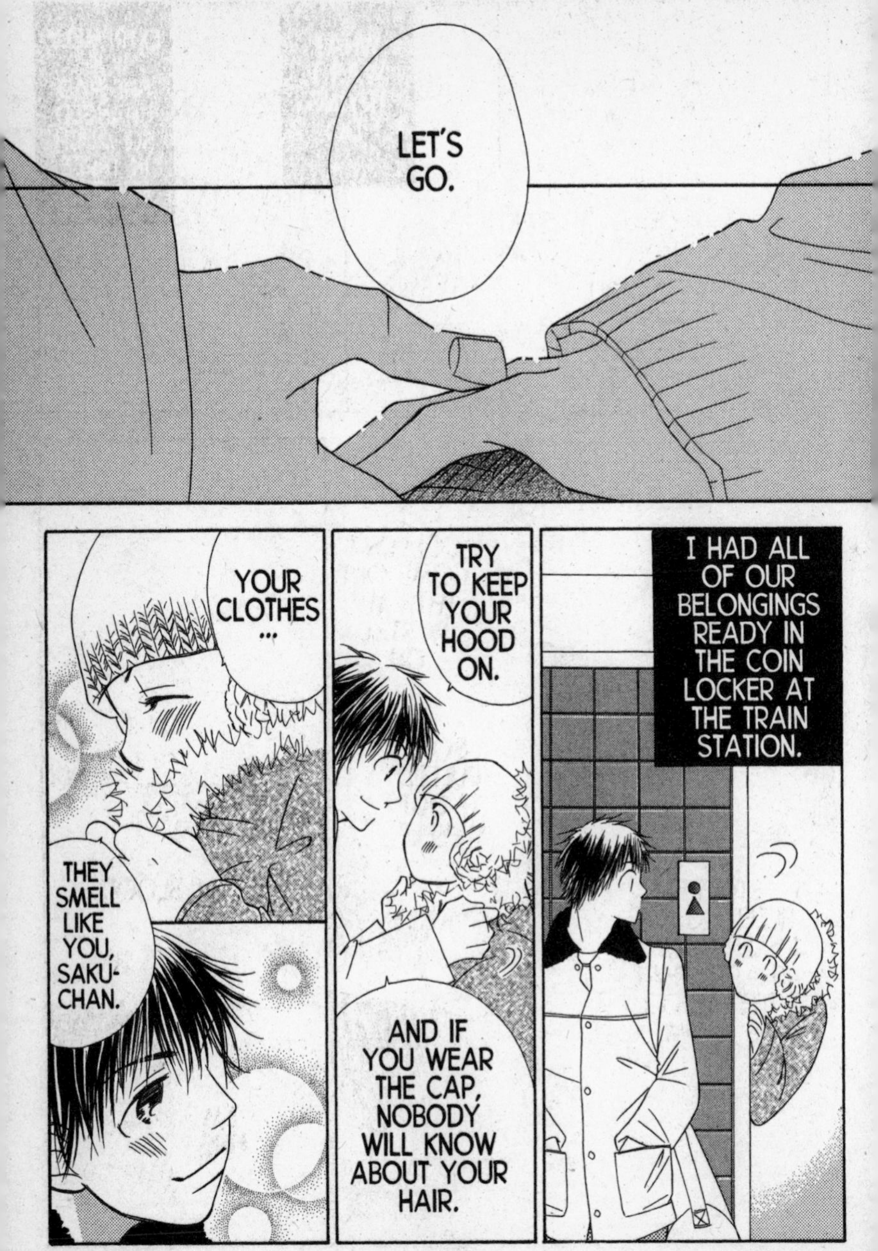
LET'S GO.
I HAD ALL OF OUR BELONGINGS READY IN THE COIN LOCKER AT THE TRAIN STATION.
TRY TO KEEP YOUR HOOD ON.
AND IF YOU WEAR THE CAP, NOBODY WILL KNOW ABOUT YOUR HAIR.
YOUR CLOTHES...
THEY SMELL LIKE YOU, SAKU-CHAN.

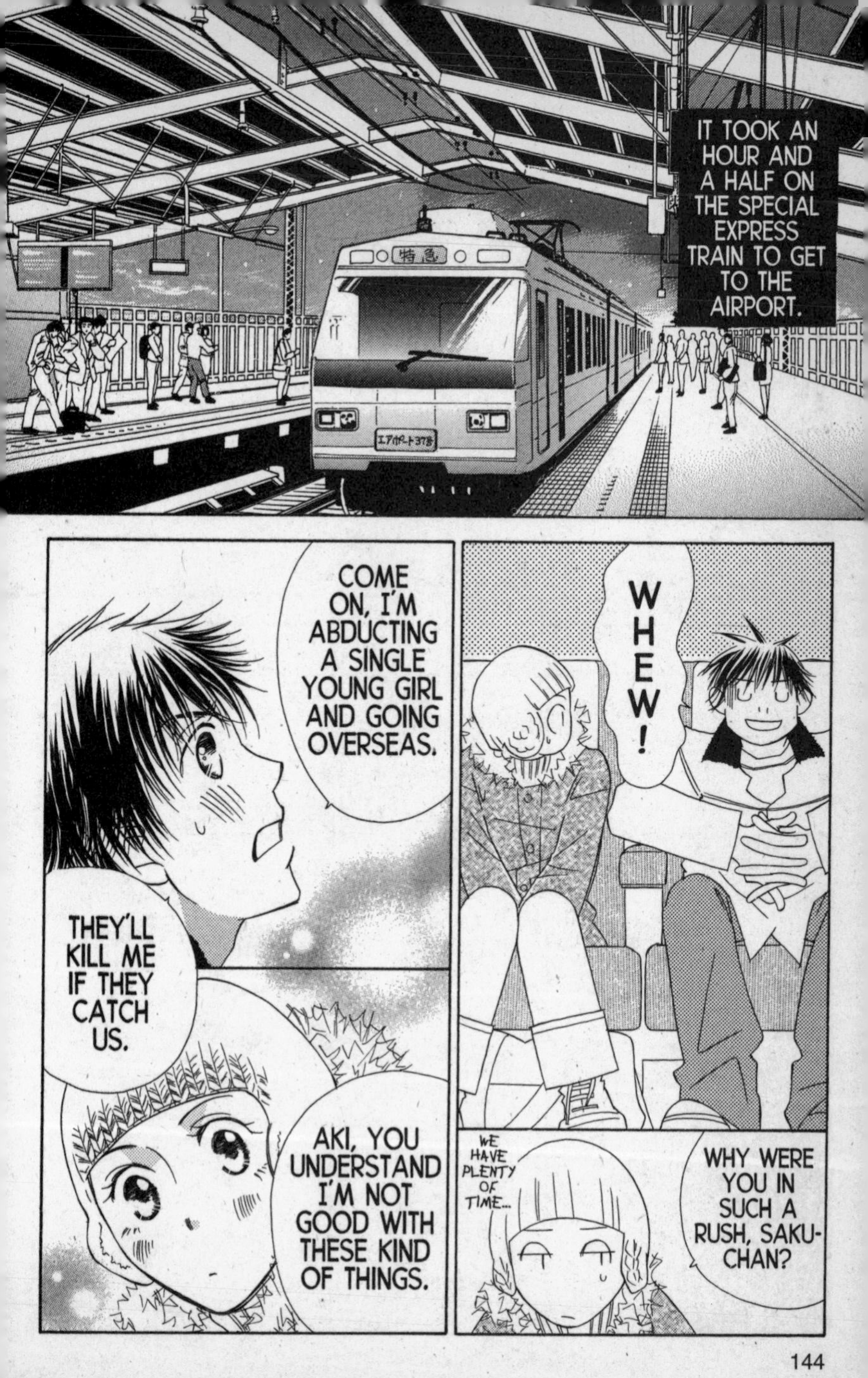
IT TOOK AN HOUR AND A HALF ON THE SPECIAL EXPRESS TRAIN TO GET TO THE AIRPORT.
特急
エアポート37号
WHEW!
WHY WERE YOU IN SUCH A RUSH, SAKU-CHAN?
WE HAVE PLENTY OF TIME...
COME ON, I'M ABDUCTING A SINGLE YOUNG GIRL AND GOING OVERSEAS.
THEY'LL KILL ME IF THEY CATCH US.
AKI, YOU UNDERSTAND I'M NOT GOOD WITH THESE KIND OF THINGS.

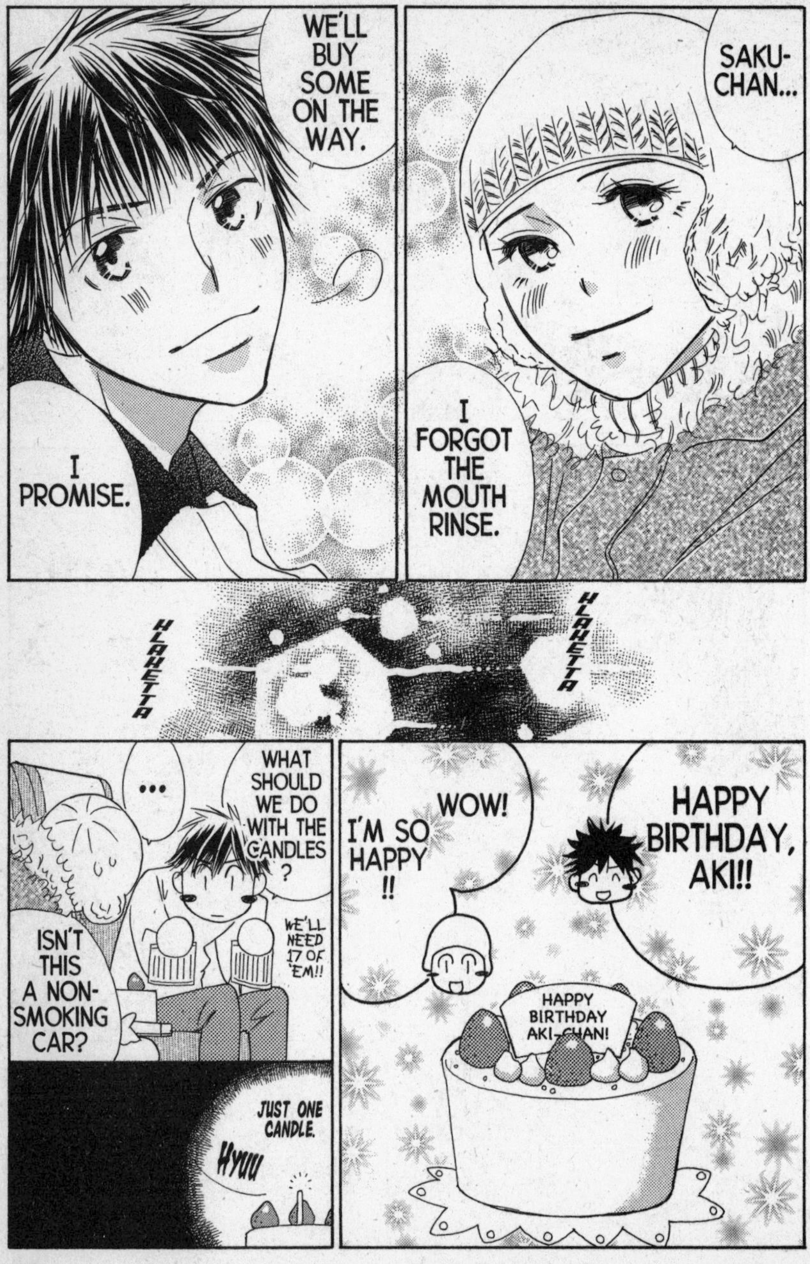
SAKU-CHAN...
I FORGOT THE MOUTH RINSE.
WE'LL BUY SOME ON THE WAY.
I PROMISE.
HLAHETTA
HLAHETTA
HAPPY BIRTHDAY, AKI!!
WOW!
I'M SO HAPPY !!
HAPPY BIRTHDAY AKI-CHAN!
WHAT SHOULD WE DO WITH THE CANDLES ?
...
WE'LL NEED 17 OF 'EM!!
ISN'T THIS A NON-SMOKING CAR?
JUST ONE CANDLE.
HYUU

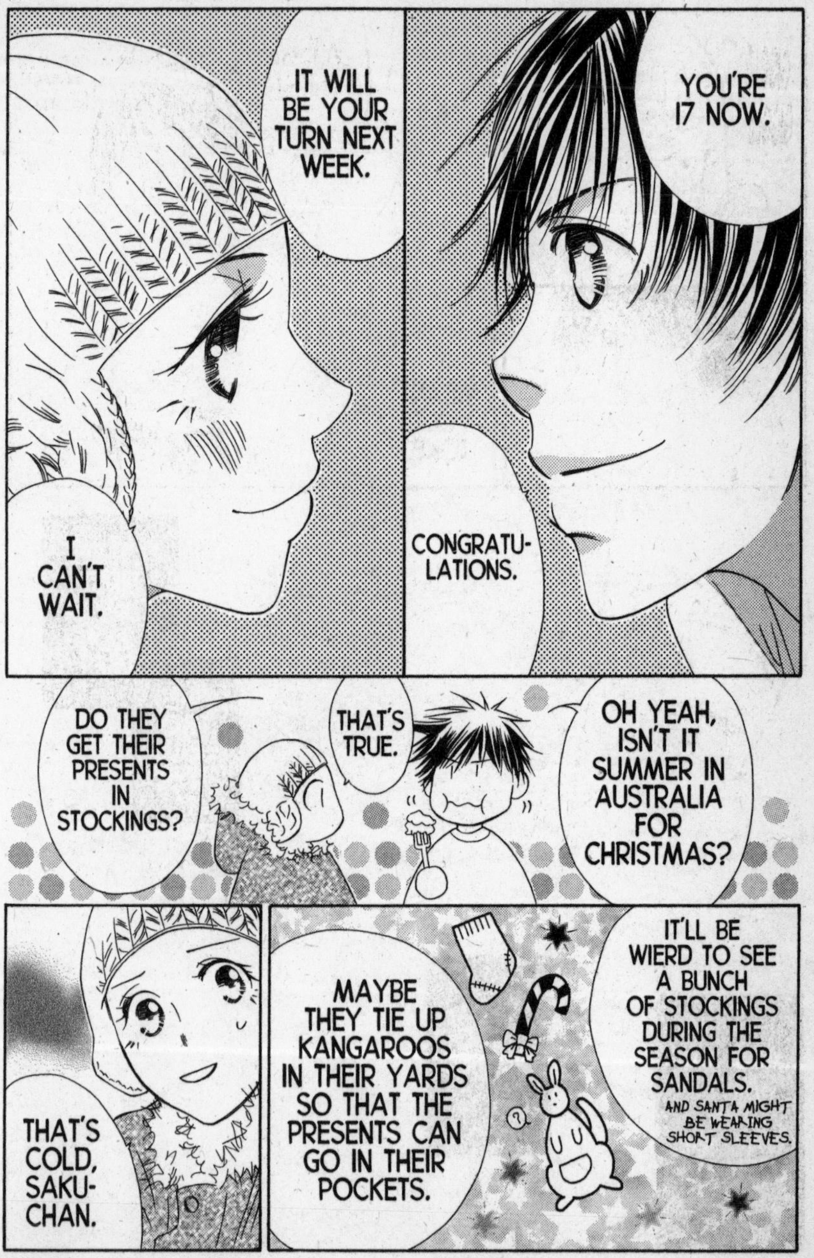
YOU'RE 17 NOW.
CONGRATULATIONS.
IT WILL BE YOUR TURN NEXT WEEK.
I CAN'T WAIT.
OH YEAH, ISN'T IT SUMMER IN AUSTRALIA FOR CHRISTMAS?
THAT'S TRUE.
DO THEY GET THEIR PRESENTS IN STOCKINGS?
IT'LL BE WIERD TO SEE A BUNCH OF STOCKINGS DURING THE SEASON FOR SANDALS.
AND SANTA MIGHT BE WEARING SHORT SLEEVES.
MAYBE THEY TIE UP KANGAROOS IN THEIR YARDS SO THAT THE PRESENTS CAN GO IN THEIR POCKETS.
THAT'S COLD, SAKU-CHAN.

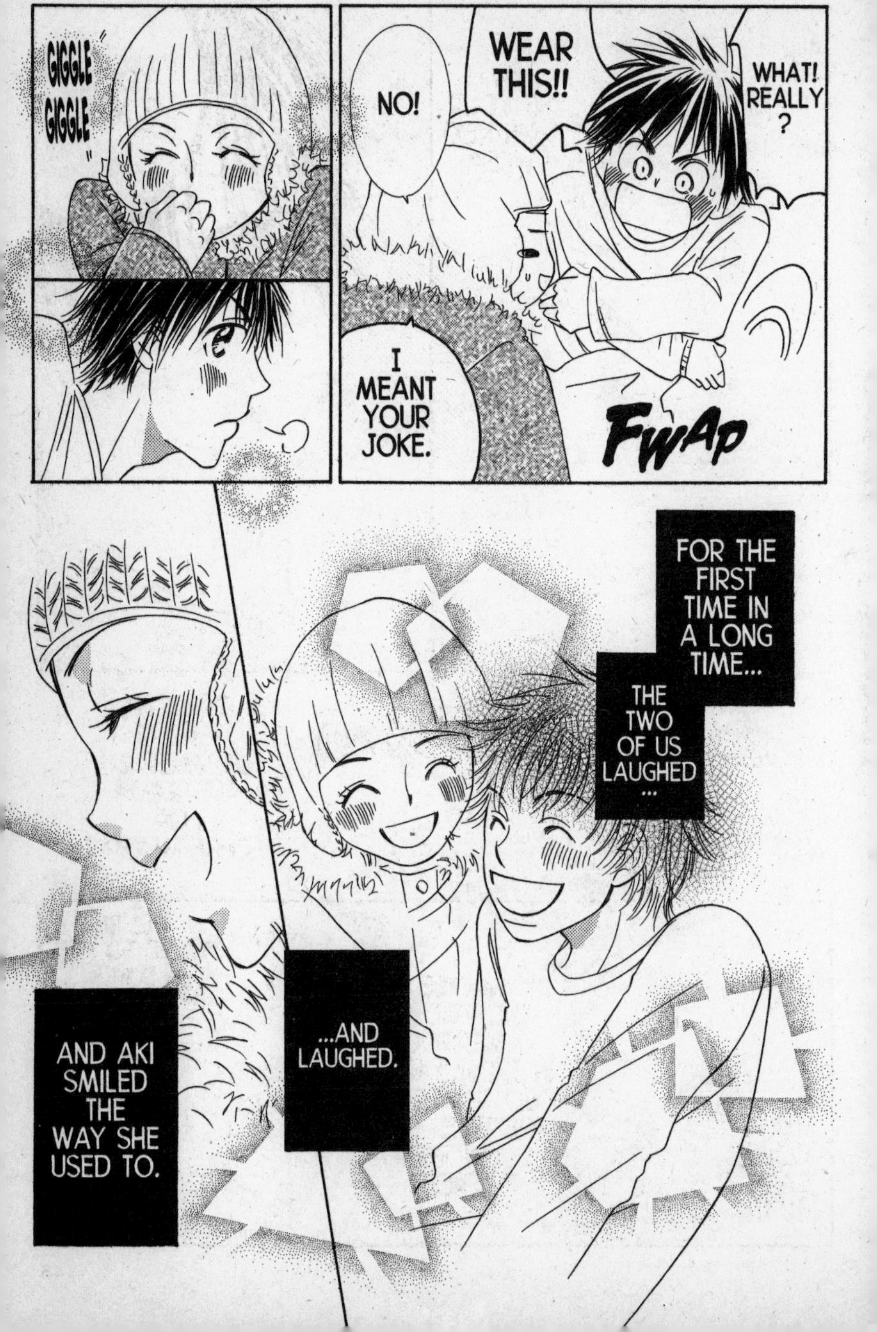
WEAR THIS!!
WHAT! REALLY ?
NO!
I MEANT YOUR JOKE.
FWAP
GIGGLE GIGGLE
FOR THE FIRST TIME IN A LONG TIME...
THE TWO OF US LAUGHED ...
...AND LAUGHED.
AND AKI SMILED THE WAY SHE USED TO.

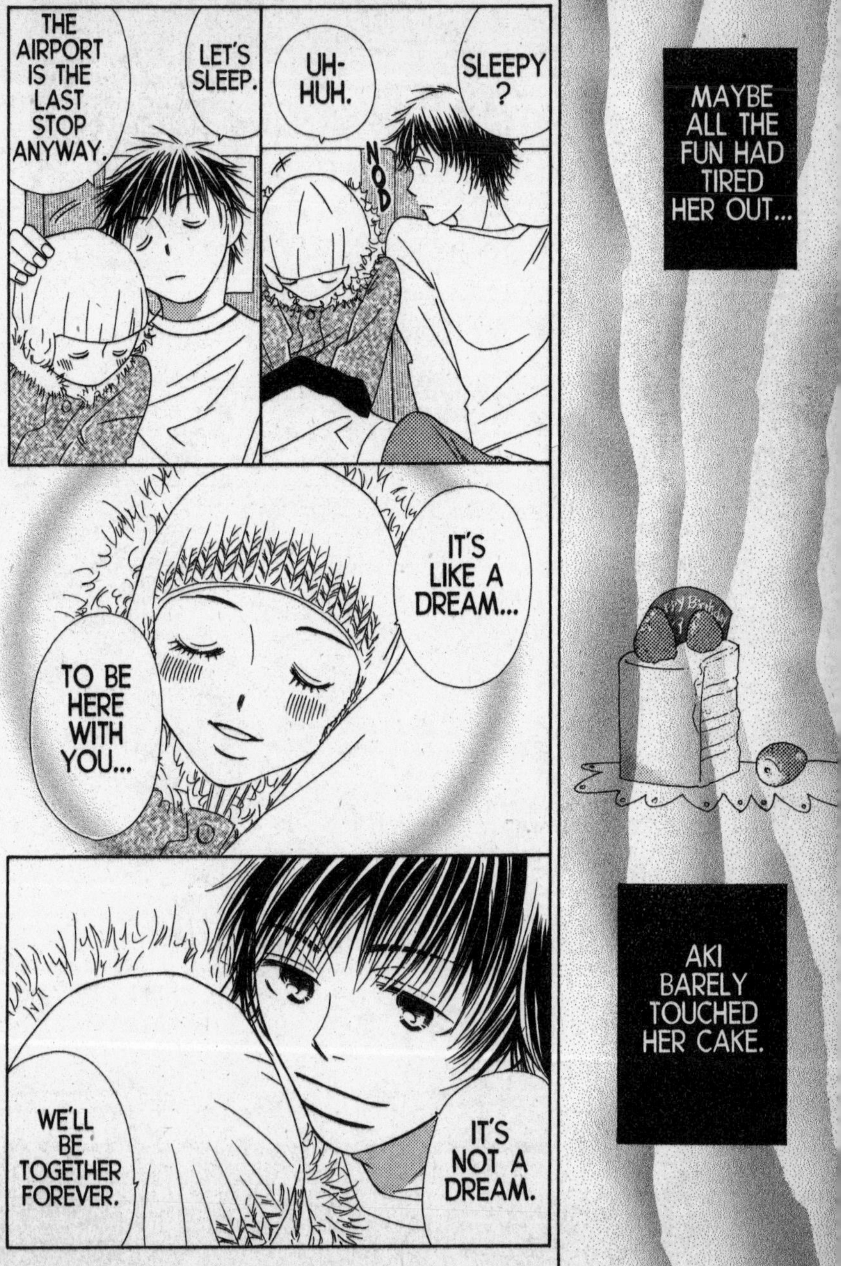
MAYBE ALL THE FUN HAD TIRED HER OUT...
AKI BARELY TOUCHED HER CAKE.
SLEEPY?
UH-HUH.
NOD
LET'S SLEEP.
THE AIRPORT IS THE LAST STOP ANYWAY.
IT'S LIKE A DREAM...
TO BE HERE WITH YOU...
IT'S NOT A DREAM.
WE'LL BE TOGETHER FOREVER.

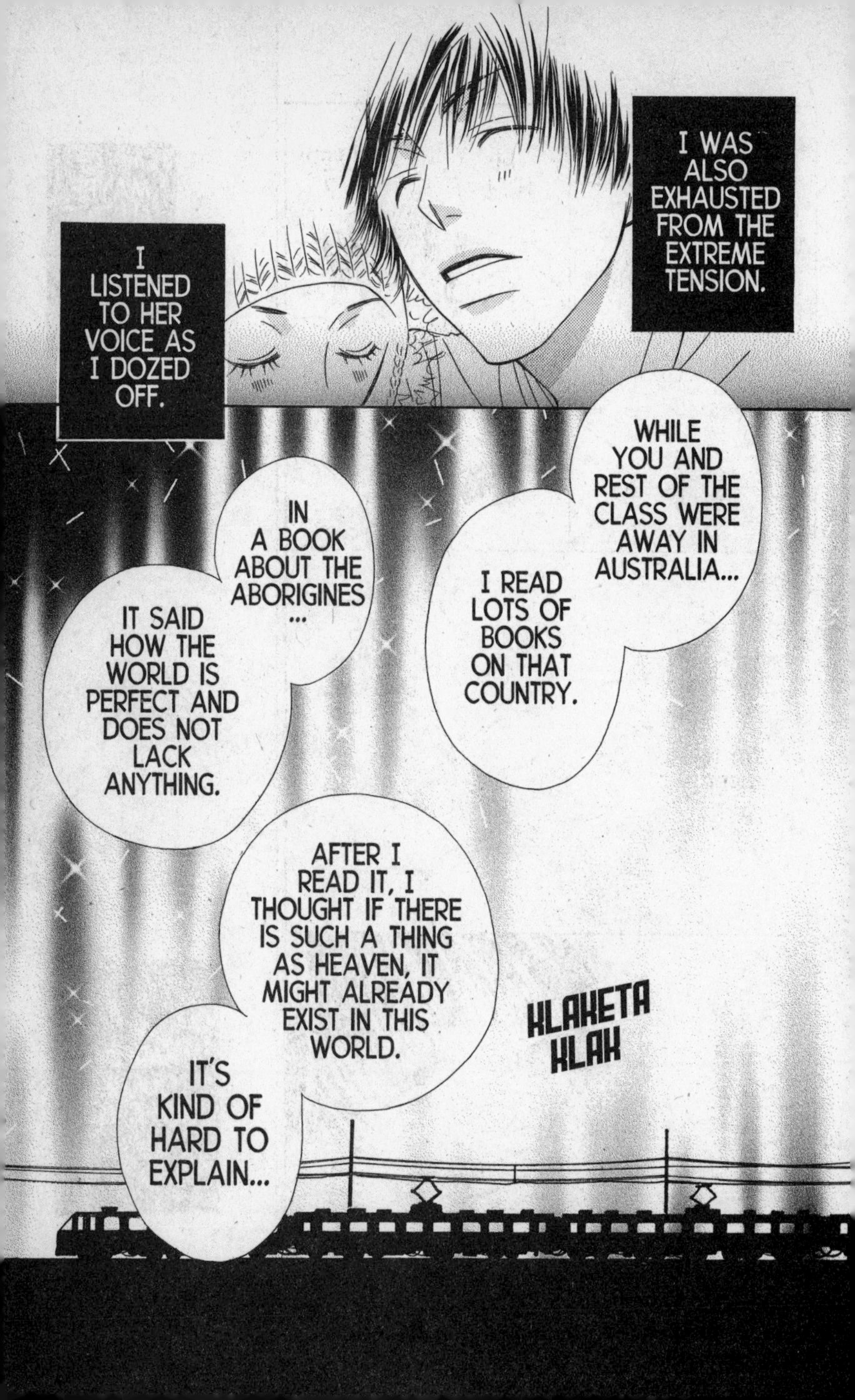
I WAS ALSO EXHAUSTED FROM THE EXTREME TENSION.
I LISTENED TO HER VOICE AS I DOZED OFF.
WHILE YOU AND REST OF THE CLASS WERE AWAY IN AUSTRALIA...
I READ LOTS OF BOOKS ON THAT COUNTRY.
IN A BOOK ABOUT THE ABORIGINES ...
IT SAID HOW THE WORLD IS PERFECT AND DOES NOT LACK ANYTHING.
AFTER I READ IT, I THOUGHT IF THERE IS SUCH A THING AS HEAVEN, IT MIGHT ALREADY EXIST IN THIS WORLD.
KLAKETA KLAK
IT'S KIND OF HARD TO EXPLAIN...

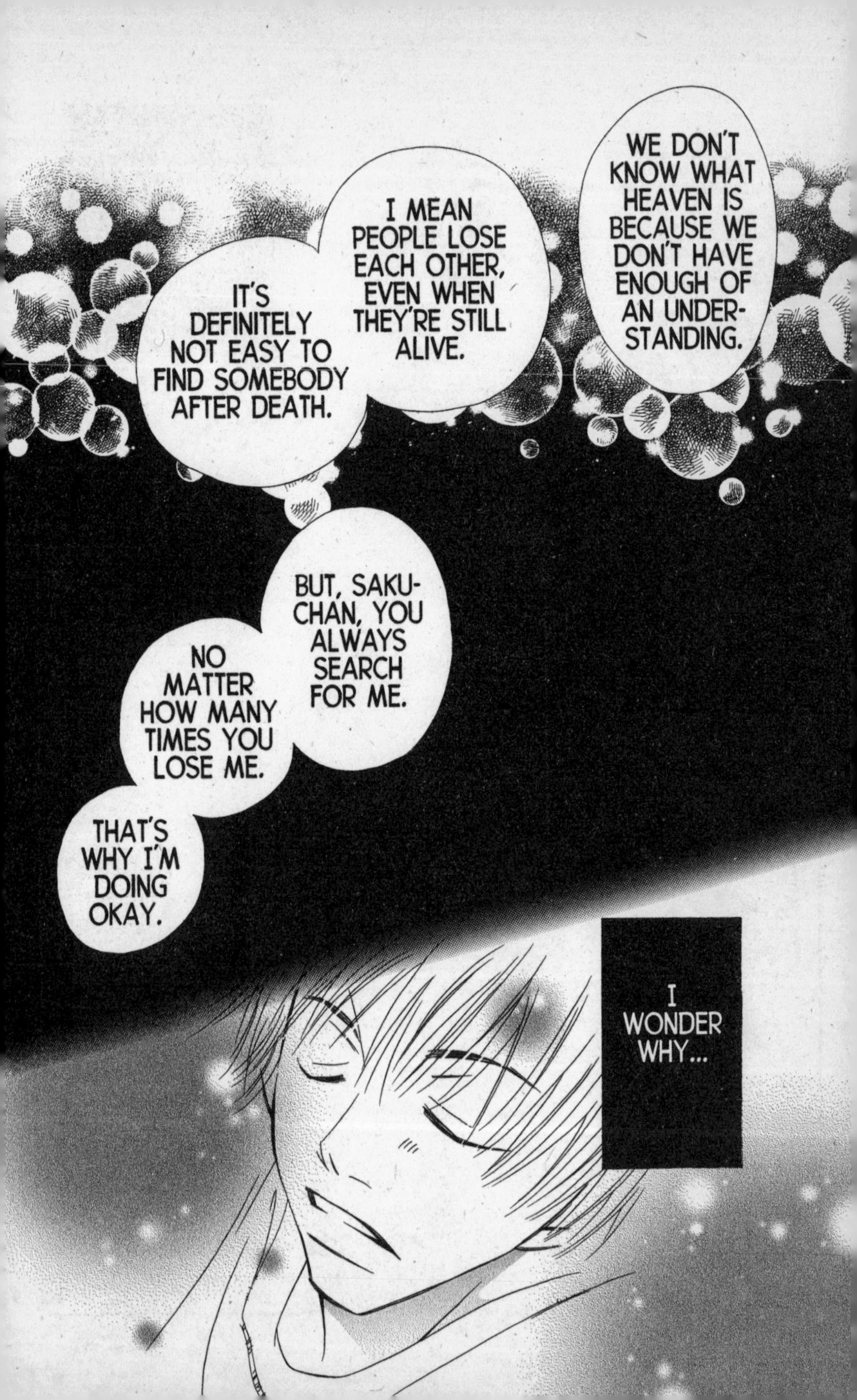
WE DON'T KNOW WHAT HEAVEN IS BECAUSE WE DON'T HAVE ENOUGH OF AN UNDER-STANDING.
I MEAN PEOPLE LOSE EACH OTHER, EVEN WHEN THEY'RE STILL ALIVE.
IT'S DEFINITELY NOT EASY TO FIND SOMEBODY AFTER DEATH.
BUT, SAKU-CHAN, YOU ALWAYS SEARCH FOR ME.
NO MATTER HOW MANY TIMES YOU LOSE ME.
THAT'S WHY I'M DOING OKAY.
I WONDER WHY...

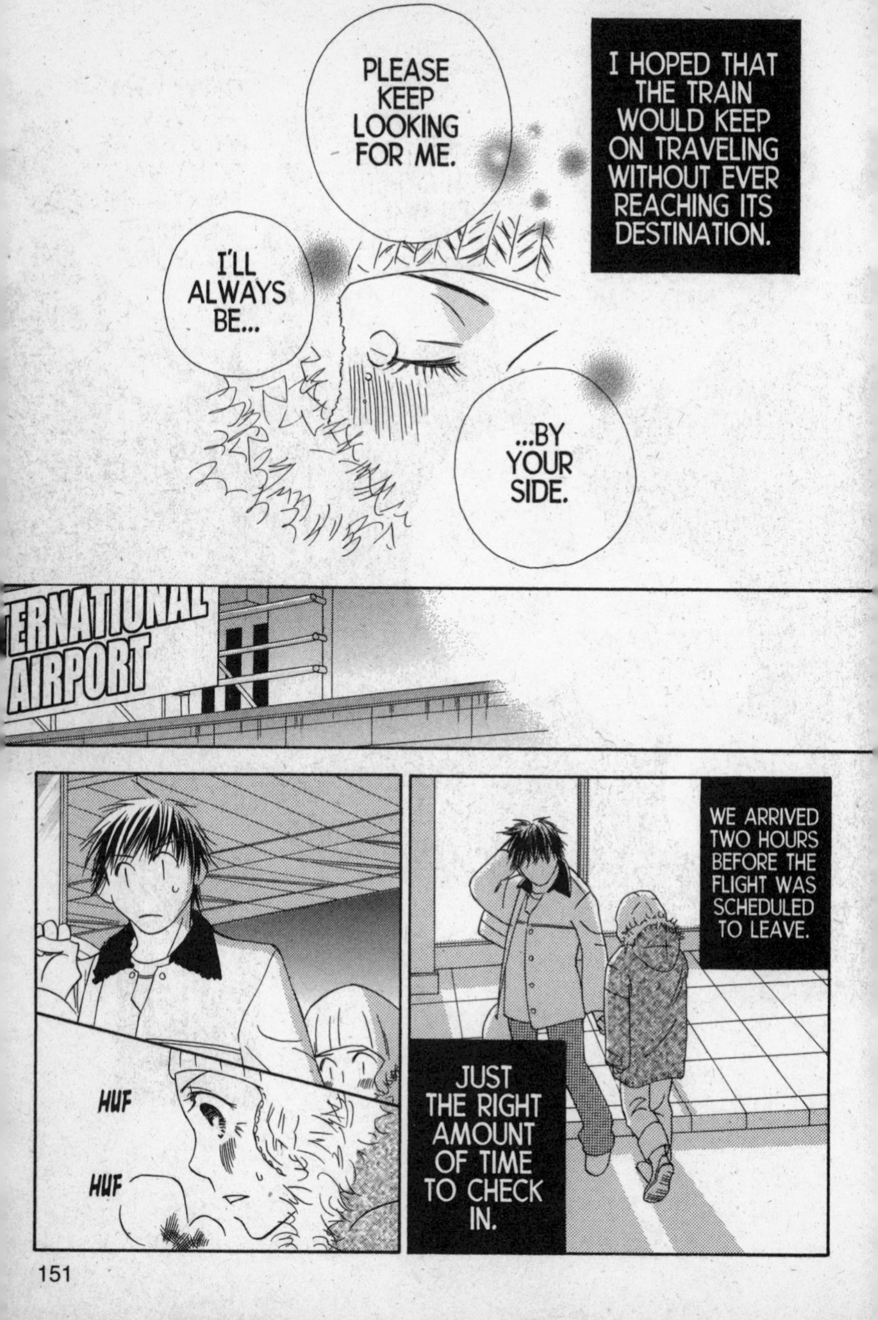
I HOPED THAT THE TRAIN WOULD KEEP ON TRAVELING WITHOUT EVER REACHING ITS DESTINATION.
PLEASE KEEP LOOKING FOR ME.
I'LL ALWAYS BE...
...BY YOUR SIDE.
ERNATIONAL AIRPORT
WE ARRIVED TWO HOURS BEFORE THE FLIGHT WAS SCHEDULED TO LEAVE.
JUST THE RIGHT AMOUNT OF TIME TO CHECK IN.
HUF
HUF

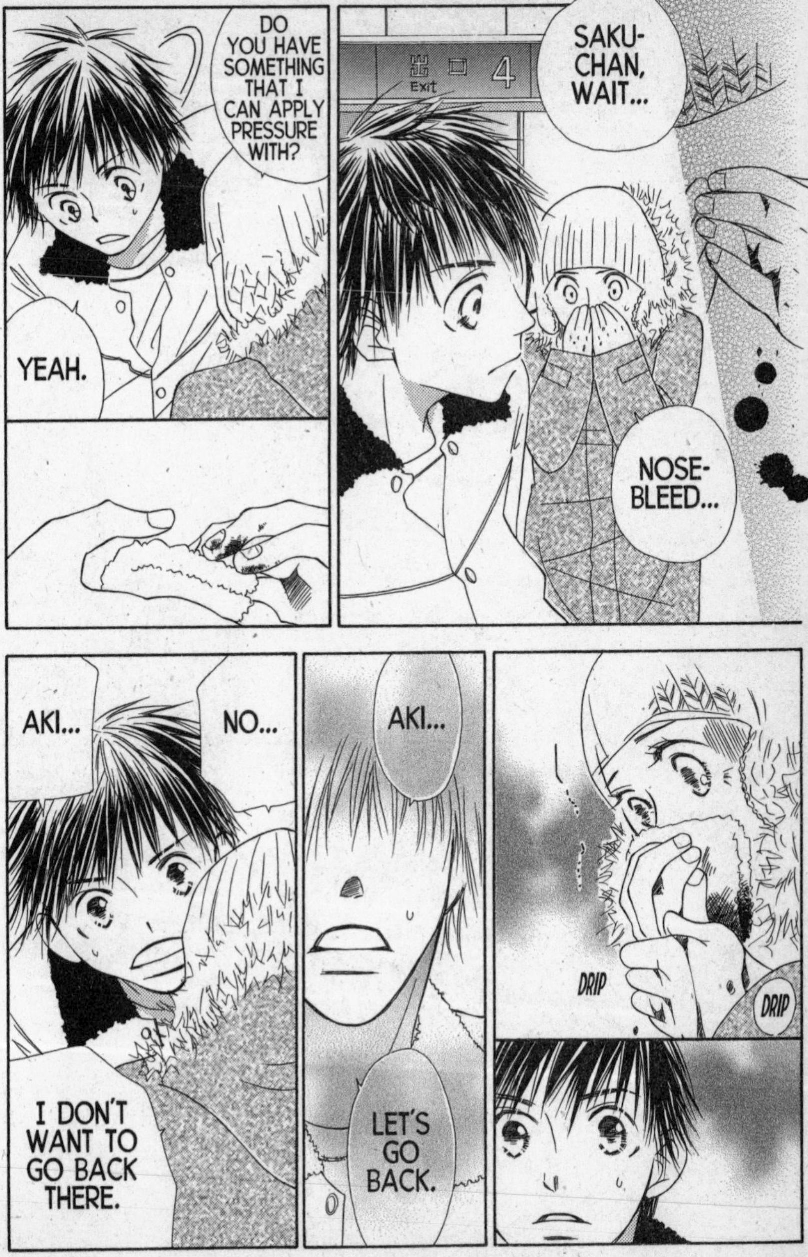
SAKU-CHAN, WAIT...
出口 4
Exit
NOSE-BLEED...
DO YOU HAVE SOMETHING THAT I CAN APPLY PRESSURE WITH?
YEAH.
DRIP
DRIP
AKI...
LET'S GO BACK.
NO...
AKI...
I DON'T WANT TO GO BACK THERE.

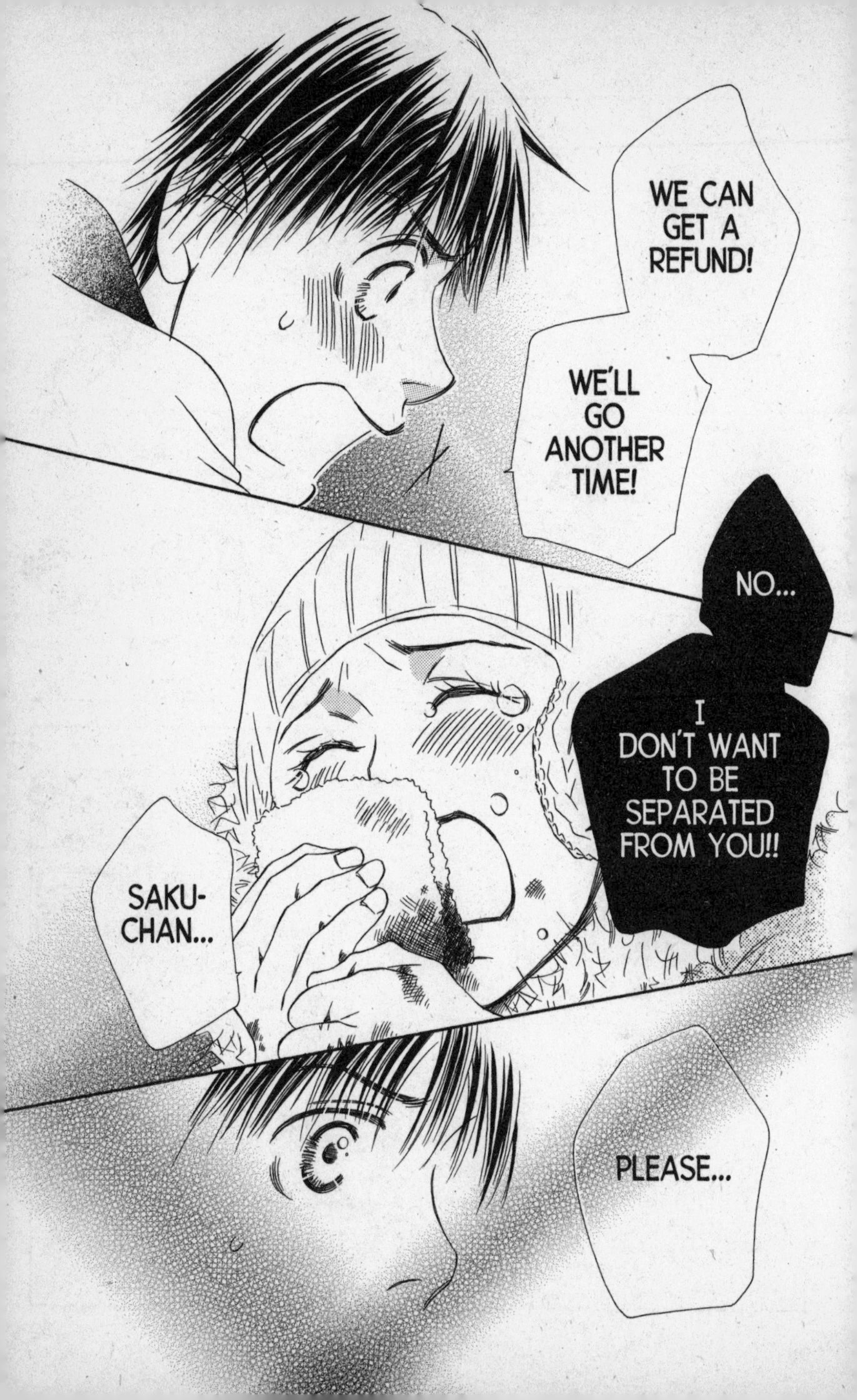
WE CAN GET A REFUND!
WE'LL GO ANOTHER TIME!
NO...
I DON'T WANT TO BE SEPARATED FROM YOU!!
SAKU-CHAN...
PLEASE...

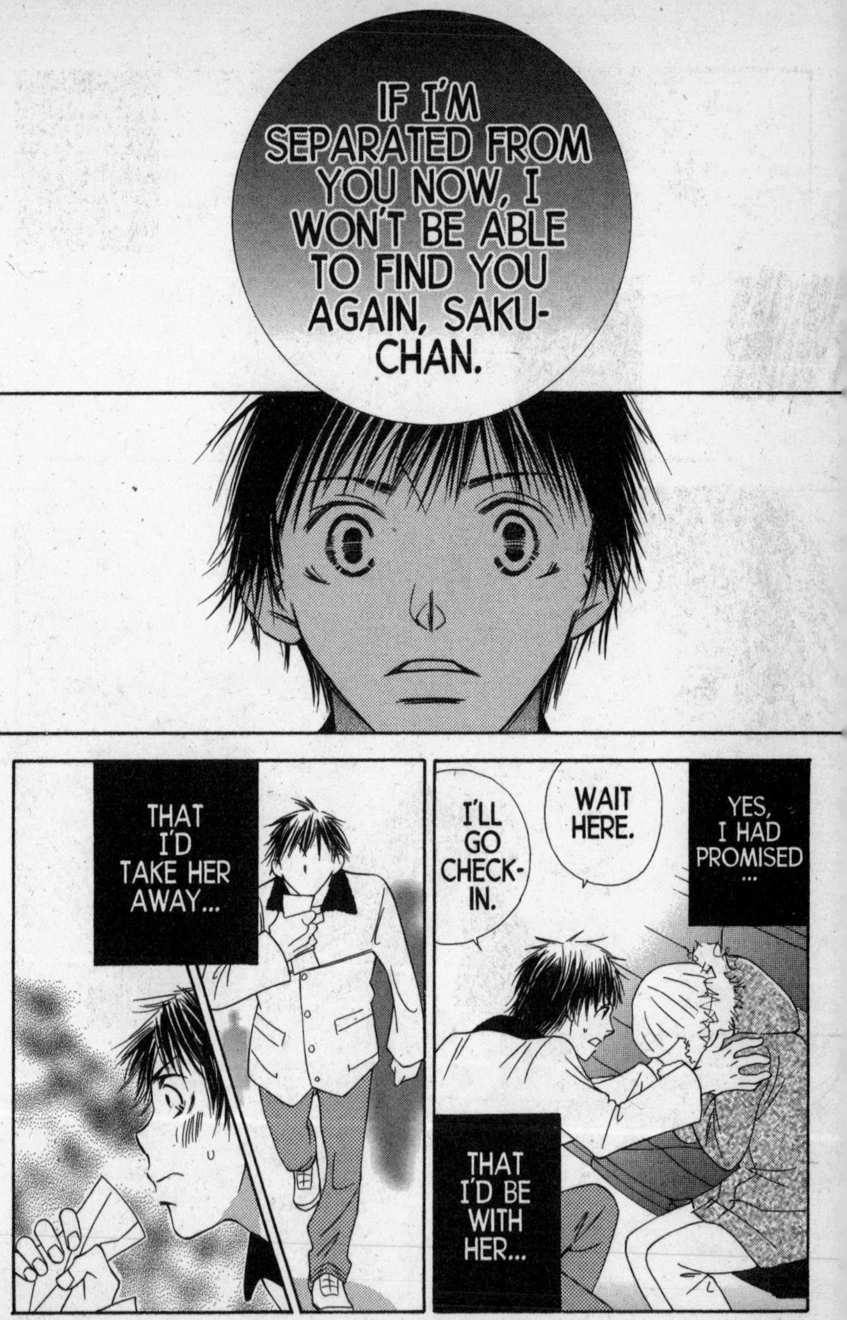
IF I'M SEPARATED FROM YOU NOW, I WON'T BE ABLE TO FIND YOU AGAIN, SAKU-CHAN.
YES, I HAD PROMISED ...
WAIT HERE.
I'LL GO CHECK-IN.
THAT I'D BE WITH HER...
THAT I'D TAKE HER AWAY...

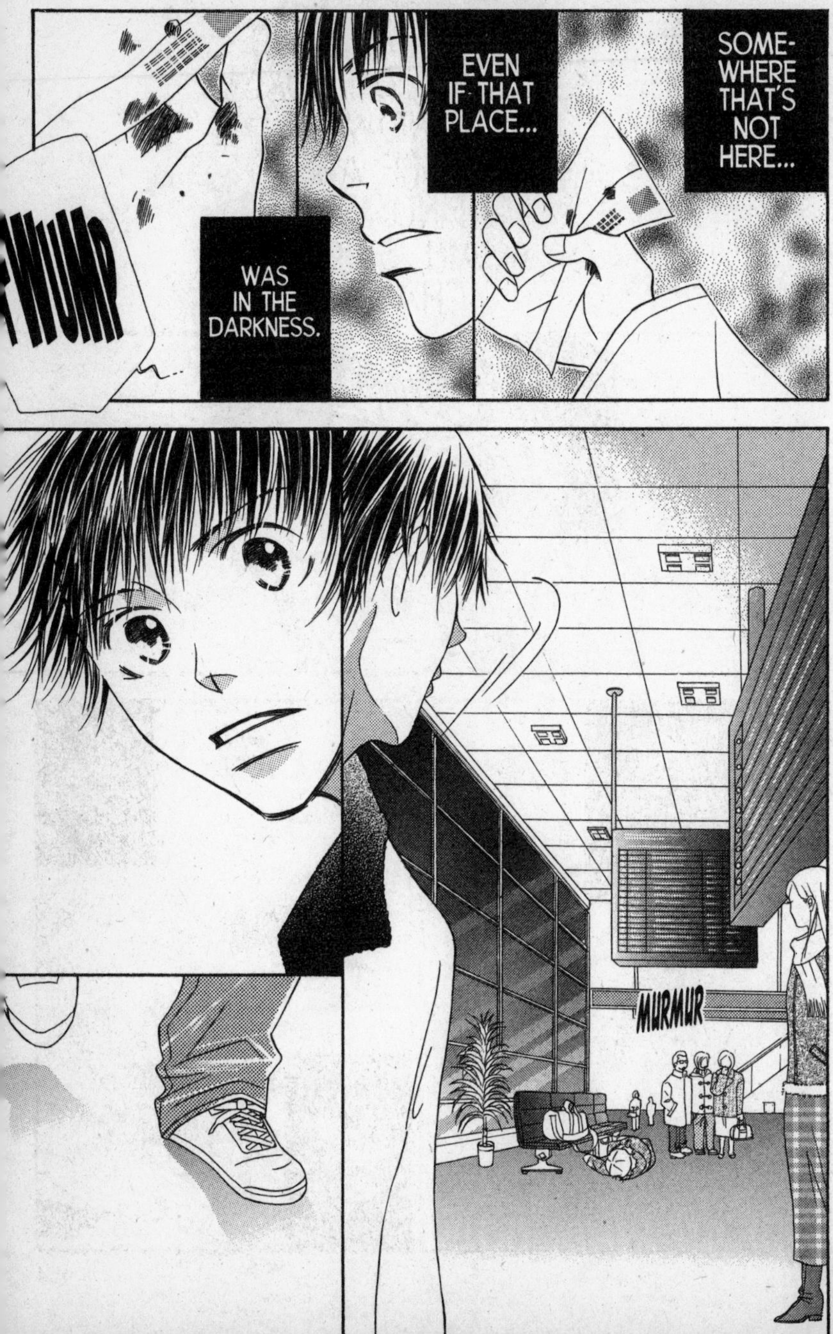
SOME-WHERE THAT'S NOT HERE...
EVEN IF THAT PLACE...
WAS IN THE DARKNESS.
HWUMP
MURMUR

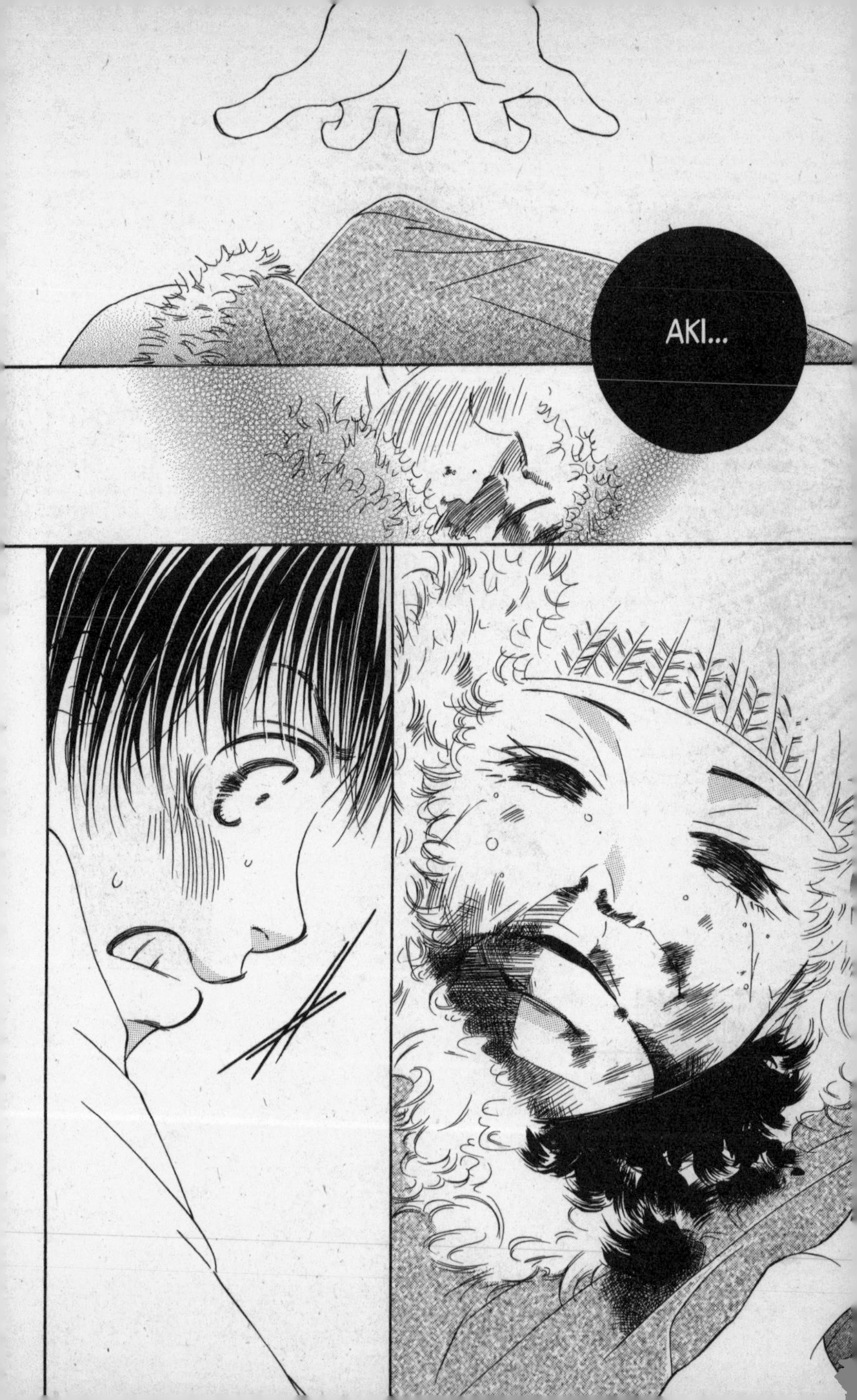
AKI...

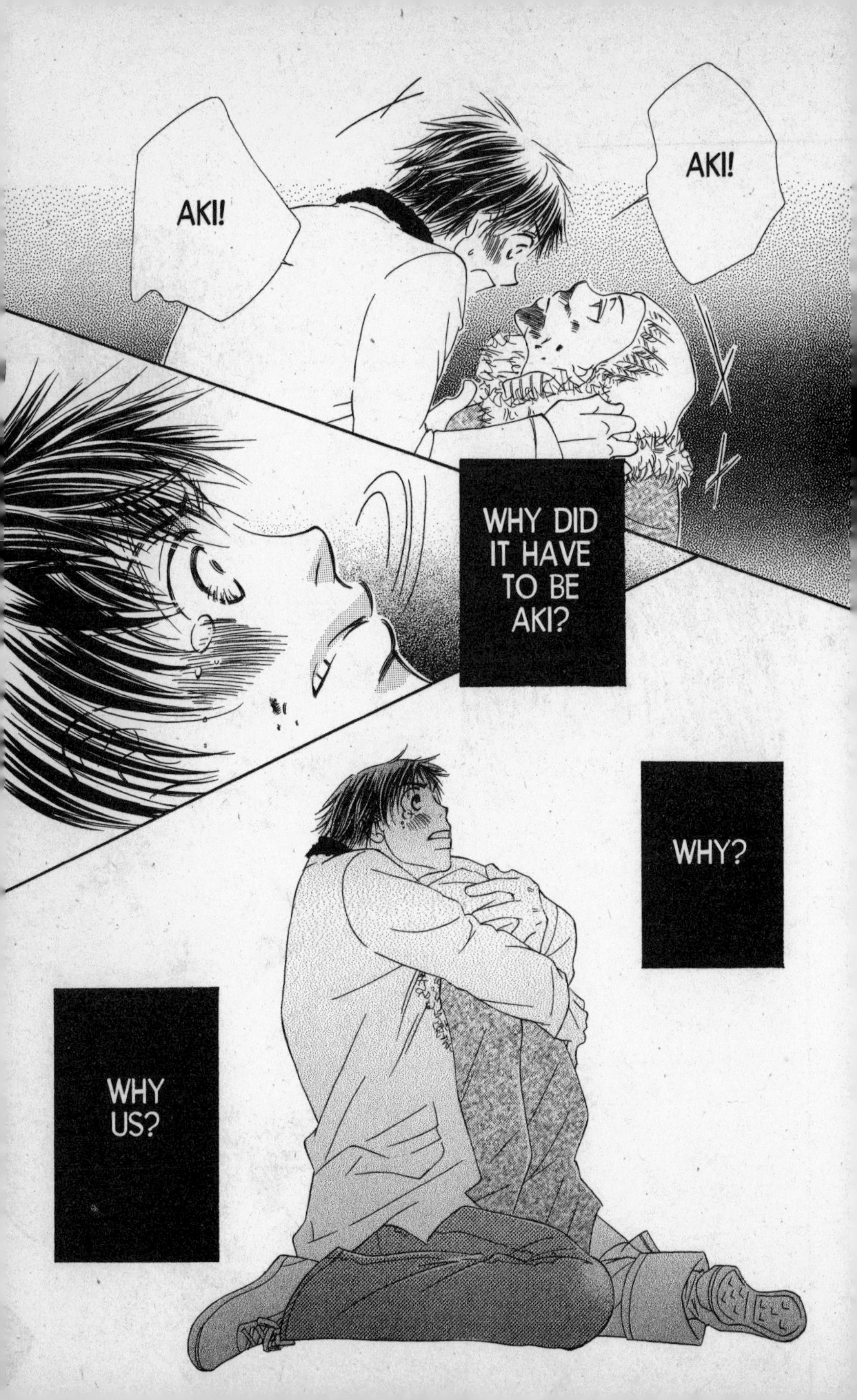
AKI!
AKI!
WHY DID IT HAVE TO BE AKI?
WHY?
WHY US?

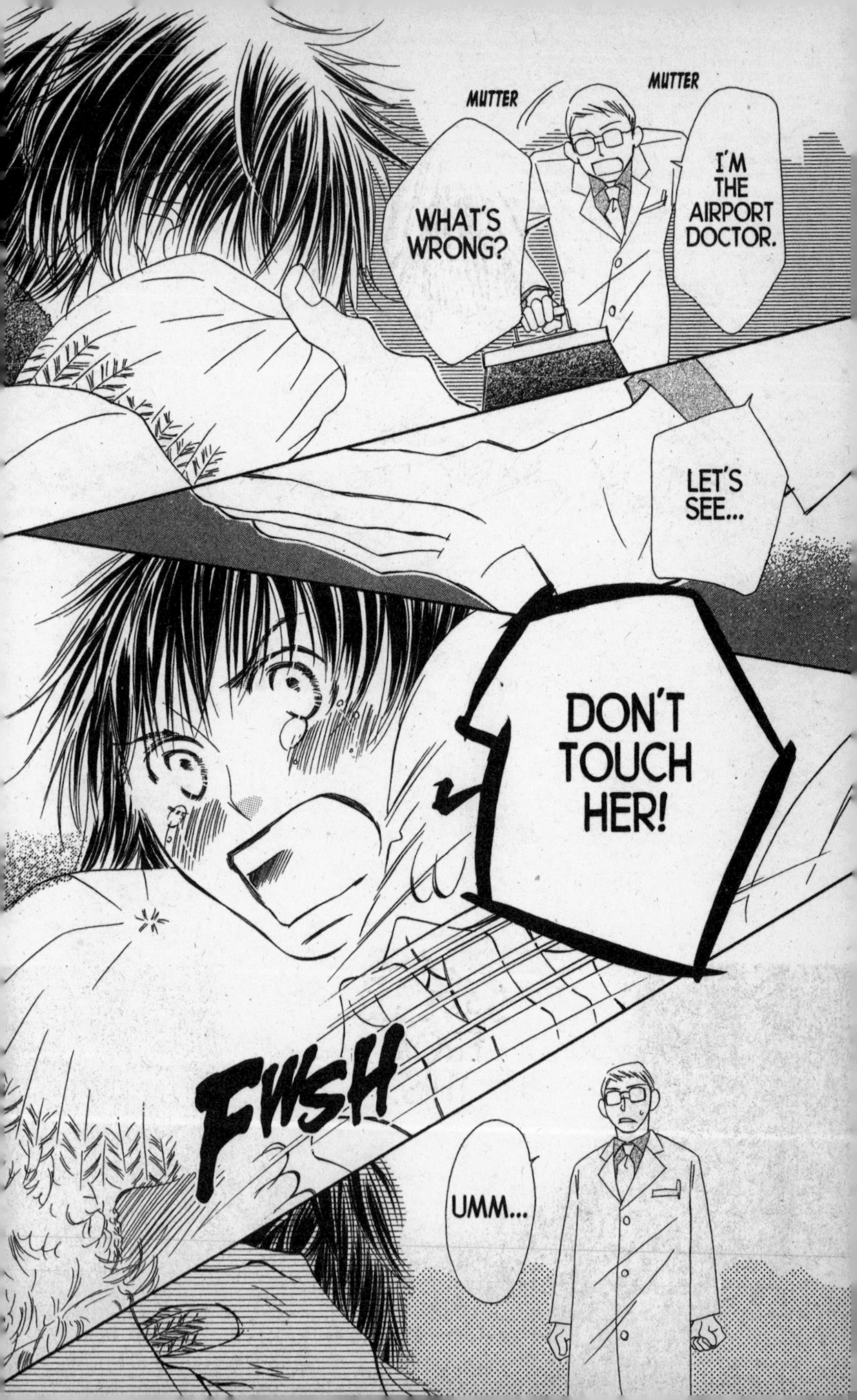
MUTTER
I'M THE AIRPORT DOCTOR.
MUTTER
WHAT'S WRONG?
LET'S SEE...
DON'T TOUCH HER!
FWSH
UMM...

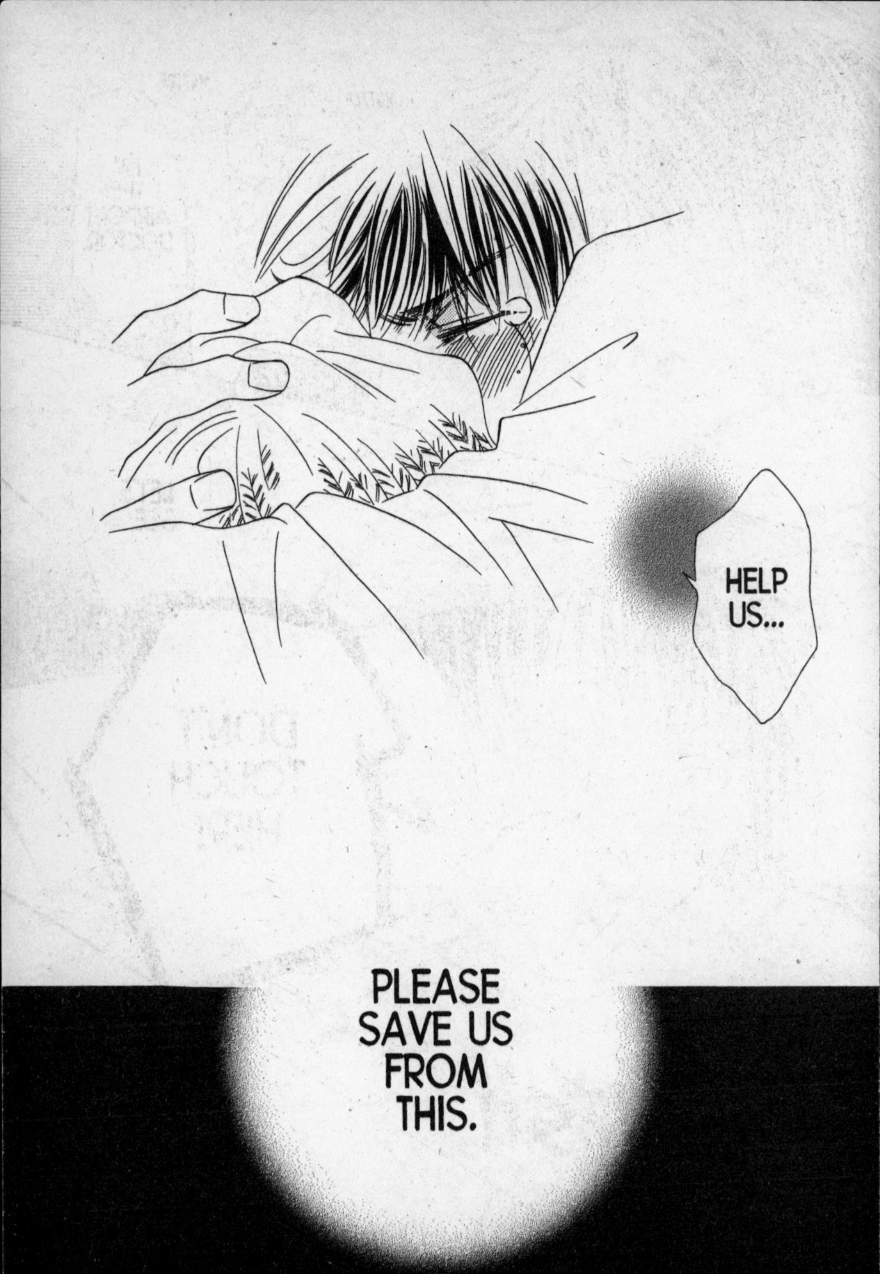
HELP US...
PLEASE SAVE US FROM THIS.

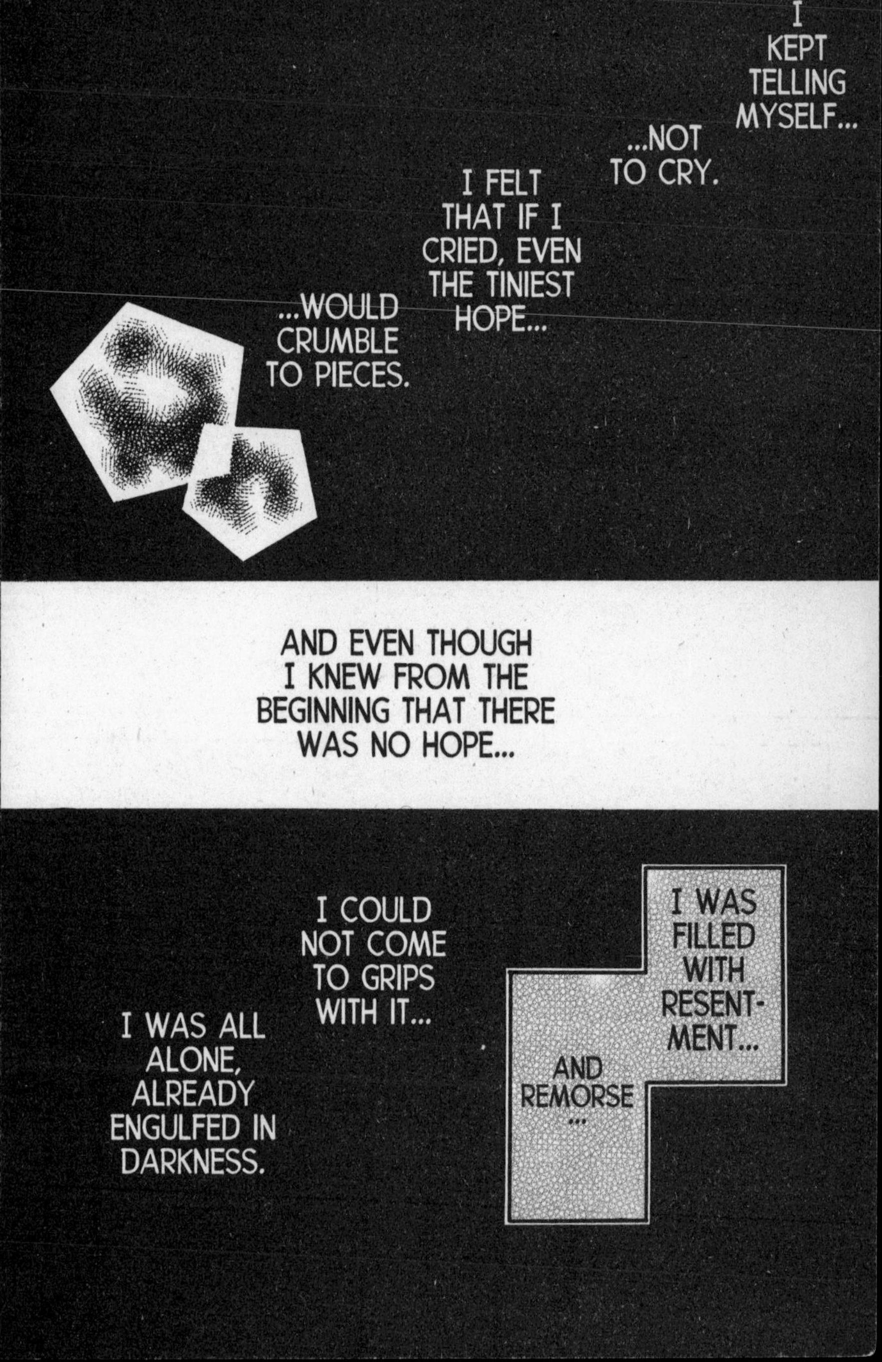
I KEPT TELLING MYSELF...
...NOT TO CRY.
I FELT THAT IF I CRIED, EVEN THE TINIEST HOPE...
...WOULD CRUMBLE TO PIECES.
AND EVEN THOUGH I KNEW FROM THE BEGINNING THAT THERE WAS NO HOPE...
I WAS FILLED WITH RESENT-MENT...
AND REMORSE...
I COULD NOT COME TO GRIPS WITH IT...
I WAS ALL ALONE, ALREADY ENGULFED IN DARKNESS.

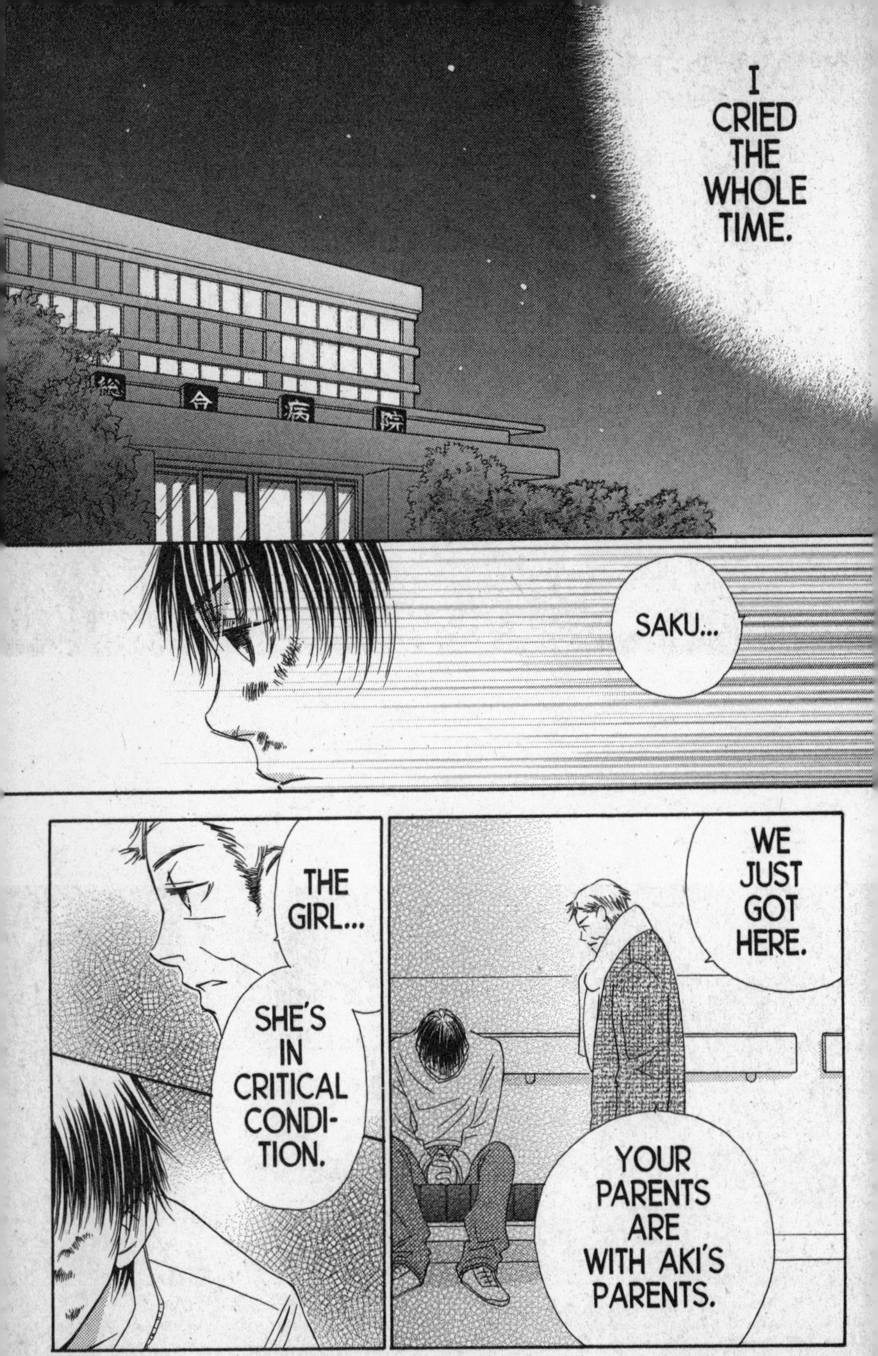
I CRIED THE WHOLE TIME.
総合病院
SAKU...
WE JUST GOT HERE.
YOUR PARENTS ARE WITH AKI'S PARENTS.
THE GIRL...
SHE'S IN CRITICAL CONDI-TION.

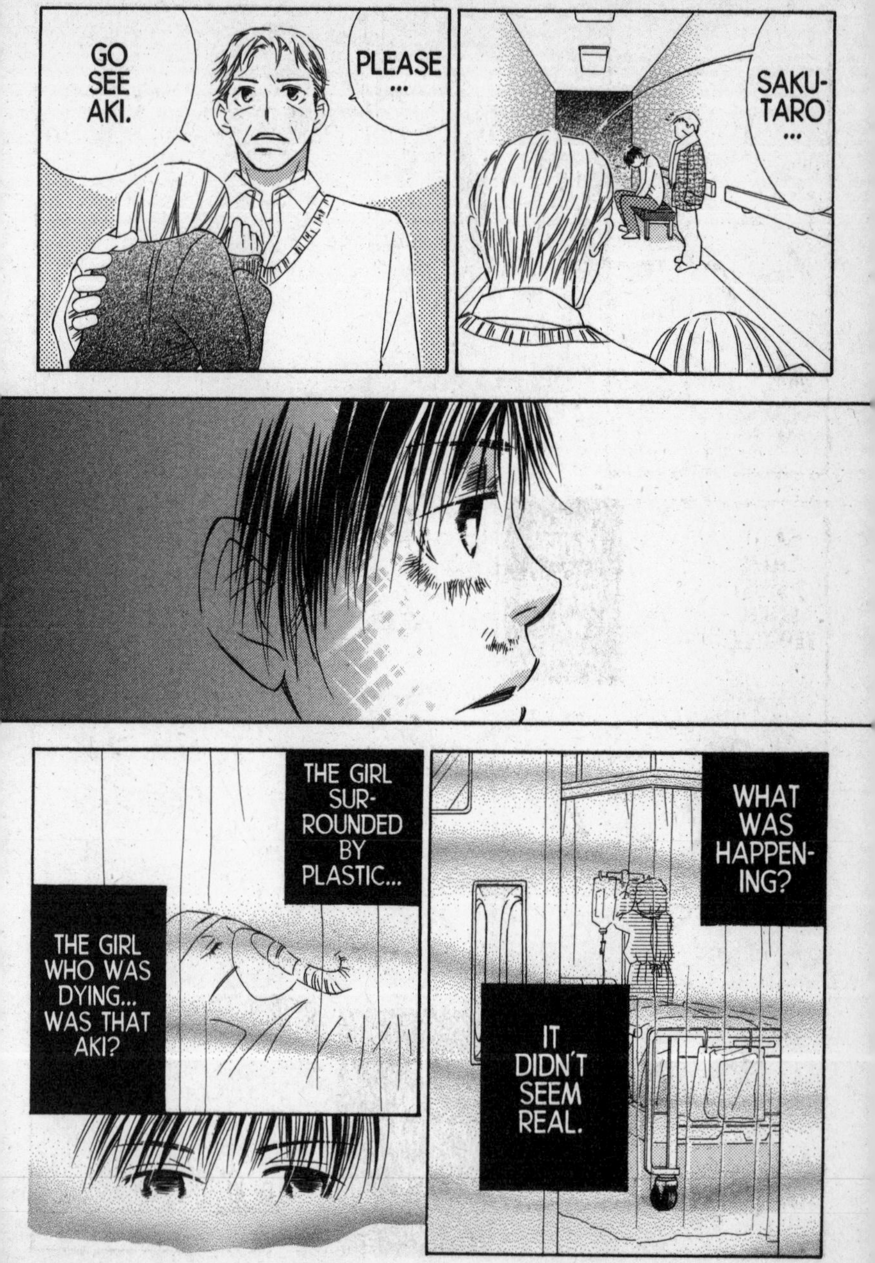
SAKUTARO...
PLEASE...
GO SEE AKI.
WHAT WAS HAPPENING?
IT DIDN'T SEEM REAL.
THE GIRL SURROUNDED BY PLASTIC...
THE GIRL WHO WAS DYING... WAS THAT AKI?

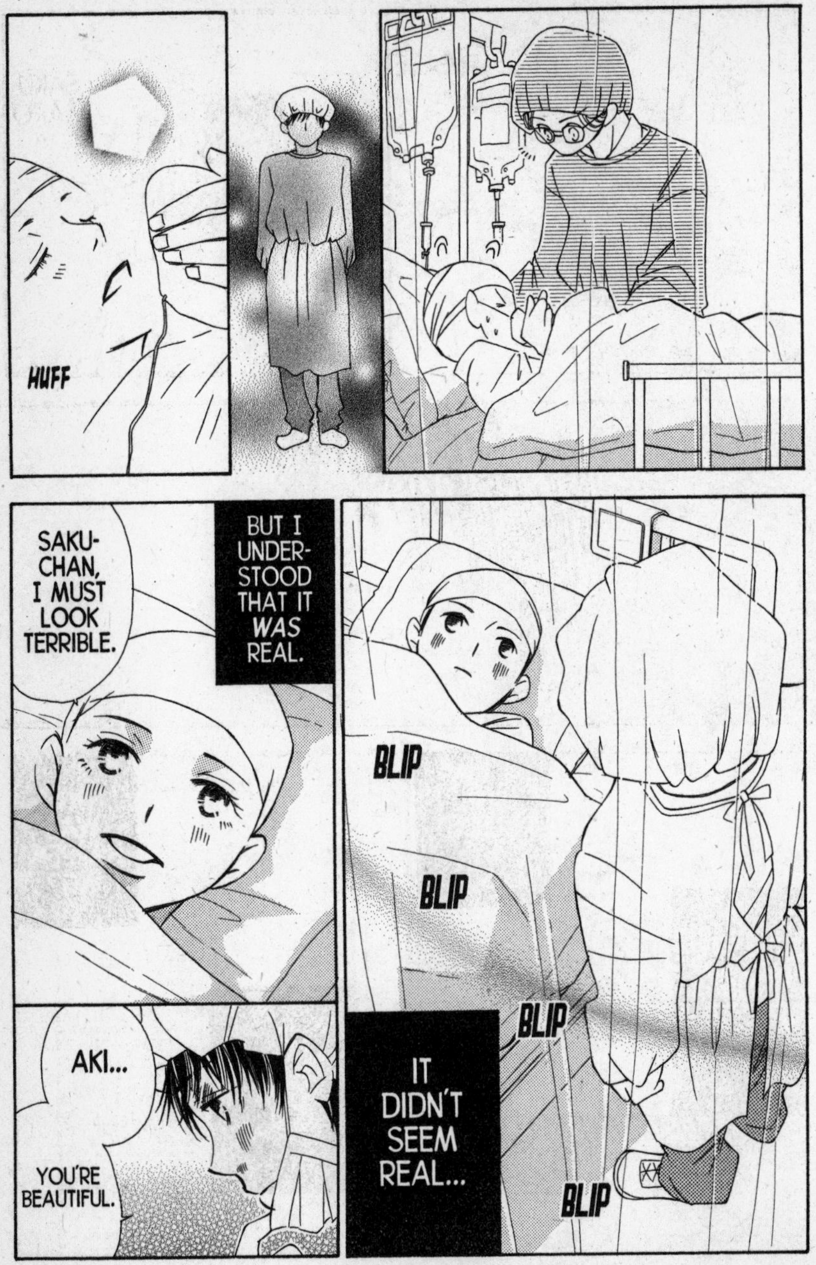
HUFF
BLIP
BLIP
BLIP
IT DIDN'T SEEM REAL...
BLIP
BUT I UNDER-STOOD THAT IT *WAS* REAL.
SAKU-CHAN, I MUST LOOK TERRIBLE.
AKI...
YOU'RE BEAUTIFUL.

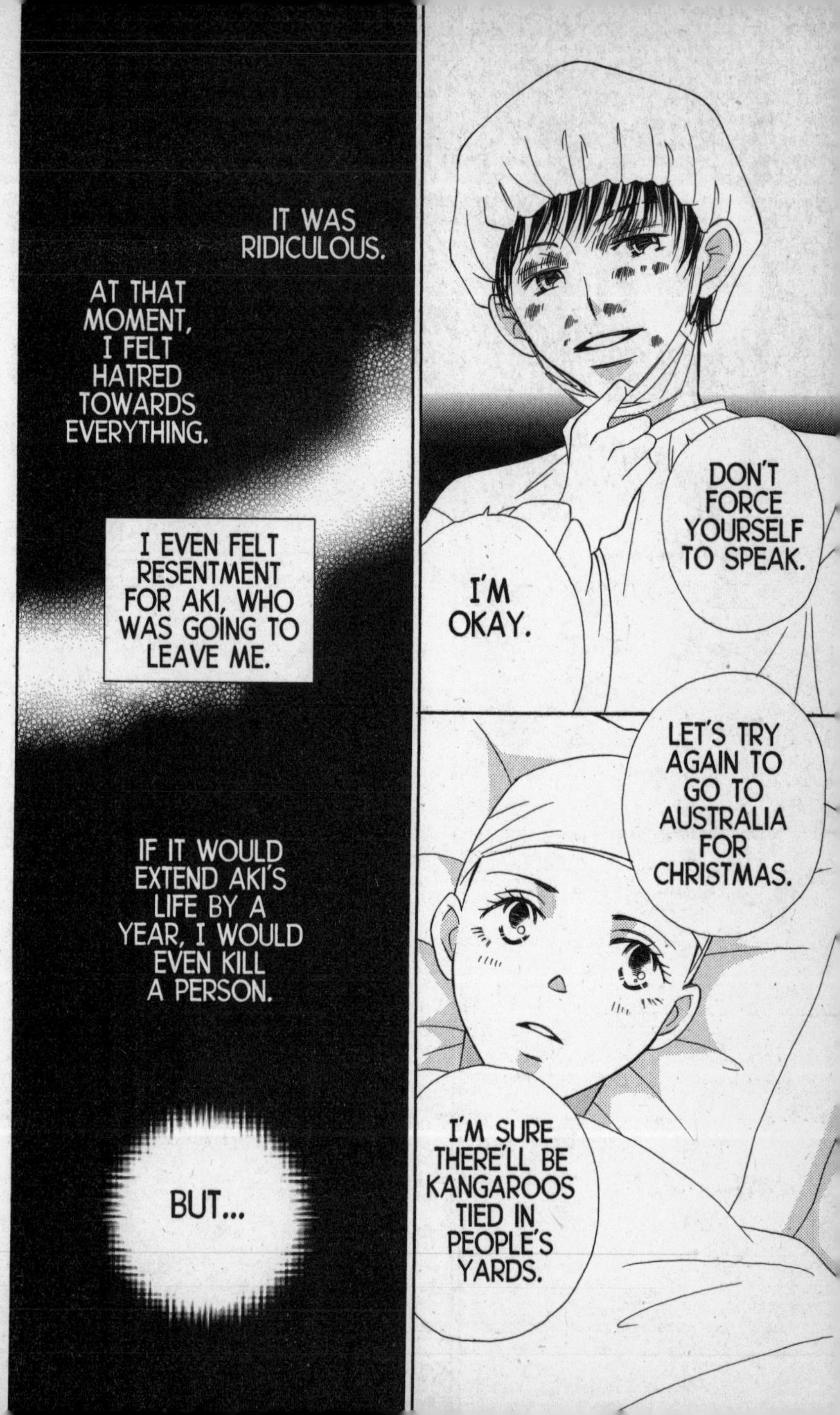
DON'T FORCE YOURSELF TO SPEAK.
I'M OKAY.
LET'S TRY AGAIN TO GO TO AUSTRALIA FOR CHRISTMAS.
I'M SURE THERE'LL BE KANGAROOS TIED IN PEOPLE'S YARDS.
IT WAS RIDICULOUS.
AT THAT MOMENT, I FELT HATRED TOWARDS EVERYTHING.
I EVEN FELT RESENTMENT FOR AKI, WHO WAS GOING TO LEAVE ME.
IF IT WOULD EXTEND AKI'S LIFE BY A YEAR, I WOULD EVEN KILL A PERSON.
BUT...

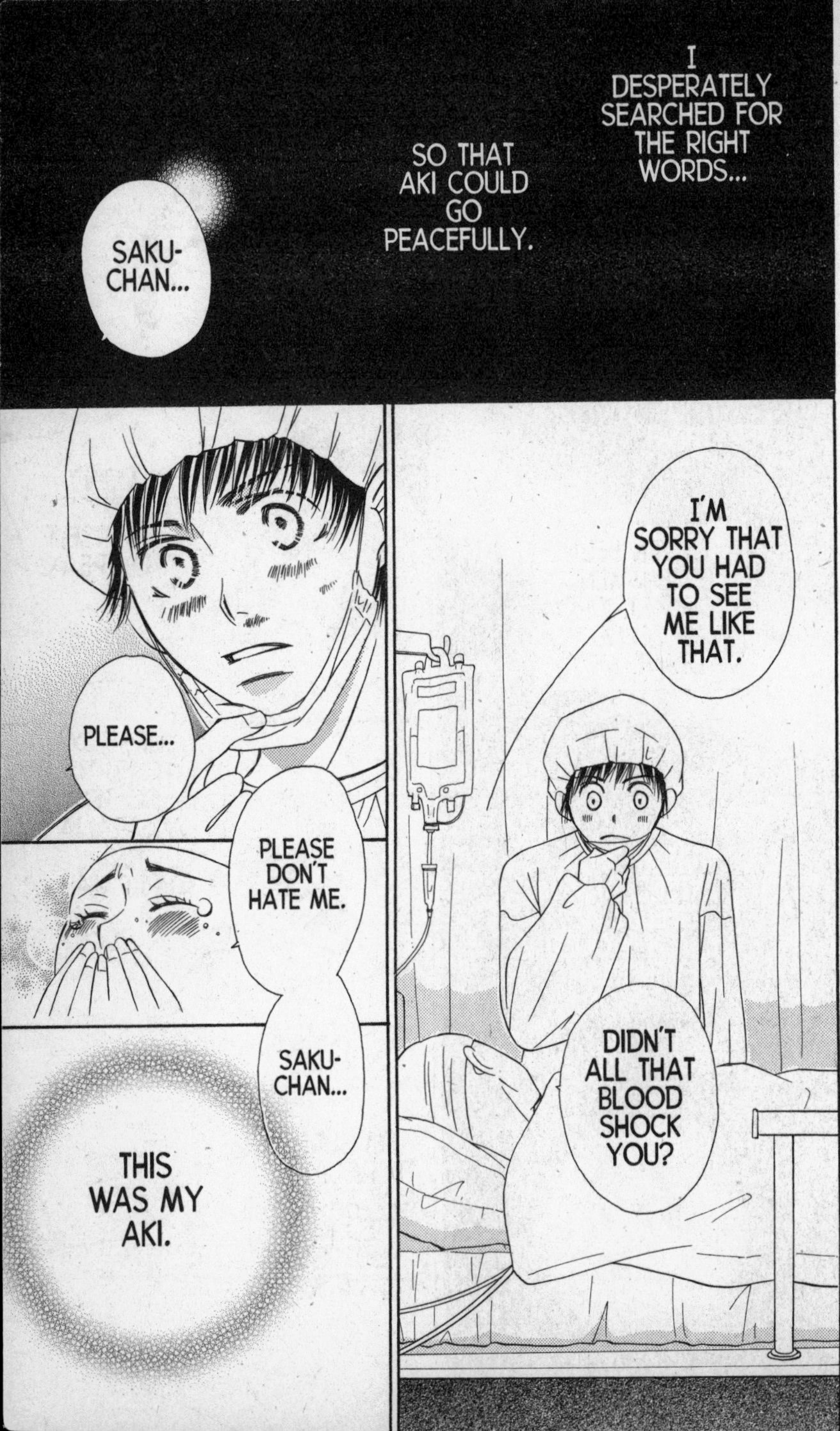
I DESPERATELY SEARCHED FOR THE RIGHT WORDS...
SO THAT AKI COULD GO PEACEFULLY.
SAKU-CHAN...
I'M SORRY THAT YOU HAD TO SEE ME LIKE THAT.
DIDN'T ALL THAT BLOOD SHOCK YOU?
PLEASE...
PLEASE DON'T HATE ME.
SAKU-CHAN...
THIS WAS MY AKI.

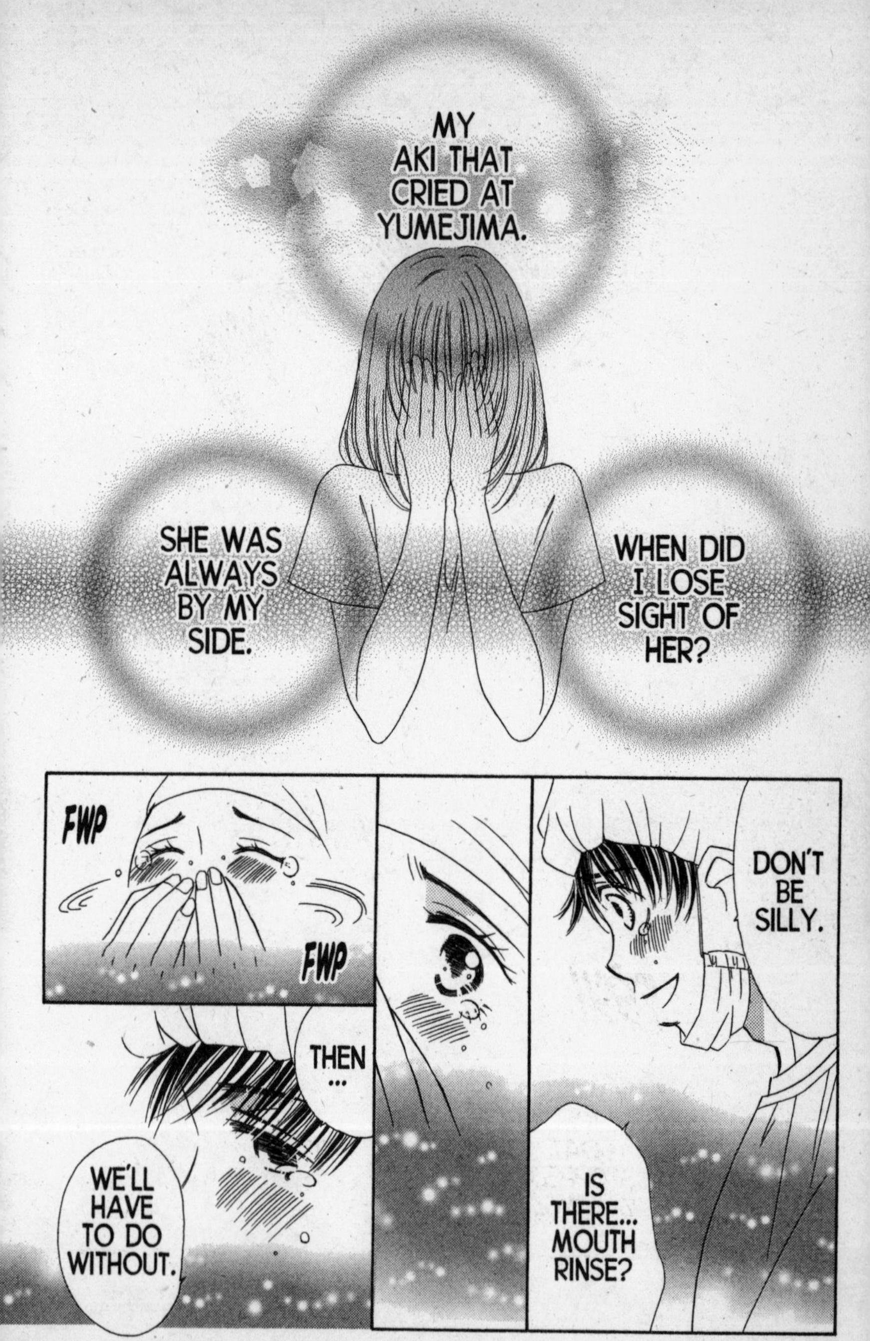
MY AKI THAT CRIED AT YUMEJIMA.
WHEN DID I LOSE SIGHT OF HER?
SHE WAS ALWAYS BY MY SIDE.
DON'T BE SILLY.
IS THERE... MOUTH RINSE?
FWP
FWP
THEN...
WE'LL HAVE TO DO WITHOUT.

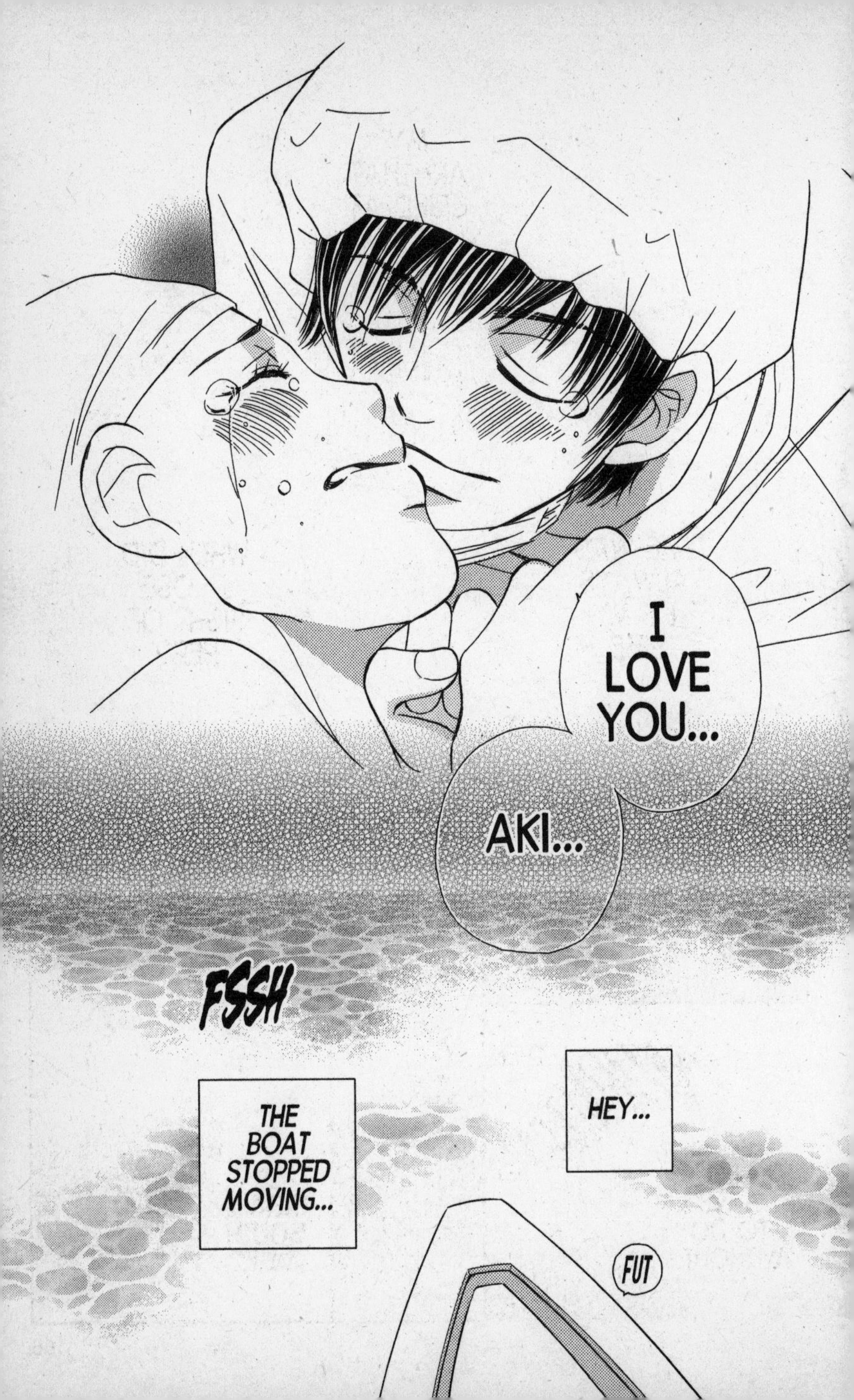
I LOVE YOU...
AKI...
FSSH
HEY...
THE BOAT STOPPED MOVING...
FUT

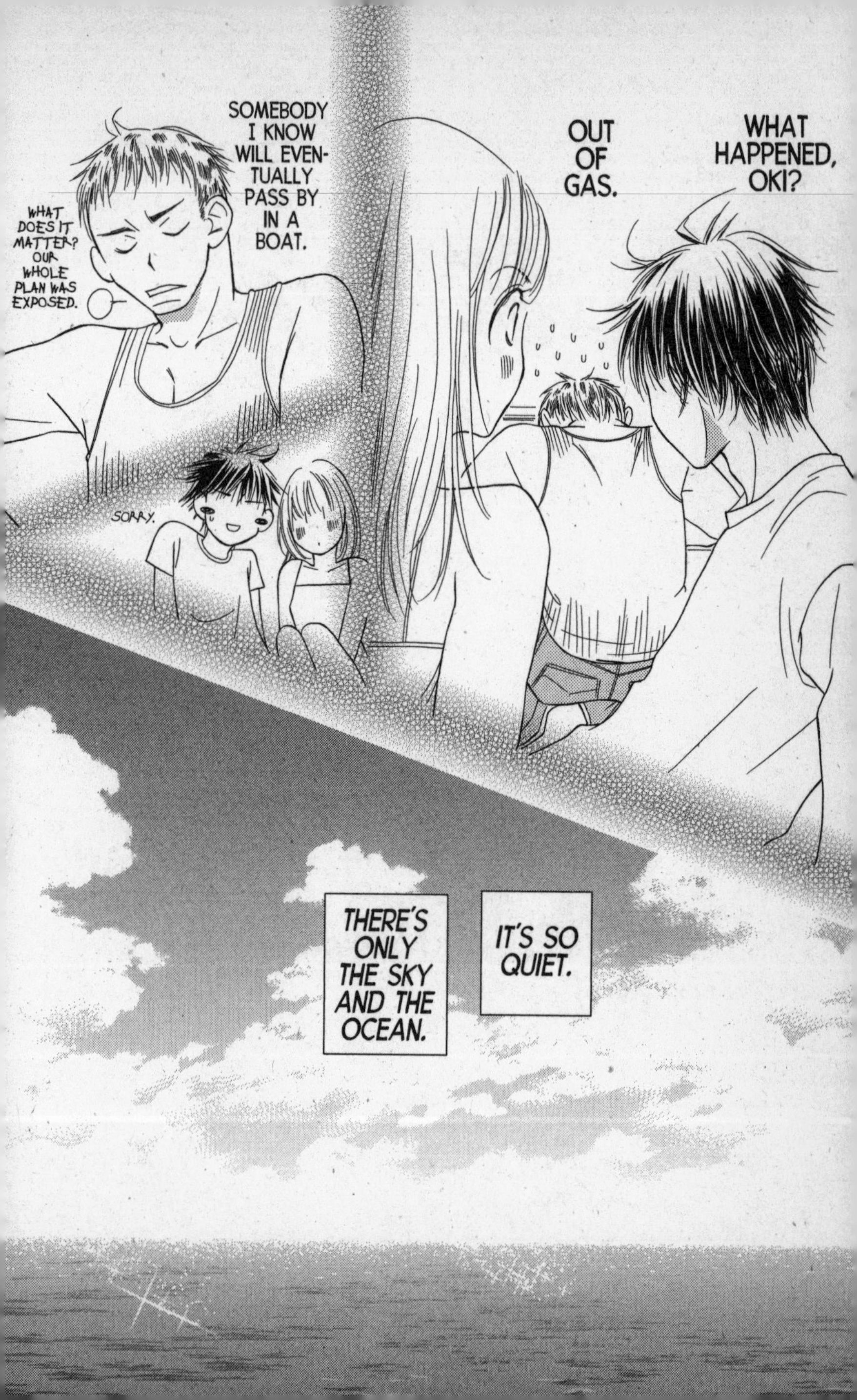
WHAT HAPPENED, OKI?
OUT OF GAS.
SOMEBODY I KNOW WILL EVENTUALLY PASS BY IN A BOAT.
WHAT DOES IT MATTER? OUR WHOLE PLAN WAS EXPOSED.
SORRY.
IT'S SO QUIET.
THERE'S ONLY THE SKY AND THE OCEAN.

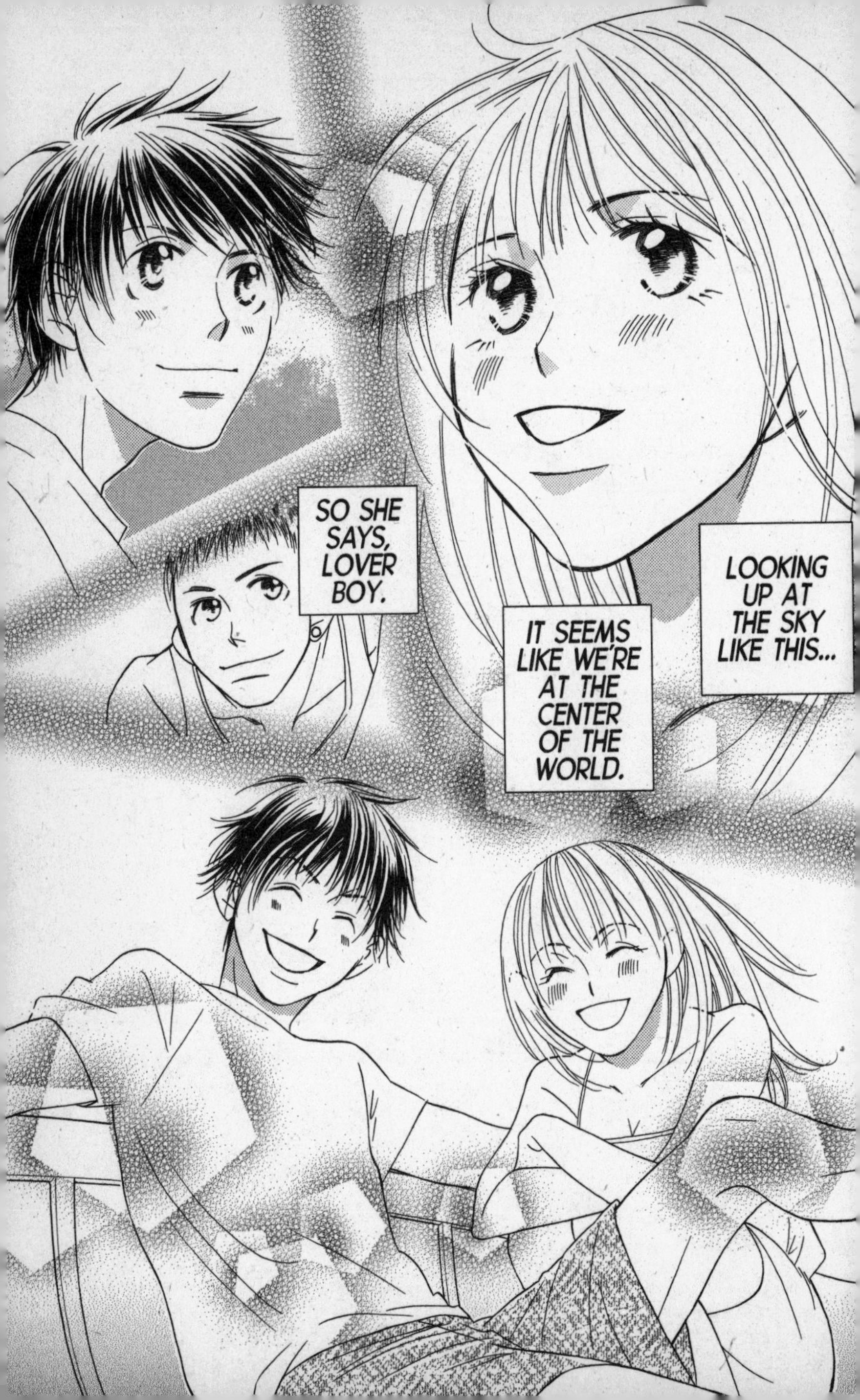
LOOKING UP AT THE SKY LIKE THIS...
IT SEEMS LIKE WE'RE AT THE CENTER OF THE WORLD.
SO SHE SAYS, LOVER BOY.

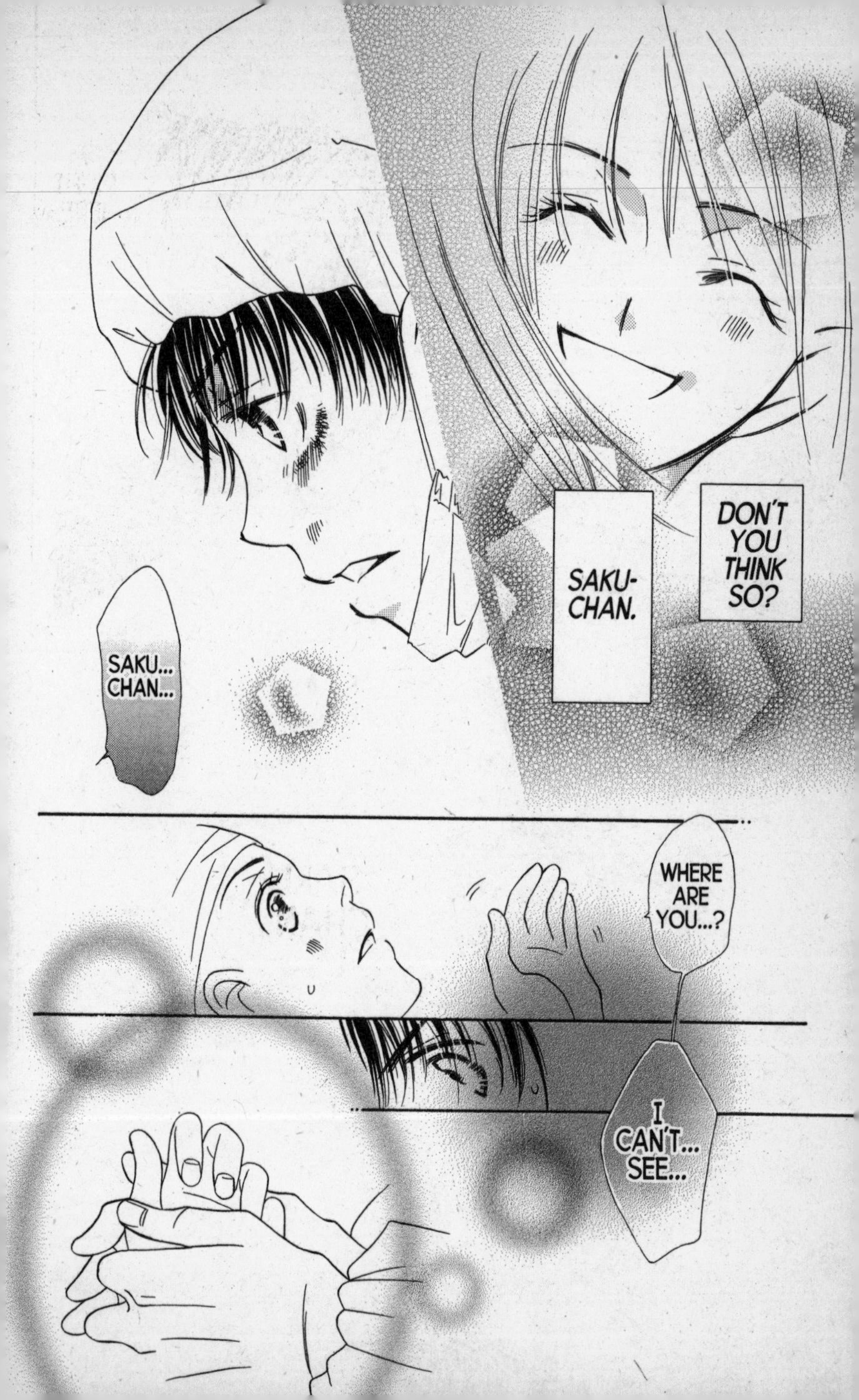
DON'T YOU THINK SO?
SAKU-CHAN.
SAKU... CHAN...
WHERE ARE YOU...?
I CAN'T... SEE...

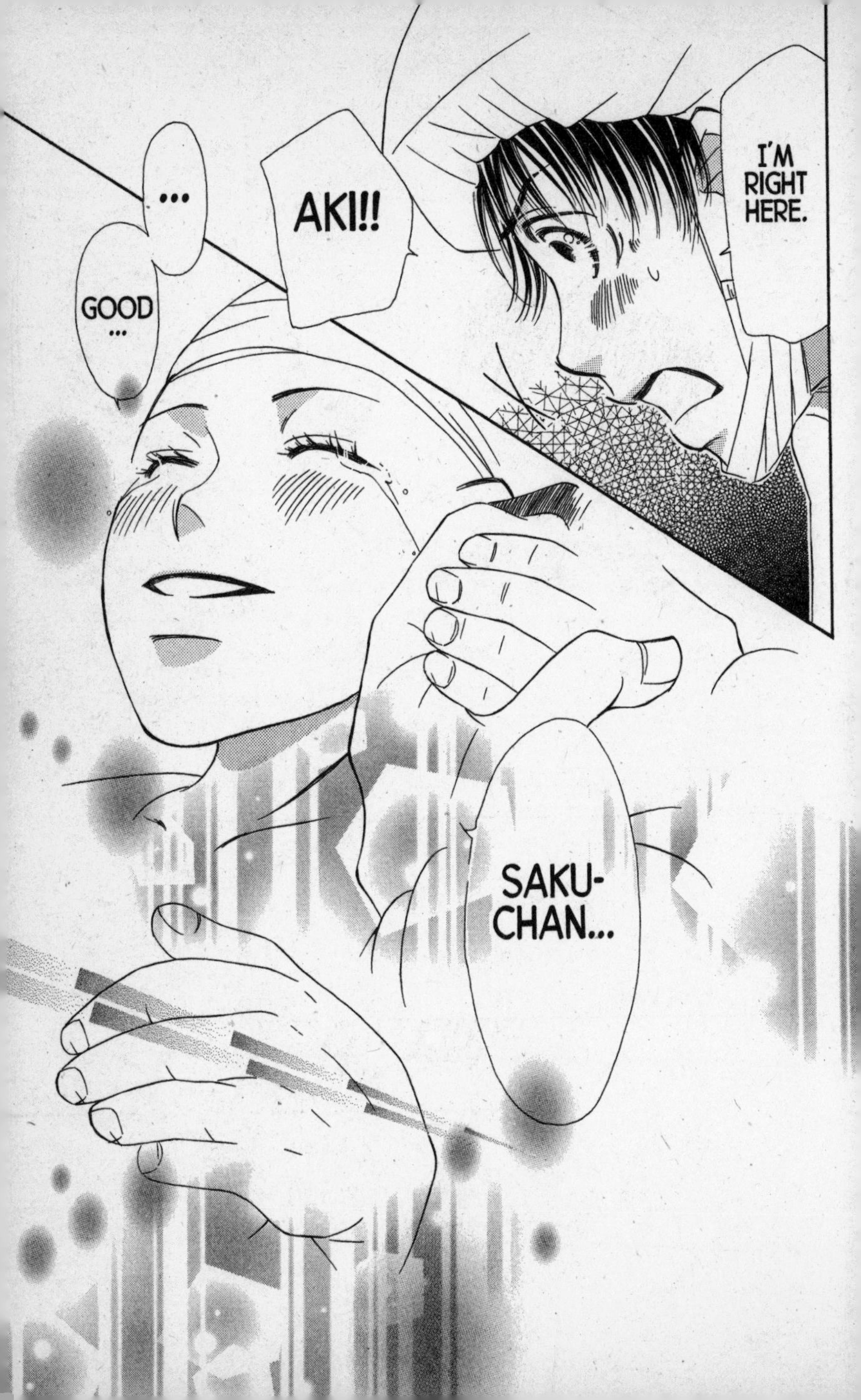
I'M RIGHT HERE.
AKI!!
...
GOOD ...
SAKU-CHAN...

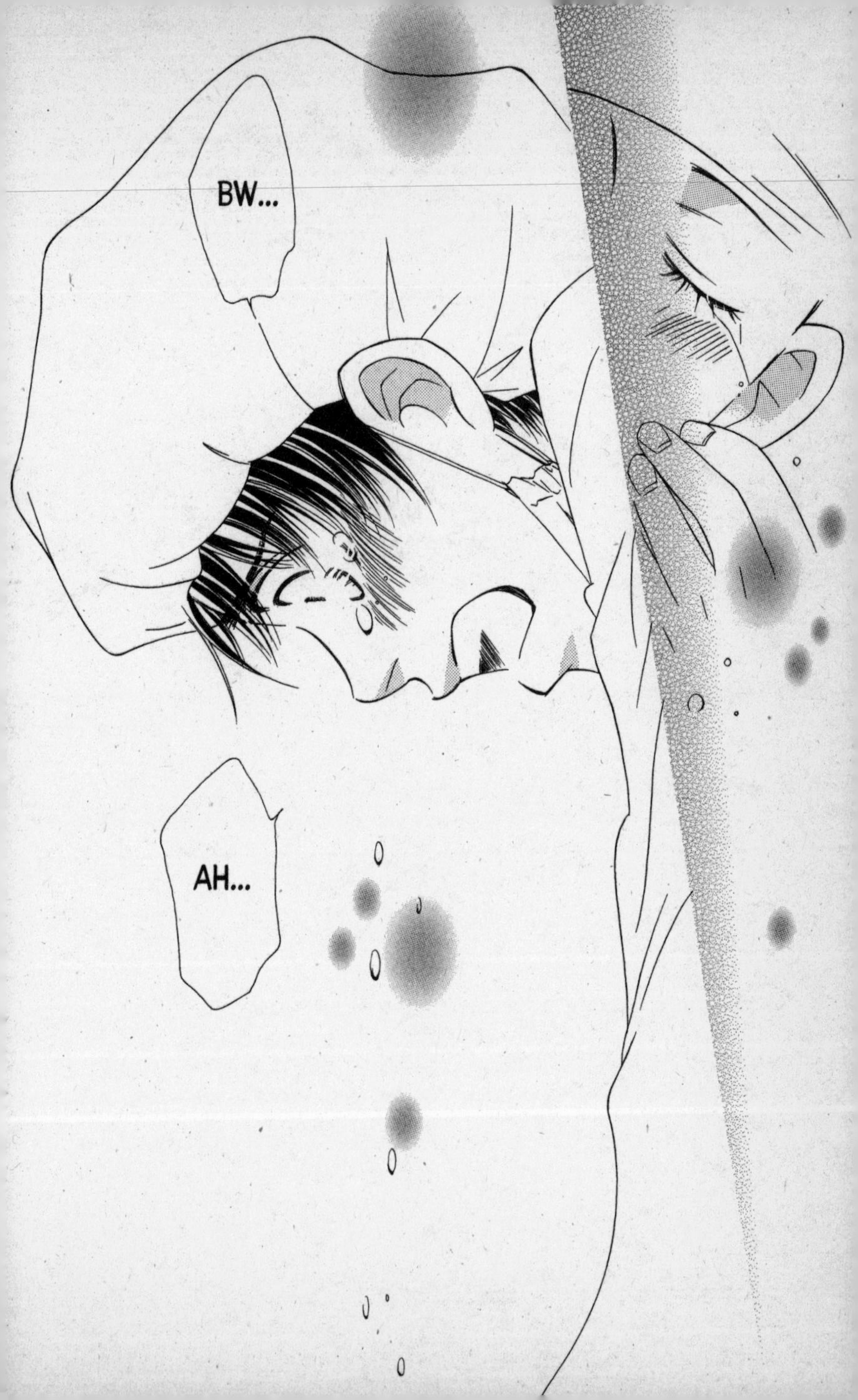
BW...
AH...

I SHOUTED
AT THE TOP
OF MY LUNGS,
BUT COULD
NOT MAKE
A SOUND.

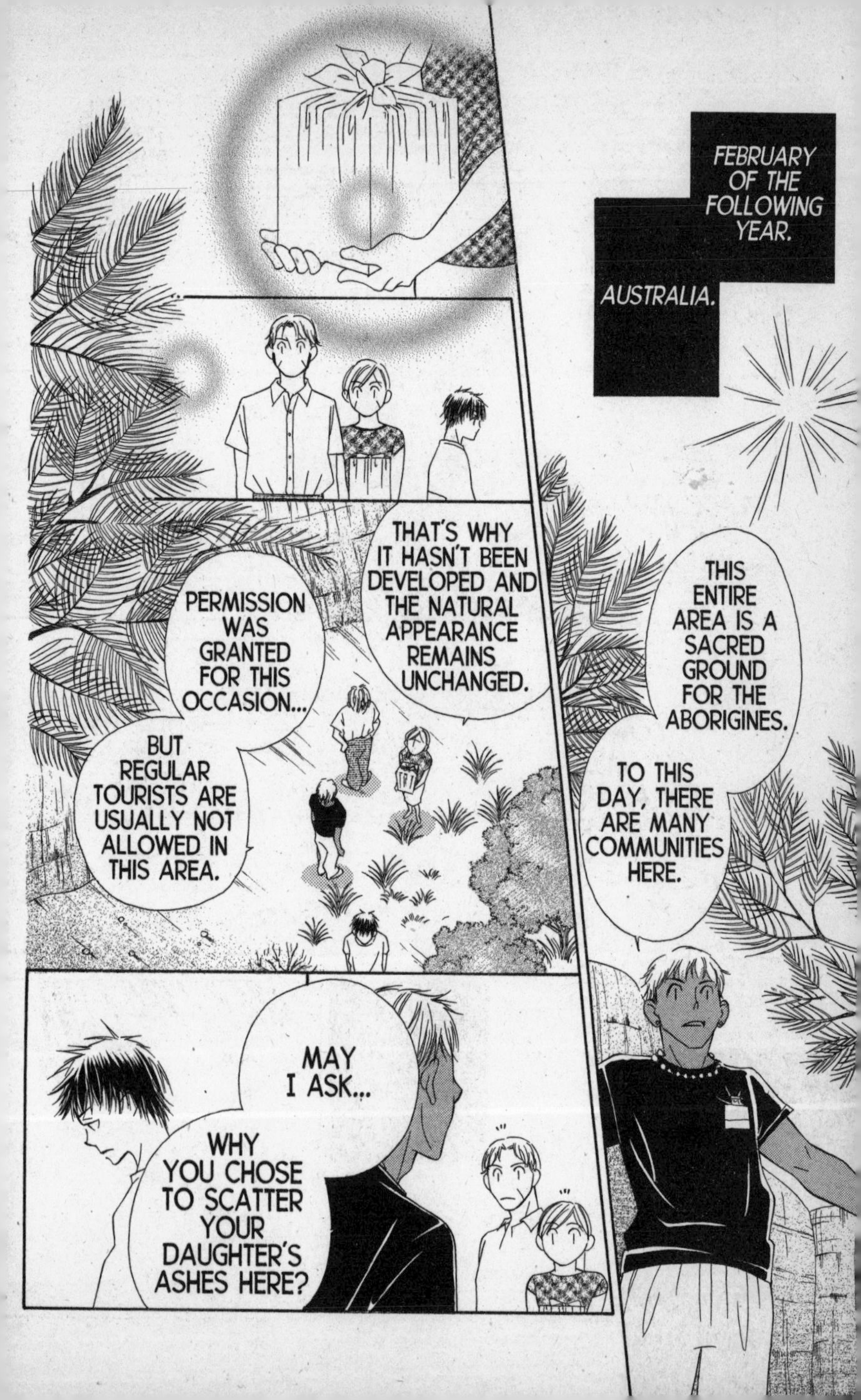

FEBRUARY OF THE FOLLOWING YEAR.
AUSTRALIA.
THIS ENTIRE AREA IS A SACRED GROUND FOR THE ABORIGINES.
TO THIS DAY, THERE ARE MANY COMMUNITIES HERE.
PERMISSION WAS GRANTED FOR THIS OCCASION...
BUT REGULAR TOURISTS ARE USUALLY NOT ALLOWED IN THIS AREA.
THAT'S WHY IT HASN'T BEEN DEVELOPED AND THE NATURAL APPEARANCE REMAINS UNCHANGED.
MAY I ASK...
WHY YOU CHOSE TO SCATTER YOUR DAUGHTER'S ASHES HERE?

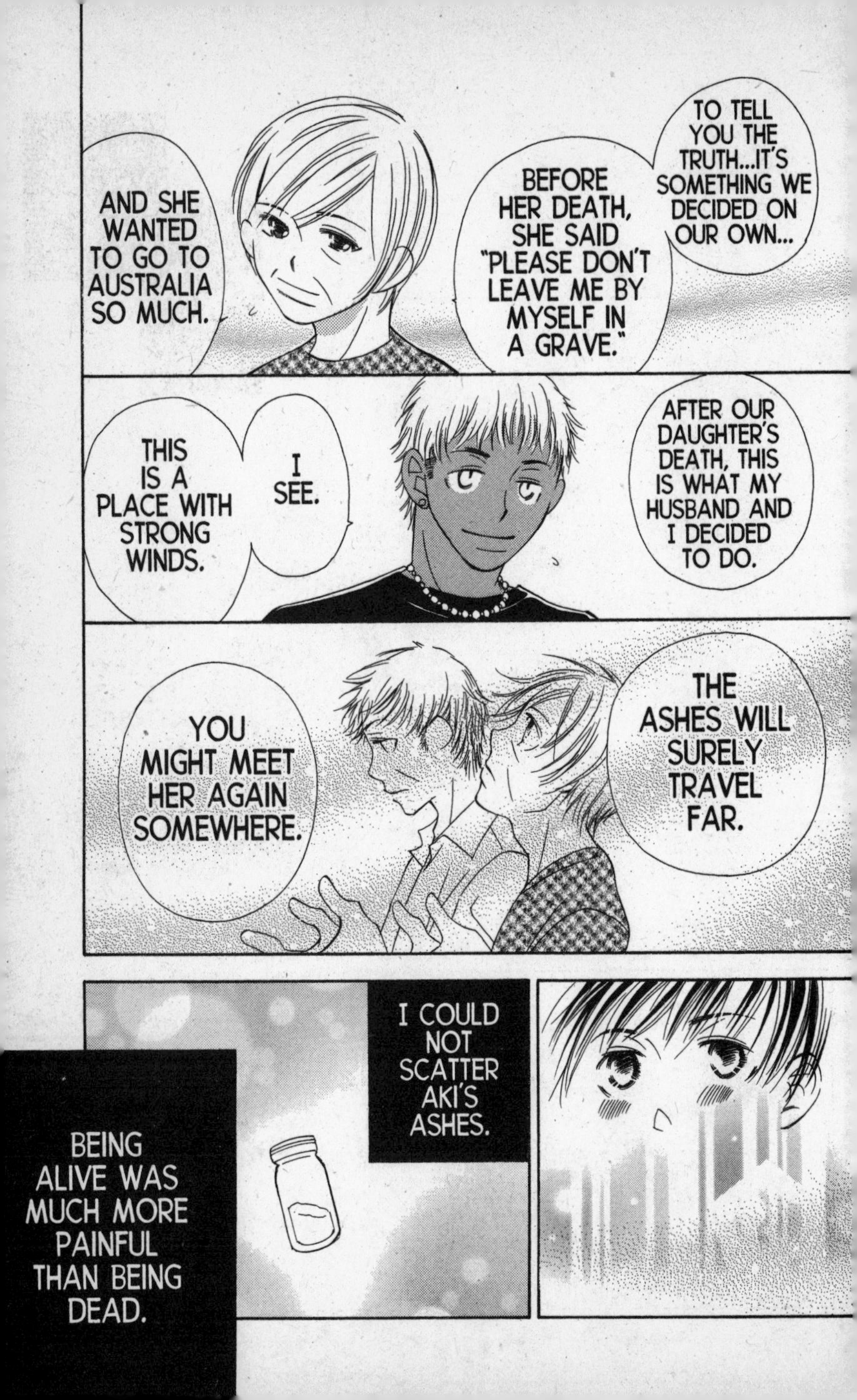
TO TELL YOU THE TRUTH...IT'S SOMETHING WE DECIDED ON OUR OWN...
BEFORE HER DEATH, SHE SAID "PLEASE DON'T LEAVE ME BY MYSELF IN A GRAVE."
AND SHE WANTED TO GO TO AUSTRALIA SO MUCH.
AFTER OUR DAUGHTER'S DEATH, THIS IS WHAT MY HUSBAND AND I DECIDED TO DO.
I SEE.
THIS IS A PLACE WITH STRONG WINDS.
THE ASHES WILL SURELY TRAVEL FAR.
YOU MIGHT MEET HER AGAIN SOMEWHERE.
I COULD NOT SCATTER AKI'S ASHES.
BEING ALIVE WAS MUCH MORE PAINFUL THAN BEING DEAD.

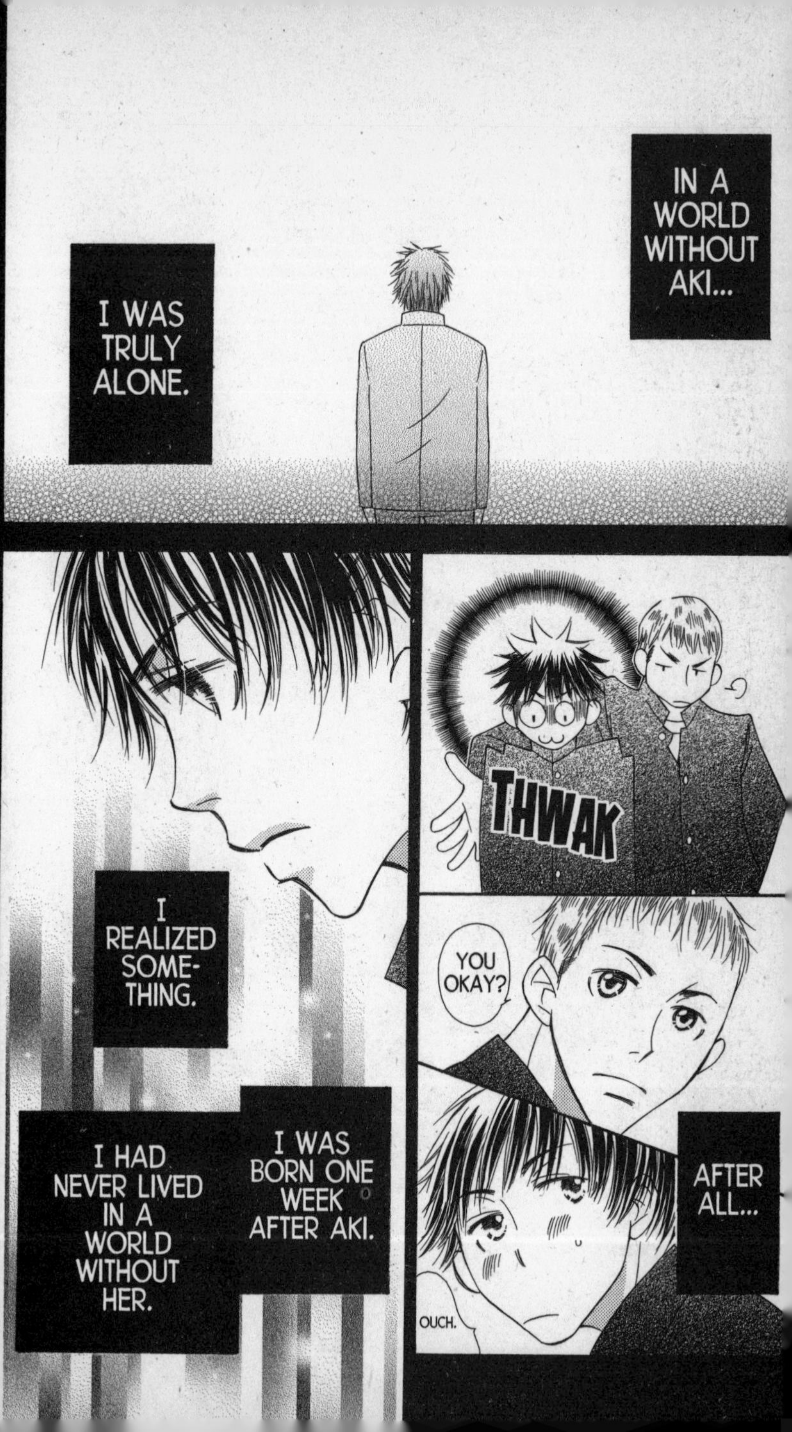
IN A WORLD WITHOUT AKI...
I WAS TRULY ALONE.
THWAK
YOU OKAY?
AFTER ALL...
OUCH.
I REALIZED SOMETHING.
I WAS BORN ONE WEEK AFTER AKI.
I HAD NEVER LIVED IN A WORLD WITHOUT HER.

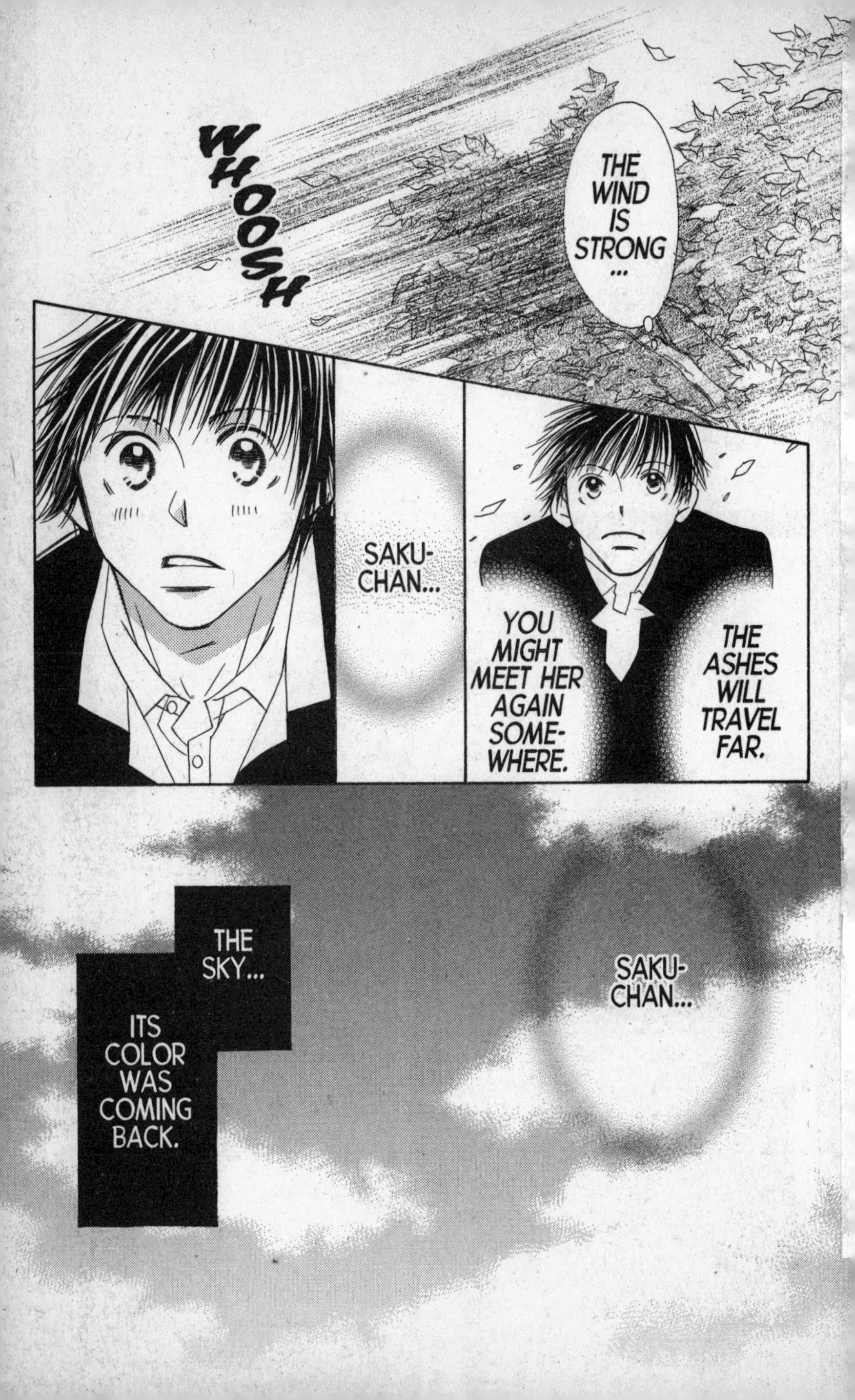
THE WIND IS STRONG...
WHOOSH
THE ASHES WILL TRAVEL FAR.
YOU MIGHT MEET HER AGAIN SOME-WHERE.
SAKU-CHAN...
SAKU-CHAN...
THE SKY...
ITS COLOR WAS COMING BACK.

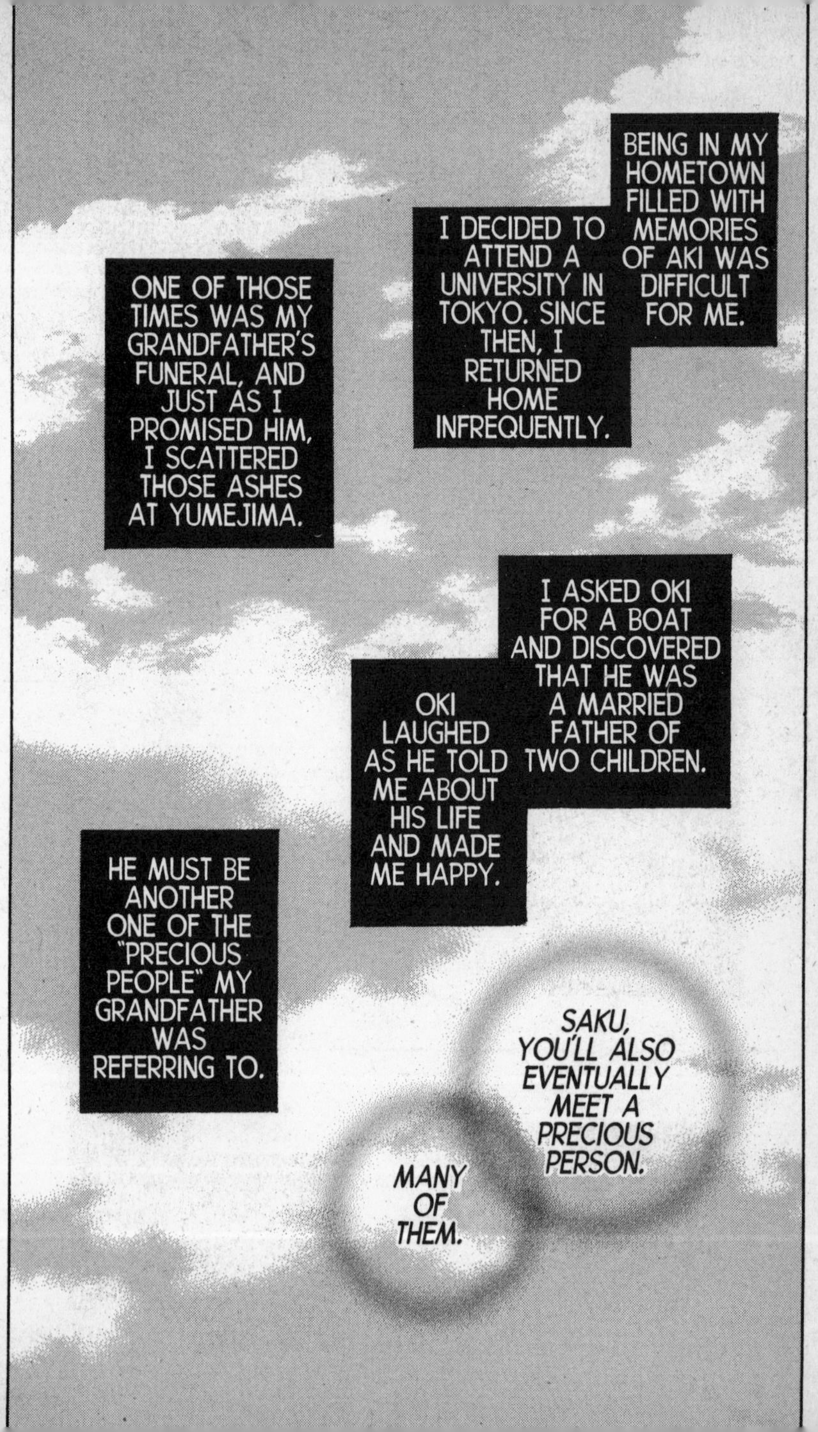
BEING IN MY HOMETOWN FILLED WITH MEMORIES OF AKI WAS DIFFICULT FOR ME.
I DECIDED TO ATTEND A UNIVERSITY IN TOKYO. SINCE THEN, I RETURNED HOME INFREQUENTLY.
ONE OF THOSE TIMES WAS MY GRANDFATHER'S FUNERAL, AND JUST AS I PROMISED HIM, I SCATTERED THOSE ASHES AT YUMEJIMA.
I ASKED OKI FOR A BOAT AND DISCOVERED THAT HE WAS A MARRIED FATHER OF TWO CHILDREN.
OKI LAUGHED AS HE TOLD ME ABOUT HIS LIFE AND MADE ME HAPPY.
HE MUST BE ANOTHER ONE OF THE "PRECIOUS PEOPLE" MY GRANDFATHER WAS REFERRING TO.
SAKU, YOU'LL ALSO EVENTUALLY MEET A PRECIOUS PERSON.
MANY OF THEM.

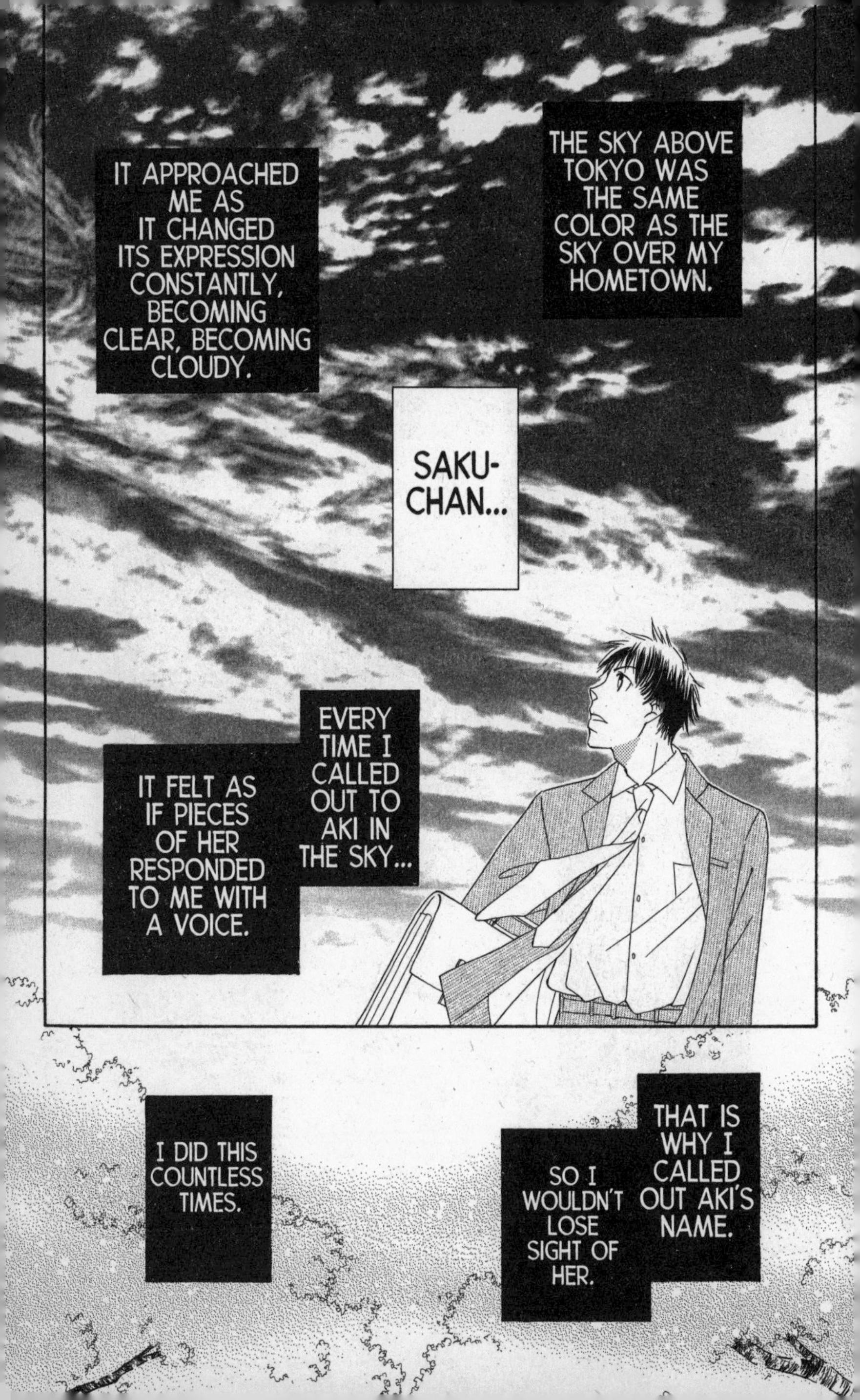
THE SKY ABOVE TOKYO WAS THE SAME COLOR AS THE SKY OVER MY HOMETOWN.
IT APPROACHED ME AS IT CHANGED ITS EXPRESSION CONSTANTLY, BECOMING CLEAR, BECOMING CLOUDY.
SAKU-CHAN...
EVERY TIME I CALLED OUT TO AKI IN THE SKY...
IT FELT AS IF PIECES OF HER RESPONDED TO ME WITH A VOICE.
THAT IS WHY I CALLED OUT AKI'S NAME.
SO I WOULDN'T LOSE SIGHT OF HER.
I DID THIS COUNTLESS TIMES.

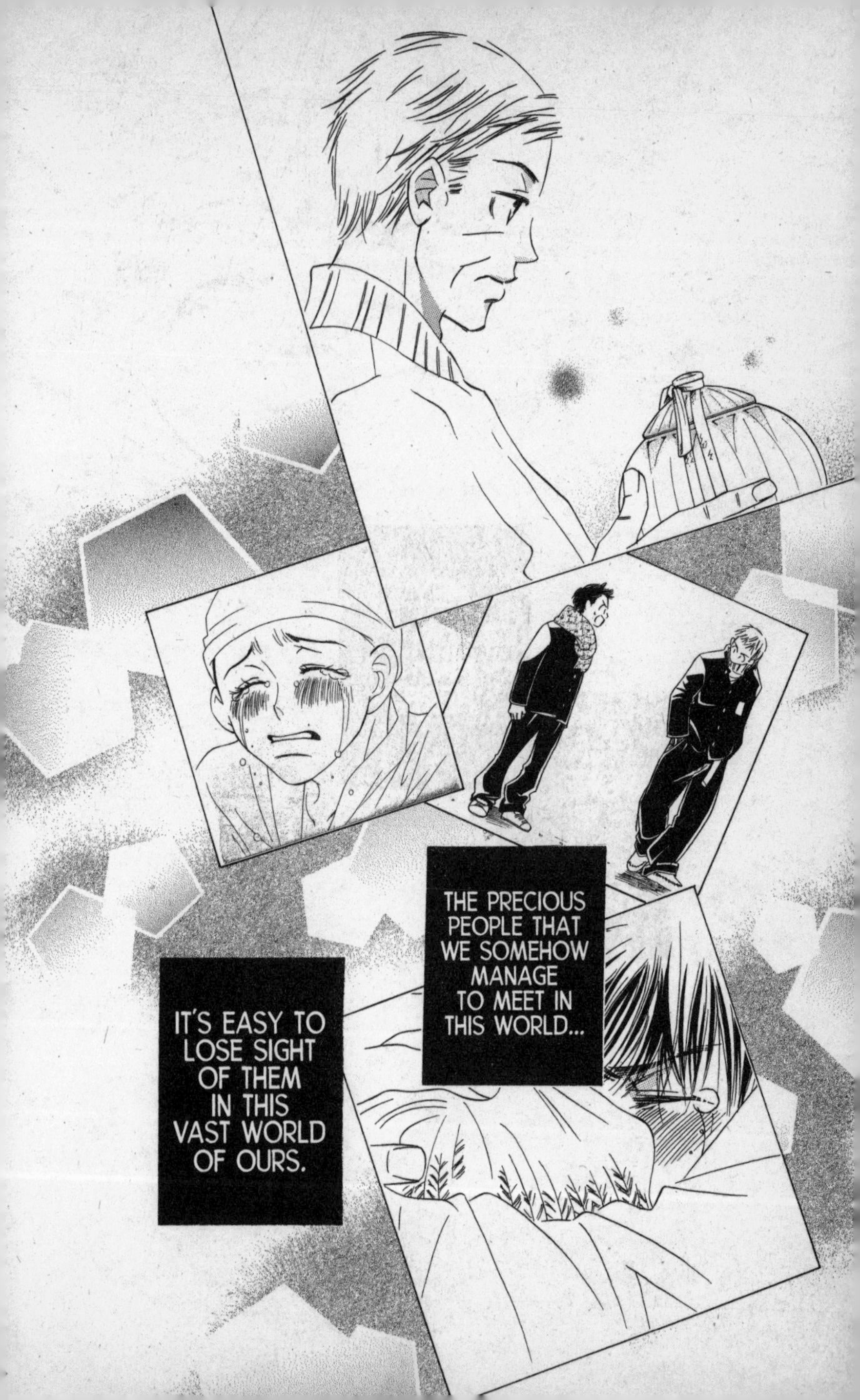
THE PRECIOUS PEOPLE THAT WE SOMEHOW MANAGE TO MEET IN THIS WORLD...
IT'S EASY TO LOSE SIGHT OF THEM IN THIS VAST WORLD OF OURS.

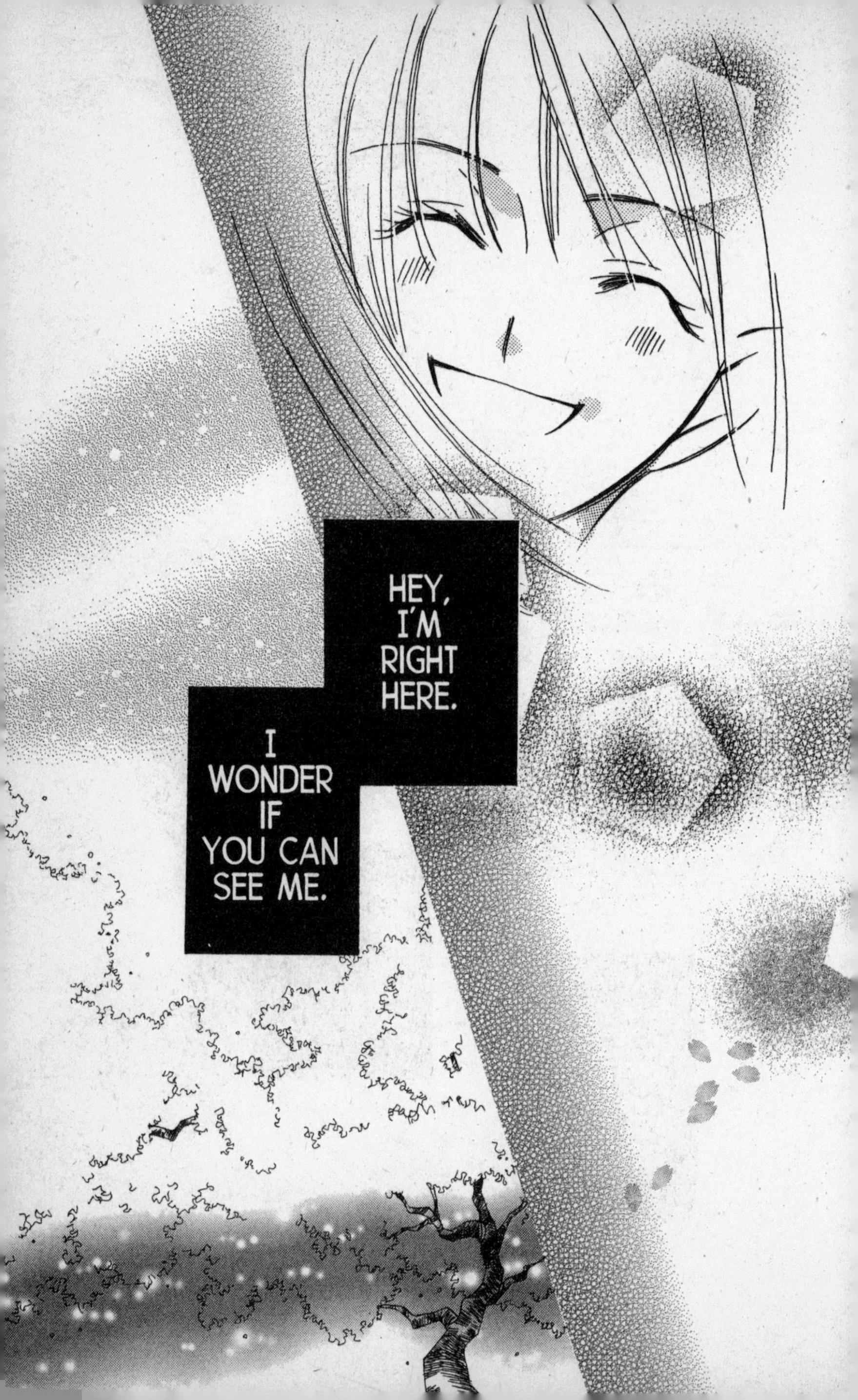
HEY, I'M RIGHT HERE.
I WONDER IF YOU CAN SEE ME.

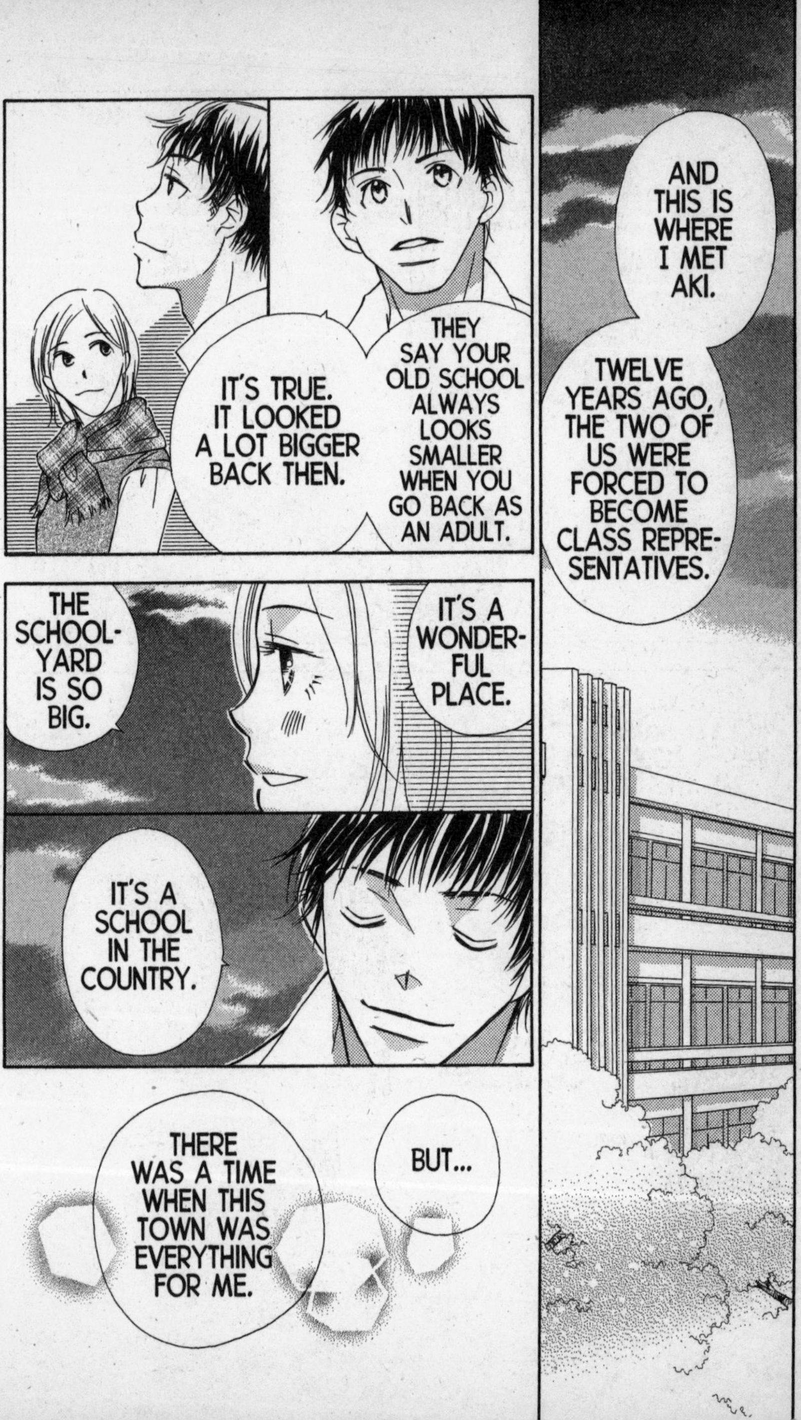
AND THIS IS WHERE I MET AKI.
TWELVE YEARS AGO, THE TWO OF US WERE FORCED TO BECOME CLASS REPRE-SENTATIVES.
THEY SAY YOUR OLD SCHOOL ALWAYS LOOKS SMALLER WHEN YOU GO BACK AS AN ADULT.
IT'S TRUE. IT LOOKED A LOT BIGGER BACK THEN.
IT'S A WONDER-FUL PLACE.
THE SCHOOL-YARD IS SO BIG.
IT'S A SCHOOL IN THE COUNTRY.
BUT...
THERE WAS A TIME WHEN THIS TOWN WAS EVERYTHING FOR ME.

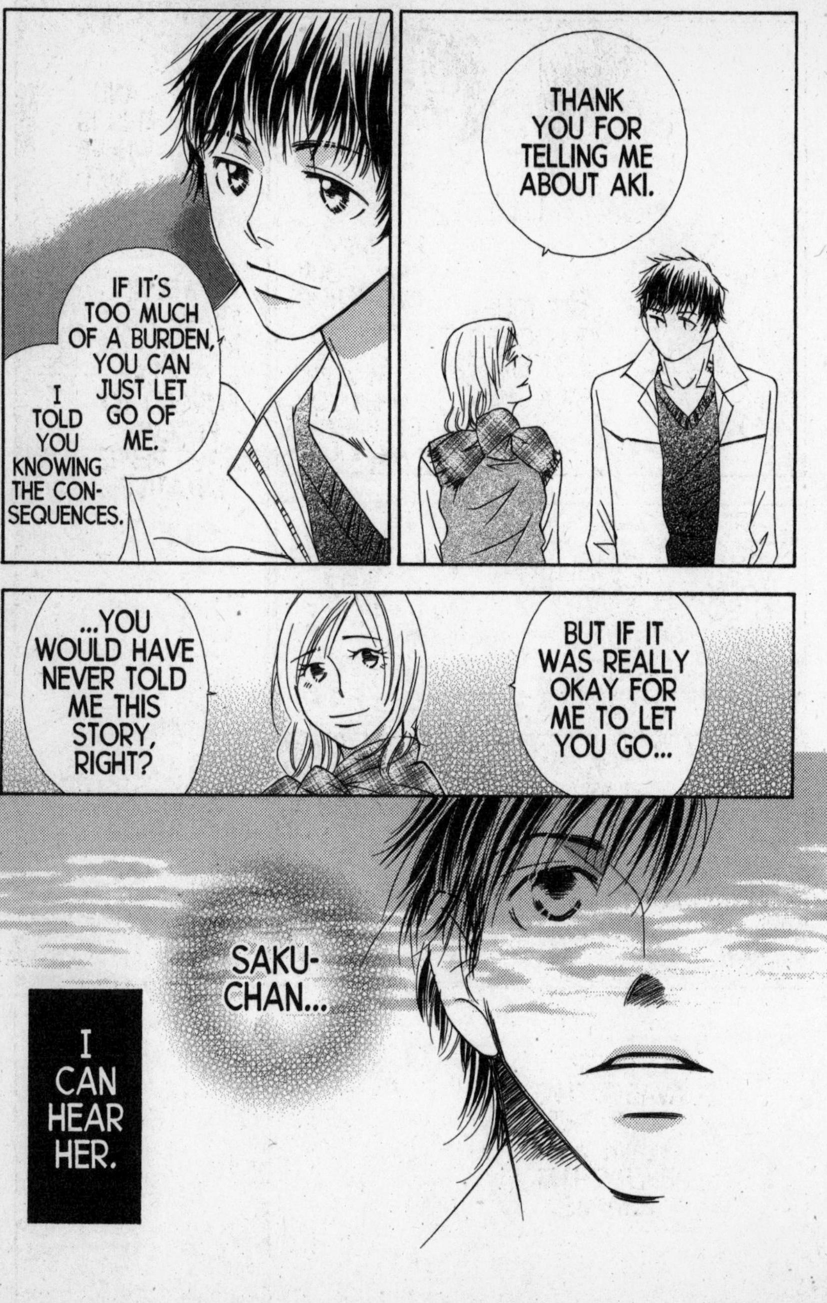
THANK YOU FOR TELLING ME ABOUT AKI.
IF IT'S TOO MUCH OF A BURDEN, YOU CAN JUST LET GO OF ME.
I TOLD YOU KNOWING THE CON-SEQUENCES.
BUT IF IT WAS REALLY OKAY FOR ME TO LET YOU GO...
...YOU WOULD HAVE NEVER TOLD ME THIS STORY, RIGHT?
SAKU-CHAN...
I CAN HEAR HER.

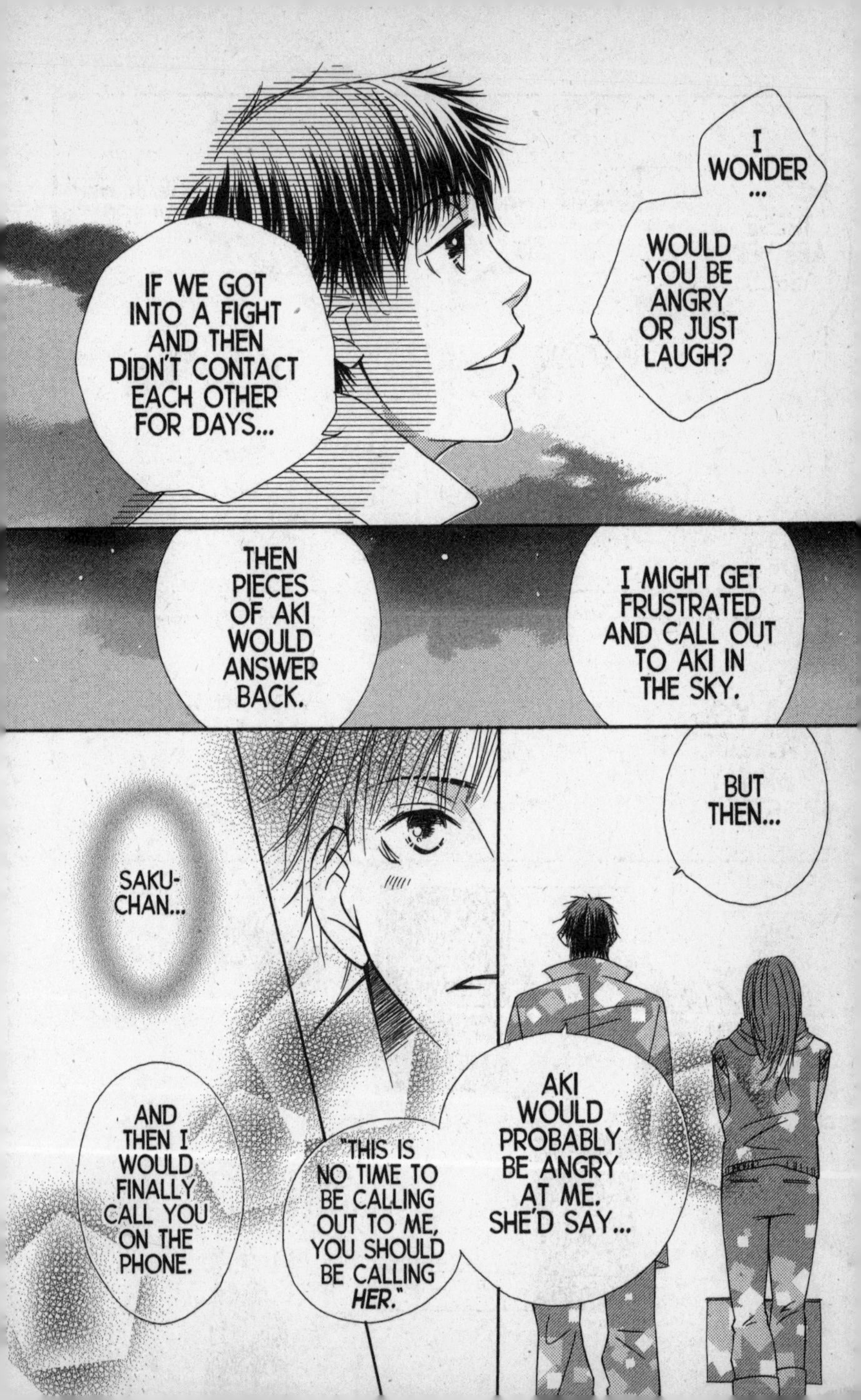
I WONDER ...
WOULD YOU BE ANGRY OR JUST LAUGH?
IF WE GOT INTO A FIGHT AND THEN DIDN'T CONTACT EACH OTHER FOR DAYS...
I MIGHT GET FRUSTRATED AND CALL OUT TO AKI IN THE SKY.
THEN PIECES OF AKI WOULD ANSWER BACK.
BUT THEN...
AKI WOULD PROBABLY BE ANGRY AT ME. SHE'D SAY...
"THIS IS NO TIME TO BE CALLING OUT TO ME, YOU SHOULD BE CALLING *HER*."
SAKU-CHAN...
AND THEN I WOULD FINALLY CALL YOU ON THE PHONE.

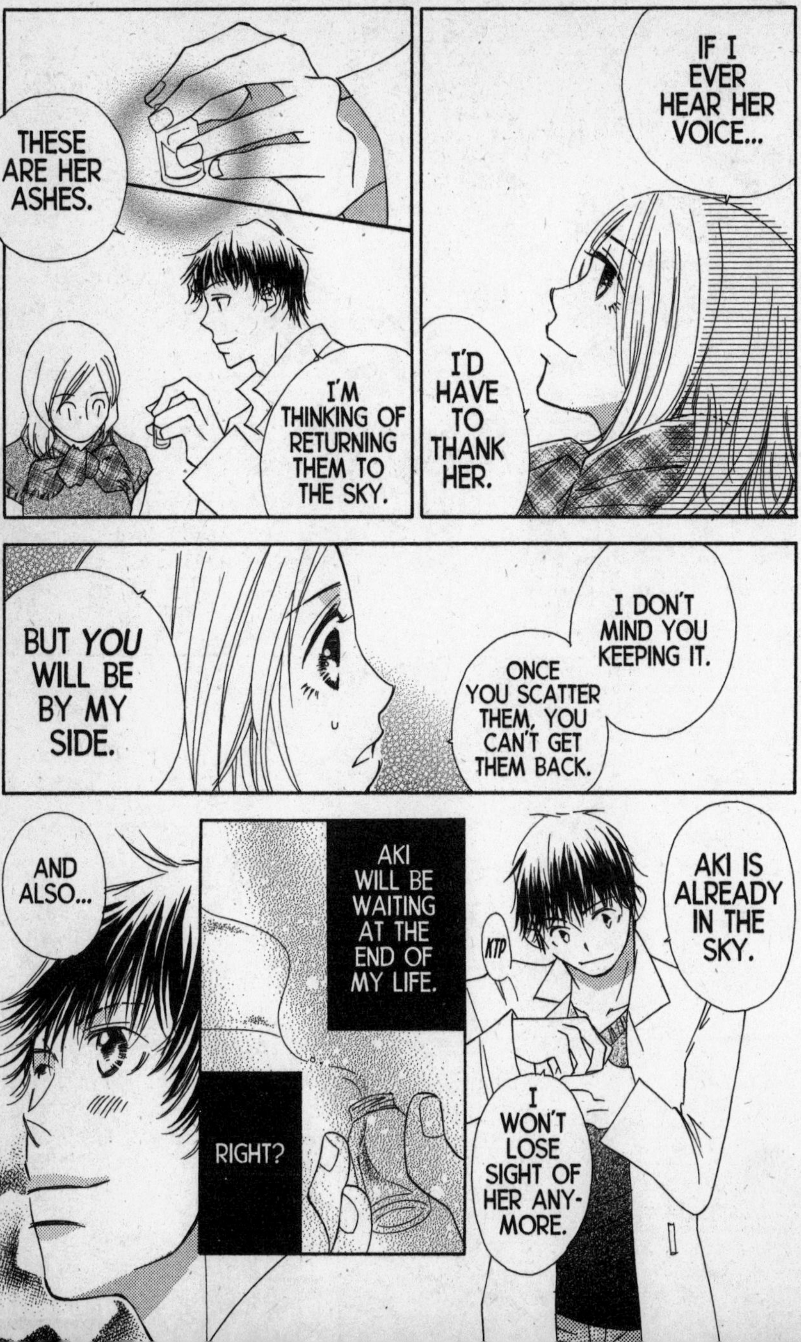
IF I EVER HEAR HER VOICE...
I'D HAVE TO THANK HER.
THESE ARE HER ASHES.
I'M THINKING OF RETURNING THEM TO THE SKY.
I DON'T MIND YOU KEEPING IT.
ONCE YOU SCATTER THEM, YOU CAN'T GET THEM BACK.
BUT *YOU* WILL BE BY MY SIDE.
AKI IS ALREADY IN THE SKY.
KTP
I WON'T LOSE SIGHT OF HER ANY-MORE.
AND ALSO...
AKI WILL BE WAITING AT THE END OF MY LIFE.
RIGHT?

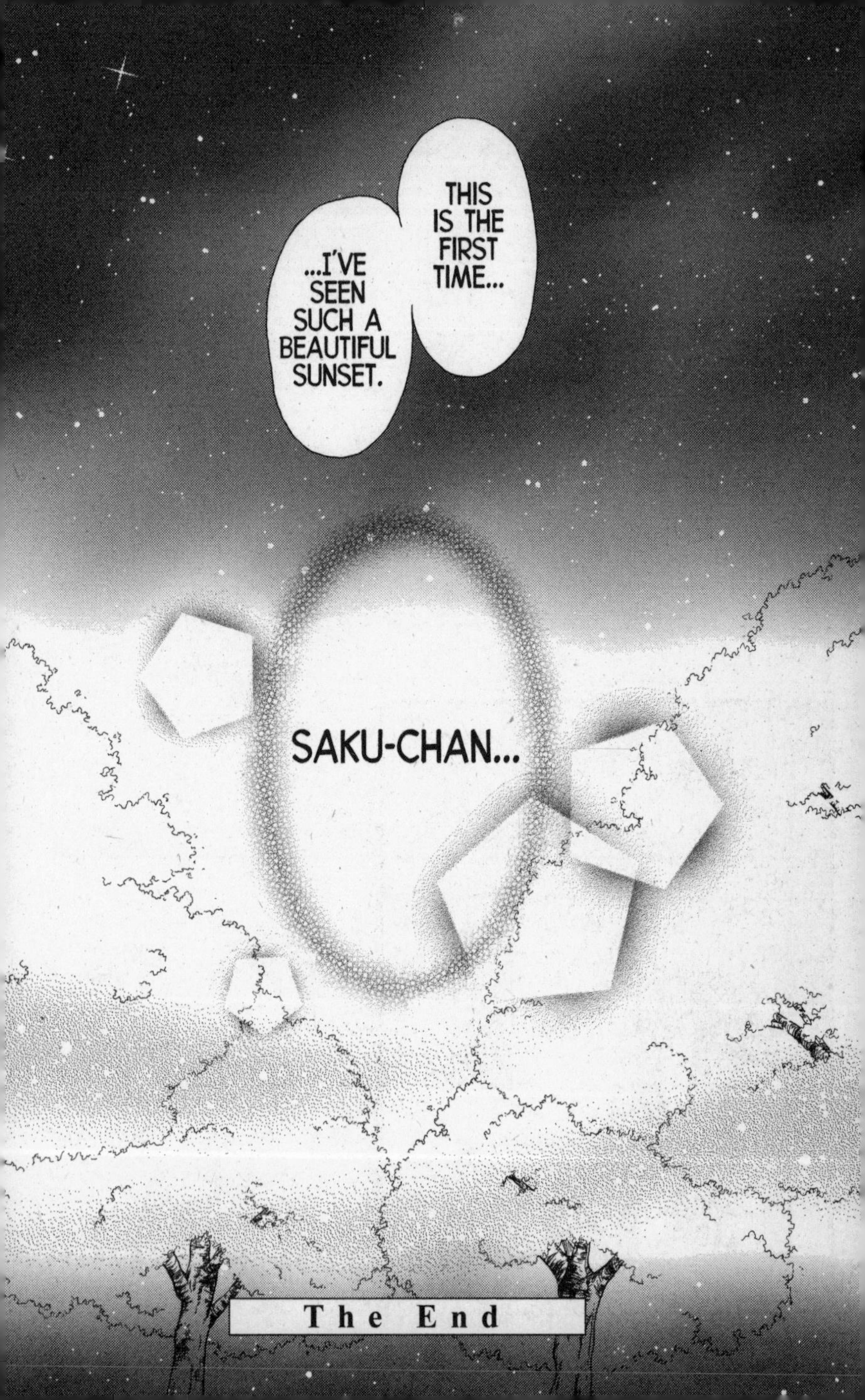
THIS IS THE FIRST TIME...
...I'VE SEEN SUCH A BEAUTIFUL SUNSET.
SAKU-CHAN...
The End

Hello, my name is Kazumi Kazui. Usually, it would be strange for an illustrator like me to chatter on like this, but if you don't mind, please read on. The comic version of *Socrates in Love* was published in the January and February 2004 issues of "Petit Comic." Taking into consideration the readership of the magazine, the content of the manga is slightly different from the original story. If you have not read the original novel yet, please give it a read. Now, I'll write a little bit about myself.

Before the actual images are drawn in a manga, rough storyboards are created. While I was creating the storyboards for the second half of the story from where Sakutaro is taking Aki away from the hospital up until Aki's death, I could not stop crying. This was the first time this kind of thing happened to me. I think I am one blessed reader of the novel *Socrates in Love*.

I would like to thank the original creator, Mr. Kyoichi Katayama, who not only accepted having his story adapted into a comic, but also provided me with his assistance. I would like to also thank my editor Mr. Kikuchi who gave me this opportunity and gave me guidance when I was worn out. I hope I succeed in communicating to the reader, even slightly, the inspiration I received from the novel.

Kazumi Kazui

Kyoichi Katayama

Born in 1959 in Ehime Prefecture. Currently resides in Fukuoka. After graduating from Kyushu University, Katayama made his literary debut in 1986 with *Kehai* (Sign), which won the Bungakkai Newcomers Award. Katayama's novel, *Sekai no Chushin de Ai o Sakebu* (released in English as *Socrates in Love*) was a national phenomenon and became the all-time best-selling novel in Japan. Affectionately known as "Sekachu," Katayama's novel brought innocent love and romance to the forefront of Japan's mass market.

Kazumi Kazui

A native of Aichi Prefecture, Kazui made her debut in 2000 in a special edition of *Petit Comic* with *Watashi no Iru Basho* (The Place Where I Am).

SOCRATES IN LOVE
The Shojo Beat Manga Edition

BASED ON THE NOVEL BY
KYOICHI KATAYAMA
ART BY
KAZUMI KAZUI

Translation/Noritaka Minami
Touch-up Art & Lettering/Steve Dutro
Design/Yukiko Whitley
Editor/Andy Nakatani

Managing Editor/Megan Bates
Director of Production/Noboru Watanabe
Vice President of Publishing/Alvin Lu
Vice President & Editor in Chief/ Yumi Hoashi
Sr. Director of Acquisitions/Rika Inouye
Vice President of Sales & Marketing/Liza Coppola
Publisher/Hyoe Narita

Published by VIZ Media, LLC
P.O. Box 77010
San Francisco, CA 94107

Shojo Beat Manga Edition
10 9 8 7 6 5 4 3 2 1
First printing, September 2005

store.viz.com

Thank you for reading
the *Socrates in Love* manga.
Please turn to the back and
enjoy a special sample of the
Socrates in Love novel,
written by Kyoichi Katayama.

"Thanks a lot, huh?"

"Hey, Ryunosuke isn't so bad. Coulda been worse."

"Like what?"

"What if they'd named you Kinnosuke?"

"Kinnosuke? Why?"

"That's Soseki's real first name."

"Huh. I didn't know that."

"Think about it. If your parents' favorite book'd been *Kokoro*, you'd be Kinnosuke Oki now."

"No way," he said, laughing. "Come on, nobody would name their kid Kinnosuke."

"Hey, just suppose. Suppose your name *was* Kinnosuke Oki. You'd be the laughingstock of the entire school."

Oki's expression darkened.

I went on, "You'd blame your parents, run away from home, and become a pro wrestler."

"A pro wrestler? How come?"

"What else could you do with a name like Kinnosuke Oki?"

"Yeah, you're right!"

Aki put the flowers we'd brought into a vase. Oki and I opened the box of cookies and dug in while we kept on about our oh-so-literary parents.

"Hey, come back soon," Oki called out as we were going. "It gets boring, lying around here all day."

"Don't worry. All the kids from class are gonna start taking turns coming by to fill you in on what you're missing."

"That I could do without."

TO BE CONTINUED...

to visit a classmate named Oki, who'd broken his leg the first day of school. On the way there, we bought cookies and flowers with the money we'd collected from our teacher and classmates.

Oki was lying on his back in bed, with his leg in a huge plaster cast. I hardly knew anything about him, so I kept quiet while Aki, who'd been in the same class with him the year before, did the talking. I stared out the fourth-floor window at the town. A flower shop, fruit market, candy store, and other businesses formed a small shopping area along the bus route. Beyond that, I could see Castle Hill. Its white tower peeped out from behind the trees, which were bright with new leaves.

"Hey, Matsumoto." Oki suddenly turned toward me. "Your first name's Sakutaro, right?"

"Yeah." I turned from the window.

"Must drive you nuts, huh?" he said.

"What drives me nuts?"

"I mean, it's because of Sakutaro Hagiwara, right?"

I didn't answer.

"Know what *my* first name is?"

"Yeah. Ryunosuke."

"Because of Ryunosuke Akutagawa."

I understood what Oki was getting at.

"They should make it illegal to name your kids after famous writers," he said, nodding. He seemed pleased with himself.

"Actually, it was my grandfather," I said.

"Your grandpa picked your name?"

"Yeah."

looked at, Aki was looking at with me, *through* me. But now, no matter what I looked at, I felt nothing. What was I supposed to look at here?

That's what it meant for Aki to be gone, what it meant to lose her. I had nothing to look at anymore, whether in Australia or Alaska, the Mediterranean or the Antarctic. No matter where in the world I went, it would be the same: no landscape could move me, nothing beautiful could please me. The person who'd given me the ability to see, know, and feel—the will to live—was gone. She wasn't with me anymore.

Four months. Everything had happened in the time for one season to change to the next. In that time, one girl had disappeared from this world. If you thought of it as one person out of six billion, it didn't mean a thing. But I wasn't there with the six billion. I was in a place where one death had wiped out every emotion. That was where I was. I didn't see anything, hear anything, or feel anything. But was that where I really was? If not, then where was I?

Two

THE FIRST TIME AKI AND I were in the same class together was our second year of junior high. Until then I'd never even heard of her, but by chance we ended up in the same class, out of nine, and by chance our teacher appointed us male and female class representative.

As class representatives, our first job was to go to the hospital to sad reality, there's a chasm you have to step across, and you can't cross it without shedding tears. It doesn't matter how many times you do it.

The place we'd left was covered in snow, but the place we landed was a city scorching under the summer sun: Cairns, a beautiful town on the Pacific Ocean. A promenade of palm trees and choking tropical vegetation spread their greenery around luxury hotels facing the bay. Large and small cruise ships waited at the wharf. The taxi taking us to our hotel followed the shore, where strolling tourists were out enjoying the sunset.

"It's like Hawaii," Aki's mother said.

To me, the place was cursed. Nothing about it had changed from four months ago, except for the seasons. Australia had gone from early spring to midsummer. That was all. That was all that had happened.

We were going to spend the night at a hotel and take a morning flight the next day. There was hardly any time difference, so the time when we'd left Japan had just continued its flow. After dinner, I sprawled out on my hotel bed and stared up at the ceiling. And I told myself that Aki wasn't here.

When I'd come to Cairns four months ago, Aki hadn't been here, then, either. Our class had come for our high school graduation trip and left her in Japan. We'd flown from a Japanese city close to Australia, to an Australian city close to Japan. That was the only nonstop route, and for this odd reason, this city had entered my life. I'd thought it was a beautiful place. Everything was strange and new and interesting, because everything I'd the treetops fell to the ground with a dry sound. When I looked back, beyond the guardrail, I could see the winter ocean. It was calm and gentle, utterly blue. No matter what I looked at, my memories would suck me in. I closed the lid on my heart and turned my back to the ocean.

The snow in the woods was deep. There were broken branches and hard, stump-like growths that made it hard to walk. Suddenly, somewhere in the grove, a wild bird let out a sharp cry and flew off. I stopped and listened for other noises, but it was as quiet as if the world had nobody left in it. When I closed my eyes, though, I could hear the chains of cars on the nearby road, like the sound of bells. I started not to know where I was or who I was. Then I heard my father calling me.

After we got over the hill, the rest of the drive went smoothly. We arrived at the airport on time, checked in, and headed to the gate.

"Thank you for everything," my father said to Aki's parents.

"We should be thanking you," Aki's father answered, smiling. "I'm sure Aki's very happy to have Sakutaro coming with us."

I glanced at the small urn in Aki's mother's hands. That urn, nestled in its beautiful brocade bag . . . was Aki truly in there?

After the plane took off, I fell asleep and had a dream. It was about Aki when she was still healthy, and in the dream she was smiling, with that slightly embarrassed smile of hers. She called out to me—"Saku-chan." Her voice lingered in my ears. I wished the dream were real, and this reality a dream. But that wasn't the case. And that was why, whenever I woke up, I'd be crying. It wasn't because I was sad. When you return from a happy dream

PART

1

THAT MORNING I woke up crying, as usual. I didn't know anymore whether I was sad or not—my feelings had flowed away with the tears. I lay there listlessly in bed until my mother came in and told me to get up.

It wasn't snowing, but the road was frozen white. Half of the cars we saw had their chains on. My dad drove, while Aki's father sat beside him. Aki's mother and I sat in back. The men up front kept talking about the snow. Would we make it to the airport in time? Would the plane take off on schedule? Aki's mom and I hardly said anything at all. I stared out the window at the passing landscape. The fields on either side of the road were covered in snow as far as the eye could see. Rays of sunlight cut through the clouds, coming down on a distant mountain ridge. Aki's mother held the small urn containing ashes in her lap.

The snow got deeper as we neared the crest of the hill. My father stopped the car, and he and Aki's father went out to put chains on the tires. To pass the time, I went for a short walk. On the other side of the parking area was a grove of trees. Untrampled snow covered the undergrowth, while snow that had piled up on

Socrates
in Love

Kyoichi Katayama

TRANSLATED BY
Akemi Wegmüller

WELCOME TO THE EXCITING NEW WORLD OF VIZ MEDIA FICTION!

What you hold in your hands is a sneak preview of a bold step in publishing: this fall, America's No.1 manga publisher, VIZ Media, debuts its fiction line, featuring the very best in new writing from Japan!

Our debut titles include *Fullmetal Alchemist: Land of Sand*, a spin-off based on the smash-success manga and anime; *Socrates in Love*, a stirring love story and the all-time best-selling novel in Japan; and *Ghost in the Shell 2: Innocence, After the Long Goodbye*, a powerful vision of the future set in the world of Mamoru Oshii's hit anime film.

Forthcoming titles include *Steamboy*, a novelization of the latest epic from anime auteur, Katsuhiro Otomo (director of *Akira*), and *Kamikaze Girls*, the Japanese cult classic exploring Japan's outré "Goth Lolita" subculture.

In 2004, VIZ released its first foray into fiction, the surprise best seller, *Battle Royale*, which demonstrated that there was a hungry audience for new fiction from Japan.

Now with the *Shojo Beat* fiction imprint, we hope you'll discover that when it comes to the exploding universe of Japanese pop culture, manga is just the beginning!

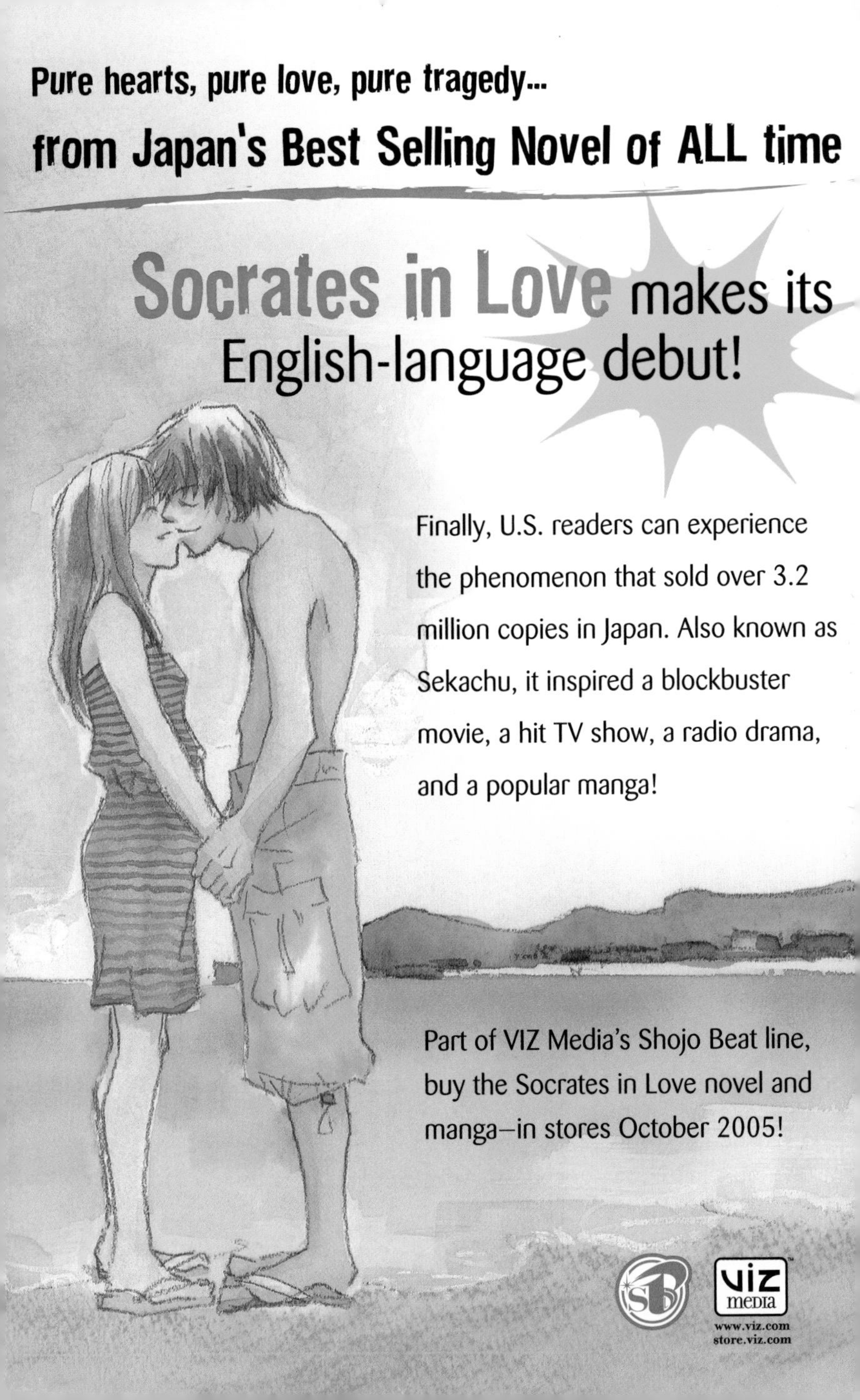
Pure hearts, pure love, pure tragedy...
from Japan's Best Selling Novel of ALL time
Socrates in Love makes its English-language debut!
Finally, U.S. readers can experience the phenomenon that sold over 3.2 million copies in Japan. Also known as Sekachu, it inspired a blockbuster movie, a hit TV show, a radio drama, and a popular manga!
Part of VIZ Media's Shojo Beat line, buy the Socrates in Love novel and manga—in stores October 2005!
VIZ MEDIA
www.viz.com
store.viz.com

When an average boy meets a
beautiful girl, it's a classic
case of young love—instant, all
consuming, and enduring. But
when a tragedy threatens their
romance, they discover just how
deep and strong love can be.

Manga

only
$8.99!

Socrates in Love
Story by Kyoichi Katayama
Art by Kazumi Kazui

Novel

Socrates in Love
Written by Kyoichi Katayama

$17.99
hardcover

www.viz.com
store.viz.com

Find the Beat online!
Check us out at

www.shojobeat.com!

Shojo Beat MANGA FROM THE HEART

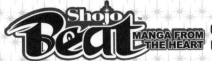

COMPLETE OUR SURVEY AND LET US KNOW WHAT YOU THINK!

☐ Please do NOT send me information about VIZ Media and Shojo Beat products, news and events, special offers, or other information.

☐ Please do NOT send me information from VIZ Media's trusted business partners.

Name: ____________________

Address: ____________________

City: ____________ **State:** ______ **Zip:** ______

E-mail: ____________________

☐ **Male** ☐ **Female** **Date of Birth** (mm/dd/yyyy): ___/___/_____ (Under 13? Parental consent required)

1 Do you purchase *Shojo Beat* magazine?

☐ Yes ☐ No **(if no, skip the next two questions)**

If **YES**, do you subscribe?

☐ Yes ☐ No

If you do **NOT** subscribe, how often do you/will you purchase *Shojo Beat* magazine?

☐ 1-3 issues a year

☐ 4-6 issues a year

☐ more than 7 issues a year

2 Which Shojo Beat Graphic Novel did you purchase? (please check one)

☐ Full Moon ☐ Fushigi Yûgi: Genbu Kaiden ☐ MeruPuri

☐ Ouran High School Host Club ☐ Tokyo Boys & Girls ☐ Ultra Maniac

Will you purchase subsequent volumes?

☐ Yes ☐ No

3 How did you learn about this title? (check all that apply)

☐ Advertisement ☐ Article ☐ Favorite creator/artist

☐ Favorite title ☐ Gift ☐ Recommendation

☐ Read a preview online and wanted to read the rest of the story

☐ Read introduction in *Shojo Beat* magazine ☐ Special offer

☐ Website ☐ Other ____________________

④ Of the titles that are serialized in *Shojo Beat* magazine, do you plan to purchase the Graphic Novels?

☐ Yes ☐ No

If **YES**, which one(s) do you plan to purchase? (check all that apply)

☐ Absolute Boyfriend ☐ Baby & Me ☐ Crimson Hero
☐ Godchild ☐ Kaze Hikaru ☐ Nana

If **YES**, what are your reasons for purchasing? (please pick up to 3)

☐ Favorite title ☐ Favorite creator/artist
☐ I want to read the full volume(s) all at once ☐ I want to read it over and over again
☐ There are extras that aren't in the magazine ☐ Recommendation
☐ The quality of printing is better than the magazine
☐ Other _____

If **NO**, why would you not purchase it?

☐ I'm happy just reading it in the magazine ☐ It's not worth buying the graphic novel
☐ All the manga pages are in black and white ☐ There are other graphic novels that I prefer
☐ There are too many to collect for each title ☐ It's too small
☐ Other _____

⑤ Of the titles NOT serialized in the magazine, which ones have you purchased? (check all that apply)

☐ Full Moon ☐ Fushigi Yûgi: Genbu Kaiden ☐ MeruPuri
☐ Ouran High School Host Club ☐ Tokyo Boys & Girls
☐ Ultra Maniac ☐ Other _____

If you did purchase any of the above, what were your reasons for purchase?

☐ Advertisement ☐ Article ☐ Favorite creator/artist
☐ Favorite title ☐ Gift ☐ Recommendation
☐ Read a preview online and wanted to read the rest of the story
☐ Read introduction in *Shojo Beat* magazine ☐ Special offer
☐ Website ☐ Other _____

Will you purchase subsequent volumes?

☐ Yes ☐ No

⑥ What race/ethnicity do you consider yourself? (please check one)

☐ Asian/Pacific Islander ☐ Black/African American ☐ Hispanic/Latino
☐ Native American/Alaskan Native ☐ White/Caucasian ☐ Other _____

THANK YOU! Please send the completed form to:

Shojo Survey
42 Catharine St.
Poughkeepsie, NY 12601

VIZ MEDIA

All information provided will be used for internal purposes only. We promise not to sell or otherwise divulge your information.